THE
HISTORY OF
GHANA

ADVISORY BOARD

THE HISTORY OF GHANA

Roger S. Gocking

The Greenwood Histories of the Modern Nations
Frank W. Thackeray and John E. Findling, Series Editors

Greenwood Press
Westport, Connecticut • London

Library of Congress Cataloging-in-Publication Data

Gocking, Roger.
   The history of Ghana / Roger S. Gocking.
      p. cm. — (The Greenwood histories of the modern nations, ISSN 1096–2905)
   Includes bibliographical references (p.   ) and index.
   ISBN 0–313–31894–8 (alk. paper)
     1. Ghana—History. I. Title. II. Series.
  DT510.5.G63 2005
  966.7—dc22   2004028236

British Library Cataloguing in Publication Data is available.

Library of Congress Catalog Card Number: 2004028236
ISBN: 0–313–31894–8
ISSN: 1096–2905

First published in 2005

Greenwood Press, 88 Post Road West, Westport, CT 06881
An imprint of Greenwood Publishing Group, Inc.
www.greenwood.com

Printed in the United States of America

The paper used in this book complies with the
Permanent Paper Standard issued by the National
Information Standards Organization (Z39.48–1984).

10 9 8 7 6 5 4 3 2 1

Contents

A photo essay follows p. 145

Series Foreword

The *Greenwood Histories of the Modern Nations* series is intended to provide students and interested laypeople with up-to-date, concise, and analytical histories of many of the nations of the contemporary world. Not since the 1960s has there been a systematic attempt to publish a series of national histories, and, as editors, we believe that this series will prove to be a valuable contribution to our understanding of other countries in our increasingly interdependent world.

Over thirty years ago, at the end of the 1960s, the Cold War was an accepted reality of global politics, the process of decolonization was still in progress, the idea of a unified Europe with a single currency was unheard of, the United States was mired in a war in Vietnam, and the economic boom of Asia was still years in the future. Richard Nixon was president of the United States, Mao Tse-tung (not yet Mao Zedong) ruled China, Leonid Brezhnev guided the Soviet Union, and Harold Wilson was prime minister of the United Kingdom. Authoritarian dictators still ruled most of Latin America, the Middle East was reeling in the wake of the Six-Day War, and Shah Reza Pahlavi was at the height of his power in Iran. Clearly, the past thirty years have been witness to a great deal of historical change, and it is to this change that this series is primarily addressed.

With the help of a distinguished advisory board, we have selected nations whose political, economic, and social affairs mark them as among the most important in the waning years of the twentieth century, and for each nation we have found an author who is recognized as a specialist in the history of that nation. These authors have worked most cooperatively with us and with Greenwood Press to produce volumes that reflect current research on their nation and that are interesting and informative to their prospective readers.

The importance of a series such as this cannot be underestimated. As a superpower whose influence is felt all over the world, the United States can claim a "special" relationship with almost every other nation. Yet many Americans know very little about the histories of the nations with which the Untied States relates. How did they get to be the way they are? What kind of political systems have evolved there? What kind of influence do they have in their own region? What are the dominant political, religious, and cultural forces that move their leaders? These and many other questions are answered in the volumes of this series.

The authors who have contributed to this series have written comprehensive histories of their nations, dating back to prehistoric times in some cases. Each of them, however, has devoted a significant portion of the book to events of the last thirty years, because the modern era has contributed the most to contemporary issues that have an impact on U.S. policy. Authors have made an effort to be as up-to-date as possible so that readers can benefit from the most recent scholarship and a narrative that includes very recent events.

In addition to the historical narrative, each volume in this series contains an introductory overview of the country's geography, political institutions, economic structure, and cultural attributes. This is designed to give readers a picture of the nation as it exists in the contemporary world. Each volume also contains additional chapters that add interesting and useful detail to the historical narrative. One chapter is a thorough chronology of important historical events, making it easy for readers to follow the flow of a particular nation's history. Another chapter features biographical sketches of the nation's most important figures in order to humanize some of the individuals who have contributed to the historical development of their nation. Each volume also contains a comprehensive bibliography, so that those readers whose interest has been sparked may find out more about the nation and its history. Finally, there is a carefully prepared topic and person index.

Readers of these volumes will find them fascinating to read and useful in understanding the contemporary world and the nations that comprise it. As series editors, it is our hope that this series will contribute to a heightened sense of global understanding as we embark on a new century.

Frank W. Thackeray and John E. Findling
Indiana University Southeast

Preface and Acknowledgments

The main purpose of this work is to present in concise form the history of Ghana from the earliest times to the present. The work describes the emergence of early precolonial states, the increasing contact with Europeans, and eventual colonial rule at the end of the nineteenth century. The remaining two-thirds of the book describes the struggle for independence and the challenges that have followed. Ghana's colonial past and the subsequent struggle to achieve independence shares much in common with other African countries that have passed through similar historical experiences and wrestle with the contemporary challenges of nationhood. In this sense the nation's history can serve as an introduction to the history of many other African countries. Yet at the same time there is a uniqueness to Ghana's particular historical experience that contributed to it being the first former colony in West Africa to achieve independence. Kwame Nkrumah, Ghana's first president, maintained that Ghana's "independence [was] meaningless unless it [was] closely linked up with the total liberation of Africa."[1] Ghana's history also finds meaning in a wider pan-African context, but at the same time it retains its own individual character.

It was at the invitation of Professors Frank Thackeray and John E. Findling, the series editors of *Greenwood Histories of the Modern Nations*, that I undertook to write this book. Along with Greenwood's editors Barbara

Rader, Kevin Ohe, and Sarah Colwell, they helped to shape the format that the book has taken.

In addition, I owe a major debt of gratitude to many other people who over the years have played important roles in helping me to develop my understanding of Ghana's past and present. I owe special thanks to the staff at the Ghana National Archives, now known as the Public Records and Archives Administration Department (PRAAD). Over the years I have benefited from the help of its directors, Mr. C. K. Gadzekpo and Mr. C. A. Azangweo, as well as from its principal archivist, Mr. Anthony Mensah, and members of the staff, who have helped me to track down files, newspapers, pictures, and biographical material. Most of all I must mention Mr. Kenneth Sowah and Mr. Frank Ablorh. The latter, especially, has been for more years than I can remember my personal archivist in Ghana, collecting local newspapers and documents for me as well as accompanying me on trips to find contemporary material and seek out local informants. His detailed knowledge of Ghana's immediate past has also been invaluable on numerous occasions. In Ghana I have also benefited from the assistance of the staff at the library of the Institute of African Studies as well as the Balme Library, both at the University of Ghana at Legon.

Closer to home, a number of my Africanist colleagues have also helped me to complete this work by providing leads and advice on focus and emphasis. I must single out my Mercy College colleague Dr. Donald Morales, who functioned very much as my Internet adviser, and Dr. Joseph McLaren, formerly of Mercy College but now at Hofstra University, who was also particularly helpful and constructive in his suggestions, since he too has published with Greenwood Press and could offer advice from this experience. Both of these colleagues share my interest in Africa and supplement it with a literary perspective. My former advisers at Stanford University, Kennell Jackson and Richard Roberts, who always challenged me to think about Africa's past in innovative ways, have also made important suggestions about the focus and content of this history. Corinne Nyquist, a fellow board member of the New York African Studies Association and a librarian at the State University of New York at New Paltz, also provided help in tracking materials that I needed from local libraries. I must also thank my colleagues in the Ghana Studies Council, especially Emmanuel Akyeampong, David Killingray, Takyiwaa Manuh, David Owusu-Ansah, and Richard Rathbone, for helping me find answers to some of the teasing questions I have faced.

The Faculty Development Committee and the provost's office at Mercy College have also played an important role in providing funding for my many research trips to Ghana over more than two decades. Without this continual return to the field it would have been difficult to keep abreast of new developments in Ghana, explore new sources of information, and acquire the latest local publications on the country.

My two sisters, Gillian Gocking-Conrad and Rosalind Bucher, have also played an indirect role in the completion of this work. For many years Rosalind lived in London and provided the most comfortable base of operations for research in such incomparable sources of information as the Public Records Office and the library collections of London University and the British Library. The contribution was more than this alone. We all grew up in a colonial situation, and they were able to share their insights derived from this experience, which have stimulated me to think about issues that I might otherwise have ignored. They have always shown an enthusiastic interest in my travels and experiences in Ghana and in other areas of the African continent. In a similar fashion, my fellow outdoor enthusiast, Gidon Schwarcz, has, over the last four years, maintained an unflagging interest in the project, never failing to greet me with "how is the book coming?"

Most of all I owe a debt of gratitude to the people of Ghana. During the 30 years I have been associated with their country they have invariably been enthusiastic and honored to find someone who was deeply interested in their history. They have given generously of their time to answer questions about themselves, deceased relatives, and prominent and not-so-prominent members of their community, and to explain the complexities of a society made up of extended families with very different structures and customs from those outside of Africa. As the Akan proverb says: A single person cannot cover God's eyes (the sky). I have clearly needed much local help in covering this relatively small canvas of Ghanaland.

NOTE

1. Kwame Nkrumah, "Africa Must Be Free," in *Selected Speeches of Kwame Nkrumah*, vol. 2, comp. S. Obeng (Accra, Ghana: Afram Publications, 1997), 67.

Abbreviations

ACDR	Association of Communities for the Defense of the Revolution
AFC	Alliance for Change
AFRC	Armed Forces Revolutionary Council
AGC	Ashanti Goldfields Corporation
A.M.E. Zion Church	African Methodist Episcopal Zion Church
ARPB	Association of Recognized Professional Bodies
AYA	Asante Youth Association
BBC	British Broadcasting Corporation
BNI	Bureau of National Investigations
CAP	National Coalition Against the Privatization of Water
CDR	Committees for the Defense of the Revolution
CIA	Central Intelligence Agency

CNC	Central National Committee
CPP	Convention People's Party
CSSV	cocoa swollen-shoot virus
CVC	Citizens Vetting Committee
CYO	Committee on Youth Organization
DPP	Democratic People's Party
DWM31st	December Women's Movement of Ghana
EAC	Economic Advisory Committee
EC	Electoral Commission
ECOWAS	Economic Community of West African States
EGLE	Every Ghanaian Living Everywhere
ERP	Economic Recovery Program
FBI	Federal Bureau of Investigation
GAF	Ghana Armed Forces
GBA	Ghana Bar Association
GCARPS	Gold Coast Aborigines Rights Protection Society
GCP	Ghana Congress Party
GCPP	Great Consolidated Popular Party
GDP	gross domestic product
GIHOC	Ghana Industrial Holding Company
GNP	gross national product
GWCL	Ghana Water Company Limited
HIPC	heavily indebted poor country
IAS	Independent African States
IMF	International Monetary Fund
INCC	Interim National Coordinating Committee
INEC	Interim National Electoral Commission
ISODEC	Integrated Social Development Centre

JFM	June Fourth Movement
MAP	Moslem Association Party
MFJ	Movement for Freedom and Justice
MP	member of Parliament
NAL	National Alliance of Liberals
NAO	Native Administration Ordinance
NCBWA	National Congress of British West Africa
NCC	National Commission on Culture
NCD	National Commission on Democracy
NCP	National Convention Party
NDC	National Democratic Congress
NDM	New Democratic Movement
NEPAD	New Economic Partnership for Africa's Development
NGO	nongovernmental organization
NIC	National Investigating Committee
NIP	National Independence Party
NLC	National Liberation Council
NLM	National Liberation Movement
NPP	New Patriotic Party
NPP	Northern People's Party
NRC	National Reconciliation Commission
NRC	National Redemption Council
NRP	National Reform Party
NUGS	National Union of Ghana Students
OAU	Organization of African Unity
OFY	Operation Feed Yourself
OPEC	Organization of Petroleum Exporting Countries
PAC	Political Advisory Committee

PAMSCAD	Program of Action to Mitigate the Social Cost of Adjustment
PANAFEST	Pan-African Historical Theater Festival
PCP	Peoples' Convention Party
PDC	People's Defense Committee
PFP	Popular Front Party
PHP	People's Heritage Party
PMFJ	People's Movement for Freedom and Justice
PNC	People's National Convention
PNDC	Provisional National Defense Council
PNP	People's National Party
POGR	President's Own Guard Regiment
PP	Progress Party
PPP	public-private partnership
PSP	private-sector participation
PURC	Public Utilities Regulatory Commission
RTU	Real Tamale United
SAP	structural-adjustment program
SIB	Special Investigations Board
SMA	Societas Missionum ad Afros
SMC	Supreme Military Council
SRC	Students Representative Council
SSNIT	Social Security and National Insurance Trust
SSS	Senior Secondary School
TOR	Tema Oil Refinery
TRC	Truth and Reconciliation Commission
TUC	Trades Union Congress
UAC	United Africa Company

UFGC	United Ghana Farmers' Council
UGCC	United Gold Coast Convention
UGM	United Ghana Movement
UNC	United National Congress
UNESCO	United Nations Educational, Scientific, and Cultural Organization
UNIA	Universal Negro Improvement Association
UNIGOV	Union Government
UP	United Party
VAT	value-added tax
VBGC	Veranda Boys and Girls Club
WAYL	West African Youth League
WDC	Workers' Defense Committee

Orthography

The spelling of place names as well as for traditional offices and office holders has gone through considerable change over time. In this work I have used contemporary spellings except when quoting from earlier times when different spellings were in use. Nevertheless, there still remain inconsistencies. The most notable is the use of *Asante* and *Ashanti*. I have followed contemporary usage in Ghana, where the region is spelled *Ashanti* and the people/culture is spelled *Asante*.

Currency

Until Ghana became independent in 1957, the British pound was the currency in circulation in the country. However, the pound devalued during the course of the twentieth century. In the first three decades of the twentieth century, the pound was officially worth 4.86 U.S. dollars, but after the First World War the pound began to decline in value, and in 1931 it was devalued by 25 percent. It was then officially worth 3.75 dollars, but its actual value continued to fluctuate. In 1949 the pound was once again officially devalued. The new value was 2.80 U.S. dollars to the pound. From 1957 to 1965 the Ghana pound was worth the same as the British pound. From 1965 on the Ghana currency was the cedi, worth $1.16. From February 1967 to July 1967 the new cedi was worth $1.40. In July 1967 the new cedi was devalued so as to be worth $0.98. In December 1971 it was devalued again so as to be worth $0.55, but in 1972 it was revalued to $0.65. In 1978 it was devalued by 58 percent. Eventually, by 1980 the official exchange rate was one cedi (¢) to $0.36 dollars, or 2.75 cedis to the dollar. By that time there was a considerable black market for cedis, with the exchange rate around 30 cedis to the U.S. dollar.

With the introduction of the PNDC's Economic Recovery Program (ERP) in 1983, the cedi was officially devalued to 30 cedis to the U.S. dollar. It progressively devalued from then onward, and in April 1988, when the government allowed foreign exchange (forex bureaus) to be legal in Ghana, the cedi was officially valued at 185 cedis to the dollar. In the forex bureaus it traded at 270 cedis to the dollar, but gradually the two exchange rates began to merge. At the end of 2004 the Interbank rate for the cedi was slightly over 9,000 cedis to the U.S. dollar, and in the forex bureaus it was trading at around 9,125 cedis to the dollar.

Timeline of Historical Events

50,000 B.C.E.	Earliest evidence of human habitation within modern Ghana.
10,000 B.C.E.	The development of late-stone-age Kintampo culture.
2000 B.C.E.	Farming and cattle raising develops in the savanna areas.
ca. 100 C.E.	Iron-smelting technology enters the savanna and spreads into the rain forest.
ca. 1000	The Akan and Ga-Adangbe people emerge in the rain forest and the Shai Hills.
ca. 1450	First centralized states in the savanna: Mamprugu, Dagbon, and Nanumba.
1471	The Portuguese arrive on the coast.
1482	The Portuguese begin construction of Castle of São Jorge da Mina.
1515–26	The Portuguese construct Fort São Antonio and Fort São Sebastian.

1637	The Dutch conquer the Castle of São Jorge da Mina from the Portuguese.
1661	The Danes begin the construction of Christiansborg Castle.
1665	The English capture Cape Coast Castle from the Swedes. The castle becomes the headquarters of the Royal African Company.
1667	The Akan state of Akwamu invades and destroys Great Accra.
1670s	Asantehene Osei Tutu lays the foundations of the Asante state.
1720–50	Asantehene Opoku Ware conquers neighboring Akan and states.
1730–80	The Asantes conquer Gonja and Dagomba.
1750	The Royal African Company loses its monopoly on the coast and is replaced by the African Company.
1764–77	Asantehene Osei Kwadwo "bureaucratizes" the Asante state. Qualification for office becomes more important than birth.
1807–14	Numerous Asante invasions of the coast.
1808	The British government abolishes the transatlantic slave trade.
1821	The British government takes over the administration of the Gold Coast Settlements in the control of the African Company.
1824	Sir Charles Macarthy, governor of the British forts and settlements, killed in a skirmish with the Asante.
1826	The British and local allies defeat the Asante at the Battle of Dodowa. Peace treaty signed.
1828	The British government returns control of British coastal forts and settlements to their merchants trading with the Gold Coast.
1828	Basel Evangelical Missionary Society established with Christiansborg as its headquarters.

1835	The first Methodist missionaries arrive in Ghana. Cape Coast becomes their headquarters.
1841	Dr. R. R. Madden investigates administration of coastal forts and settlements.
1844	The British government resumes control of the coastal forts and settlements. Lieutenant governor signs Bond of 1844 with local chiefs.
1850	The British purchase the Danish castle and forts on the coast.
1852	The British introduce a poll tax to help pay for local administration.
1853	The British establish a supreme court for their coastal possessions.
1857	The *Accra Herald* become the first independent source of news in the Gold Coast.
1863	The Third Asante War results in a humiliating British retreat.
1865	The Select Parliamentary Committee recommends withdrawal from the coast.
1868	Exchange of castles and forts between the Dutch and the British.
1870	The British buy all the Dutch castles and forts on the coast.
1871–72	Attempts to create a Fante confederation.
1873	The Asante invade the coast. A British expedition invades and burns Kumasi.
1874	The British settlements on the coast become a formal colony. Slavery abolished.
1876	The establishment of a supreme court for the colony.
1877	Capital of the Gold Coast Colony moved from Cape Coast to Accra.
1878	Cocoa introduced into Ghana from Fernando Po by Tetteh Quarshie.

1880	Arrival of the Roman Catholic Societas Missionum ad Afros (SMA) fathers. They make Elmina their headquarters.
1883	Passage of the Native Jurisdiction Ordinance.
1886	Africans appointed to the Legislative Council.
1887	Ruling in *Oppon v. Ackinnie* upholds judicial power of native kings and chiefs.
1896	Outbreak of hostilities with Asante. Asantehene Prempeh I deported to Sierra Leone.
1897	Gold Coast Aborigines' Rights Protection Society (GCARPS) established in Cape Coast to oppose British government's attempt to establish crown lands and regulate sale of concessions. Deputation goes to Great Britain.
1898	A highly controversial town council established for Accra.
1900	Governor Hodgson's search for the Golden Stool of Asante precipitates last Asante revolt. Asantehene Prempeh I and other Asantes exiled to the Seychelles Islands.
1901–2	Ashanti Protectorate and Northern Territories become part of the Gold Coast Colony.
1902	Secretariat of Native Affairs established.
1903	Railway from Sekondi reaches Kumasi.
1904	Town council established for Sekondi.
1906	Town council established for Cape Coast.
1910	Outbreak of yellow fever claims 12 lives in the colony.
1910	Passage of the Native Jurisdiction Bill.
1912	The West African Lands Committee recommends state intervention to halt transition to individual ownership of the colony's public land.
1916	Governor Hugh Clifford appoints three chiefs to an expanded legislative council.

1920	First meeting of the National Congress of British West Africa held in Accra.
1922–37	Asamangkese dispute over the control of diamond-producing areas.
1924	Korle Bu hospital in Accra completed.
1924	Prempeh I repatriated from the Seychelles and allowed to be chief of Kumasi.
1925	Governor Gordon Guggisberg introduces a new constitution that creates Provincial Councils of Chiefs and expands chiefly representation in the legislative council.
1927	Achimota College formally opened.
1929	West African Court of Appeal established.
1930	Deepwater harbor at Takoradi completed.
1930	Governor Ransford Slater's attempts to introduce income tax in the colony greeted with riots that dooms legislation.
1930–31	First major cocoa "holdup" organized by African cocoa farmers.
1934	Governor Shenton Thomas introduces the "Obnoxious Ordinances" to curb dissent in the colony. The CNC and GCARPS send separate deputations to London to protest this legislation.
1935	Ashanti Confederacy restored. Prempeh II enstooled as *asantehene*.
1935–38	I.T.A. Wallace-Johnson convicted for sedition, eventually banned from the Gold Coast, and sent back to Sierra Leone.
1937	Second major cocoa holdup. The Nowell Commission established to investigate marketing of cocoa in the colony.
1939	Passage of the Native Administration Ordinance, which creates treasuries for native states.
1942	Governor Alan Burns appoints two Africans to the colony's executive committee.

1943   Scientists determine how the swollen shoot of cocoa disease spread.

1944   The Native Courts Ordinance places native courts under the control of the government.

1946   A new constitution comes into force that gives Africans a majority in the legislative council and links Ashanti and the colony.

1947   Establishment of the Cocoa Marketing Board.

1947   The establishment of the United Gold Coast Convention (UGCC). Kwame Nkrumah appointed secretary of the organization.

1948   Anti-Inflation Campaign forces European firms to reduce prices.

1948   Ex-servicemen demonstration ends in shooting and riots that leave 29 dead and vast amounts of property destruction. Executive of UGCC arrested.

1949   Nkrumah breaks from the UGCC and forms the Convention People's Party (CCP). The CCP initiates "Positive Action." Government imprisons Nkrumah and the CPP's leadership.

1951   The CPP wins a majority of the seats in the newly established legislative council. Nkrumah released from prison and becomes leader of government business.

1951   Five-Year Development Plan drawn up to cost 120 million pounds.

1954   The CPP win 72 out of 104 seats in the expanded legislative council. The National Liberation Movement (NLM), primarily an Asante political party, is founded and challenges the CPP.

1955   The NLM and other anti-CPP groups unite to form the United Party (UP). They advocate a federal form of government.

1956   A plebiscite in the former German Togoland favors union with an independent Ghana.

1957	The CPP wins the final election before independence with 71 of the 104 seats contested.
1957	Ghana becomes independent.
1958	The CPP government passes the Preventive Detention Act, which allows for the detention of opponents without trial.
1958	All-African Peoples Conference takes place in Accra.
1959	Nkrumah announces new Five-Year Development Plan that is to cost $700 million.
1959	Brong-Ahafo separated from the Ashanti Region and becomes its own region.
1960	Ghana becomes a republic, with Nkrumah as the first president.
1961	The Casablanca meeting. The Ghana-Guinea-Mali Union announced.
1962	Attempted assassination of Nkrumah at the border town of Kulungugu.
1963	Organization of African Unity (OAU) formed with Addis Ababa in Ethiopia as its capital.
1964	A national referendum makes Ghana a one-party state.
1964	Construction of Akosombo Dam completed.
1965	Accra hosts the OAU.
1966	Nkrumah overthrown by the army in a bloodless coup. The army and police establish the National Liberation Council (NLC).
1967	General Kotoka, one of the NLC leaders, killed in an attempted military coup.
1969	Dr. Kofi Busia's Progress Party (PP) wins 105 of the 140 seats in national elections, ushering in the era of the Second Republic.
1969	The Busia government passes the Aliens Compliance Order. About 150,000 West Africans without residence papers forced to leave Ghana.

1972	The Busia government devalues the Ghanaian currency. A month later the army stages a bloodless coup.
1972	Colonel Ignatius Acheampong, the leader of the military coup, becomes leader of the new National Redemption Council (NRC) government.
1972	The NRC government launches Operation Feed Yourself (OFY).
1972	Exiled former president Nkrumah dies while seeking medical attention in Rumania.
1975	The Supreme Military Command (SMC) replaces the NRC.
1976	The SMC seeks to promote Union Government for Ghana (UNIGOV).
1978	People's Movement for Freedom and Justice (PMFJ) formed to oppose the idea of UNIGOV.
1978	Middle-ranking officers force Acheampong to resign; SMC II formed.
1979	Flight Lieutenant Jerry Rawlings leads a coup against the SMC, and the Armed Forces Revolutionary Council (AFRC) takes over the country's government.
1979	General Acheampong and seven other NLC and SMC military leaders publicly executed by firing squad.
1979	The AFRC allows national elections to take place, and Dr. Hilla Limann's People's National Party (PNP) wins. Dr. Limann becomes the president of Ghana's Third Republic.
1981	Rawlings stages another coup. The Third Republic dissolved, and the Provisional National Defense Council (PNDC) takes control of the country with Rawlings as chairman.
1982	Three high-court judges and a retired army major kidnapped and murdered. Members of the PNDC accused of being involved.
1982–83	Two major coup attempts by disaffected soldiers.

1983	Over a million Ghanaians forcibly repatriated back to Ghana from Nigeria.
1983	A year of terrible drought. Bushfires in the rain-forest regions of the country.
1983	Five killers tried by the Accra Public Tribunal and found guilty, and the three in custody executed by firing squad.
1983	Ghana devalues its currency and turns to the International Monetary Fund (IMF) and the World Bank for financial support, and establishes an economic-recovery program designed to suit World Bank guidelines.
1986	The PNDC introduces ERP II.
1988–89	Elections held for new district assemblies.
1990	The Movement for Freedom and Justice (MFJ) established. It calls for a return to multiparty democracy.
1991	The PNDC agrees to create a new Consultative Assembly to draw up a new constitution.
1992	A referendum approves a new democratic constitution and multiparty system. The PNDC becomes the National Democratic Congress (NDC) and wins the election.
1993	Rawlings, as leader of the NDC, inaugurated and becomes the president of Ghana's Fourth Republic.
1994	Outbreak of serious ethnic fighting in northern Ghana.
1996	NDC wins second term.
1997	Introduction of a value-added tax (VAT).
2000	The New Patriotic Party (NPP) wins the third election in Ghana's Fourth Republic.
2001	John Agyekum Kufour installed as president of Ghana.
2001	Ghana joins the Heavily Indebted Poor Countries (HIPC) Initiative.
2004	President Kufuor wins the fourth election in Ghana's Fourth Republic.

1

Introduction: Ghana in Perspective

At midnight on March 6, 1957, the former British colony of the Gold Coast became the modern nation of Ghana. This newly independent nation took its name from the great Sudanic Empire of Ghana, which existed from the fifth to the thirteenth centuries several hundreds of miles to the northwest of modern Ghana in the Sudanic zone (a combination of the savanna and the sahel) of West Africa. Modern Ghana, in contrast, is located on the West African coast and is the eighth-largest country of the region's 16 nations. It has an area of 238,540 square kilometers, or roughly 92,000 square miles, which makes it slightly larger than the United Kingdom and slightly smaller than the U.S. state of Oregon. The country's main city and seat of government is the coastal city Accra, with a population estimated in 2004 to be almost 3 million, while the country's overall population is estimated at 20.8 million. The gross domestic product (GDP) per capita (purchasing power parity) is $2,200 (2003 estimate).[1] Though relatively small in size, Ghana has the second-largest population in West Africa, after Nigeria. Since January 9, 1993, Ghana has officially been known as the Fourth Republic of Ghana; it is a constitutional democracy in which the head of state is also the head of government. The country is divided into 10 administrative regions.

THE LAND

Ghana lies in the middle of the West African coastline between three degrees west longitude and one degree east longitude. Its most southern point, Cape Three Points, is 4.5 degrees north latitude, and its most northern point is 11 degrees north latitude. This location means that Ghana enjoys a tropical climate in which the main seasonal change is the difference between the wet season and the dry season. In the southern half of the country, much of which consists of various forms of rain forest, there are two rainy seasons: the most extensive is between May and June, and then there is a shorter rainy season in September. In the north of the country, which is primarily savanna woodland, there is only one rainy season, which usually peaks between August and September. Rainfall varies from over 80 inches a year in the area of tropical rain forest north of Half Assini to less than 30 inches a year for the capital, Accra, which is located in a strip of coastal savanna.

From November to April the northeast trade winds, known as the Harmattan, sweep in from the Sahara Desert, bringing dry and dusty conditions as far south as the coastal areas. In the south these winds last only from December to February. This is the coolest time of the year for this part of the country, while the months between the end of the Harmattan season and the onset of the rainy season are the hottest. In the rain-forest region the daytime temperature during the year varies only slightly between 80 and 90 degrees, but in the far north daytime temperatures can rise to over 110 degrees during the Harmattan and be no higher than 75 degrees during the rainy season.

The Rain Forest

Much of the southern part of the country consists of two types of rain forest: evergreen and semideciduous forests. Trees in the evergreen forests get more rain and tend to retain their leaves throughout the year, while those in the semideciduous forest shed off foliage during the dry season, though this kind of forest can often be a mixture of evergreen and semideciduous trees. In the latter the vegetation tends to be more dense since sunlight can more easily penetrate, while in the evergreen forests large trees, often over 150 feet in height, form canopies that block out sunlight. Both types of forest provide important commercial species like mahogany, *odum, wawa, sapele,* and *makoré.* There are over 300 timber-producing species, many of which are only used domestically. In 2003 timber exports were valued at $174 million and amounted to 7.5 percent of total exports.[2]

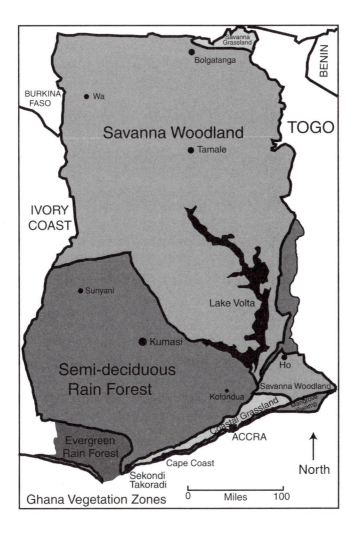

Ghana Vegetation Zones

Generations of lumbering operations and shifting cultivation have resulted in large areas within the rain-forest region that have been cleared.
These areas can grow back as secondary forest with very dense vegetation
and trees that are much smaller in size than the original rain forest, but it
is possible for this secondary forest to return eventually to rain forest.
Unfortunately, pressure for farmland makes this unlikely.

Ghana's most important cash crop, cocoa, grows in a large diagonal belt
that stretches across the center of the rain-forest region, but with the greatest concentration in the Ashanti and Brong-Ahafo regions. Cocoa requires

well-drained land with high and regular amounts of rainfall as well as shade from larger forest trees, so that much of the rain forest is left standing in areas of heavy cocoa cultivation. Cocoa is Ghana's second-largest export after gold. In 2003 cocoa exports were valued at $803 million and were equivalent to about 35 percent of total exports.[3] Oil palms are another important cash crop from this region, many of which grow wild since, unlike cocoa, the oil palm is indigenous to this part of Africa. The main area of cultivation is a long, narrow belt a short distance in from the coast. The coast itself is studded with coconut palms, which, like cocoa, are a relatively recent import to this area. Oil from coconuts and especially oil-palm nuts is an important source of vegetable oil, and most of this is consumed locally. Oil palm trees are also tapped by making a small hole into the trunk of the tree. The sap that comes out is known as palm wine. As it ferments it becomes increasingly more alcoholic. Palm wine is also distilled to produce a potent alcoholic beverage known as *akpeteshie*. Kola nuts from the kola tree, a mild stimulant, have historically been one of the important exports from the rain forest to the Sudanic interior. Some coffee and citrus fruit, and more recently increasing amounts of pineapple, make up the important cash crops that grow in this region of the country.

The main food crops of the rain-forest region have traditionally been root crops or tubers. The cocoyam is indigenous to this area, as are other types of yam, while the Asian yam is a more recent arrival. Yams are important staples in the Ghanaian diet. Today more varieties of yam are grown in the savanna woodland than in the rain-forest region of the country. Root crops like cassava are also imports, in this instance from South America, and represent one of the few reverse benefits of the transatlantic slave trade. This root crop grows in a wide range of locations and is one of the most important sources of starch in the local diet. Maize is another important South American import, and like cassava it can grow both in rain-forest regions and in the savanna woodland. Wetland rice is also cultivated in areas that can easily be flooded, which include both the rain-forest region and the savanna woodland. Bananas, plantains, and a wide array of tropical fruits are also grown in these regions. Much of the farming in Ghana has been shifting cultivation with mixed cropping, which helps to preserve fertility since tropical soils rapidly deteriorate when stripped of all vegetation. However, increasing use of chemical fertilizers is changing this pattern of agriculture.

The Savanna

More than half of Ghana is savanna woodland, which consists of high grass and a wide array of semideciduous trees, the most commercially important of which is the shea tree, a source of vegetable oil. A small portion of this area in the far northeast is even drier Sudan savanna, where the grass is lower and large baobab trees and thorny acacia trees dominate the environment. A significant area of savanna woodland and grassland is found along Ghana's eastern coast. The country's capital is located in this area, where the average rainfall is among the lowest in the country. The most important cash crops from the savanna region are shea nuts, peanuts (known in West Africa as groundnuts), and more recently cotton. Food crops are primarily grains like rice, millet, and sorghum (known in Ghana as guinea corn), with maize, cassava, and yams in areas of higher rainfall. In general, agriculture is more precarious in this region due to the ever-present possibility of drought. Much of the savanna is too dry for tsetse flies, unlike the rain forest, and is consequently free of sleeping sickness so that cattle raising is often the most important economic activity in this region. Goats, sheep, and chickens are not affected by the trypanosomes that cause sleeping sickness and consequently are found all over Ghana. As is the case in the rain-forest region, there is extensive fruit and vegetable farming in the savanna woodlands, particularly near sources of water for irrigation and close to large urban populations.

Coastal Scrub and Grassland

This zone begins as a narrow strip near the mouth of the River Pra and widens to about 20 miles in width near the delta of the Volta River. The western section of this zone consists of dense scrub and reaches almost all the way to Accra, the country's capital. From this point scrub gives way to grassland, and what is known as the Accra Plains stretch almost all the way to the Volta Delta. This is the area of Ghana that receives the lowest amount of rainfall in the country, and has benefited most from the construction of the Akosombo Dam on the Volta River and the irrigation schemes associated with this project. Cassava is the most widespread crop, which is often intercropped with maize, okras, peppers, tomatoes, and eggplants. Near the Volta Delta, shallots (a type of small onion) are extensively cultivated, while in the savanna-grassland area, which is free of tsetse flies, there is considerable cattle raising. Along much of the coast there are stands of coconut palms that are an important source of copra (the flesh of the nut), from which oil is extracted. The coast itself is open, without bays, and the water offshore is shallow. Consequently, Ghana has few natural harbors. Nevertheless, there is considerable fishing along this coast, and most of the over 360,000 tons of fish caught yearly in Ghana come from these waters.[4]

Topography

Ghana's topography can best be described as rolling with dark-green hills dominating the panorama for large distances. There are no real mountains, or highlands, though in some areas, like the Ashanti Uplands, the Kwahu Plateau, and the Akwapim-Togo Ranges, summits do rise to between 2,300 to 2,900 feet above sea level. This is not enough to have a significant impact on climate and environment, which remains tropical with only small temperature changes. Several major river systems drain the country's surface area. The largest is the Volta River system. The main arms of this system, the Black, the White, and the Red Volta, originate in the neighboring countries of either the Ivory Coast or Burkina Faso. Since 1966 these rivers and their tributaries have been impounded by the Akosombo Dam to form one of the world's largest artificial lakes. The Volta Lake stretches for over 240 miles, most of which is navigable by large ships. It covers about a sixth of Ghana's surface area, and apart from providing transportation and generating most of the country's electricity, the lake also supplies water for irrigation and sustains an important fishing industry. The other three major river systems are the Pra, the Ankobra, and the Tano Rivers, which drain the rain-forest region of the country. Their flows are very much affected by the rainy season, and on all of them there are either rapids or waterfalls that restrict their navigable use.

Geology and Minerals

Ghana's geology is complex. Large areas in the savanna consist of sedimentary rocks that make up what is known as the Voltain Basin. To the north and south there are plateaus made up of older shales, sandstones, and basalt, some of which are derived from ancient volcanoes. Particularly in the south there is considerable folding that has given rise to the ranges of hills known as the Akwapim-Togo Ranges. Further southward and to the west and north of the Voltain Basin there are older Precambrian rocks with intruded granites. There are two main series recognized, the Birrimian and the Tarkwaian, which are economically the most important geologic formations in the country. Most of the gold, diamonds, and manganese obtained in Ghana comes from Birrimian and Tarkwaian rocks, while rich deposits of bauxite are also found in areas with these rocks.

Of all these minerals, gold has been and remains the most important. Before the coming of Europeans in the fifteenth century, gold was mined in this area, which Europeans came to call the Golden Coast of Guinea

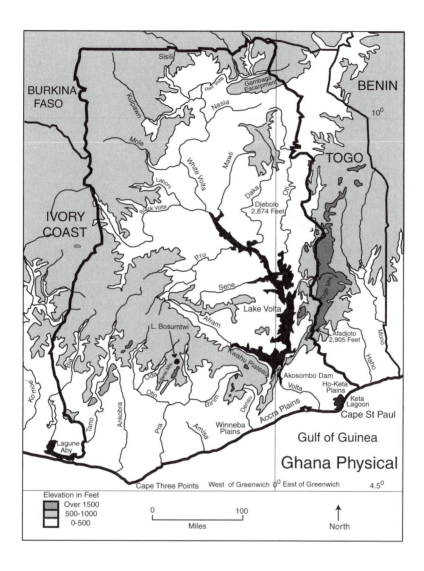

Ghana Physical

Elevation in Feet
Over 1500
500-1000
0-500

0   100
Miles

North

and later on simply the Gold Coast. In the past much of this gold came from alluvial deposits in streams and rivers in the rain forest and in coastal sands, where it had been washed down from the interior by rivers and rains.[5] There was also shaft mining, which continues using traditional techniques and is referred to in Ghana today as *galamsey* mining, but most of the gold now mined is lode, or reef, gold, which requires heavy machinery and vast amounts of capital to extract. These deep mines, which in some cases go down over 5,000 feet, are concentrated in the narrow Tarkwaian system that stretches from Tarkwa in the south to Konongo in the north at the edge of the rain forest region. In 2003 Ghana produced over 2.27 million ounces of gold, valued at $830 million, or equivalent to 36 percent of the country's total exports.[6] Ghana was the second-most-important gold producer in Africa, after the Republic of South Africa.

Of lesser importance is diamond mining, most of which is for industrial diamonds. There are two main producing areas: the larger Birim area around the Birim River, a tributary to the Pra located in the Eastern Region, and in the Bonsa valley in the Western Region. In the former area, large-scale multinational companies dominate, while in the latter, mining is in the hands of thousands of African prospectors. Most of the diamonds found are of the alluvial type. In 2002 diamond exports were worth $21 million. The country also possesses important deposits of manganese, most of which come from very rich mines at Nsuta in the Western Region. In 2002 manganese exports were worth $31.6 million. There are also vast deposits of bauxite, with the deposits in the Sefwi Bekwai region some of the world's largest. Mining did not start until 1941, but in 2002 over 663,000 tons were mined, which were shipped to alumina-processing plants outside of Ghana. Export earnings from this resource amounted to $14.8 million.[7]

THE PEOPLE

About 44 percent of Ghana's population are Akans, who live primarily in the forest regions of the country. Akans can be further subdivided into 11 subgroups, the largest of which are the Asante, the Fante, the Akyem, the Akwamu, and the Nzimas. Their languages are all closely related and form part of the larger Kwa group of languages to which most of the people of West Africa belong. Traditionally they are matrilineal. Membership in the *abusua,* or lineage, is determined through the female line, which means that property passes from maternal uncles to nephews, as does succession to traditional offices like that of chieftaincy. This means that women, the "stool mothers," play an important role in determining succession.[8] Some offices, especially those in traditional military associations known as *asafos,* are inherited patrilineally, as are paternal characteristics (*sunsum*), which has prompted some anthropologists to suggest that these groups, especially the Fante, follow a system of double descent.[9] But even among the coastal Fante, where the *asafo* system has been most developed, matrilineal links are clearly dominant, even to the point where today important offices in these institutions are often passing to maternal nephews.

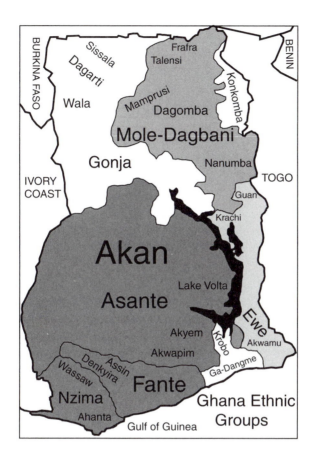

The Mole-Dagbani (also known as the Moshi-Dagomba) are the second-largest ethnic group in Ghana, comprising about 16 percent of the population, and are located primarily in the north. They can be subdivided into smaller groups like the Nanumba, Mamprusi, Mossi, Frafra, Talensi, and Dagomba. Linguistically they belong to the Gur language group, which is one of the two major language groups of the savanna region of West Africa. Like other cattle-raising savanna peoples, they are patrilineal, and the long-standing influence of Islam in this area has also reinforced this characteristic.[10] Some of these people, like the Dagomba and the Mamprusi, live in centralized states like the Akan, while others, like the Nanumba and the Talensi, live in small clans that are bound together by kinship ties.

The third-largest ethnic group are the Ewe, who comprise about 13 percent of the country's population. They live mainly on the eastern side of Lake Volta, and many spread over into the neighboring country of Togo. They speak many different dialects but constitute a single linguistic entity, though there are small non-Ewe groups among them, like the Akpafu, Lolobi, and Likpe, who live in the northern part of this area and speak different languages. Supposedly they are patrilineal, but among the southern Ewe especially, where Akan influence has been greatest, matrilineal influence has been spreading.

Undoubtedly it is among the Ga, who along with the Dangme (also known as the Adangbe) people make up about eight percent of the population and live in the most cosmopolitan part of Ghana, around the country's capital, Accra, where Akanization has gone furthest. Not only have their languages been affected by the influence of Twi, the main Akan language, but as one historian has suggested, there has been considerable "Gaisation" of Akan institutions and culture.[11] Most notable has been the matrilineal influence. Traditionally the Ga are patrilineal, but given the extensive history of intermarriage with Akans, from as early as the seventeenth century, it is not surprising Ga systems of inheritance have a long history of being influenced by Akan customs. Geography and history, however, have conspired to make it much harder for centralized states to emerge in this area, and up until the coming of colonial rule the people of this area lived primarily in coastal settlements divided into small, fiercely independent *akutsei,* or quarters. The modern Dangme, who include people like the Shai, the Ningo, and the Krobo, live further away from Accra and have also been affected by Akanization.

The remaining 19 percent of Ghana's population consists of smaller ethnic groups like the highly dispersed Guan peoples, who now live scattered in a great curve from Gonja in the Northern Region all the way south to Winneba on the coast, and the Lodagaa in northwestern Ghana, who number no more than a few hundred thousand people. Ghana also has a long history of attracting Africans from neighboring countries. In many cases ethnic groups overlap these borders, which can make it difficult to distinguish citizen from noncitizen. Undoubtedly it is in the Volta Region among the Ewe people that this problem has been most acute in recent times. At the time of independence there was a significant faction who wanted unification with other Ewes in Togo to form a separate nation.

Other Africans have come from further afield. The links between fellow British colonies in West Africa (and even the Caribbean) facilitated this process. Sierra Leoneans, Gambians, and most of all Nigerians took advantage of these opportunities, but today it is undoubtedly the Nigerians who predominate. Many of them have been many generations in Ghana and absorbed into the local population. Finally, among these nonnatives must also be included people of non-African origin, like Syrians, Lebanese, and Asians, some of whose ancestors migrated to Ghana in the late nineteenth and early twentieth centuries. Along with small numbers of expatriates, predominantly from Europe, they add a cosmopolitan character to the Ghanaian population. Particularly since independence, a small population of African Americans also reside in Ghana. They number about 1,000 and live primarily in the capital area. In general, Ghana's population is young, like that of other Third World societies, with 38 percent of the population between 0 and 14 years of age.[12]

About 63 percent of Ghanaians profess to believe in some form of Christianity.[13] Between 15 and 25 percent of this population is Catholic. As an indication of their increasing importance to the Catholic Church, in 2003 Archbishop Peter Appiah Turkson was appointed the first cardinal of the Ghanaian Catholic Church. Protestants, comprising Methodists and Presbyterians, make up the second-largest segment of the Christian population, 25 percent. There are smaller numbers of other Christians, like Anglicans, Seventh-Day Adventists, Jehovah's Witnesses, and vast numbers of independent Christian churches variously referred to as *spiritual* or *pentecostal*. These independent churches are the fastest-growing segment of the Christian population, and they draw away members from the established churches. A recent estimate puts their number as high as 22 percent of all Christians.[14] Muslims make up about 16 percent of the population, most of whom are to be found in the north, but there are also sizeable communities (known as *zongos*) in many of Ghana's southern cities. About 21 percent of the population is classified as professing indigenous religious beliefs.[15] There are also other religions, like Hinduism, Buddhism, and Judaism, that attract small numbers of followers.

HISTORICAL OVERVIEW

Much of what is now Ghana has been inhabited as far back as the early Stone Age, or more than 50,000 years ago. By the beginning of the second millennium B.C.E., farming and cattle raising had developed in the savanna areas, and were soon followed by settled village communities. The coming of iron technology into this area, beginning in the second century C.E., made it easier to farm the denser vegetation of the rain-forest region to the south. Small bands of migrants with this superior technology were able to impose themselves on earlier inhabitants, who in the long run absorbed them. Around the tenth century, the Akan and the Ga-Dangme were the first to emerge as distinct people in this region.

However, it was in the savanna north that centralized states first began to emerge. Many came under the influence of Islam, and these states became important centers of Islamic culture. In the seventeenth century the people of this region acquired a powerful neighbor in the rain forest to the south, the Akan state of Asante. By the eighteenth century most of the northern people had been incorporated into what had become the Asante Confederacy.

State building in the south was influenced by the coming of Europeans, who, beginning with the Portuguese, established themselves on the coast at the end of the fifteenth century. Other Europeans soon followed. They entered into alliances with local people, the most important of which was the British with the Fante, an Akan people. In the early nineteenth century this alliance served to check the expansion of the Asante to the coast.

The expansion of British power on the coast inevitably caused conflict with the Asantes. In the nineteenth century the Asante invaded the coast several times. The British government shifted between formally taking control of the coastal area and handing it over to the British merchants who traded on the coast. Eventually, in 1874, after successfully invading the Asante empire, the British government proclaimed the coastal area the Colony of the Gold Coast. After a final Asante rebellion in 1901, the British incorporated Asante into their colony. Concerns that other European powers might annex the north prompted the British to proclaim the Northern Territories a protectorate in 1902. For all practical purposes these three territories became a single political unit administered by a single governor.

Colonial polices, particularly over the control of land, resulted in the creation of the Gold Coast Aborigines Rights Protection Society (GCARPS). In 1898 this organization sent a delegation to London to protest colonial land policies. It succeeded in radically altering colonial land policies. The government's adoption, at the turn of the twentieth century, of what was to be known as an indirect-rule policy, in which the traditional chiefs were incorporated into the administration of the colony, also gave rise to protest. The Western-educated elite felt that they could better represent the interests of the African population. The National Congress of British West Africa (NCBWA), which was established after the First World War, brought this rivalry to the forefront, as many of the colony's most important chiefs refused to join this attempt to create a pan-British West African political-pressure group.

Even more fundamental in effecting change was the colony's emergence in the early twentieth century as the world's leading producer of cocoa. The cash economy that cocoa created transformed notions about the ownership of land and the inheritance of property. Economically, the colony was drawn into the world economy and became subject to its vagaries, like the Great Depression. In the 1930s there were two major "cocoa hold-ups" in which Gold Coast farmers tried to force a rise in prices by with-holding their crops. The marketing of cocoa became a central issue in the stirring of nationalist sentiment.

The Second World War and the winds of change that followed quickly accelerated the pace of nationalist demands. Under the charismatic lead-ership of Kwame Nkrumah and his Convention People's Party (CCP), the Gold Coast made rapid strides toward independence, and in 1957 became the first colony in West Africa to attain this status.

In 1960 Ghana became a republic, and for a while was the leading pro-ponent of pan-Africanism in Africa, as more and more former colonies became independent in the 1960s. However, reaction to what was seen in Ghana as Nkrumah's increasing authoritarianism resulted in a military coup that overthrew his government in 1966. The new leadership, the National Liberation Council (NLC), moved to return Ghana to civilian rule and authorized a new constitution for the Second Republic.

In 1969 a former academic, Dr. Kofi Busia, was elected as Ghana's prime minister. Austerity measures that his government introduced rapidly un-dermined its popularity, and in 1972 the army once again seized power.

The National Redemption Council (NRC), under the leadership of Colo-nel Ignatius Acheampong, reversed many of the Busia government's aus-terity measures and repudiated many of the country's foreign debts. The NRC resisted handing power back to civilians, but eventually conceded. In 1979, before the elections took place, a group of junior officers led by Lieutenant Jerry Rawlings staged a coup.

The new military government, the Armed Forces Revolutionary Coun-cil (AFRC), eventually allowed elections to take place, but before the new government could take charge eight former members of the NRC govern-ment were executed.

The new president of what was now Ghana's Third Republic, Dr. Hilla Limann, faced high inflation, a budget deficit, and a rash of strikes that rapidly eroded his government's popularity, and in 1981 Rawlings led yet another coup and established a new government that called itself the Pro-visional National Defense Council (PNDC).

This eighth government in the 15 years since the fall of Nkrumah was to remain in power until 1994. For a short while the PNDC government seemed socialist, but by 1983 it was following the advice offered by the International Monetary Fund (IMF) and the World Bank and adopted a structural-adjustment program (SAP). Eventually, in 1991, Rawlings agreed to return to civilian rule. In the elections held in 1992 Rawlings ran as the leader of what was then called the National Democratic Congress (NDC). His party won, and Rawlings became the fourth civilian president of Ghana's Fourth Republic.

In 1996 there were highly contested elections, with the NDC again victorious. Unlike in the 1992 elections, when the opposition had refused to take part in the parliamentary elections and had not been represented in Parliament, in 1996 the opposition was more united and won almost half of the parliamentary seats. Along with a vibrant independent press, the NDC government had to listen to considerable criticism of what were now basically free-market policies.

The elections of 2000 resulted in victory for the New Patriotic Party (NPP), the NDC's main opposition, which won 100 of the 200 parliamentary seats in contention and was able to wrest control of that body from the NDC. No candidate received an outright majority, which necessitated a runoff that was eventually won by the NPP's flag-bearer, John Agyekum Kufuor.

In December 2004 the country faced its fourth democratic election, which was again won by John Agyekum Kufuor, and the NPP won 129 of the 230 parliamentary seats that were in contention.

NOTES

1. Central Intelligence Agency, "Ghana," in *The World Factbook* (2004), http://www.cia.gov/cia/publications/factbook/geos/gh.html.

2. "Budget 2004: A *Daily Graphic* Special 8-page pull-out" presented by Mr. Yaw Osafo-Maafo, the Minister for Finance and Economic Planning. *Daily Graphic,* February 7, 2004.

3. Ibid.

4. J. Atta-Quayson, ed., *Macmillan Atlas for Ghana* (London and Basingstoke: Unimax Publishers and Macmillan Educational, 1995), 13.

5. Raymond Dumett, *El Dorado in West Africa: The Gold-Mining Frontier, African Labor, and Colonial Capitalism in the Gold Coast, 1875–1900* (Athens: Ohio University Press, 1998), 31.

6. "Budget 2004."

7. The Institute of Statistical, Social and Economic Research, *The State of the Ghanaian Economy in 2002* (Legon, Ghana: Institute of Statistical, Social, and Economic Research, University of Ghana, 2003), 74.

8. The stool, usually carved out of wood, is the most important symbol of office among the Akan people.

9. James Christensen, *Double Descent among the Fanti* (New Haven, Conn.: Human Relations Area Files, 1954).

10. Anthropologists argue that cattle-raising people are invariably patrilineal, since they give cattle as brideprice, which are high in value, and consequently children belong to their father's lineage.

11. John Parker, "Ga State and Society in Early Colonial Accra, 1860–1920s" (Ph.D. diss., University of London, 1995), 25.

12. Central Intelligence Agency, *The World Factbook*. In contrast, the figure for the United States is 20.8 percent.

13. Ibid.

14. David B. Barett, George T. Kurian, and Todd M. Johnson, *World Christian Encyclopedia* (Oxford: Oxford University Press, 2001), 307. Statistics in general for Third World countries are always open to question.

15. Central Intelligence Agency, *The World Factbook*.

2

Precolonial States and Societies

PREHISTORY

There have been many hypotheses to explain the origins of the present people of Ghana. British anthropologist Eve Meyerowitz and Ghanaian nationalist Dr. J. B. Danquah have suggested that the Akan migrated from the ancient empire of Ghana. Danquah was tirelessly to champion this theory, and it was very much on account of his efforts that when the Gold Coast became independent in 1957 the country changed its name to Ghana. The nineteenth-century Ghanaian historian Dr. Carl C. Reindorf has suggested that the Ga came to Ghana from Benin. Others have mentioned Togo, Dahomey, Yorubaland, and even the Biblical land of Canaan as points of origin. However, as one archaeologist has observed, "Ghana has a fairly long prehistory, probably going back to around 50,000 B.C.," and these Stone Age ancestors "bequeathed to Ghana a legacy of human population on which the future population of the country was to be built."[1]

Not until about 10,000 B.C.E., with the flourishing of what has been identified as the Kintampo culture, does the archeological record become extensive and precise. Many of the sites associated with this culture have been found in the vicinity of the present-day market town of Kintampo in the Brong-Ahafo Region, about 90 miles north of Kumasi. Significant technological changes in tool making, especially the fashioning of small implements, were followed by pottery making, and eventually by animal raising, farming, and village community life. Somewhere between the third and the second millennium, cattle, sheep, and goats were domesticated, and shortly afterward food plants like cowpeas, hackberry, oil palms, and white and yellow yams (*Dioscorea* sp.). Significantly, Kintampo culture was not restricted to the savanna, where it probably first emerged, but so far over 16 sites have been excavated in the savanna grassland and woodland as well as further south into areas of the rain forest.

It was the coming of iron technology, somewhere between the second and the fourth century C.E., that was to have "a profound effect on many aspects" of these early societies.[2] Apart from making it easier to farm areas in the rain forest, iron technology contributed to the development of specialization, urbanization, state formation, and territorial expansion. Gold mining that developed in the rain forest, sometime in the fourteenth century C.E., was one of these new specializations, and the long-distance trade that it stimulated contributed to establishing trading links between different vegetation zones as well as state formation, first of all in the savanna, and later on in the rain-forest regions to the south. Increased trade gave rise to local currencies. Cowry shells from the Indian Ocean found in settlement mounds at Kisoto in the Volta Basin date back to the fourteenth century and indicate how extensive long-distance trade had become. What eventually followed from these developments was that

> old Ghana had two faces. One face looked towards the middle Niger and Hausaland [present-day northern Nigeria] and the trans-Saharan caravan routes which linked West Africa with Roman and Islamic north Africa and north-east Africa. The other face looked southward towards the maritime coast, the scene of contact with the commercial representatives of several European nations.[3]

STATE BUILDING

Archeological evidence indicates that much of the early Iron Age activity was located in the Volta Basin of northern Ghana. The common occurrence of low-grade iron ore and wood for fuel stimulated iron-smelting industries in this region. As a result, it was not surprising that it was here that centralized states first developed. Mande-speaking invaders from the north and the northeast seemed to have superimposed themselves on indigenous peoples to form such states as Mamprugu (the state of the Mam-

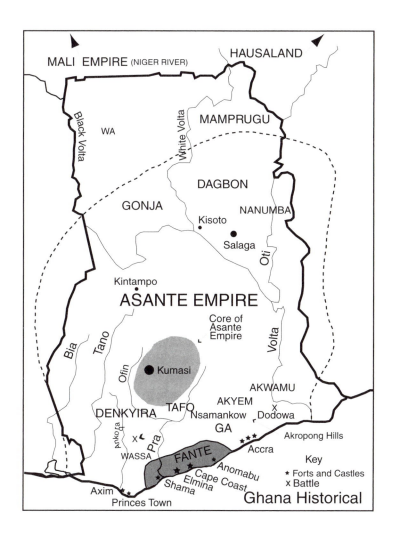

prusi people), Dagbon (the state of the Dagomba people), Nanumba, and later Gonja.[4] These states belonged to what some historians have referred to as the middle-belt neo-Sudanic states: those between the multiethnic Sudanic kingdoms and empires that emerged in the sahel and the savanna of West Africa (the Sudanic zone) in the first millennium C.E. and the kingdoms of the rain forest to the south. Some suggest that the wanderings of these invaders probably began in the thirteenth century.[5]

However, it was not until the end of the fifteenth century that centralized states came into existence in this area. The savanna location allowed these states to control the long-distance trade between the rain forest and the trading centers to the north located on the Niger River or in Hausa-land. Gold and kola nuts were exchanged for salt, cloth, and grain. The need to protect merchants and at the same time tax their transactions must have contributed to the growth of centralization. Disputes over succession led to further migrations and the founding of new states. Oral tradition indicates that this is how Dagbon developed from Mamprugu, and the kingdoms of Buna and Wa developed from the latter.

To the southwest of these states emerged the centralized kingdom of Gonja, whose founders were probably Mande-speaking people of Bam-bara origin. They may have come from the disintegrating Mali empire.[6] King lists would seem to indicate that Gonja was not founded until the second half of the sixteenth century. Nevertheless, its strategic location astride the trade routes both to the Niger Bend to the north and to Hau-saland in the northeast rapidly made it the most powerful of these sa-vanna kingdoms. By the seventeenth century its principal market town, Salaga, was the most important terminus for caravans and traders coming from the rain forest and the northern Sudan. In the seventeenth century, under the most famous of its kings, Lata (1623?–67?), Gonja extended south all the way to the confluence of the White and the Black Volta, and eastward as far as the borders of Nanumba.

In all of these savanna states the early invaders seized the land from the *tindanas,* or earth priests, who were the principal mediators between the people, the Earth God, and the ancestors. However, in some cases, notably among the Dagbon, the *tindanas* were allowed to remain as village chiefs under Dagbon divisional chiefs, and this contributed to lessening the degree of centralization that developed. These new rulers were known as *nas.* They sat on skins, the symbols of authority, akin to the stool in Akan states, and they were assisted by a council of elders. Succession to office was patrilineal.

Initially the invading peoples who established these early states were not Muslims, but had at least been exposed to Islam before their migration southward. As trading links with the Sudanic north expanded, the neo-Sudanic states came under the influence of Islam as Muslims dispersed into this area. The next phase consisted of "the incorporation of Islamic elements into the culture of these states, then the integration of foreign Muslims into the socio-political systems of these states and finally the conversion of members of the local society, mainly from the chiefly es-tate."[7] In Dagbon this process of Islamization went furthest, to produce the most homogeneous society of these Middle Volta Basin states, with a common culture and one language. Mamprugu's involvement in the af-

fairs of neighboring stateless peoples created political tensions that undermined the cohesiveness of the state, and Muslims tried to assert a
semiautonomous status that brought them into conflict with both commoners and chiefs. In Gonja, even though there was contact between Muslims and chiefs before the conquest of the state and the two shared in
its conquest, the two "estates remained distinct," and three social estates
(chiefs, Muslims, and commoners) became rigidly defined.[8]

In all these Middle Volta Basin states Muslims were predominantly
traders and urban-based. In this area Islam was the religion of a small
elite and did not serve to energize conflicts between commoners, who
were farmers or cattle herders, as happened in areas further north. The
process of Islamization was basically peaceful and accommodative. Instead, the main military challenge to these states was to come from the
rain forest to the south with the expanding power of the Akan state of
Asante. They were to become part of the Asante Confederacy, which by
the end of the eighteenth century covered much of present-day Ghana.

In the 1730s first central and western and then eastern Gonja were conquered, but not until the 1750s was a civilian administration established.
A decade later Dagbon experienced the same fate, but continuing opposition to Asante rule meant that it was not until the 1770s that a civilian
administration was established. In both cases this meant recognition of
previous rulers as vassals who paid annual tribute, usually in the form of
slaves. The open savanna terrain favored large-scale Asante military
operations. The Asante had the added advantage of possessing firearms,
which were imported from Europeans on the coast. Forces from both vas-
sal states were incorporated into the Asante army, and as part of the reorganization of the Dagbon fighting forces, a corps of gunmen were
created and the Asante allowed them to import firearms.[9] The incorporation of these conquests into the Asante Confederacy accentuated how
much the latter were a savanna power rather than strictly a rain-forest
kingdom, particularly after the confederacy was forced to retrench its
southern interests in the eighteenth century.[10]

Indeed, Akan traditions in general emphasize savanna origins, and it
seems likely that the original Akan farmers, up until the fifteenth century,
only entered the rain forest for hunting or small-scale, seasonal gold mining. Dyula traders from the Mali empire probably stimulated this development with their interest in gold and kola nuts from the rain forest. In
the fifteenth century some of these Akan began to use slave labor to clear
the forest and to mine for gold using slaves acquired from the Dyula.
Other Akan were attracted to these cleared areas and became subjects of
the "owners of the land" so that the original settlers who controlled the

mines became the founders of new Akan chiefdoms.[11] According to tradition the earliest Akan states to emerge were Bono-Manso in the northwest, at the edge of the rain forest and the savanna, and Adansi at the confluence of the Ofin and the Pra, a center of gold mining in the rain forest. Both of them must have been able to benefit from the north-south long-distance trade in gold and kola nuts. Some suggest that this was in the first half of the fifteenth century, while others think this was somewhere around the middle of the sixteenth century.[12]

As Akan people moved along the northward trade routes, in the late sixteenth and early seventeenth centuries states such as Tafo, Amoakom, Kaase, Akrokyere, Edweso, Mampon, and Kumawu were established. Movements southward and eastward from Adansi resulted in the foundation of such kingdoms as Kwahu, Akyem Abuakwa, Akyem Kotoku, and Akwamu; the Etsi states of Asebu, Fetu, and Sunkwa; and the kingdoms of Fante and Agona even further to the south and Wassa, Sefwi, and Aowin to the southwest. From a Dutch map of 1629 it is clear that all these Akan kingdoms and states had already emerged.[13] However, it was not until the second half of the seventeenth century that what were to be the most powerful of Akan states, Asante and Denkyira, emerged. Initially it was Denkyira that came to monopolize the gold and kola trade of the Pra-Ofin basin, but by the beginning of the eighteenth century it was eclipsed by the Oyoko state of Asante. A century later this powerful kingdom had become dominant in much of what is modern Ghana.

In the 1670s Osei Tutu, a military leader and head of the Oyoko clan, grouped other clan leaders around himself and began establishing control over a trading center that was to become the present-day city of Kumasi. Many of these people were under the rule of the kings of Denkyira and wanted to throw off this yoke. Osei Tutu and his Oyoko brothers were able to take advantage of this dissatisfaction. To endow this union with a spiritual force, Osei Tutu and his priestly adviser, Okomfo Anokye, magically brought into being the Golden Stool of Asante, which came to symbolize the spiritual nature of this union. They also created a constitution for this confederacy. The head of the Oyoko clan was recognized as the king of the confederacy, or the *asantehene*, while two of the powerful non-Oyoko clans of Mampon and Asumenya were made the head of the right and left wings into which the other non-Oyoko clans were divided. Kumasi became the capital of the confederacy. The army was reorganized and armed with guns rather than traditional weapons. In 1700 this army scored a great victory over Denkyira at the battle of Feyiase, eight miles southeast of Kumasi. Between 1700 and 1715 Osei Tutu also conquered the neighboring Akan states of Twifu, Wassa, and Aowin, and he was probably killed in 1717 in one of his wars against Akyem.

Osei Tutu's successor, Opoku Ware, was an even greater conqueror. During his long reign from, 1720 to 1750, he incorporated into the Asante Confederacy the Akan states of Takyiman, Akyem, Kwahu, and the Ga-Dangme principalities near the coast, as well as the savanna states of Gonja, Dagbon, and Krakye. If Osei Tutu was the founder of the Asante state, then Opoku Ware was the founder of the Asante empire.[14] However, it was under Osei Kwadwo, who ruled from 1764–77, that the "bureaucratization" of the Asante state took place. He was the first to "emphasize as credentials for office qualifications other than descent," which was to greatly augment the power of the *asantehene*.[15] Many of the stools or offices in the Kumasi state became appointive rather than hereditary, as well as the regional commissioners for the conquered states. By the beginning of the nineteenth century Asante was no larger than it had been under Opoku Ware, but it was much more effectively administered, and *asantehenes* enjoyed unrivaled power all over the confederacy. Playing an important role in the administration of this large area were a small group of Muslims, mostly from conquered states of the north, who conducted trade with the Sudan. By the early nineteenth century there must "have been over a thousand Muslims more or less permanently settled in Kumasi."[16]

Apart from Denkyira, the other important Akan state to challenge Asante was the kingdom of Akwamu, which also began to gain control over its neighbors at the end of the seventeenth century. This kingdom had one of the longest histories of any Akan state, and though few dates "can be fixed with certainty," it probably began sometime in the early sixteenth century.[17] Originally its people were a part of the Akan coastward migration, and they eventually settled at Nyanawase, Abakrampa, and Asamangkese, in what today is the Eastern Region. However, Nyanawase, the best defensive location of all these sites, eventually became the capital of their kingdom. By this time the Portuguese had already established a fort on the coast, and the opportunities for trade with these Europeans stimulated Akwamu expansion in the direction of the Accra plains. In 1667 they invaded and destroyed Great Accra, the capital of the fledgling Ga state, and then three years later conquered even the settlements on the coast to where the Ga had escaped, even though they were under the protection of European forts. In 1730 Akwamu was defeated by other Akan people, the Akyem chiefdoms, but in 1742 the Asante defeated the Akyem, and the entire area, all the way to the coast, was incorporated into the southern provinces of the Asante empire.

Powerful kingdoms did not develop in the coastal area even though there was considerable migration into this region. The Guan-speaking peoples, part of the larger Akan migratory movement, had begun populating an area from the Volta river basin to beyond the plains of Winneba by the fifteenth century. They never seemed to have established centralized states. Instead, the "the thickly wooded vegetation" and the presence of diseases that affected livestock forced people in this area to live in small states or chiefdoms.[18] They were the people that the Ga-Dangme conquered in the sixteenth century to form Great Accra. Later Akan migrants, the Borbor Fante, whose traditions say they migrated from Brong Takyiman across the Pra and the Ofin rivers to the coastlands, were also able to displace or conquer the Etsi, a Guan people who had spread along the coast from the Pra river to the Plains of Winneba. By the beginning of the eighteenth century Fante territory consisted of a narrow strip of coast that stretched from the Iron Mount, near the coastal settlement of Mori, eastward to the Plains of Winneba.

By that time trade with Europeans on the coast was extremely important, and to maintain their middleman position the Fante sought to gain control of small coastal states like Eguafo, Fetu, Asebu, and Agona, which had established trading contact with the European forts on the coast. Asante expansion in the interior also stimulated Fante expansion and consolidation. By the middle of the eighteenth century the Fante controlled the coast from the Pra river all the way to the borders of Accra in the east. However, unlike the Asante or the Akwamu, they never really became a centralized state, but nevertheless they entered into a number of defensive and offensive alliances with Asante dependencies like Akyem, Denkyira, and states to the west such as Nzima, Twifu, and Wassa. Their primary concern was "to check the expansionist powers of the Asante kings and to maintain their political and economic independence."[19]

The settlement of the Accra coastlands by the Ga-Dangme people was also affected by considerable migration. Archeological evidence indicates that the plains of Accra were inhabited as far back as four millennia B.C.E. by late-Stone-Age hunter-gatherers. Between 500 and 1400 C.E. iron technology developed in this area and contributed to the rise of towns and later kingdoms. Ga traditions indicate that by the fifteenth century over 30 settlements in the central Accra area had been amalgamated into a centralized kingdom, which eventually located its capital at the inland town of Ayawaso. The closeness to the gold-producing regions of the southern Akan stimulated this development, and rapidly the Ga became the most important suppliers of this commodity to the European traders who by the sixteenth century began to frequent this area of the West African coast. In general the Ga played an important role as middlemen, exchanging Ga-produced salt, fish, and corn as well as European goods like firearms, textiles, metal goods, and alcohol for commodities like gold, slaves, ivory, foodstuffs, and livestock obtained from people in the hinterland. As an indication of how important this trade was to the Europeans involved, in the seventeenth century the Dutch (1642), Danish (1661), and English (1672) companies engaged in this trade built forts on the coast.

The Dangme peoples of the eastern Accra plains also developed in a similar fashion. Perhaps a little later than the Ga, they established a centralized state with its inland capital at La. They too became important middlemen between the Europeans on the coast and African people in the hinterland. Indicative of this development, eventually, in the eighteenth century, Europeans also built a few small forts and lodges on the coast in this area. La was particularly famous for its cotton textiles, which undoubtedly came from Europe and were much in demand as far north as the Akwamu settlements in the hinterland. Sometime in the early seventeenth century civil war destroyed La, and its people moved to Labadi on the Atlantic coast. Originally, the rulers of the Dangme peoples were religious figures known as *wulomei*, but contact with Europeans on the coast enhanced the role of secular leaders, the most important of whom became the state father, or *mantse*. It was a development that was to be mirrored in Ga communities when the center of the Ga world also moved to the coast in the late seventeenth century to escape the aggressively expansionist Akan kingdom of Akwamu.[20]

THE COMING OF EUROPEANS

The coming of Europeans to the coast radically affected the face of old Ghana. The Portuguese arrival on the coast in 1471 was to set in motion a gradual refocusing of power and influence away from the interior to the coast. Eleven years after their initial contact with West Africa, they began the construction of what is still the most impressive of European fortifications on this coast, the Castle of São Jorge da Mina. They were able to choose a choice site close to sources of gold in the rain-forest interior and located at the mouth of the Benya River, which provided one of the few natural harbors on this otherwise open coastline. Initially this location was known as A Mina ("the mine" in Portuguese), but the name was eventually corrupted to become Elmina. It was from this castle and others that they built on this coast—São Antonio (1515, close to the mouth of the Ankobra River and near the town of Axim) and São Sebastian (1520–26, at the mouth of the Pra River in the town of Shama)—that the Portuguese monopolized the trade of this area until the early seventeenth century. Initially it was the gold of Guinea that brought them to West Africa. Pepper and ivory also became important trade items, and in exchange they offered textiles, copper- and brass-ware, iron bars, and iron products.

From their first contact with West Africa the Portuguese and their earliest rivals, the Castilians, had bought slaves for sale in Europe.[21] To help carry their trade items into the Gold Coast interior, in the early sixteenth century the Portuguese started importing slaves from the kingdom of Benin. Some of these slaves they used for their own needs on the Gold Coast or took back to Portugal, while others were sold to the gold miners in the interior in exchange for gold and ivory. In the sixteenth century the Portuguese also introduced the cultivation of sugar cane to the previously uninhabited equatorial islands of Príncipe and São Tomé using slave labor from Benin. These interregional slave-trading activities were to be the launching pad for the transatlantic slave trade that came to define the relationship between Europe and Africa.

Other European traders, like the Spaniards, French, and English, tried to break the Portuguese monopoly on the coast, but it was not until 1637 that the Dutch were successfully able to dislodge the Portuguese from Elmina Castle. In 1642 the Dutch managed to expel the Portuguese entirely from the Gold Coast. Quickly following behind them were the English, Swedes, Danes, French, and Brandenburgers, all of whom built fortifications. The most important of them were Christiansborg, which the Danes constructed in 1661 near Accra, and Cape Coast Castle, which the English seized from the Swedes in 1665. As an indication of how important and intense the competition for the trade of this area became, of the roughly 110 fortifications that Europeans erected on the coast of West Africa, about 100 of them were located on the Gold Coast.[22] They consisted of large castles like Elmina, Cape Coast, and Christiansborg; smaller forts like Fort Crèvecoeur (Dutch, 1649) and James Fort (English, 1673), both in Accra, and Gross-Friedrichsburg (Brandenburg, 1683), near Princes Town; and numerous fortified lodges that varied from being miniature forts to merely fortified trading stations built out of *swish*, local clay.

Erecting these fortifications required approval from the Africans who lived in these locations. In general the sparseness of population on the coast and the absence of powerful kingdoms in this area made these negotiations fairly easy. Oral traditions indicate that African coastal settlements in many of these sites only antedate by a few generations the coming of the Europeans. These coastal settlements tended to be fishing or salt-making outposts of parent inland states that were willing to trade interior products like gold, ivory, elephant teeth, skins, dyewoods, pepper, beeswax, and small numbers of slaves to Europeans, but by the seventeenth century the trade in slaves became the main trading activity.

Over time, as European trade continued, there developed outside the walls of these European fortifications what Dutch slave trader William Bosman described as "very populous negroe towns."[23] The result was that they began to challenge the inland states to which they had originally been subordinate. Sometime around 1515 Elmina achieved its independence from the kingdoms of Eguafo and Fetu. Instead, as an anonymous Dutch cartographer was to maintain in 1629, the Elminians lived "as a republic on their own and mostly governed by the Portuguese Governador."[24] How much power this European official enjoyed is debatable, since when the Dutch attacked in 1637, the people of Elmina basically remained neutral. In the case of Cape Coast, it was probably the Seven Years War (1756–63) that contributed to breaking the inland state of Fetu's control over the town. The fighting in Europe between Britain and France during this war spilled over into West Africa, and in this fighting Fetu lost control of its offshoot, Cape Coast. The coastward expansion of the Asante in the late eighteenth century completed this process by forcing the Fetu ruling class to flee to Cape Coast for protection.

In the case of the Ga, when the Akwamu invaded in 1677 and destroyed the capital of Great Accra at Ayawaso, many survivors sought refuge under the protection of the European forts on the coast at Accra. In 1680–81 the Akwamu conquered even these sanctuaries. Briefly the Ga were able to regain a measure of independence when the Akyem defeated the Akwamu in 1730, but in 1742 the Asante defeated the Akyem and incorporated much of the Accra plains into the southern provinces of the Asante empire. Consequently, in contrast to Elmina, Cape Coast, and many other coastal settlements that had begun by the seventeenth century to crystallize into independent states, the process of state formation was much less developed in Accra. The presence of three competing European trading companies with a castle and forts in close proximity to one another also undermined state crystallization. The towns that developed around them were able to retain their separate identities well into the nineteenth century.

The long history of interaction with Europeans was to have a profound effect on these coastal settlements, which in turn acted as points for the further dispersion of this influence into the interior. Probably the most ubiquitous was the wide range of fruits and food crops that were introduced from the Mediterranean, Asia, and the Americas. Among them were lemons, sugar cane, oranges, bananas, coconuts, pineapples, yams, rice, sweet potatoes, peanuts, maize, and cassava. Initially these crops were grown in gardens around European fortifications to supplement the food supply, and also to provision slave ships for the journey across the Atlantic Ocean to the Americas, known as the Middle Passage, but gradually they spread into the interior. European trade goods, like firearms, alcohol, metalware, and textiles also became an integral part of coastal economies. Just as Sudanic architectural styles spread into northern Ghana, so too did European building styles affect local construction. Rich African traders built stone houses similar to those built by Europeans. Eventually this influence was to spread into the interior. For example, the cult shrines that the Asante built as early as the seventeenth century were modeled after the elliptical arches of the coastal forts and castles.[25]

African institutions also came under substantial European influence. Most notably among them were the *asafos,* or military companies, of the coastal towns. There has been considerable debate over the origin of these institutions. Some historians have suggested that Europeans were responsible for their establishment, while others have seen an indigenous origin.[26] Clearly some of the *asafos* in Cape Coast, Elmina, and Anomabu did owe their origins to the European presence in these towns. At critical periods in the defense of their respective towns, European governors seemed to have played important roles in numbering these organizations and organizing them into military formations. In a far more unstructured fashion, all of them adopted as part of their paraphernalia and rituals European objects and symbols, the most notable of which were the Dane gun (muskets) and European military flags. The *asafo* system eventually was to spread all along the coast. Either the Fante or the Akwamu were responsible for its introduction among the Ga and Dangme peoples of the Accra plains. Here it developed more as a military organization, with membership based primarily on age rather than associated with specific town quarters, as is the case among the Akan peoples.

European languages also became the lingua francas of trade. Initially this was Portuguese, which outlasted Portugal's dominance on the coast, but eventually the languages of successor nations began to replace the former. In 1679 French traveler Jean Barbot found that "good English" was spoken by the canoe men he encountered at sea within sight of Elmina, but Portuguese was still being used in the area around Axim even though the Dutch had evicted the Portuguese 37 years ago.[27] Eventually, however, it was English and pidgin English that were to emerge as the lingua francas of the coast.

Of great long-term significance was the impact of Christianity. Initially the Portuguese made significant efforts to spread Catholicism, and soon after their settlement at Elmina there were over 1,300 baptized Catholics in the town.[28] In 1573 six Augustinian friars were sent from Portugal to expand this effort, but after some initial success the people of Komenda and Eguafo attacked and killed the monks. Perhaps it was the incompatibility of slave trading and proselytizing that doomed this effort. Neither did the unhealthy nature of the coast for Europeans argue well for missionary efforts into the interior, and for most of the era of the transatlantic slave trade, Christian proselytizing was confined to the forts and castles and their populations. The Portuguese and later on the Dutch continued to maintain chaplains on their staff who were also responsible for the education of the children born to their soldiers and their African concubines. Clergymen were also attached to the other European castles and forts, but frequent sickness and death interrupted their efforts. In the eighteenth century Africans were trained for these positions, and the three most successful, Elisa Johannes Capitein of Elmina, Christian Protten of Christiansborg, and Philip Quaque of Cape Coast, served for several decades.

However, it was not until the nineteenth century, with the abolition of the slave trade, that Christian missionary work really began in earnest in West Africa. The Danes were the first European nation to abolish the transatlantic slave trade, and appropriately it was at their settlement at Christiansborg where the Basel Evangelical Missionary Society began missionary work in 1828. They were followed by the Methodists in 1835, and much later, in 1880, by the newly established Catholic Societas Missionum ad Afros (SMA) fathers. West Africa's reputation as the white man's grave proved all too real for these early missionaries. Three of the four Basel missionaries died within three weeks of their arrival in the Gold Coast. Five months after the first Methodist missionary, Joseph Dunwell, arrived in Cape Coast, he also died. The Basel Mission survived by relocating to the more healthy uplands of Akropong. The Methodists in Cape Coast established their residence on Standfast Hill, where sea breezes contributed to reducing the health hazards associated with mosquitoes. But in general, mortality rates for European missionaries remained extremely high and influenced these fledgling churches to rely heavily on a native ministry. Undoubtedly the most successful of these African missionaries was Thomas Birch Freeman. He had been born in England of a Ghanaian father and an English mother and served on the Gold Coast and Nigeria from 1838 to 1890.

There had always been a link between Christian proselytizing and the spread of Western education, and rapidly the nineteenth-century missionaries expanded this connection. Particularly was this the case for the Methodists, who rapidly realized that there was a close correlation between their success in converting Africans to Christianity and providing Western education. In 1858, when membership in the church's seven circuits stood at 2,000, with 6,000 attending public worship, there were roughly 1,250 boys and girls receiving education in some 31 schools.[29] Earlier in the century Christian missionaries had hoped that the "Bible and the plough" would civilize Africa. Instead, on the West African coast the far more important link that developed was between the schoolbook and the store. The expanding trade economy of the nineteenth century required more and more knowledge of Western education, and this ensured that there would be close link between Christianity, Western civilization, and commerce.

THE EXPANSION OF BRITISH POWER

Christian missionary activity also coincided with the expansion of British power on the coast. One major reason for this increase in British influence came as a result of Asante expansion toward the coast. For the Asante this was vitally necessary to ensure a ready supply of European firearms to maintain their hold over their outlying provinces. However, especially to British merchants on the coast, this expansion raised the fear of an Asante monopoly of coastal trade. It would mean that the main trade items, like slaves, gold dust, and ivory, would came from Ashanti-controlled areas, and that the latter would be able to charge whatever prices they liked. In 1806 the Asante, under their dynamic leader, Asantehene Osei Bonsu, defeated the Fante and besieged the British fort at Anomabu. In 1811, 1814, and 1816 the Asante again invaded the Fante area and finally established domination over the coast. Fearful that they might lose their share of trade to the Dutch, who had more friendly relations with the Asante, in 1817 the British Company of Merchants sent a mission headed by T. E. Bowditch, a company employee, to Kumasi, the Asante capital, to negotiate a treaty. Nevertheless, few concessions were made to the Asante, and the treaty reflected the hostility of the coastal people to Asante overlordship.

One year later the British government appointed its own agent and consul, Joseph Dupuis. In 1820 he also went to Kumasi and negotiated a new treaty that abrogated the earlier agreement and recognized the *asantehene*'s sovereignty over the Fante people. But neither the home government nor the local British merchants were willing to accept this treaty, and there remained considerable confusion over how to deal with the Asantes. Britain's abolition of the slave trade in 1808 also contributed to tension with the Asantes. The Spanish and Portuguese, who were not subject to British law, moved into the vacuum created by the absence of British merchants, who had dominated the transatlantic slave trade in this area of the West Africa.[30] In Britain the British merchants on the coast were criticized for not having effectively stamped out the slave trade, and their policies were blamed for harming British trade in general.

The result was that in 1821 the British parliament relieved the Company of Merchants of the responsibility for administering the British forts and settlements on the coast and placed them under the authority of the Crown's officers. Sir Charles Macarthy, the governor of Sierra Leone, took over the administration of the British forts and settlements on the coast, and he rapidly formed an unfavorable opinion of the Asantes. He felt that they were barbarians with whom it was impossible to trade. A dispute over jurisdiction eventually led to war, but Macarthy's forces proved no match for the Asantes. In 1824, at the battle of Nsamankow, they were ambushed and the governor and seven of his officers were killed. At this point the Asante empire was at the height of its power.

However, in 1826, at the battle of Dodowa (also known as Akantamansu), on the Accra plains, the British, with the assistance of Fante, Ga, Denkyira, Akyem, and Akwamu forces, were able to avenge this defeat, and effectively ended Asante domination of the coast. After a long series of negotiations the Asante signed a treaty in 1831. Apart from depositing 600 ounces of gold and sending the British two Asante princes as security, they agreed that trade should be free and recognized the independence of Denkyira, Assin, and the Fante states.

Conflict with the Asante had stimulated a heated debate in Great Britain over the benefits of "protected" versus "unprotected" trade. Those who felt that the latter inevitably drew Britain into messy conflicts overseas in unhealthy parts of the world were successful in getting Parliament to relinquish British control of the forts and settlements on the coast and handing their administration back to the British merchants on the coast. In 1828 they appointed Captain George Maclean as their governor. He had served as a lieutenant in Sierra Leone in the Royal African Corps and also had some familiarity with the area, since from 1827 he had been the private secretary to the officer commanding the British troops in the Gold Coast.

He quickly moved to maintain peace and promote trade. He proved to be a remarkable diplomat and gained the trust of both the Fantes and the Asantes. Undoubtedly his most important contribution was adjudicating disputes. Neither was he above using force if necessary to maintain peace. In 1835 he even organized a military expedition against the king of Appollonia, near Axim, who was accused of murdering traders in his area. It was a measure of his success that by 1840 exports from Cape Coast had risen to £325,000 from £131,000 in 1831. Maclean also made something of a celebrity of himself by marrying a well-known London actress, Letitia Elizabeth Landon, who accompanied him to Cape Coast in 1838 but died shortly after her arrival.

Rumors about her death and, more importantly, accusations that he had not done enough to stop the slave trade and suppress domestic slavery undermined Maclean's reputation, and in 1841 the British government sent a commissioner, Dr. R. R. Madden, to Cape Coast to investigate the charges against the governor. The select committee parliament appointed to inquire into the state of the British possessions on the West Coast of Africa did not accept Dr. Madden's hostile findings, but did recommend that Maclean's de facto rule of the Fante area be made legal, and once again the Gold Coast was placed under the governor of Sierra Leone.

In 1844 Captain H. W. Hill took over the Gold Coast forts and settlements as lieutenant governor and Maclean was made judicial assessor and magistrate. Together they negotiated a number of treaties with local Fante that came to be known as the Bond of 1844. Apart from recognizing the "power and jurisdiction" of British officials, the chiefs conceded the adjudication of serious crimes to British officials with the long-term purpose of "moulding the customs of the country to the general principles of British law."[31] The establishment of a supreme court in 1853, three years after the forts and settlements had become a separate colony from Sierra Leone, continued the process of establishing English common law in the colony. The chief justice continued to serve as the judicial assessor, and acting in the latter position he applied customary law, but after Maclean died in 1847, his successors tended to be shorter-serving and less knowledgeable about customary law and sympathetic to local customs.

How to pay for the administration of the colony was also a controversial issue. The British parliament had provided an annual grant of £4,000, but it wanted the colony eventually to become self-sufficient. This was the purpose behind the purchase of the Danish castle and forts on the coast in 1850, since it lessened the opportunities for smuggling, which seriously undermined attempts to raise revenue by taxing imports and exports. The introduction of a poll tax in 1852 was an even more direct attempt to increase local revenue, but collecting this tax was very difficult, especially in the Accra area, where in 1854 a British warship had to bombard the settlements of Labadi, Teshi, and Christiansborg to suppress an armed rebellion against British rule. This unpopular form of direct taxation lingered on until 1862 and left a legacy of antagonism on the part of the coastal peoples toward any such form of revenue collection.

In conjunction with this inability to generate local revenue, the outbreak of war with the Asante in 1862 and a humiliating British retreat that followed raised the question, once again, of whether the British government should be responsible for the administration of the area. A select parliamentary committee in 1865 recommended withdrawal and handing over of the administration of all the West African colonies, with the exception of Sierra Leone, to the local inhabitants. It was an electrifying proposition to the Western-educated elite in the Gold Coast, who were inspired by the development of nationalist movements in Europe at that time, and two of them traveled to London to give evidence before the committee. However, to British administrators on the coast, the committee seemed to be calling for more efficient administration, and there was the potential for serious conflict between them and the African elite. Most particularly was this so in Cape Coast, where in 1866 the recently enstooled King Aggrey, who was supported by many of the town's educated elite, challenged Governor Conran's authority and was deported to Sierra Leone.

Rather than withdrawing, British control increased, and in 1868 there was an exchange of castles and forts with the Dutch, the remaining European power on the coast. All those from Elmina westward became Dutch, while all those to the east became British, and the intermingled nature of the European settlements on the coast came to an end. Previously this interspersing of possessions had made imposing significant customs duties impossible. None of the African people involved were consulted in this exchange. The Fante were particularly worried that the Asante would invade the coastal area to protect their trading interests that the exchange had upset. As a result, the Fante chiefs assembled at their ancient headquarters of Mankessim to form a "Fantee Council." It was soon organizing resistance against the Dutch, who were perceived as allies of the Asante. The ideas of Sierra Leonean Dr. James Africanus Horton, who was stationed as a British military physician on the Gold Coast, also played an important role in transforming this council into a Fante confederation that would be able to implement the self-government recommended by the select parliamentary committee.

However, the reasons for the military alliance were temporarily removed in 1870 when the British agreed to buy the Dutch possessions on the coast, but to many supporters of the confederation movement this seemed only "preliminary to handing over the Gold Coast to a united native government."[32] In 1871 there was a concerted effort to draw up a constitution and elect the officers for the confederation. The governor saw this as a challenge to British authority on the coast, and he arrested members of the confederation's executive. The appointment of a more sympathetic governor general in Sierra Leone gave the framers of the previous confederation another chance, in 1872, to put together a scheme for a more limited form of self-government that was less challenging to British authority. It raised the question of just what the relationship should be between the British and the coastal peoples and what role their chiefs should have in the administration of the area and their powers of adjudication.

All these questions were put on hold when in 1873 the Asante again invaded the coast. The sale of the Dutch possessions to the British had created considerable dissatisfaction in Elmina. One Dutch officer had been killed in a riot, and in 1872 the British had deported the town's king, Kobina Gyan, to Sierra Leone for his resistance to the transfer. To the Asantes the transfer meant that they lost the rent that the Dutch had paid to them, and even more importantly threatened their trade with the coast and their source of firearms, which they had obtained through a disguised slave trade with the Dutch. On the other hand, the British were determined not to be driven from the coast by the Asante, and appointed General Sir Garnet Wolseley with full power to free the Gold Coast from the Asante "menace."[33]

The British had learned something about campaigning in West Africa and managed to conduct operations before the onset of the rainy season. Wolseley, along with his subordinate Captain J. H. Glover, who took an eastern route, entered Kumasi, the Asante capital, early in 1874; burned it; and forced the Asante to pay an indemnity, give up their claims to Elmina, guarantee freedom of inland trade routes, and agree to "check the practice of human sacrifice."[34] The Sargrenti War, as it was known locally (a corruption of Sir Garnet Wolesley's name) was seen by the British as a fitting victory for the humiliations of 1863, even though it did not result in the capitulation of the Asante and contained the seeds of future conflicts. However, the war did indicate how much the British were committed to the area. There was still a strong minority opinion in Parliament in favor of withdrawal from the coast as stipulated in the 1865 recommendations, but the government in Great Britain decided to transform the settlements into the Gold Coast Colony, which was to be linked administratively with Lagos rather than Sierra Leone. An unspecified area adjacent in the interior became the Protected Territories, and the Legislative Council of the colony was empowered to legislate for it also.

NOTES

1. James Anquandah, *Rediscovering Ghana's Past* (Harlow, United Kingdom: Longman Group, 1982), 126–27.

2. Ibid., 127.

3. Ibid., 128.

4. Jack Goody, "The Mande and the Akan Hinterland," in *The Historian in Tropical Africa,* ed. J. Vansina, R. Mauny, and L. V. Thomas (London: Oxford University Press, 1964), 193–218.

5. Nehemia Levtzion, *Muslims and Chiefs in West Africa: A Study of Islam in the Middle Volta Basin in the Pre-Colonial Period* (London: Clarendon Press, 1968), 85.

6. Ibid., 53. The Mali empire was the largest of the Sudanic empires and lasted from the thirteenth to the fifteenth centuries. The Bambara were an ethnic group within this empire.

7. Ibid., xxv.

8. Ibid., 190.

9. Ivor Wilks, *Asante in the Nineteenth Century: The Structure and Evolution of a Political Order* (London: Cambridge University Press, 1975), 22.

10. Ibid., 243.

11. Kevin Shillington, *History of Africa* (New York: St. Martin's Press, 1995), 194.

12. Adu Boahen, *Ghana: Evolution and Change in the Nineteenth and Twentieth Centuries* (Accra, Ghana: Sankofa Educational Publishers, 2000), 10; W.E.F. Ward, *A History of Ghana,* 4th ed. (London: George Allen and Unwin, 1967), 53.

13. Boahen, *Ghana: Evolution and Change,* 11.

14. Ibid., 18.

15. I. Wilks, *Asante in the Nineteenth Century: The Structure and Evolution of a Political Order* (London: Cambridge University Press, 1975), 446.

16. Ivor Wilks, "The Position of Muslims in Metropolitan Ashanti in the Early Nineteenth Century," in *Islam in Tropical Africa,* ed. I. M. Lewis (London: Oxford University Press, 1966), 319.

17. Ward, *A History of Ghana,* 54–55.

18. John Fynn, "Trade and Politics in Akanland," *Tarikh* 26 7, no. 2: 23.

19. Ibid., 30.

20. Anquandah, *Rediscovering Ghana's Past,* 124.

21. In 1469 Castile and Aragon were joined through marriage, and gradually a Spanish state emerged from this union.

22. A. W. Lawrence, *Trade Castles and Forts of West Africa* (Stanford, Calif.: Stanford University Press, 1963), 42.

23. William Bosman, *A New and Accurate Description of the Coast of Guinea* (1704; reprint, London: Frank Cass, 1967), 43.

24. Kwame Daaku and Albert van Dantzig, "An Annotated Dutch Map of 1629," *Ghana Notes and Queries* 9 (November 1966): 15.

25. Anquandah, *Rediscovering Ghana's Past*, 133.

26. Ansu Datta and R. Porter, "The Asafo System in Historical Perspective," *Journal of African History* 12, no. 2 (1971): 282–83.

27. Anquandah, *Rediscovering Ghana's Past*, 131.

28. Helene Pfann, *A Short History of the Catholic Church in Ghana* (Cape Coast, Ghana: Catholic Mission Press, 1965), 4.

29. F. L. Bartels, *The Roots of Ghana Methodism* (Cambridge: Cambridge University Press, 1965), 76.

30. Mary McCarthy, *Social Change and the Growth of British Power in the Gold Coast: The Fante States 1807–1874* (Lanham, Md.: University Press of America, 1983), 76.

31. J. J. Crooks, *Records Relating to the Gold Coast Settlements from 1750 to 1874* (1923; reprint, London: Frank Cass, 1973), 296.

32. David Kimble, *A Political History of Ghana, 1850–1928* (London: Oxford University Press, 1963), 243.

33. Crooks, *Records Relating to the Gold Coast*, 460.

34. Ibid., 522–23.

3

Colonial Rule

ESTABLISHING THE COLONY

In defining the extent of British power, the lieutenant governor, Captain G. C. Straham, proceeded by way of proclamation rather than by signing bonds with the local chiefs, as had been done in 1844. The Crown's powers were to include the preservation of the peace, the administration of both civil and criminal adjudication, the enactment of laws, the encouragement of trade commerce, and, most controversial of all, a unilateral abolition of slave trading and the emancipation of existing slaves. There was protest on the part of African slave owners, both chiefs and commoners, over the latter provision, since there was no attempt at compensation. Straham maintained that by providing protection against the Asante the British government had more than met this obligation. Extensive coverage of the 1873–74 Asante war had familiarized people in Britain with the widespread nature of local slavery in the Gold Coast, and Straham's precipitous actions did much to solve what otherwise would have been an embarrassing situation in a British colony. He also eliminated any debate over compensating slave owners.

However, the government made no attempt to pursue a vigorous abolition policy, and the small number of cases involving illegal slave dealing that did come before the colony's courts after 1874 would seem to indicate that abolition was not particularly disruptive. Of more immediate importance were the administrative and judicial changes. The colony's Legislative Council was authorized to legislate for the colony and the vaguely defined area in the interior known as the Protected Territories. The civil commandants of the forts became district commissioners in preparation for the exercise of more judicial powers. In 1876 the Supreme Court Ordinance and the associated Criminal Procedure Ordinance were enacted, which abolished the judicial assessor's court and established a single supreme court headed by a chief justice.[1] Decisions from district commissioners' courts as well as from chiefly courts could be appealed in the supreme court, and after 1877 provision was made for final appeal to the Privy Council in London.

The result of these changes was to increase the importance of English common law in the colony. English rules of evidence and methods of procedure were followed, and the chief justice was empowered to admit barristers and solicitors to appear in court. The "country advocates," members of the Western-educated elite who lacked formal legal training but had represented clients in court cases and had existed in an uneasy relationship with judges prior to 1876, had their status regularized. However, they were soon to be replaced by lawyers who had been trained in Great Britain. In theory the Supreme Court Ordinance gave preference to customary law unless it was specifically excluded by a contract. Nevertheless, it seemed initially as if the changes privileged English common law since many of the British judges knew little about customary law, but over time there did develop a body of "case law based on native law."[2]

One of the immediate questions that these administrative and judicial changes raised was the status and judicial power of the chiefs in this new order. The Native Jurisdiction Ordinance of 1878 sought to define the power and judicial authority of "head chiefs" and "minor chiefs," but was never enacted, partly because of opposition on the part of Africans. Neither were British administrators in agreement over what role the chiefs should play in the colony's administration. Herbert Ussher, who became lieutenant governor in 1879, felt that the chiefs were "useless, tyrannical and not to be trusted to administer justice."[3] He preferred direct government exercised by European officials. His successor, Sir Samuel Rowe, held diametrically opposed ideas, as he felt that "the proper way to administer the Gold Coast [was] by acting through the chiefs."[4] In 1883 he repealed the 1878 ordinance and reenacted it with one major modification: decisions in chiefly courts could be appealed in the British courts.

Initially the ordinance was applied to only six head chiefs in the pro-

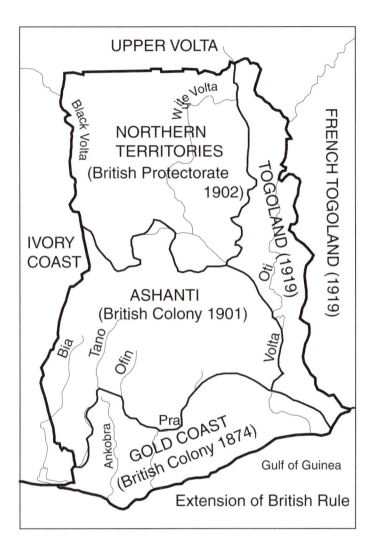

UPPER VOLTA

White Volta

Black Volta

NORTHERN
TERRITORIES
(British Protectorate
1902)

FRENCH TOGOLAND (1919)

TOGOLAND (1919)

Oti

IVORY
COAST

ASHANTI
(British Colony 1901)

Bia

Tano

Ofin

Volta

Ankobra

Pra

GOLD COAST
(British Colony 1874)

Gulf of Guinea

Extension of British Rule

tectorate, and there was no intention to apply it to the coastal area. Here it was felt that the chiefs were eventually going to lose their power, and the relationship between them and the government was hostile. In 1880 Governor Ussher had deported King Taki Tawia, the *Ga mantse* of Accra, to Elmina for trying to exercise judicial authority that challenged the British courts. Seven years later, when Kojo Mbra was enstooled as the *omanhen* of Cape Coast, the government was opposed and refused to recognize him. However, the 1887 ruling by the supreme court in the case of *Oppon v. Ackinnie* that the Supreme Court Ordinance of 1876 had "in no way impaired the judicial power of native kings and chiefs" once again provoked debate over the role of the native order.[5] In addition, many officials had recognized that to carry out badly needed sanitary improvements in the coastal towns they needed cooperation from the chiefs. To act in this fashion the latter needed judicial authority, and in 1888 the Native Prisons Ordinance gave them the power to fine and imprison. The outbreak of hostilities with the Asante in 1894 also indicated how dependent the government was on the chiefs to supply porters to transport supplies into the interior. Not surprisingly, those chiefs who had lost the most power were least able to cooperate, and this indicated the need for a new policy toward the native order all over the colony.

In 1895 Governor Sir William Maxwell, who had come from the Straits Settlement (Malaya), where an indirect rule form of government was already well developed, sought to implement a similar policy for the Gold Coast. He wanted chiefs to have more judicial power and a role in developing the colony's road system, and he was even willing to recognize coastal chiefs so long as they were not "too close to native lawyers."[6] His early death and conflict with the Asante cut short these plans. It was not until the annexation of Asante and the Orders in Council that defined the boundaries of the Northern Territories and the Gold Coast Colony in 1902 that it became possible to end the ambiguous relationship that had existed with the chiefs since the Bond of 1844. Governor Mathew Nathan, who became the colony's governor in 1900, argued that chiefly powers were not inherent, but derived from the Crown, so that the government could then determine how to formalize the relationship with the chiefs. In 1902 he began this process by establishing a Secretariat of Native Affairs.

There still remained an important dissenting voice in the colony's chief justice, Sir William Brandford Griffith, who was particularly concerned about the judicial standards in the chiefly courts. If there were to be such courts, he was determined that they should be under the control of the supreme court rather than administrative officers. It was not realistic given the minuscule size of the judiciary, and chiefly courts were to remain under the supervision of administrative officers for almost all of the colonial period. As an indication of how contentious this policy remained, when Governor Rodger finally introduced a new native jurisdiction ordinance in 1910, he resorted to amending aspects of the 1883 Native Jurisdiction Ordinance so that every clause of the new bill would not be open to discussion. The most important of these amendments was the extension of chiefly courts to the entire colony. Appeal from these courts lay with the district commissioner's court rather than with the divisional court, which African lawyers would have preferred. Most controversial of all was the power the bill gave to the governor to "suspend for a stated time, or [to] depose any chief, who shall appear to him to have abused his power, or be unworthy, or incapable of exercising the same justly."[7] The bill was a fundamental challenge to the chiefs' position that their power was inherent and not derived from the power of the Crown.

The role of what at that time was referred to as the "educated natives" also underwent considerable change. The challenge to British rule that many officials had seen the Fante Confederation posing had contributed to souring relations between officials and these educated natives, whom one official was to describe as the "curse of the West Coast."[8] Nevertheless, the establishment of the colony did much to increase their ranks. The expansion of the colony's administration provided considerable opportunities for educated Africans. In 1867 the civil staff consisted of only 85 people, but three decades later had increased more than 10-fold, to 863.[9] Many of these were junior-level positions filled by Africans educated in the mission schools, but some were senior positions filled by both Africans from the Gold Coast and from other areas of West Africa, like Sierra Leone, and even some West Indians. For a while in the 1880s seven of the colony's nine district commissioners were Africans. In the 1890s the colony's most senior judge, Justice Francis Smith, was a Sierra Leonean. From 1894 to 1897 the colony's chief medical officer was also a Sierra Leonean, Dr. James Farrell Easmon. At that time 4 out of the 22 medical officers in the Gold Coast were Africans, and they enjoyed the same pay scale as their European counterparts.

The mission churches were also an important source of employment for educated natives. Many were simple catechists, but as the missions had turned to Africans to replace Europeans, who had great difficulty surviving in the climate, even the hierarchy had become African. This was particularly so for the Methodists. At the time of their golden jubilee in 1885, there were 15 African ministers and only three Europeans. Undoubtedly the best-known of all of these was the veteran Reverend Thomas Birch Freeman. In the 1840s and 1850s he had served as the superintendent of the mission. During his long period of service he made three major attempts to spread Christianity to Asante.[10] In 1859 he established in Cape Coast the *Christian Messenger and Examiner,* which along with the *Accra Herald* of 1857 was among the earliest attempts in the Gold Coast to provide a local source of news.

The establishment of Crown colony rule coincided with a major expansion in trade between a rapidly industrializing Europe and the Gold Coast. By the end of the nineteenth century this trade was worth three times what it had been in 1874. The advent of steam ships in the 1870s made it easier for African merchants to participate in this trade and gave rise to a number of commercial kings. Cape Coast merchants like Francis Grant and John Sarbah played a dynamic role in the development of the rubber trade in the 1880s. A fellow Cape Coaster, Charles Barnes, was a pioneer in the timber industry, and King Ghartey of Winneba, in his merchant days, was the first to introduce palm-nut-cracking machinery in the Gold Coast.[11] Some were successful enough to be in business for themselves, while others worked as agents for European trading concerns. Far more numerous were the shopkeepers who sold the merchandise imported from Europe and America and the petty traders who hawked their wares in marketplaces and along the roads of the colony's busy towns. By the end of the nineteenth century, trade dominated the colony's economy. In 1891 over 30 percent of the working population in Cape Coast were estimated to be involved in trading, and over 20 percent of the Accra population.[12] It also drew in the colony's fishermen, who manned the surf boats that brought cargo to and from the oceangoing ships that anchored as much as a mile offshore. Even after the Gold Coast acquired a deep-water harbor at Takoradi in 1928, much of the colony's trade was still carried out from surf ports like Cape Coast, Saltpond, Winneba, Accra, and Keta.

Trade also stimulated the growth of related activities that served to increase the importance of educated natives in the colony. There was a need for auctioneers, photographers, pharmacists, doctors, and engineers, the latter stimulated by the growth of gold-mining activities, but most visible of all were lawyers. The untrained country advocates of the past gave way to lawyers trained in Great Britain. Initially they were either from Great Britain or Sierra Leone, but in 1887, John Mensah Sarbah of Anomabu and Cape Coast was the first African from the Gold Coast to join their ranks. By the end of the century he had been joined by about 10 other Inns of Court–trained Gold Coast barristers.[13] The first Africans appointed to the Legislative Council were merchants, but significantly, by the end of the nineteenth century they were lawyers, and for the rest of colonial period lawyers dominated these positions.

Highly visible also were newspaper editors and publishers. In 1874 James Hutton Brew, who was also a country advocate and had been deeply involved in the Fante Confederation scheme, started in Cape Coast the colony's first printed newspaper, the *Gold Coast Times*. Brew's newspaper efforts continued in the 1880s with the *Western Echo*, which provided a spirited criticism of government policy until 1887, when Brew left for England on professional business. The Wesleyan Methodist Mission also started a newspaper in Cape Coast in 1886, the *Gold Coast Methodist Times,* under the editorship of the Reverend Attoh Ahuma, and it also became an outlet for criticism of the government. Not until 1890 did Accra acquire its own newspaper, the *Gold Coast Chronicle.* In 1895 it was challenged by a rival, the *Gold Coast Independent,* which was to foreshadow the development of competing presses in the colony's main towns in the twentieth century. None of these newspapers were long-lived. Political conflicts in the colony tended to spark their existence, and as they faded so too did the paper. In 1897 the Cape Coast newspaper the *Gold Coast Aborigines* was established as the organ of GCARPS to oppose Governor Maxwell's Lands Bill, but by 1898 it had folded. In 1912 it was resurrected under the new name of the *Gold Coast Nation.* It was not until the twentieth century that the colony got a truly regular press. Often it was the colony's professional classes, lawyers and doctors, who sustained these publications.

Government policies regarding customs duties, expansion into the interior, the question of African representation on the Legislative Council, and most of all attempts to make what seemed like unowned land Crown land were some of the controversial issues that the press covered. In 1882 James Hutton Brew, in his newspaper, the *Gold Coast Times,* made the suggestion of sending a deputation to London to ask for "popular representation that through an assembly would virtually rule the country."[14] The cost of such an deputation defeated the scheme, but in 1886 Governor Brandford Griffith did appoint two unofficial members to the legislative council, which also served to defuse the deputation movement. However, in 1894, when the governor introduced the Crown Lands Bill, which was designed to control what was described as unowned crown land protest exploded again, and eventually did give rise to a deputation to London in 1898.

The rise of gold mining and the timber trade after 1874 had brought the issue of land ownership to the forefront, since the government felt that the granting of land concessions was badly in need of supervision. The Crown Lands Bill was designed "to vest Waste Lands, Forest Lands and Minerals in the Queen."[15] It immediately sparked protest both from the chiefs, who saw their control over stool lands threatened, and from the educated natives, who were often deeply involved in the concessions business themselves. The opposition to the bill eventually meant that it had to be withdrawn, but in 1897 the new governor, Sir William Maxwell, introduced more limited legislation that only sought to give the Crown "rights of administration but not ownership" of "waste land."[16] Nevertheless, what was still seen as the threat to African rights of ownership resulted in the formation of the colony's first political organization. GCARPS was established in Cape Coast in 1897 and soon had branches all over the colony.

In a remarkable show of unity, GCARPS brought together both the colony's chiefs and the educated elite. They also got support from commercial interests in Great Britain, who indicated that the bill might discourage investment in the colony. Neither did Governor Maxwell's sudden death, on his way home on leave, increase the bill's chances of being approved by the secretary of state. Shortly afterward, a three-man GCARPS deputation arrived in London, and they were able to get the secretary of state, Sir Joseph Chamberlain, to agree to a "judicial court" that would observe "native law," which would deal with the issue of concessions rather than making the Crown the administrator of "waste lands."[17] This very considerable victory guaranteed the continued existence of GCARPS, which the colony's chiefs empowered to act on their behalf. The new governor, Sir Frederic Hodgson, even met the Society's officials in Cape Coast, after the deputation's three members returned from Great Britain, and for a short while relations with officialdom were "cordial."[18] A new Concessions Bill was accepted in 1900 that established a special concessions court under the control of the colony's judiciary, which was mainly concerned with establishing security of title for concession holders and protecting landowners from fraud.[19]

Only indirectly did the Lands Bill controversy involve the colonial government in the question of the colony's boundaries and the nature of the protectorate inland. More challenging was the relationship with the Asante Confederation, which had not broken up, as had been anticipated, after 1874. Many of the subordinate territories, like Gonja, Dagbon, and Mamprugu, had broken away. There was internal dissension, particularly over succession to the Golden Stool, in addition to considerable instability in areas of the protectorate that bordered on Asante. Inevitably this affected trade, which meant that British policy toward the Asante concerned a wide array of interest groups. Further complicating the relationship with the Asantes and the north in general were the activities of the French and Germans. As the scramble for Africa intensified in the 1880s, the British government had somewhat reluctantly been drawn into signing treaties of friendship and protection with people in the hinterland. In 1892 the colony's governor, Sir William Brandford Griffith, sent his Fante agent, George Ekem Ferguson, to conclude treaties with the chiefs of Dagbon, Gonja, Mamprugu, and Mossi. In 1893 and 1894 he continued this effort even signing treaties in what was known as the Neutral Zone, an area between the Gold Coast and German territory in what was to become Togoland.

In 1894 another African, Traveling Commissioner Hendrick Vroom, was sent to Kumasi to ask the Asante to accept a British officer as their "friend and advisor."[20] The new *asantehene*, Agyeman Prempeh I, declined this request as well as others, but pressure was building for this kingdom to be brought under British control to prevent the French from doing so. There was considerable feeling in the colony in support of this move. In 1894 a deputation from the Cape Coast Chamber of Commerce, many of whose members had links to merchants in Great Britain, put pressure on the governor to appoint a permanent resident. Eventually the Asante sought to bypass the authority of the British governor by sending an eight-person deputation to London to plead for their state's independence, but it was neither recognized nor received, and they were told to deal directly with the governor in the Gold Coast. Instead, the British government had decided to settle what was now officially referred to as a quarrel by sending an expedition across the Pra to enforce all of the terms of the 1874 peace treaty, which had been ignored for over 20 years.

Early in 1896, to make sure that the operation was over before the beginning of the rainy season, an expedition under Sir Francis Scott and R. S. Baden Powell entered Kumasi without any resistance. They arrested the *asantehene* and most of his leading divisional and wing chiefs on the grounds that they failed to pay immediately the indemnity of 50,000 ounces of gold imposed on them by the terms of the 1874 treaty, and they were sent first to Elmina Castle and then to Sierra Leone. Nevertheless, there remained considerable support for the exiled *asantehene* and anger at what was seen as British treachery. In 1900 the new governor of the Gold Coast, Sir Frederic Hodgson, visited Kumasi and while there demanded that the Golden Stool of the Asante be surrendered to him as a right, and to prevent any new *asantehene* from being enstooled. To the Asante the Golden Stool was more than a throne. It was seen as a symbol of Asante nationhood containing all of their *sunsum,* or souls, and consequently this demand was seen as a great insult. Under the leadership of the queen mother, Yaa Asantewaa, the Asante besieged the British in their fort in Kumasi, and several months of hard fighting followed before the revolt was put down. Forty-six Asantes were rounded up and sent to Cape Coast. Fourteen of them, including Yaa Asantewaa, were sent to the Seychelles to join Prempeh and his party, who had been sent there soon after the relief of Kumasi in 1900. They were to remain in this Indian ocean outpost of the British Empire until 1924.

Affairs in Asante served to settle the question of the protectorate, which became part of the Gold Coast Colony in 1901 and subject to laws passed by its Legislative Council. However, Asante was annexed as a separate protected territory, and the governor, not the Legislative Council, was empowered to legislate in this territory, and the court system kept separate. The area to the north of Asante was also annexed in 1902 as a protectorate called the Northern Territories, where once again the powers of jurisdiction and legislation were kept separate from the colony. In each of the two protected territories the governor's powers were exercised by a chief commissioner. There was no protest on the part of Africans to this final definition of British power, mostly because it came so soon after they had been assured that the government would not lay claim to their land. However, the manner in which this had been done tended to emphasize regional differences. When Asantes and northerners were to become politically conscious later on in the colonial period, they tended to see themselves as different from the Gold Coast Colony, and it took a while to break down these perceived differences.

The Orders in Council defining what in essence was one colony also gave the governor the power to raise revenue. There was an effort in Asante to collect some payment for the war debt, but the fear of inciting more discontent and a mutiny in the West African Regiment in Kumasi contributed to the abandonment of this plan. In the Northern Territories there was a brief attempt to collect a maintenance tax, but what in essence was a form of compulsory labor was soon abandoned due to the difficulty of obtaining it and a preference for free labor, which was seen as a more traditional form of tribute. In general, officials in the Gold Coast were against direct taxation. Past experiences had been disappointing, and the colony's revenue was expanding dramatically through import duties, so that by 1901 more than half of total expenditure could be financed from this source.

Economically the colony was enjoying boom conditions. Palm-oil exports had peaked around the turn of the century, as did those for wild rubber, but there was great hope that the Gold Coast would become another South Africa. By 1911 gold exports were valued at over £1 million and amounted to 30 percent of the colony's exports. Railway construction had begun very much influenced by the needs of the gold-mining industry. In 1901 a narrow-gauge line from Sekondi reached Tarkwa, the center for mining in the western area of the colony. In 1902 it reached Obuasi in the Asante region, the site of the colony's richest gold mine, and in 1903 Kumasi. But most important was the rapid expansion of the cocoa industry. From a minuscule £4 in 1891, cocoa exports rose to £43,000 in 1901 and ranked third in the list of the colony's exports. By 1911 cocoa was to amount to nearly half of the colony's exports, and the Gold Coast became the world's leading producer of this tropical crop. At that time it was worth over £6 million.[21]

However, boom conditions did not necessarily favor African entrepreneurs. European companies began to establish their own operations in the colony, with European agents in charge. These businesses were far better capitalized than their African counterparts and had access to credit not available to even the African commercial princes. These large merchant houses were given special rates by shipping companies like Elder Dempster and the Woerman Line that monopolized trade with West Africa, and in 1895 formed a West African Shipping Conference that raised freight rates but offered rebates to larger concerns.[22] Significantly, of the 19 merchants who signed a petition to the secretary of state in 1894 requesting the annexation of Asante, only 5 were African.

More than just shifting economic conditions underlay these changes. At the turn of the century the rise of pseudoscientific racism undermined the relationship between Africans and Europeans in general. A younger generation of businessmen, officials, and even missionaries came to believe that Europeans where inherently superior to even the best-trained Africans, and that the latter should be, at best, in subordinate positions. Developments in tropical medicine made it possible to think in these terms even in areas as unhealthy for Europeans as West Africa, which had been known as the white man's grave. The Europeanization of the upper positions in the civil service and in the mission churches were some of the most visible aspects of this deteriorating relationship.

Indicative of this more racially motivated attitude toward Africans in the Gold Coast, at the end of the century the careers of such shining examples of African advancement in the civil service as those of Dr. John Farrell Easmon and Hendrik Vroom ended in disgrace. In 1897 Governor Maxwell, one of the most hostile of Gold Coast governors to educated Africans, removed Easmon from his position as the colony's chief medical officer and then forced him to resign entirely from the Colonial Medical Service.[23] In 1901 Governor Maxwell reduced District Commissioner Vroom's salary by half, on the grounds that he was a native of the Gold Coast, and he was sent to the interior, away from his family. When he tried to retire, he was offered a pittance of a pension even after 29 years in government service. Ironically, both men had received promotions for meritorious service. The abrasive young missionary Reverend Dennis

Kemp publicly castigated his fellow African ministers in the Methodist Church for not "living the Christian life in Africa."[24] This conflict was underscored by the continuing existence of a European Missionaries' Synod and a General Synod even though many of the church's African ministers were far senior in service to their European counterparts.

One response to this kind of discrimination was the establishment of independent African Christian churches all over West Africa. This movement began in the Gold Coast in 1898 with the establishment of the African Methodist Episcopal Zion Church (AME Zion Church) by Bishop B. J. Small. Originally from Barbados in the West Indies, he had first come to the colony as a sergeant in the West India Regiment in the 1870s, but after his period of service he had gone to the United States to be ordained as a minister in the AME Zion Church. Through his efforts a young man, Frank Ata Asam Pinanko, from a village near Cape Coast, was selected for training at Livingstone College in the United States, and in 1903 he returned to the Gold Coast and began the difficult task of establishing the AME Zion Church, first of all in Cape Coast and then in other towns along the coast.[25] Initially there was a great deal of enthusiasm on the part of the leading members of the Cape Coast Christian community for this independent African church, but few, even Methodists, were willing to take so radical a step as giving up their membership in an established Christian church. In general there was a great deal of cultural ambiguity on the part of what Cape Coast barrister and early nationalist Kobina Sekyi was to describe in the early twentieth century as an "Anglo-Fanti" society.[26]

It was hardly surprising that in the 1890s newspaper reports of African advancement in the civil service were invariably tempered with a fatalism that somehow the recipients of these honors would not prove worthy of their race. The early pan-Africanist Edward Wilmot Blyden argued that too much Europeanization was responsible for this "degeneracy" and sparked an interest in African customs in Sierra Leone.[27] There were similar expressions of cultural assertion in the Gold Coast. In 1889 John Mensah Sarbah, along with other members of the educated elite in Cape Coast, established the Mfantsi Amanbuhu Fékuw. For the founders of this organization its purpose was to counter "the demoralizing effects of certain European influences," and "to stop further encroachments into their nationality."[28] Suspicion between Europeans and Africans long antedated the late nineteenth century, but the way in which this found expression in the climate of pseudoscientific racism of the late nineteenth century was to have important implications for how colonial rule was to develop in the following century.

NOTES

1. The judicial assessor's court was abolished, and there was only one British court system in operation.

2. Lord Hailey, *An African Survey Revised 1956: A Study of Problems Arising in Africa South of the Sahara* (London: Oxford University Press, 1957), 599.

3. David Kimble, *A Political History of Ghana, 1850–1928* (London: Oxford University Press, 1963), 461.

4. Ibid., 462.

5. John Mensah Sarbah, *Fanti Customary Laws* (1897; reprint, London: Frank Cass, 1968), 237.

6. Governor Maxwell's dispatch to the secretary of state, January 16, 1897, CO/96/294, Public Record Office (PRO), London.

7. An Ordinance to Facilitate and Regulate the Exercise of Certain Powers and Jurisdiction by *Native Authorities* (Accra, Ghana: Government Printer, 1910), chapter 29.

8. Minute by A.W.L. Hemming (an official in the Colonial Office, London), July 24, 1886, CO/96/174, PRO.

9. Government of the Gold Coast, *Gold Coast Colony Blue Book* (Accra, Ghana: Government Printer, 1867), and Government of the Gold Coast, *Gold Coast Colony Blue Book* (Accra, Ghana: Government Printer, 1897).

10. T. B. Freeman, *Journal of Various Visits to the Kingdom of Ashanti, Aku, and Dahomi* (1842; reprint, London: Frank Cass, 1968), l.

11. Much of the oil from the palm fruit comes from the exterior of the nut, the pericarp. Traditionally this has been the main source of oil, but the interior of the nut, the kernel, also contains oil. Machinery is necessary to squeeze out this oil.

12. J. F. Easmon, report to Governor William Brandford Griffith, 1891, enclosed in Sir William Brandford Griffith's dispatch to the secretary of state, November 11, 1892, CO 96/226, PRO.

13. Ray Jenkins, "Gold Coasters Overseas, 1890–1919: With Specific Reference to Their Activities in Britain," *Immigrants and Minorities* 4, no. 3 (1985): 45–46. The British legal profession is divided into barristers and solicitors. The former represent clients in court and the latter provide legal services.

14. *Gold Coast Times*, August 26, 1882.

15. Letter of July 26, 1894, from Hutchinson to Governor Brandford Griffith, CO 96/247. Quoted in Kimble, *A Political History of Ghana*, 334.

16. Ibid., 340.

17. *Report of the Proceedings of the Deputation* (1898). Ibid., 354.

18. Ibid., 355.

19. Ibid., 356.

20. Confidential Dispatch of February 26, 1894, from Governor Hodgson to the secretary of state, CO 96/243. Quoted in Ibid., 283.

21. Government of the Gold Coast, *Gold Coast Colony Blue Book* (Accra, Ghana: Government Printer, 1911).

22. Elder Dempster was British, while the Woerman Line was German.

23. Adell Patton, "Dr. John Farell Easmon: Medical Professionalism and Colonial Racism in the Gold Coast, 1856–1900," *International Journal of African Historical Studies* 22, no. 4 (1989): 623.

24. Cited in F. L. Bartels, *The Roots of Ghana Methodism* (Cambridge: Cambridge University Press, 1965), 139.

25. I. S. Ephson, *Gallery of Gold Coast Celebrities* (Accra, Ghana: Illen Publications, 1969), 111.

26. K. Sekyi, "The Anglo-Fanti," *West Africa,* May 25–September 18, 1918. This is a fictional account of a young Fante who tries to remain true to his own culture in the face of his society's Anglomania. In many aspects it is autobiographical.

27. E. W. Blyden, *Christianity, Islam and the Negro Race* (London: W. B. Whittingham, 1889), 234–35. Quoted in L. Spitzer, *Creoles of Sierra Leone: Responses to Colonialism, 1870–1945* (Madison: University of Wisconsin Press, 1974), 115.

28. John Mensah Sarbah, *Fanti National Constitution* (1906; reprint, London: Frank Cass, 1968), xvii.

4

Politics and Protest in the Model Colony

FROM TOWN COUNCILS TO THE NCBWA

In spite of the concessions to chiefs in the coastal towns, the colonial government felt that there should be different political institutions for these areas of the colony. Officials felt that the educated elite, who were concentrated in the main coastal towns, had through their exposure to Western society become "detribalized and even denationalized," and some sort of elected municipal government was necessary for them.[1] In 1858 Governor Pine had tried to bring this into being with his Municipalities Ordinance, and there had also been more informal attempts on the part of "educated natives," especially in Cape Coast, to "train up their people in the art of self-government."[2] The growth of coastal towns after 1874 made some kind of municipal government even more pressing. In 1888 the colonial government offered Africans in the three main coastal towns, Accra, Cape Coast, and Sekondi, municipal councils that initially were to have elected African majorities. Controversially, however, these municipalities were to finance their activities out of local taxation. To the colonial rulers this was an important principle to establish, but this provision was enough to doom any voluntary acceptance of the ordinance.

In 1894 the government once again attempted to pass the Town Councils

Bill, but more realistically recognized that local property taxes would not be enough to finance these institutions. There would have to be some subvention from general revenue. However, greater financial dependence meant less political power for Africans and coincided with the increasing distrust of Africans holding senior positions in government. The new bill gave official members a majority and ensured that this proposed municipality would be even less popular than its predecessor. As a result, when the government finally established a town council for Accra in 1898, it was in the face of considerable opposition.

Apart from undermining African ideas of private property, the Town Councils Bill also contributed to tension between the educated elite and the chiefs. To the latter, town councils represented yet another challenge to what little authority they still possessed, and initially in Accra, to overcome this criticism, the government appointed the town's second-most-important *mantse* to a position on this body. In 1904, when the ordinance was applied to Sekondi, this question of competing authorities was less controversial, since the native order in that town was too bitterly divided over who should be the town's chief to organize opposition to the ordinance. Sekondi was more of a colonial creation that had grown up around the turn of the century as the gold-mining and timber industries had developed in the Western Province. Significantly, four Europeans were returned unopposed to the unofficial positions on the town council.

However, in 1906, when the ordinance was applied to Cape Coast, with its long history of opposition to colonial policies, there was considerable protest. It came at a time when the town's fortunes were in decline. Accra had become the colony's capital, and gold mining and the concessions business had moved to Sekondi. To Cape Coast's wide awake citizens it seemed as though their town was being penalized for its past history of opposition to colonial policies, and initially the Cape Coast–based GCARPS worked closely with the town's *omanhen*, Kojo Mbra, to oppose the bill. Controversy over a hurried one-man deputation to England and who should address the government soon caused a split in this show of unity, with a younger, more activist faction within the educated elite siding with the *omanhen*. Colonial polices were based on the assumption that there was a fundamental divide between what officials considered to be the Westernized and traditional aspects of colonial society. The Cape Coast situation indicated that the boundaries between these two orders were far more blurred than officialdom realized. The polarization in the town ensured that no Africans stood for election to the town council and none of those whom Governor John Rodger nominated took their seats.

An outbreak of plague in 1908 and a yellow-fever epidemic in 1910 served to transform even further these institutions into little more than an arm of the colonial government. Ten Europeans and two Africans died in the yellow-fever epidemic of 1910, and the climate of fear that this created was more than enough to override any pretension that the town councils were training grounds for African self-government. To make these institutions more effective in eradicating rodents and mosquitoes, provincial commissioners became their presidents, and the councils lost the power of appointing their own health officers. The African unofficial members were powerless to check what they saw as the excesses of the appointed health officers, European officials. Since 1902, when the West African Medical Service had been closed to African doctors, medical officers had rapidly become exclusively Europeans. They had relatively few African patients, and consequently there was little sympathy for those who violated the regulations governing water storage that town councils passed. Eliminating stagnant water where yellow-fever mosquitoes could breed took precedent over all else at that time.

The yellow-fever epidemic also spurred the government into building segregated housing for European officials. Africans, according to medical thinking then, were a reservoir of both the malaria parasite and the yellow-fever virus. Particularly at night, when the mosquitoes that spread these illnesses were most active, Europeans needed to be separated from African populations. So frantic was the haste to create these segregated housing areas that in 1913 Governor Hugh Clifford remarked it had "reduced" the colony's Public Works Department "to a state of partial paralysis."[3] Complete segregation was obviously impossible, and town councils were also charged with decongesting crowded African quarters, which were seen as prime breeding grounds for mosquitoes. It meant passing regulations restricting building materials and removing unsafe and unsanitary structures, which inevitably pitted European officials against the African unofficial members. The provincial engineer, the European official who issued building permits, came to rival in importance the town council's medical officer.

By the beginning of the second decade of the twentieth century, the pseudoscientific racism of the late nineteenth century had been reinforced by what now was seen as medical science. African unwillingness to accept its findings was evidence that even the best-educated among them could not be trusted as reliable partners in the challenging task of developing the colony. Significantly, even though the colony's finances improved at this time and during the first decade of the twentieth century the civil service almost doubled in size, Africans were no longer appointed to senior positions in the administration.[4] Improving health conditions made it possible for European officials to bring their wives from Britain, which also served to undermine what in the past had been a significant degree of social interaction between Africans and Europeans. It was in recognition of this development that Governor Rodger in 1908 established in Accra the club that was named after him to cater to Africans who were excluded from the Accra Club, which was exclusively for Europeans.

The establishment of the town councils coincided with a new challenge to the African ownership of land. In 1910 the government introduced a forestry bill to set up forest reserves. Titles to ownership were not necessarily affected, "but might lapse if not claimed within a given time-limit."[5] This potential threat to ownership was enough to bring the chiefs and the educated elite together in a show of unity to oppose what they felt was violation of the pledge given by the secretary of state, Joseph Chamberlain, in 1898. It was enough to force the government to amend the bill to allay African suspicions, but in 1912 the secretary of state appointed a special commissioner, H. C. Belfield, to investigate land alienation in the Gold Coast. Shortly after, the West African Lands Committee was appointed to look at what some critics in Great Britain felt was the threat to communal ownership that the excessive commercialization of land posed all over West Africa. GCARPS sent a four-man deputation to London to challenge the committee's recommendations that there should be "sweeping state intervention to halt the transition to individual tenure."[6]

Instead, it was the development of the cocoa industry, based on peasant farming; fear of upsetting the chiefs, who were playing an active role in the administration of the colony; and most immediately the interruption of the First World War that served to undermine any attempt at reforming land policies in the Gold Coast. Nevertheless, this struggle over something so fundamental as land once again seemed to underscore GCARPS's inability to combat what was seen as hostile colonial policies. In 1911 Governor James Thorburn, in the face of opposition from the society, had appointed one of the colony's best-educated chiefs, Mate Kole, the *konor* of Manya Krobo, to the Legislative Council. To the society this undermined their claim to represent and speak for the colony's chiefs. Governor Clifford, Thorburn's successor, was even more in favor of having the chiefs participate in the administration of the colony, and in 1916, along with three educated Africans, he appointed three paramount chiefs to an expanded Legislative Council. They were to represent the Twi, Fante, and Ewe-speaking peoples of the colony.[7] Once again the Cape Coast–based GCARPS seemed powerless to affect these developments, and a younger generation of the educated elite led by Cape Coast lawyer J. E. Casely Hayford began to argue in favor of a new organization that was less parochial.

Examples of the need for a much broader focus already existed. The first Pan-African Conference, organized in London in 1900 by Trinidadian barrister Henry Sylvester Williams, had included the barrister A. F. Riberio, from the Gold Coast, along with other delegates from Nigeria, Sierra Leone, and Liberia. The Gold Coast press carried reports of the conference and extolled the need for "the Negro" to "be protected" from white conspiracies by depending largely on himself.[8] The unprecedented spectacle of such race solidarity was inspirational for Casely Hayford, who from as far back as the period of his secondary education had come under the influence of pan-African thinker Wilmot Edward Blyden. At that time, in the 1870s, Blyden was already the leading advocate of the "African personality," and was a frequent visitor from Liberia to Freetown, Sierra Leone, where Casely Hayford was a student at Fourah Bay College.[9]

Indeed, in Casely Hayford's second book, appropriately entitled *Ethiopia Unbound*, the main character in this semiautobiographical work praises Blyden as "the foremost thinker of the race."[10] His call for a West African community and his interest in the creation of a West African university and a West African church had a particular appeal to the West African elite at a time when pseudoscientific racist beliefs were undermining their self-esteem.

In 1912 Casely Hayford's brother, Reverend Mark Hayford, had attended Booker T. Washington's International Conference on the Negro, held at Tuskegee Institute in Alabama, where he gave an address and read a letter from his brother.[11] Blyden's death in the same year provided further stimulus for something similar for West Africa as a commemoration of his passing. Along with Dr. R. A. Savage, who had been the Nigerian delegate at the 1900 London Pan-African Conference, Casely Hayford began to contact influential people in the British West African colonies, soliciting their opinions on a West African conference. In 1912–13 he used his newspaper, the *Gold Coast Leader*, to popularize the idea. The interregional approach that the British government had taken to the land question further vindicated the need for a British West African organization that would include all of Britain's West African colonies: Nigeria, the Gold Coast, Sierra Leone, and The Gambia. Together they would constitute what Casely Hayford hoped would be a "united West Africa." The First World War intervened, and it was not until 1919 that, along with other Gold Coast professionals, he was able to organize the Gold Coast Section of the projected West African Conference.

Allied war aims and the Versailles Peace Conference that was going on at that time had popularized the idea of self-determination. In the Gold Coast this translated into greater representation for Africans on the Legislative Council, but the question of who should be these representatives was publicly to split the educated natives and the chiefs. Casely Hayford felt that it was time for the "educated natives" to establish themselves as the "natural leaders" of their country, and he antagonized the leadership of GCARPS as well as the colony's most prominent chief, Nana Ofori Atta, the *okyenhene* of Akyem Abuakwa.[12] Ofori Atta had been appointed to the Legislative Council in 1916 to represent the Twi-speaking peoples of the Gold Coast, and had become an articulate and important voice in the council. Indeed, he had been thinking along similar lines to that of Casely Hayford, and was highly irate to discover he had been left out of the latter's deliberations. GCARPS also refused to go along with this new initiative, fearing that the ancient society would lose its identity in the wider association Casely Hayford proposed.

Nevertheless, in 1920 the first meeting of what was to be known as the National Congress of British West Africa (NCBWA) took place in Accra with representatives from the four British West African colonies. The most senior Gold Coast lawyer who was in favor of the congress, T. Hutton Mills, was elected president, and Casely Hayford was elected vice president. Most of the officers were from the Gold Coast, but five additional vice presidents were elected to give some voice to the other West African colonies. The congress passed 83 resolutions that dealt with issues as diverse as elected representative government, the government's relation to the land question, the creation of a British West African university, opportunities for Africans in the upper ranks of the civil service, opening up the judicial service and the West African Medical Service to qualified Africans, and calling for the repatriation of Syrians, who were seen as offering unfair economic competition to African entrepreneurs. Most of these Syrians were in reality from Lebanon. They had begun coming to West Africa in the 1890s, and by pooling their resources and cutting costs they had been able to displace African merchants from the retail trade all over the area. In the volatile economic conditions after the First World War, tension between Africans and their Lebanese competitors had become so heated that it had resulted in serious rioting in Sierra Leone in 1919. It was not surprising that the congress's representatives wanted to see the government do something about they described as the "Syrian Peril."[13]

However, in general these resolutions were reformist rather than radical, even though they were couched in the language of self-determination. President Wilson of the United States had included self-determination for all peoples as one of his Fourteen Points for establishing a lasting and just peace after the First World War, and this had inspired colonial people all over the world. Initially the new governor, Gordon Guggisberg, who was himself reformist in sentiment, was mildly sympathetic, but when the congress hastily organized a nine-person deputation from the four West African colonies to go to London to press for reforms, this sympathy evaporated. The chiefs, under the leadership of Nana Ofori Atta, also attacked the idea that the educated elite were the natural rulers and undermined whatever chance Casely Hayford and his fellow deputation members might have had in influencing the Colonial Office in London.

This conflict between the chiefs and the educated elite allowed the government in the Gold Coast to dismiss the congress as unrepresentative. To challenge this evaluation, the congress captured control of GCARPS, and Casely Hayford became its vice president. In the Legislative Council, where he had been a member since 1916, he "impeached" Nana Ofori Atta and his supporters as "traitors to the cause of British West Africa."[14] However, the damage to the cause of West African unity had been done, and though there were a number of joint sessions in the capitals of the other British West African colonies (Freetown, 1923; Bathhurst, 1925–26; and Lagos, 1929) it was only at these times that the movement actually came alive. As a political force, the NCBWA had only an indirect impact on the legislatures of the British West African colonies. Only one of its many suggestions, the establishment of the West African Court of Appeal (1929), was actually implemented during the organization's existence. More importantly, the organization indicated that the educated elite wanted more say in the administration of their colonial societies.

THE GUGGISBERG ADMINISTRATION

Much of the reason for the upstaging of the congress movement was due to the energetic administration of the colony's 12th governor, Gordon Guggisberg, who was to serve from 1919 to 1927. Apart from being Canadian by birth, Guggisberg was also different from his predecessors by coming from an engineering background. He had graduated from the Royal Military Academy at Woolwich in 1889 and had served in a number of technical positions in the colonies and in Great Britain. From 1901 to 1908 he had been the assistant director of the Gold Coast Survey Department and had surveyed almost all the colony and about a quarter of the Ashanti Region. His experiences in the field made him particularly sensitive to the colony's need for improved systems of communication and transportation.

Guggisberg arrived in the Gold Coast after the First World War at a time of boom conditions. Cocoa exports had gone from almost £1.8 million in 1918 to over £8 million in 1919, and though there were significant ups and downs, the value of the colony's main export continued to increase during the 1920s. He recognized that the colony's future prosperity depended on the development of its infrastructure, without which it would not be able "to attract the overseas capital on which further development would depend."[15] One of the first things that he did was to outline a 10-year development program in which he intended to spend the unheard-of sum of £25 million. More than half of this expenditure was to be on railroad construction, without which Guggisberg felt the colony's economy was doomed. A great deal was eventually spent on extending the colony's already-existing railroad network, but the ambitious Northern Province Railroad that was to open up the north to development was never built. In addition, his administration also spent over £1.2 million on road construction, much of it in the north. In 1924 the construction of Korle Bu hospital was completed, the "finest hospital in Africa," which Guggisberg envisaged would become a teaching hospital.[16] In 1927 Achimota College was formally opened, which rapidly became the foremost educational institution in the colony. Of particular pride to Africans was that the position of vice principal for the school was held for a short while by an African educator, James E. K. Aggrey, who had been trained in the United States.[17] Guggisberg envisaged that this elite secondary school would eventually be the nucleus of the colony's first university. Undoubtedly the centerpiece of Guggisberg's program was the construction of a deepwater harbor at Takoradi, which was to cost well over £3 million and was not finished until 1930.

Projects of this nature were not without opposition. Financing the construction of Takoradi Harbor and other infrastructure improvements meant floating a loan of £4.5 million on the London financial market. There were some officials in the colonial office who felt that the long-term indebtedness that this loan represented indicated that the governor was "tainted with the disease of reckless extravagance."[18] Also, in the colony there was a great deal of opposition to the harbor, and especially the Central Province Railroad, an important part of its feeder system, which was seen as likely to drain away upcountry produce from surf ports such as Winneba, Saltpond, and Cape Coast. Indeed, so great was this threat seen to Cape Coast, since exports from its hinterland would much more easily go by railroad to Takoradi, that it was enough to bring together GCARPS, bitterly divided over the congress movement, to oppose the Central Province Railroad and any government plans to close the town as a surf port.

Guggisberg also introduced a number of political reforms. Some, like

the repatriation of the former *asantehene* Prempeh I in 1924, and his in-
stallation in 1926 as *kumasihene,* were unreservedly popular. Similarly appreciated was the governor's determination to increase the numbers of
Africans holding senior positions in the civil service. Governor Clifford
had begun this process in 1919 by appointing two police magistrates, new
judicial positions in the colony's court system, and a temporary medical
officer. By the time Guggisberg left office in 1927 there were 31 such appointments. Most of these were "special class" appointments reserved for
Africans.[19] Guggisberg believed that the secondary-school system, with
Achimota College at its center, would provide a stream of qualified Africans for such posts. In general, finding positions for Africans in the civil
service was not difficult. The civil service needed rebuilding after the de-
pletions caused by the First World War. During the eight years of Guggisberg's administration the civil service expanded by over 63 percent.[20]
Guggisberg believed that such employment, though it would result temporarily in "a slight loss of efficiency," would in the long run save the
colony money, since Africans holding European positions were to receive
20 percent less pay, and they were not entitled to the same generous leave
provisions.[21] This was a source of friction between the governor and the
African members of the Legislative Council.

Even more controversial were the governor's constitutional reforms. In
1924, partly in response to African demands for more representation in
government and partly to improve the operation of the town councils,
Guggisberg introduced the Municipal Corporations Bill. It provided for a
majority of elected African councillors with powers to levy new rates and
with the franchise limited to owners or occupiers of a house of ratable
value of £5. Initially Casely Hayford welcomed this legislation, but there
were other members of the educated elite who argued that the bill did
not extend African participation in the Legislative Council. Others bitterly
opposed the provisions for direct taxation, and eventually Guggisberg
withdrew the bill. Instead, he merely amended the 1894 Town Council
Ordinance to increase the number of appointed members.

Guggisberg's new constitution of 1925 produced even more controversy. He expanded the legislature from 21 to 30 members, 16 of whom
were to be officials and the rest unofficials. Five of the unofficials were to
be Europeans representing commercial interests in the colony, and the rest
elected Africans. Each of the colony's three municipalities were to elect
one representative, with the franchise open to all those over 21 years of
age and in occupation of a house with a ratable value of at least £8 per
annum. The remaining six African members were to be elected by newly
created bodies known as Provincial Councils of Chiefs. The Western Prov-

ince, with the smallest population, was entitled to one representative; the Central Province had two representatives; and the Eastern Province, with the largest population, had three. The government sought to maintain that this system was both democratic and representative, and tried to trace its roots back into the nineteenth century. However, to the educated elite this attempt to preserve native institutions was seen as a blow to their aspirations to become what Casely Hayford had described as the "natural leaders." It supported the educated elite's contention that colonial policy was divide and rule and favored "semi-illiterate" chiefs over the educated elite.[22]

The immediate reaction of GCARPS was an "absolute refusal to cooperate."[23] The society, controlled by Casely Hayford and his supporters, ruled that no head chiefs should attend any of the provincial councils. With great difficulty the government did manage to get the three provincial councils to meet, but only the Central and the Eastern councils elected representatives. Nana Ofori Atta, who had failed to be elected as a representative from the Eastern Province, was later nominated to fill the vacancy for the Western Provincial Council. The Society was more successful in preventing anyone from running for office as a municipal member. Guggisberg had wanted to make municipal self-government for the coastal towns a stepping-stone to elective representation on the Legislative Council. Instead, he was forced to nominate Africans to these positions, which served to split the ranks of the educated elite. E.J.P. Brown, who was Casely Hayford's main political rival in Cape Coast, resumed his seat on the Legislative Council. A. W. Kojo Thompson, a young lawyer from Accra, took advantage of a bitter rivalry between sections of the town to have one of these factions submit his name for nomination, while George Grant, a timber merchant from Axim, accepted nomination for Sekondi.

Neither did a hasty one-man deputation to London by the indefatigable Casely Hayford prevent the new Legislative Council from meeting in 1926. By 1927, when elections for municipal members to the Legislative Council were due, he decided that further opposition was useless. Along with his supporters in the Congress of British West Africa, he formed the Accra Ratepayers Association, which succeeded in electing Accra lawyer Glover-Addo. In Sekondi, Casely Hayford himself stood successfully for election. However, in Cape Coast, with its long history of opposition to colonial policies, there was considerably more defiance. A younger section of the educated elite, led by Cape Coast lawyer W.E.G. Sekyi, who had already disagreed with Casely Hayford over the Municipal Council Bill, attacked him for what he now described as "his servile habit of mind."[24] Fear of being left behind politically eventually brought a significant section of the town together to form the Cape Coast Ratepayers Association, and a young lawyer, K. A. Korsah, was eventually elected. The Noncooperators, as they came to be known in Cape Coast, led by Sekyi, challenged the legality of this election. Here they were unsuccessful, but as an indication of how much municipal politics were to become intertwined with those of the native order, they successfully destooled the town's *tufuhen*, W. Z. Coker, who had allowed himself to become president of the Cape Coast Ratepayers Association.

Like Casely Hayford before, Sekyi took control of GCARPS and used this body to disrupt the functioning of the provincial councils. He was most successful in the Central and Western Provinces, where he was able to take advantage of succession disputes and conflicts between paramount chiefs and their subordinates. In Cape Coast he was able to gain control over the town's *omanhen*, Mbra III. In the Eastern Province, Sekyi was able to attack Nana Ofori Atta by representing, in a series of court cases, the latter's subchiefs who wanted to break away from Akyem Abuakwa's control. At stake was the control over revenues from diamond mining. What was known in the colony as the Asamangkese dispute began in 1922 and was to continue until 1937 when the *ohene*, the chief of the town of Asamangkese, the most recalcitrant of Nana Ofori Atta's subchiefs, eventually withdrew an appeal he had pending before the Privy Council in Great Britain. Over £160,000 was spent in legal fees by both sides.

Fueling even more opposition from GCARPS and other members of the educated elite was the new Native Administration Ordinance (NAO), which the Guggisberg administration allowed the chiefs to introduce in 1927. Apart from giving the chiefs experience in framing legislation, the ordinance strengthened their administrative and judicial powers. One of the ironies of the government's policy of indirect rule was that as it had become more formalized it had resulted in creating a very unstable native order. Destoolments of paramount chiefs in the colony had shown an alarming increase, from 7 in 1904–8 to 41 in 1919–24.[25] There was also a growing tendency for subchiefs to break off their allegiance to their paramount chiefs. The Asamangkese dispute was hardly unique. The NAO was to help counteract this trend, but to its opponents it was once again seen as giving powers to the chiefs that went counter to tradition, and stimulated even more opposition.

The Guggisberg reforms and especially the NAO represented a shift from what had been a noninterventionist to an interventionist indirect-rule policy.[26] Rather than being primarily interested in the smooth functioning of the traditional state's judicial machinery and the resolution of disputes, indirect rule was now to incorporate the chiefly order into the machinery of colonial government. It clearly required a better understanding of traditional societies and their institutions, and to achieve this Guggisberg established in 1921 an Anthropological Department. It was placed under the direction of Captain R. S. Rattray, who had already published in 1916 a collection of Asante proverbs that he regarded as "the very soul of this people."[27] Altogether Rattray published seven works on the Akan people and the "tribes" of the northern hinterland. His main focus was the Asante, and rapidly he came to the conclusion that there were fundamental similarities between them and all other Akan peoples. Earlier African commentators, like John Mensah Sarbah and Casely Hayford, had already made this observation. Now, however, it received official acceptance. The result was that, more consciously than in the past, interventionist indirect rule was to be based on this Akan model of statecraft.

This interest in understanding native societies also extended to the north, which lacked the centralized states of the south. Sizable kingdoms like Gonja and Mamprugu had been dislocated by slave raiding and civil wars in the nineteenth century. Especially in the northwest and northeast, many people had no chiefs at all, which the administration had sought to rectify by creating paramount chiefs over particular areas. In general very little was known about local traditions and customs. The north had developed as little more than a labor reserve for the mines, cocoa farms, the Public Works Department of Ashanti and the south, and the colony's military and police force. To colonial officials it was described as the Cinderella of the country.

In the 1920s the Guggisberg administration turned its attention to what was hoped would be a more systematic development. The projected Northern Territories Railroad was to be the central component in this process. Better understanding of northern society also seemed necessary, and commissioners were encouraged to make reports on the people under their control. Eventually Rattray turned his attention to the people of the northern hinterland. He was able to provide considerable information about the dual system of government that derived from the *ten'dana*, the priest kings of the indigenous inhabitants, who conducted all "religious or magico-religious concerns," and the secular rulers, who were the descendants of the invading warriors from further north.[28] Nevertheless, Rattray found that there were still considerable similarities between these northern peoples' constitutions and those of the Akan south. Not surprisingly, indirect-rule policies for the north were also influenced by Akan ideas of statecraft.

Like much of the anthropological work of the time, this research was based on assumptions about what should happen and not what really happened. Significantly, Rattray avoided those areas where there had been "frequent intercourse" with Europeans. He studiously avoided the Ashanti capital of Kumasi and did his fieldwork for his studies of Asante society among "the older men and women who [had] few dealings with the foreigner, [and] lived secluded lives in remote villages."[29] In general his work portrays ordered and even timeless societies that contrast vividly with the highly contested nature of the traditional order that is described in the administrative records of the time. It was a vision that appealed to colonial administrators, since it reinforced their assumptions about how different this traditional order was from the Westernized societies of the coast. They assumed also that colonial rule itself had a timeless quality, and that change would come only gradually. A system of government rooted in an unchanging past seemed best suited to preserving the authority of the chiefs on whom they depended.

THE DEPRESSION YEARS

For a short while after Sir Ransford Slater succeeded Sir Gordon Guggisberg as the governor of the colony, the boom in cocoa prices continued. However, by 1929, with the onset of the Great Depression, prices began to plunge, and by 1930 they were a little more than a third of what they had been in 1927. Almost 60 percent of the colony's revenue derived from cocoa exports, and the economy was in crisis. For much of the decade of the 1930s this remained the case. Guggisberg's ambitious plans for the colony were shelved, and instead unpopular attempts to cut back on spending and raise revenue stimulated African opposition to colonial rule. The collapse of cocoa prices also triggered African responses, most notably in the form of holdup actions. In general the crisis in the world economy subjected the capitalist countries of the West to searching criticisms of their institutions. Defending colonies from anti-imperialist ideologies that subjected colonialism to hostile scrutiny became an important task for colonial legislatures, and they passed legislation to achieve this purpose. In the Gold Coast challenging such obnoxious ordinances as well as revenue-raising measures characterized much of colony's political life in the 1930s.

Even before the onset of the Depression, Governor Slater demonstrated his difference from his predecessor by showing little enthusiasm for the Africanization of the civil service. Even more unpopular was his reduction of starting salaries for probationary African clerks in 1930. A year later he really inflamed protest by trying to introduce an income tax. It was to be modest in scale and apply only to those who had an income of more than £40 per annum. Coming at a time when many Africans and Europeans had already been retrenched, or had suffered serious income loss, the bill meet with major opposition. In Sekondi, Shama, and Cape Coast there was sporadic rioting that disrupted business and court proceedings, targeting the police and sometimes Europeans. Most upsetting of all to the government was that the intelligentsia were able to exploit the situation, and received support from members of the European commercial community.

The governor was forced to retreat on the issue to protect what he considered his more important initiative, which was the introduction of a more general direct taxation though the native authorities. He considered his most important objective the implementation of a full-scale indirect rule policy, patterned after that of Nigeria, which would "make the native authority . . . a living part of the machinery of government."[30] Indeed, it was during his administration that the term *indirect rule* became officially part of government terminology. To achieve his aim he felt it was necessary to raise revenue that would allow the chiefs "to pay the salaries of their officials and to inaugurate schemes of development."[31] In 1932 he tried to do this with the Native Administration Revenue Ordinance, but once again there was considerable protest. Apart from a few chiefs like Sir Nana Ofori Atta (who had been knighted in 1927) and Nana Ayirebi Acquah, the *omanhen* of Winneba, there was no more support for direct taxation in the countryside than there had been in the towns.

It was not surprising that this was so, since there was already extensive turmoil in the colony's rural areas. As cocoa prices had collapsed, the European firms had joined together to form a pool led by the United Africa Company (UAC), which itself had come into being in 1929 as a combination of three major metropolitan firms. The colony's cocoa farmers had responded by forming a Gold Coast and Ashanti Cocoa Federation, and in 1930–31 organized a holdup of limited success. It was not the first time that Gold Coast cocoa farmers had resorted to holdups. As far back as 1921, Akwapim cocoa farmers had formed an association for this purpose. In the past these attempts at holdup had tended to be local. However, the 1930–31 holdup was colony-wide and also extended to the Ashanti Region. For a few months it was extremely successful in the colony, but much less so in the Ashanti Region, where the political officers put considerable pressure on the chiefs not to participate. Unfortunately, when the holdup finally collapsed early in 1931, the price of cocoa plunged, and there were various competing schemes to market cocoa independently of the pool firms, but without much success. Cocoa prices continued to fall, and there remained considerable discontent in the colony's rural areas. It was hardly a propitious time for introducing any form of direct taxation.

Instead, Sir Shenton Thomas, who succeeded Slater in 1932, was forced to continue with unpopular cost-cutting measures as well as trying to raise revenue from other sources. One such initiative was his Waterworks Ordinance Bill, which was to make the citizens of towns that had water systems pay for their water, which previously had been furnished free. Coupled with this "obnoxious" ordinance was the Criminal Code Amendment Bill, which was designed to prevent "the entry of subversive literature into the colony."[32] The later bill was an indirect way of controlling what the government felt was a local press that had become too "race-conscious and anti-colonialist."[33] One source of growth during the depression was the colony's press. Particularly was this so in Accra, where by 1934 there were four newspapers, one of which (the *Times of West Africa*) was a daily. Often, to the annoyance of colonial officials, this press could be highly critical of government actions. Some of the more radical publishers and editors were also in contact with anti-imperialist front organizations for the Comintern, like the International League against Imperialism and Marcus Garvey's Universal Negro Improvement Association (UNIA).[34] The literature disseminated by these organizations was the main target of the Criminal Code Amendment Bill, popularly known as the Sedition Bill.

The discontent in the cocoa-growing areas and protests in the towns served to bring the chiefs and the intelligentsia together to form what was known as the Central National Committee (CNC). Indeed, this unity had been building with the establishment of the Youth Conference Movement as far back as 1929. Professionals recently returned from their studies in Great Britain were the driving force behind this movement that sought to have "the chiefs using the intelligentsia and the intelligentsia using the chiefs."[35] Nana Sir Ofori Atta's nephew, Dr. J. B. Danquah, who had returned from Great Britain in 1927 after completing a degree in law and Ph.D. in ethics, was the main force behind this movement. It was not surprising that this was so, since in his student days in Great Britain he had been involved in politics and had been the president of the West African Students' Union. When, in 1934, the CNC decided on yet another deputation to London, the eight-person Gold Coast and Ashanti Delegation comprised many of the leading figures of the Youth Movement from the colony and Ashanti. To give the deputation as much legitimacy as possible, the organizers prevailed upon Nana Sir Ofori Atta to be its leader. In addition, they broadened their concerns by demanding changes in the colony's constitution. They wanted an African majority in the Legislative Council and representation on the Executive Council.

There were too many divisive issues in the colony for there to be complete unity, and after much wrangling with the CNC, GCARPS eventually sent its own two-person deputation to London. Neither had much success, since the government in Britain was also confronting a red scare and engaged in the passage of its own sedition bill. It was relatively easy for officials in the colonial office to sympathize with their subordinates in the Gold Coast, whom they saw as facing similar threats. With the possible exception of Danquah, the other members of the Gold Coast and Ashanti Delegation were moderates and studiously avoided doing anything unconstitutional while they were in the United Kingdom. Even after they had failed to secure any concessions from the secretary of state, they refused to make contacts with left-wing elements in the Labor Party. However, in the Gold Coast there were far more radical elements who seemed to epitomize the threat that communist ideas offered to the colony.

Undoubtedly the most important of these was Sierra Leonean I.T.A. Wallace-Johnson. In the early 1930s he had attended the People's University of the East in Moscow and had graduated, one colonial official maintained, "in the art of subversive propaganda."[36] He had arrived in the Gold Coast in 1933 after being expelled from Nigeria by the colonial authorities for organizing the Nigerian Workers' Union. Wallace-Johnson went well beyond the established noncooperative radicalism in the Gold Coast by linking his opposition to colonial rule with international leftist causes, which made him particularly threatening to colonial officials. Rapidly he became involved in labor agitation. In the 1920s, labor unions had begun to form in the colony, with the Sekondi Railway Association (1923) among the first. However, it was during the depression years of the 1930s that labor agitation increased dramatically, and Wallace-Johnson threw himself into such conflicts. The struggle for workman's compensation was one of his major concerns. The Prestea mine disaster in 1934, in which 40 miners lost their lives, provided him with a platform for attacking the hazardous conditions that existed in the colony's gold mines. He used the colony's more radical press for this purpose, and he also contributed articles to the *Negro Worker*, as well as making sure that this mouthpiece of the International Trade Union Committee of Negro Workers was distributed in the Gold Coast. Even more directly he sought to link Gold Coast struggles with international campaigns for racial justice, like the defense of the Scottsboro Boys in the United States.[37]

Neither did the passage of the Criminal Code Amendment Bill deter Wallace-Johnson. In 1935 he sided with the Friends of Ashanti Freedom

Society, which was opposed to the restoration of the Ashanti Confederacy, and by so doing he was able to attack indirect rule. He joined with Nigerian Nnamdi Azikiwe to form the West African Youth League (WAYL). The latter had come to the Gold Coast in 1935 to be the editor of one of Accra's most radical newspapers, the *African Morning Post*. The WAYL went beyond what Casely Hayford had conceived by seeking to establish links with French-speaking and Portuguese-speaking Africans. In spite of its name, it was not restricted to youth, but comrades could be both "the youth in age and the youth in mind," and the league sought to popularize anti-imperialist marxist ideas.[38] In the hotly contested municipal elections for Accra in 1935, the league supported A. W. Kojo Thompson against the conservative Dr. Nanka-Bruce. They were able to intimidate many of the latter's older supporters, and though the first election was nullified, in the second they were still able to have their candidate elected.

The WAYL also established a branch of the Ethiopia Defense Committee, which had been formed in Paris in 1935 when the Italians invaded Ethiopia. The pan-African protest that followed linked anti-imperialism with race consciousness and found a ready response among the colony's workers and others adversely affected by the depression. In 1936, Governor Sir Arnold Hodson was able to take advantage of a particularly hostile attack on European civilization, Christianity, and imperialism that Wallace-Johnson published in the *African Morning Post* under the title "Has the African a God?"[39] The government arrested and prosecuted him and the paper's editor, Nnamdi Azikiwe, under the Criminal Code Amendment Bill. Both were found guilty and fined. Azikiwe successfully appealed his conviction before the West African Court of Appeal, but soon after, he returned to Nigeria. In 1937 Wallace-Johnson went to the United Kingdom to appeal his conviction before the Judicial Committee of the Privy Council. Here he failed, and in 1938 he returned to his homeland, Sierra Leone, since the Gold Coast government had banned his return to that colony. Without his organizational abilities the WAYL in the Gold Coast collapsed, and Wallace-Johnson focused his attention on building a similar organization in Sierra Leone.

With Wallace-Johnson out of the way, Governor Hodson was almost immediately faced with an even more serious challenge. Cocoa prices had risen in 1936, and it seemed as if the depression was over for the Gold Coast, but in 1937 they declined precipitously. Once again the major firms, led by the UAC, entered into a buying agreement, which rapidly became the target of yet another holdup. The 1937 holdup was far more successful than that of 1930–31, and other, even less successful earlier attempts at this action. Much had been learned from the past. The lead for this holdup came from the farmers, with the chiefs playing a circumspect role that made it difficult for political officers to hold them responsible for illegal coercive actions. The buying agreement also targeted brokers by seeking to eliminate abuses they were accused of committing in the past. The holdup lasted for seven months, from October 1937 to April 1938, and at its height was over 80 percent successful. Eventually, in 1938, the colonial government was forced into appointing a commission of inquiry to investigate the marketing of cocoa in Nigeria and the Gold Coast.

To bring about a truce, the Nowell Commission (named after its chairman, William Nowell, who had been the director of the East African Agricultural Research Institute) called for an end to the buying agreement. Instead, the government passed an ordinance establishing export quotas. For the farmers this was even more disastrous, as they were forced to sell for less than half what they would have received before the holdup. For a long-term solution, the Nowell Commission recommended group cooperative marketing to eliminate the brokers, whom they saw as primarily responsible for the abuses in the system. The two committees the government established to see how this could be done were very pessimistic about the success of such a scheme. They felt that the costs would be extremely high. Neither were the farmers particularly enthusiastic. There was a long history of such marketing initiatives in the colony that had not been particularly successful. The most notorious of them, the Strickler swindle of 1924, had cost Gold Coast cocoa farmers over £250,000. In 1937 the case was still being litigated in the supreme court of New York, since F. D. Strickler was an American and had used American companies to carry out his operation.

Instead, it was the outbreak of the Second World War in 1939 that radically altered the nature of cocoa marketing all over West Africa. To prevent a repeat of the devastation that had befallen the cocoa industry during the First World War, the metropolitan government decided to buy the colony's entire cocoa crop. The price offered was very low, and all during the war there was agitation for a higher price on the part of the colony's farmers. Nevertheless, it was out of this control scheme that the postwar Cocoa Marketing Board was to emerge.

Apart from altering the manner in which cocoa was marketed in the Gold Coast, the holdup of 1937 indicated just how important the chiefs had become in the political and economic life of the colony. Initially they had been averse to the holdup, but when they decided to join, their support was crucial. Reflective of this importance during the 1930s, it was the provincial councils that became one of the main focal points for African activity in the colony.[40] However, this importance meant that the chiefs could be blamed for failures. Nana Sir Ofori Atta had come in for extensive criticism for the failure of the 1934 delegation. The disastrous fall in cocoa prices in 1938 undermined much of the elation that the appointment of the Nowell Commission created, and the chiefs were once again the losers. Moreover, these reverses came in the context of the colonial government's controversial legislative attempts to strengthen indirect rule, which made the chiefs once again vulnerable to criticism.

The most controversial of these measures was the attempt to create Native Treasuries to exercise control over the revenue that the native states generated. Significantly, this was first of all done in the Northern Territories in 1932, which in a simplified form followed what existed in Northern Nigeria and Tanganyika. In 1935 the government also enacted the Native Authority Ordinance for Ashanti, which empowered the governor to require that recognized native authorities establish Native Treasuries.[41] It was done in conjunction with the restoration of the Ashanti Confederacy, which meant that the newly enstooled *asantehene*, Prempeh II, was not likely to protest. Nor was this the case for the intelligentsia that comprised the Kotoko Society. Unlike their counterparts in the colony, many of them were co-opted into the Confederacy Council, the counterpart to the latter's Provincial Council of Chiefs. It was not until 1939 that similar legislation was enacted for the colony with the passage of the Native Administration Treasuries Ordinance. Predictably, there was more opposition, since this legislation made it possible for native states to tax their subjects.

On the surface such opposition seemed to underscore the continuing divide between the chiefs and the intelligentsia. The rebirth of the Youth Movement at the end of the decade was an important attempt to defuse this tension. Significantly, when the movement held its second conference in 1938, it was held in Cape Coast, which was an attempt to bring GCARPS on board and make the movement as national as possible. For similar reasons, the second conference, in 1939, was held in Kumasi, which was an important attempt to bridge the separation between the colony and Ashanti. At first, Dr. J. B. Danquah, the moving force behind this movement, wanted to make it as nonpolitical as possible, so as not to antagonize the colonial government in the way that the NCBWA had done in the 1920s. The movement was to bring the "thinking people" together rather than to "do something."[42] By bringing together a wide array of participants, the moderates swamped the radicals, and as indication of how all-inclusive and moderate the movement was, Governor Hodson, known in the Gold Coast as the Sunshine Governor, addressed the 1939 Kumasi conference.

By looking at the political organizations of the 1930s, historians have stressed the elitist nature of the colony's political life. The cocoa holdups clearly had mass rural participation, but significantly, the Youth Movement paid little attention to the colony's developing labor movement. The Kumasi conference members were as surprised by the Union of Railwaymen's strike that coincided with the conference as was the government. However, focusing on the elitist nature of the colony's main political organizations, or the divide between the chiefs and the intelligentsia, ignores just how much indirect rule contributed to politicizing Gold Coast society. This is most graphically indicated by how much of the colonial record is taken up with what was known as native affairs. Much of it is extremely parochial in focus and consequently ignored by historians, who have been predominantly interested in the growth of nationalist consciousness in the colony.

Destoolments and succession disputes were the lifeblood of the colony's political life in the interwar years. They involved a wide array of people that could include members of the intelligentsia as well as illiterate fishermen or farmers. Women, who played a minor roll in elite political movements, filled important positions as stool mothers, since they were responsible for selecting candidates for traditional offices. Neither was the divide between chiefs and commoners particularly rigid. The extended family system insured that there was inevitably a wide range of candidates, even to the point of including those who were considered of domestic or slave background. Disputes arising out of these selection processes could be extremely contentious, even to the point of bloodshed. Six *asafo* members were shot dead in Cape Coast in 1932 as a result of a dispute over who was the legitimate *tufuhen* of the town.[43] Disputes of this nature could also be extremely protracted and often linked to national issues. From the 1920s to the 1940s there was no officially recognized *omanhen* for the town of Elmina. The two main contending factions, ostensibly comprising "illiterate fisherman" as opposed to "literate scholars," both sought legal support from members of the intelligentsia, who were either opposed to the provincial councils or who supported them.[44] In general, indirect rule stimulated a competition for traditional office, which required new stratagems to obtain what in essence were the new spoils of office.

The bewilderingly unfamiliar nature of this political environment could leave the architects of indirect rule in despair. As one colonial official in 1939 was to describe it, "the unending stool palavers, apathy, lack of real interest, lack of policy, lack of coordination, lack of vision characterized the whole administration of the Gold Coast and the sooner it [was] given a real jolt the better for all concerned."[45] It was understandable why it was difficult for even perceptive outsiders to recognize this faction-ridden world as the stirring of nationalism. When Lord Hailey, the British authority on Africa, published *An African Survey* in 1938, he assumed that at the most it was "the intention to concede responsible self-government in West Africa when Africans [were] considered competent to exercise it." It was a distant dream, to be conceded "in the full fruition of time."[46] Yet in less than 20 years the Gold Coast was to become independent Ghana. In the 1930s, despite protests and deputations, the colonial government effectively maintained the initiative in what they considered to be their model colony in West Africa. The Second World War threw up new challenges that indicated the need for major reforms. In the new world order that followed, the initiative rapidly passed to the nationalists. Clearly they built on the protests of the past while the highly politicized nature of Gold Coast society made it that much more easy for them to "aggregate grievances" and create a mass movement for independence.[47]

NOTES

1. W.A.G. Ormsby-Gore, *Report by the Hon. W.A.G. Ormsby-Gore, M. P. (Parliamentary Under-Secretary of State for the Colonies) on his Visit to West Africa during the Year 1926* (London: HMSO, 1926), 135.

2. F. C. Grant et al., letter of May 18, 1887, to Administrator White, enclosed in his dispatch to the secretary of state, July 5, 1887, CO 96/182, PRO.

3. Governor Clifford to the secretary of state, March 8, 1913, CO Afr. 999, no. 83, 113. Cited in Raymond Dumett, "The Campaign against Malaria and the Expansion of Scientific Medical and Sanitary Services in British West Africa, 1898–1910," *African Historical Studies* 1, no. 2 (1968): 172.

4. In 1900 the civil service consisted of 829 people. In 1910 there were 1,505. *Gold Coast Colony Blue Book* (Accra, Ghana: Government Printer, 1900); *Gold Coast Colony Blue Book* (Accra, Ghana: Government Printer, 1910).

5. David Kimble, *A Political History of Ghana, 1850–1928* (London: Oxford University Press, 1963), 363.

6. Anne Philips, *The Enigma of Colonialism: British Policy in West Africa* (London: James Currey, 1989), 77.

7. Twi is the language spoken by Asantes. It is closely related to Fante.

8. *Gold Coast Aborigines*, August 31, 1900.

9. Blyden did not publicly use the term "African personality" until 1893, when he did so in a lecture he gave in Freetown, Sierra Leone. Hollis Lynch, *Edward Wilmot Blyden: Pan-Negro Patriot* (New York: Oxford University Press, 1967), 54–55.

10. J. E. Casely Hayford, *Ethiopia Unbound: Studies in Race Emancipation* (1911; reprint, London: Frank Cass, 1969), 164.

11. J. Ayodele Langley, *Pan-Africanism and Nationalism in West Africa 1900–1945* (Oxford: Clarendon Press, 1973), 32.

12. Nana Ofori Atta, Legislative Council Debates, April 27, 1921. Quoted in Kimble, *Political History of Ghana,* 379.

13. Leo Spitzer, *The Creoles of Sierra Leone: Responses to Colonialism, 1870–1945* (Madison: University of Wisconsin Press, 1974), 158.

14. Casely Hayford, Legislative Council Debates, April 25, 1921. Quoted in Kimble, *Political History of Ghana,* 394.

15. Ibid., 56.

16. Ibid., 58.

17. "Aggrey of Africa" first made a name for himself by accompanying Dr. Thomas Jesse Jones, who was sent by the New York–based Phelps-Stokes Fund in 1920–21 to conduct a survey of education in Africa. In 1927 Aggrey left Achimota to complete a Ph.D. at Columbia University, but died suddenly soon after arriving in New York. The classic work on Aggrey is W. E. Smith, *Aggrey of Africa: A Study in Black and White* (London: Student Christian Movement, 1929).

18. David Meredith, "The Construction of Takoradi Harbour in the Gold Coast 1919 to 1930: A Case Study in Colonial Development and Administration," *Transafrican Journal of History* 5, no. 1 (1976): 133.

19. R.E. Wraith, *Guggisberg* (London: Oxford University Press, 1967), 225.

20. In 1920 the civil service amounted to a little over 2,700 personnel. By 1927 it numbered a little over 4,300 personnel. *Gold Coast Colony Blue Book* (Accra, Ghana: Government Printer, 1920); *Gold Coast Colony Blue Book* (Accra, Ghana: Government Printer, 1927).

21. Wraith, *Guggisberg,* 231.

22. "An Open Letter to his Excellency Sir Gordon Guggisberg," *Gold Coast Leader,* October 23, 1926.

23. Kimble, *Political History of Ghana,* 445.

24. *Gold Coast Times,* 30 April 1927.

25. Kimble, *Political History of Ghana,* 490.

26. Robert Stone, "Colonial Administration and Rural Politics in South Central Ghana, 1919–1951" (Ph.D. diss., Cambridge University, 1975), 1–2.

27. Robert S. Rattray, *Ashanti Proverbs: The Primitive Ethics of a Savage People Translated from the Original with Grammatical and Anthropological Notes* (1916; reprint, Oxford: Clarendon Press, 1969), 12.

28. R. S. Rattray, *The Tribes of the Ashanti Hinterland,* vol. 1 (Oxford: Clarendon Press, 1932), xv.

29. R. S. Rattray, *Ashanti* (Oxford: Clarendon Press, 1923), 7.

30. Sir A. R. Slater, *Native Administration in the Gold Coast and its Dependencies* (Accra, Ghana: Government Printer, 1930). Quoted in Stone, "Colonial Administration and Rural Politics in South Central Ghana," 99.

31. Governor Slater to the secretary of state February 18, 1930, CO 96/693/6599/1930, PRO. Cited in Stanley Shallof, "The Income Tax, Indirect Rule, and the Depression: The Gold Coast Riots of 1931," *Cahiers d'Etudes Africaines* 54, no. XIV-2: 360.

32. Stanley Shallof, "Press Controls and Sedition Proceedings in the Gold Coast, 1933–39," *African Affairs* LXXI, no. 284 (July, 1972): 242.

33. H. S. Newlands to the undersecretary of state for the colonies, January 15, 1931, CO 96/707/21613/1933, PRO. Quoted in Shallof, "Press Controls and Sedition Proceedings in the Gold Coast."

34. V. I. Lenin had established the Communist International (the Comintern) in 1919 as a global organization for spreading socialism throughout the world. It was made up of many subsidiary, or front, organizations, which carried out the Comintern's policies supposedly independent of the Soviet Union. Marcus Garvey had established UNIA in Jamaica in 1914, but two years later he moved to New York City, which became the real center of UNIA. Garvey called for "Africa for Africans at home and abroad."

35. Boahen, *Ghana: Evolution and Change in the Nineteenth and Twentieth Centuries* (Accra, Ghana: Sankofa Educational Publishers, 2000), 138.

36. Shallof, "Press Controls and Sedition Proceedings in the Gold Coast," 245.

37. The Scottsboro case involved nine African Americans who were charged with raping two white women in Alabama in 1931. The Communist Party of the United States took up the defense of the accused and exposed the racism of the South.

38. Leo Spitzer and LaRay Denzer, "I.T.A. Wallace-Johnson and the West African Youth League," *International Journal of African Historical Studies* 6, no. 3 (1973): 413.

39. *African Morning Post*, May 15, 1936.

40. Baron A. Holmes, "Economic and Political Organizations in the Gold Coast, 1920–1945" (Ph.D. diss., University of Chicago, 1972), 463.

41. Lord Hailey, *An African Survey Revised 1956: A Study of Problems Arising in Africa South of the Sahara* (London: Oxford University Press, 1957), 523.

42. Holmes, "Economic and Political Organizations in the Gold Coast," 784–5.

43. Stanley Shallof, "The Cape Coast Asafo Company Riot of 1932," *International Journal of African Historical Studies* 7, no. 4 (1974): 602.

44. The provincial commissioner to the secretary of native affairs, May 3, 1934, Edina Native Affairs, ADM 23/1/749, National Archives of Ghana (NAG), Accra.

45. Minute by unnamed Colonial Office official, February 16, 1939, CO 96/757/31165D, PRO.

46. Lord Hailey, *An African Survey: A Study of Problems Arising in Africa South of the Sahara* (London: Oxford University Press, 1938), 252.

47. B. A. Holmes, "What Was the 'Nationalism' of the 1930s in Ghana?" in *Akyem Abuakwa and the Politics of the Inter-war Period in Ghana, Mitteilungen der Basler Afrika Bibliographien* 12 (1975): 18.

5

The Model Colony at War and the Aftermath

THE COLONY AT WAR

More than 11,000 Africans were recruited from the Gold Coast for military service during the First World War, while over 65,000 saw military service in the Second World War. The colony's population had increased from roughly 1.6 million to around 4 million in the intervening years, but nevertheless the impact of this latter war was far greater on the colony. As was the case in the First World War, soldiers from the Gold Coast saw active duty in different parts of the continent. There were no neighboring German colonies in West Africa to capture, as had been the case of Togoland and the Cameroons in 1914 and 1916. Neither were there German forces in East Africa as there had been during the First World War. Nevertheless, Gold Coast soldiers did see combat in 1940–41 in East Africa, where they were used to fight the Italians in Italian Somaliland and Abyssinia, the Italian colony of Ethiopia. After 1940, and the fall of France, the French colonies in West Africa also became potential enemy territories. However, there was very little actual fighting in this region, and by 1943 these colonies became part of Free France and were no longer enemies. Undoubtedly the most important military contribution that Gold Coast forces made to the Allied war effort was their participation from 1943 onward in the campaign against the Japanese in Burma. They were particularly suited to the tropical conditions of southwestern Burma, where much of this fighting took place. Altogether over 41,000 soldiers from the Gold Coast saw service overseas.

In addition, strategically the Gold Cost was important to the Allied war effort. When Italy joined the Nazis, the Mediterranean route to Britain's Far East empire was blocked, and ports and airfields in West Africa in general became important. France's surrender to the Nazis in 1940 made this even more so, since it meant the loss of North African bases. To handle the military shipments and also the increase in exports that followed, Takoradi Harbor underwent a major expansion. The Gold Coast became an important link in the air-transportation system for the Allied war effort, and both the airfields at Takoradi and Accra had to be expanded dramatically to deal with the increased air traffic that followed. In 1941 the U.S. army air force was established in Accra, and during the peak years of 1942 and 1943 between 200 and 300 planes stopped daily in Accra for checking and refueling on their way north and east.[1]

With the Japanese conquest of the Far East, West Africa also became an important source of raw materials for the war effort. Increased production of vegetable oils, such as palm oil and coconut oil, was necessary to replace what had come from Far Eastern colonies now under Japanese control. Timber and rubber were also affected. Minerals like tin and bauxite were needed, some of which, like tin, had come from the Far East. Aircraft construction required aluminum, and it was during the war that the colony's vast reserves of bauxite that had been discovered as far back as 1914 were finally exploited. An extension of the railway from Dunkwa to Awaso was constructed before the end of the war to facilitate working these deposits.

In order to save shipping space and reduce dependency on Great Britain, a wide range of secondary industries were set up for the first time in the Gold Coast and in other West African colonies.[2] There were also attempts to diversify the colony's agricultural production to replace products that had hitherto been imported. To coordinate these efforts with those of other British West African colonies, the British government appointed in 1942 a cabinet minister to be resident on the coast, former secretary of state Sir Philip Cunliffe-Lister, who was then Lord Swinton. His headquarters was in the Gold Coast, the most central of the West African colonies.

Inevitably, the wartime stimulation of the economy led to inflation. The increased concentration of Europeans and Africans in the major towns along with a shortage of imported goods contributed to a sharp rise in prices. It was impossible to implement strict rationing schemes as was the case in Great Britain, and black markets developed. The cost of living rose between 50 and 75 percent in some of the coastal towns, and the government was forced to set up price controls as well as periodically raise wages for its workers. However, since the primary goal of British policy was to stabilize prices to earn foreign exchange to support the war, in the long run the real wages of Gold Coast workers declined during the war years.

Neither did the marketing arrangements seem to favor Africans, since the way in which the government allocated import licenses benefited the large expatriate companies and made it impossible for prospective African merchants to enter either the export or the import business. Nevertheless, the people of the Gold Coast remained loyal members of the British Empire during the war. They contributed generously to the war effort by subscribing close to £1.5 million in gifts, bonds, and interest-free loans. The Spitfire Fund, which provided Spitfire aircraft for the Royal Air Force, was particularly popular. However, under the surface there existed considerable discontent, which was to explode in serious rioting in 1948.

THE NEED FOR REFORMS

The demands made by the war also underscored how ineffective the chiefs were in helping to increase production. Indeed, in this regard "chiefly rule was more of a hindrance than a help. It was hard to conceive of agencies less adapted to the work of what was now called 'development.'"[3] In general, the war stimulated an interest in reforms. In 1942 the new governor, Sir Alan Burns, appointed two Africans to the Executive Council, Nana Sir Ofori Atta and K. A. Korsah, who both had long experience as members of the Legislative Council.[4] In addition, the 1925 constitution was amended so as to make it possible for the chiefs of the Joint Provincial Council to elect nonchiefs to the Legislative Council. In 1943 the governor established a committee of inquiry chaired by the colony's attorney general, H.W.B. Blackall, to investigate the working of the Native Tribunals. The Blackall report "presented to the public a convincing picture of the defects of the existing system," and many of its recommendations were incorporated into the Native Courts Ordinance of 1944.[5] What were then styled "native courts" were "specifically declared to be constituted by a Government Order in Council."[6] Court members to the four grades of courts that were established could be appointed by the government, and they were to be paid a regular salary. By 1951 the number of these courts had declined from over 300 to 135.

The 1944 Native Authority Ordinance introduced even more far-reaching reforms. The most important aspect of this legislation was that the government finally rejected "the claim that the Chiefs or any other Stoolholders possessed any right to inherent jurisdiction."[7] It allowed the governor in the case of prolonged stool disputes to appoint a council to be responsible for the state's administration until a chief was enstooled. Most controversially, it permitted him to group together small states so as to facilitate the establishment of effective state treasuries. The legislation strengthened the chiefs' position and indicated the government's continuing hopes that indirect rule could be made to work effectively. Significantly, the Joint Provincial Council of Chiefs accepted the legislation, but there was bitter opposition from municipal members on the Legislative Council. Enhancement of chiefly power rekindled the intelligentsia's old fears that the chiefs would become more autocratic and subservient to government officials.

The municipal councils also underwent changes. In 1943 the Kumasi Board of Public Health became a town council with an unofficial majority. Between 1944 and 1945 there were similar developments in Sekondi, Cape Coast, and Accra. Their town councils were expanded from 10 to 14 members, with 7 elected Africans and 2 representatives nominated by what was now called the Native Authority. However, opposition still continued to the idea of municipal taxation, and still only a small percentage of the electorate voted in town-council elections. In addition, in 1943 the government took advantage of the wartime emergency to finally pass an income-tax bill. The municipal members staged a last-ditch fight against this measure, but significantly, the chiefs, with some small adjustments, accepted the idea that "direct taxation goes with representation." The tax fell almost entirely on non-African sources of income and was the second lowest in the British Empire.[8]

Far less controversial was the appointment of Africans to senior positions in the civil service. Most significantly, in 1943 Dr. K. A. Busia, who had recently returned from Great Britain with a doctorate in sociology, and A. L. Adu were appointed to positions in the Political Service as assistant district commissioners, positions that in the past had been reserved for Europeans. The depletion of the civil-service staff on account to the war made this easier than would otherwise have been the case, but it did represent a significant return to Governor Guggisberg's promise to Africanize senior positions in the government. Linked to this concern with African advancement in the civil service was the establishment of higher education in the British West African colonies. The Elliot Commission, named after its chairman, the British member of Parliament (MP) Walter Elliot, failed to come to a consensus and submitted in 1945 a majority and a minority opinion. The Gold Coast member, K. A. Korsah, stood with the majority, who wanted the existing colleges in Sierra Leone, the Gold Coast, and Nigeria developed as universities. The chairman's minority opinion suggested, instead, concentrating resources on a single West African university, much like what was being planned for the West Indies, which would be located in Nigeria. Initially the British government preferred the minority opinion, but later agreed to a separate Gold Coast establishment on the understanding that it would be financed primarily from local resources.

Most indicative of how different this new world order was to be for Britain's colonies in general was the passage of the Colonial Welfare and Development Act. In contrast to the Colonial Development Fund of 1932, which was primarily designed to help British West African colonies deal with their budget crises during the years of the depression, this later act was designed to make funds from the Great Britain available for colonial development. Passed just before the war began and in response to riots in the West Indies in 1938, the act set aside £5 million a year for development projects and £500,000 for research in Britain's colonies. In essence the act signified the abandonment of the principle of economic self-sufficiency that had characterized colonial policy in the past. Indicative of this new approach, one of the first tasks that Sir Alan Burns undertook when he became governor of the Gold Coast in 1942 was to draw up a five-year development plan. The contingencies of the war and lack of staff precluded much from being done. It was not until 1946 that Governor Burns inaugurated a far more ambitious 10-year development plan.

Pressure for change was also coming from Africans, with the Joint Provincial Council taking a leading role. In 1941 the paramount chiefs meeting in Saltpond "invited the views of the general public as to the social, educational, economic and other changes that were deemed desirable for the New World Order which must inevitably follow the cessation of hostilities."[9] The Youth Conference meeting later in the year responded with a 400-page memorandum entitled *Things to Change in the Gold Coast*. Eventually a small group of the colony's intelligentsia, led by Dr. J. B. Danquah, produced a draft of a new constitution. Governor Burns, in consultation with the Colonial Office, rejected this constitution, but he convened a set of conferences to work on another that in 1944 was almost completely accepted by the secretary of state. Apart from bringing officials and the intelligentsia together, these conferences also included representatives of the Ashanti Confederacy Council.

Linking with the much larger colony posed political risks to Ashanti, and historically there was a long legacy of hostility between the two regions, but during the 1930s such separatist tendencies had been counteracted by the region's participation in national movements like the 1934 delegation and the cocoa holdups. In 1933 the judicial system in Ashanti had been brought into line with that of the colony. Lawyers were now allowed to practice in the region's courts, and appeals could go to the West African Court of Appeal. Many of the leading members of the intelligentsia, both in Ashanti and the colony, were members of what was a small, close-knit legal fraternity.

The result of these negotiations was that in 1944, coinciding with the centenary of the Bond of 1844, Governor Burns announced a new constitution. The new Legislative Council was to consist of 31 members, with the governor as president and 6 ex officio members. In addition, the governor was to nominate six members. The 18 remaining members were to be elected, which meant that Africans were to be in the majority. However, chiefly dominance continued, as nine of these members were to be elected by the Joint Provincial Council and four by the Ashanti Confederacy, and there were only five positions for municipal members, with Accra getting two and Sekondi/Takoradi, Cape Coast, and Kumasi each getting one. Significantly, the new constitution linked the colony and Ashanti, but the other dependencies were not considered developed enough to merit representation. In 1946 the Northern Territories received a council of chiefs, and the way was paved for eventual incorporation into the Legislative Council. South Togoland was given a territorial council in 1949 and in 1950 was allowed to send one of its members to the Gold Coast Legislative Council. The new constitution also made some administrative changes. The colony's three provinces were consolidated into two, and the old office of secretary of native affairs was replaced by a chief commissioner, who had his headquarters in Cape Coast.[10]

It was not until 1946 that the constitution actually came into force, but to many it seemed to make "the Gold Coast people . . . the pioneers of political advance and the touchstone of political competence in Africa."[11] However, events were moving much more rapidly than anyone could have anticipated, which rapidly made this political advance obsolete. Allied war propaganda, especially the Atlantic Charter of 1941, had promised "to create a world in which people could choose their own form of government."[12] Clement Attlee, the leader of the British Labor Party, had told West African students in 1941 that these principles applied to the African colonies. In 1945 his party was voted into power in Great Britain and committed to independence for India, Burma, and Ceylon. In the same year, the United Nations was established and drew up a charter that among other articles emphasized the principle of self-determination for all peoples. The rapid development of the cold war added an ideological component to the postwar political world that gave colonial peoples an ideal battleground for attacking colonial powers.

POSTWAR CONDITIONS: PROTESTS AND POLITICS

Local conditions also added to discontent. The most important was the spread of the cocoa swollen-shoot virus (CSSV), first of all in the cocoa-growing areas of the Eastern Region, but by the end of the Second World War it had spread, in varying degrees, to all other cocoa-growing areas in the colony. This disease had been around in older cocoa-growing areas of the colony at least as far back as the 1920s, but in the 1930s it began to spread in epidemic proportions in the Eastern Region. Very much influenced by this development, in 1938 the government had established the Central Cocoa Research Institute at Tafo in the Eastern Region to investigate cocoa diseases in general.[13] By 1943 the scientists had determined that the virus, which gradually spread from infected to healthy trees and killed all such trees, was carried by mealy bugs that could not be eradicated. It meant that to contain the outbreak, both infected and healthy trees on farms affected by the disease had to be cut down and burned, even while these trees were still productive.

Wartime conditions and the depressed nature of the cocoa-growing industry undoubtedly contributed to the spread of the disease, since it meant that farmers had less incentive to care properly for their farms. In addition, the government was more interested in increasing food production and the production of vegetable oils, so that during the war little was done to combat the disease. Participation in CSSV-eradication programs was voluntary, but in 1946, as cocoa output began to decline significantly, this changed. In that year the colonial government passed an ordinance that made it obligatory for all owners of infected farms to remove infected trees. Cutting-out crews from the Department of Agriculture could, under the direction of a government-appointed farm inspector, enter farms and destroy infected plants. However, this came at a time when cocoa prices were finally on the rise, and understandably the cutting-out program met with considerable opposition from the colony's cocoa farmers. To most farmers, the cure seemed worse than the disease, since even affected cocoa trees could continue bearing fruit for at least two seasons. In 1947 the government sought to make the cutting-out program more acceptable by offering compensation, but as cocoa prices continued to rise dramatically, what was offered did not come close to compensating for the loss of cocoa crops.

By the end of 1947, 2.5 million trees had been destroyed, but there still remained over 40 million still infected, the cutting out of which, though involving a relatively small proportion of the colony's total number of 400 million, often involved most of the mature trees on a particular farm. Neither were there guarantees that the program would work, and by the end of 1947 there were protest meetings among cocoa farmers in the local state capitals of the cocoa-growing areas, and clashes between individual farmers and the cutting-out gangs employed by the Agricultural Department.[14] The farmers associations that had been active during the 1937 cocoa holdup once again came into action, and as was the case during the cocoa holdups of the 1930s, the chiefs, many of whom were also cocoa farmers, played a major role in opposing the government's eradication program. It meant that farmers "were more than ready to meet the intelligentsia leaders in any criticism of the administration."[15]

If many of the cocoa-growing areas were on the verge of revolt, the situation in the main trading towns and municipalities was equally explosive. The shortage of consumer goods that had developed during the war had continued, but the increase in the amount of money available had contributed to sending prices soaring. Even though the amount of cocoa exported had dropped by a third from 1937 to 1938, as a result of swollen shoot, in 1947–48 the value of the crop had increased almost eightfold, and there was four times the amount of money in circulation as there had been before the war. The shortage of shipping meant that it was difficult to import what few consumer goods were available, and the result was not only a sharp rise in prices but extensive black marketing. The real index of daily paid and salaried workers fell from 100 in 1939 to 74 in August 1948. The Association of West African Merchants, dominated by the UAC, which had been the target of the 1930 boycotts, once again was seen as the main villain. Consumers and petty traders who could not find goods to trade were convinced that these firms were deliberately keeping up prices to inflate their profits. African businessmen were also irate since the government's allocation of import licenses on the basis of past performance favored the big companies that had been able to survive the lean years of the depression. This meant that they were unable to take advantage of the postwar boom in prices.

In 1947 one of these businessmen, Nii Kwabena Bonne II, who was also a traditional chief in Accra, began a boycott campaign that was directed against the big firms and the Lebanese merchants who he felt "had a virtual monopoly" on the economy.[16] He first of all tried to get the Accra Chamber of Commerce to agree on an accepted set of prices, but they refused, and rapidly Nii Bonne was able to get support all over the colony for his Anti-Inflation Campaign. The high prices for imported goods seemed to be part of a larger plot on the part of the European firms, who also bought the colony's cocoa crop, to recompense themselves for the high prices they were then paying for cocoa. The government's unwillingness to become involved seemed clear evidence to Africans that it was acting in collusion with these European firms.[17] The boycott lasted for most of the month of January 1948. It was directed against imported goods like cotton textiles, canned meat, flour, and spirits, and was effective enough that major firms did agree to reduce their profit margins on these items from 75 to 50 percent. Quarrels between the boycott committee and petty traders who had run short of goods also put pressure on the organizers.

No sooner had the boycott come to an end in February than another discontented group was ready to take to the streets. These were the ex-servicemen. They had come back from the war to discover that demobilization meant no jobs and pensions that were hardly commensurable with the cost of living. At the same time, their wartime experience had shattered the prestige of the white man and the myth of his inherent superiority, and they were not willing to wait passively for conditions to improve. In 1946 some of the more political veterans had formed the Gold Coast Ex-Serviceman's Union. The union had played an active part in the boycott campaign, and as soon as it was over their secretary, B.E.A. Tamakloe, had announced that the ex-servicemen were going to march in procession to Christiansborg Castle, the seat of government, to present a petition to the governor. The procession soon departed from the authorized route and came up against a small detachment of police, which tried to prevent them from approaching the castle. Stones were thrown, and in the confusion that followed, the European superintendent in charge of the police snatched a rifle from one of his men and opened fire on the crowd. Two ex-servicemen were killed, and several other marchers were wounded.

The marchers straggled back to the commercial center of Accra and were joined by unemployed young men who claimed that the large firms were not charging the agreed-on prices. Even before, the shooting, looting, and burning of European, Syrian, and Lebanese stores had been underway and was to continue late into the night. The shooting increased the tempo of these activities. One of the government's prisons nearby was also attacked, and some prisoners released. News of the rioting spread rapidly, and during the next few days there was similar rioting in Koforidua, Nsawam, Akuse, and Kumasi. Initially the government allowed the rioting in Accra to continue for a time, since the loss of property seemed preferable to the loss of life that suppressing the riots would have required. Finally, however, the government had to declare a state of emergency and bring in troops from Nigeria. Twenty-nine people were killed, 266 were injured, and over £2 million of damage was done before order was restored. The belief in the Gold Coast as the model colony had suffered irreparable damage.

It was not surprising that the bewildered government, in looking around for an explanation for this explosion, should assume the existence of some deep-laid plot, since so many events seemed to have come together at just the right time. The most obvious target was the executive of the United Gold Coast Convention (UGCC), which had been formed just before in 1947. The governor, Sir Gerald Creasy, ordered the arrest of Dr. Danquah and five of his fellow leaders of the UGCC and detained them in distant parts of the Northern Region. Here they were kept for about six weeks to "keep them out of mischief."[18] A commission of inquiry was set up "to enquire into and report on the recent disturbances . . . and their underlying causes; and to make recommendations on any matter arising from their enquiry."[19] Unlike such commissions in the past, most of its members consisted of people not from the ranks of colonial administration. The chairman, Aiken Watson, was a prominent British barrister. Another member, Andrew Dalgleish, was an authority on trade unionism, while a third, Keith Murray, was a lecturer at Oxford University.

Undoubtedly the UGCC had taken advantage of the breakdown in public order. Dr. Danquah and the convention's secretary, Kwame Nkrumah, had sent telegrams to the secretary of state, the United Nations, and major news organizations claiming that civil government had broken down in the Gold Coast, and called for the dispatch of a special commissioner, the recall of the governor, and the convening of a constituent assembly of the chiefs and peoples to create a new constitution. In reality, the UGCC was much more conservative than these demands indicated. It had been the expectations for further constitutional advance that the Burns Constitution had aroused that inspired Sekondi timber merchant G. A. Grant (Pa Grant) to join with some of his friends, among whom was Dr. G. B. Danquah, to form a nationwide political movement. A conference had been held in Saltpond with "40 representative leaders," and in August 1947 the UGCC had been launched under the direction of a Working Committee.[20] The main aim was to see that the "control of government should pass into the hands of the people and their chiefs in the shortest possible time."[21]

The UGCC wanted to replace the chiefs on the Legislative Council with "educated commoners," but to achieve what was in reality a narrow constitutional issue they made the momentous decision of appointing a full-time organizing secretary to run the convention on their behalf.[22]

The man they chose was Kwame Nkrumah. He was a product of Achimota College, and afterward he had taught in a number of Roman Catholic schools as well as at their seminary. In 1935 he had gone to America, where he spent 10 years obtaining a bachelor of arts from Lincoln University, in Pennsylvania; a bachelor of theology from Lincoln Seminary; and a master of arts in philosophy from the University of Pennsylvania. In 1945 he had gone to Great Britain to continue his education, and at the time the UGCC contacted him he was in London studying law as well as being a doctoral student in philosophy at the London School of Economics.

Along with his academic studies, Nkrumah had been involved in political organization. He had set up an African Students' Association of America and Canada while he had been a student at the University of Pennsylvania. In London he had quickly become so involved in political organization that he was little more than a student in name. Significantly, his focus had become more West African. He had become a member of the West African Students Union and eventually became its vice president. He had served with the West Indian pan-Africanist George Padmore as the joint secretary for the Fifth Pan-African Congress, which was held in 1945 in Manchester, England, and was once again secretary for the West African National Secretariat, one of the offshoots of this congress. To promote the ideas of this organization he published a short-lived monthly paper called the *New African,* and also, as part of the secretariat's work, he had organized a Colored Workers' Association of Great Britain.

During the two and a half years that Nkrumah spent in Great Britain, he had emerged as one of the leading critics of colonial rule from Britain's African colonies. With his organizing experience he seemed to be the ideal person to give the UGCC the kind of direction it needed to become an effective political organization. However, he was hesitant at first to accept the position of general secretary since he felt that "it was quite useless to associate [himself] with a movement backed almost entirely by reactionaries, middle-class lawyers and merchants."[23] He felt that his "revolutionary background and ideas would make it impossible for [him] to work with them."[24] Nevertheless, after consulting with the West African National Secretariat, he decided to accept the offer, since it offered "the dawn of action at the end of a long and intensive training . . . but he was prepared to come to loggerheads with the Executive of the UGCC if [he] found that they were following a reactionary course."[25] Neither was the executive entirely satisfied with its choice. Dr. Danquah was particularly suspicious of how Nkrumah was going to reconcile his "interests in West African unity with the rather parochial aims of the UGCC."[26] Nor did the executive like Nkrumah's use of the term *comrade*, which they felt "might arouse the suspicions of the public as well as officialdom."[27]

Nkrumah obviously had much larger goals in mind than the UGCC executive, and he immediately drew up a plan of action with the steps itemized that would lead to self-government. In addition, he was determined to take the movement beyond the colony and to include the Ashanti Region, the Northern Territories, and the Trans-Volta Togoland. In the space of six months he had expanded the number of branches from at best 13 to over 500. He did so by traveling all over the colony, appealing to audiences that consisted of farmers, petty traders, drivers, artisans, schoolteachers, clerks and letter writers, and a growing army of elementary-school leavers, many of whom could find no jobs. They were known derisively in the Gold Coast as "verandah boys" since they had no homes and were forced to sleep at night on the verandahs of roadside trading houses. He recognized much more acutely than the other members of the UGCC that it was more than just the intelligentsia who were dissatisfied with their powerlessness under the colonial regime, and that there was "fertile ground for nationalist agitation" among the people in general.[28]

Nkrumah also recognized that new leadership was emerging to lead the radical youth groups that had sprouted in the 1940s as a flood of elementary-school leavers had moved into the southern towns and villages. There had been a dramatic increase in the numbers of scholars' unions, literary and debating societies, youth movements, and improvement societies whose membership could very easily be politicized. For example, at the same time as the UGCC was forming in Saltpond, a more radical organization was coming into being in Kumasi, the capital of Ashanti. It was known as the Asante Youth Association (AYA) and elected a local storekeeper, Atta Mensah, as its secretary-general. The main demand of this association was "self-government, not for the chiefs advised by officials, but under the control of the ordinary man."[29] One of the leading members of this association, Krobo Edusei, who at the time was a reporter and debt collector for the Kumasi newspaper the *Ashanti Pioneer*, was to become the chairman of the Ashanti Boycott Committee in the Nii Bonne Anti-Inflation Campaign. Kojo Botsio, who had been studying in Britain at the time Nkrumah was there and returned on the same boat to the Gold Coast to take up a teaching position at Akyem Abuakwa State

College, was instrumental in helping Nkrumah form the national Committee on Youth Organization (CYO) after the latter was released from prison. Komla Gbedemah, who had graduated from Achimota, like Nkrumah, was the chairman of the CYO and also editor of the *Accra Evening News*, the newspaper Nkrumah established in 1948.

Invariably hostile to the chiefs and suspicious of the professionals who dominated the UGCC, it was only a matter of time before this new leadership propelled Nkrumah into splitting from the UGCC and forming his own party. The arrest of the Big Six hastened this development, since it inevitably caused friction and recriminations, with Nkrumah being blamed for what had happened. When they appeared individually before the Watson Commission, these divisions were even more apparent, with nearly all of the executive members of the Working Committee disassociating themselves from Nkrumah's plans for organizing the UGCC. Nevertheless, the Watson Commission represented a watershed in the colony's history. Predictably enough, it exonerated the police and the government for the way in which the riots had been handled, but it was highly critical of the Gold Coast government's policies. The report listed 16 causes for the riots, 8 of which were specific and dealt with issues like how the cutting-out program had been conducted, discontent over ex-servicemen's pensions, the housing shortage, the concentration of economic power in the hands of Europeans and Lebanese, and the high cost of living. The others were more long-term, the most important and controversial of which was the government's failure to see that "the star of rule through the chiefs was on the wane."[30] Under these circumstances it was not surprising that the commissioners thought that the Burns Constitution of 1946 had been "out-moded at birth."[31]

There was already some soul-searching going in the Colonial Office in London about the role of the chiefs in the colony's future, but there was still hope that they could be "retained but democratized."[32] Significantly, however, when the Watson Commission's most important recommendation was put into place, that an all-African committee draw up a new constitution, only 9 of its 36 members were chiefs. Neither was it chaired by a senior British official, as had been the case in the past with such bodies. Instead, the chairman was the colony's most senior African member of the judiciary, Mr. Justice J. H. Coussey. The initiative had clearly passed to Africans and just as significantly away from the chiefs to the intelligentsia. The Colonial Office and Governor Burns had hoped that the 1946 constitution would "for several decades satisfy the legitimate aspirations of the political class [in the Gold Coast], and thus at the same time afford a period for the healthy growth of local government."[33] The events of 1948 rapidly undermined these hopes, and equally significantly brought a new and more radical leadership to the fore that was much more impatient than the older elite. As Governor Creasy expressed it, when he addressed the Legislative Council after the riots, he had been "overtaken by events."[34] After 1948 the speed at which events unfolded accelerated at an even more bewildering pace than any of the protagonists could have imagined before 1948.

NOTES

1. F. M. Bourret, *Ghana: The Road to Independence 1919–1957* (Stanford, Calif.: Stanford University Press, 1960), 148.

2. Adu Boahen, *Ghana: Evolution and Change in the Nineteenth and Twentieth Centuries* (Accra, Ghana: Sankofa Educational Publishers, 2000), 151.

3. Richard Rathbone, *Nkrumah and the Chiefs: The Politics of Chieftaincy in Ghana 1951–60* (Athens: Ohio University Press, 2000), 17.

4. K. A. Korsah was knighted in 1955.

5. Lord Hailey, *Native Administration in British African Territories* (London: HMSO, 1951), 211.

6. Ibid.

7. Ibid.

8. Lord Hailey, *An African Survey Revised 1956: A Study of Problems Arising in Africa South of the Sahara* (London: Oxford University Press, 1957), 666.

9. Baron Holmes, "Economic and Political Organizations in the Gold Coast, 1919–1945" (Ph.D. diss., University of Chicago, 1972), 816.

10. Bourret, *Ghana*, 164.

11. Martin Wight, *The Gold Coast Legislative Council* (London: Faber and Faber, 1947), 207.

12. Robert Paxton, *Europe in the Twentieth Century* (New York: Harcourt Brace Jovanovich, 1975), 469.

13. Francis Danquah, *Cocoa Diseases and Politics in Ghana, 1909–1966* (New York: Peter Lang, 1995), 61.

14. Dennis Austin, *Politics in Ghana: 1946–1960* (London: Oxford University Press, 1964), 66.

15. Ibid., 65.

16. Quoted in Austin, *Politics in Ghana*, 71.

17. W.E.F. Ward, *A History of Ghana*, 4th ed. (London: George Allen and Unwin, 1967), 328.

18. Ibid., 332.

19. Aiken Watson, A. Dalgleish, and Keith A. Murray, *Report of the Commission of Enquiry into Disturbances in the Gold Coast: 1948* (London: HMSO, 1948), 5.

20. Austin, *Politics in Ghana*, 52.

21. Ibid.

22. Ibid.

23. Kwame Nkrumah, *Ghana: The Autobiography of Kwame Nkrumah* (New York: International Publishers, 1957), 62.

24. Ibid.

25. Ibid.

26. UGCC, *Minute Book*, December 28, 1947.

27. Ibid.

28. Nkrumah, *Ghana*, 74.

29. Austin, *Politics in Ghana*, 56.

30. Watson, *Report of the Commission of Enquiry into Disturbances in the Gold Coast*, 7.

31. Ibid., 24.

32. R. D. Pearce, *Turning Point in Africa: British Colonial Policy 1938–48* (London: Frank Cass Publishers, 1982), 153.

33. Wight, *The Gold Coast Legislative Council*, 208.

34. Austin, *Politics in Ghana*, 11.

6

The Convention People's Party and the Road to Independence

THE SPLIT WITH THE UGCC

When the Gold Coast police arrested Nkrumah after the riots of 1948, they found on him an unsigned British Communist Party card as well as a document defining the aims of a "vanguard group" known as "the Circle." African students in London who supported the West African National Secretariat had started this group, and Nkrumah had been the chairman. Its main aim was the "national independence of West Africa, and the creation and maintenance of the Union of African Socialist Republics."[1] To the Watson Commission, this was more than enough to indicate that Nkrumah had "become imbrued with a Communist ideology which only political expediency [had] blurred."[2] His calls for colonial liberation, his attacks on imperialism and the reactionary bourgeoisie, and his use of other marxist terminology only served to reinforce this opinion.

Initially the Working Committee of the UGCC had taken advantage of the popularity that imprisonment had brought them, but rapidly they moved to the defense of law and order, and Nkrumah, officially linked with "communist enslavement," became a liability for them. The prominent members of the Working Committee had been invited to be members of the Coussey Committee, but pointedly this had not included Nkrumah.

He had described himself to the Watson Commission as the convention's "humble and obedient servant." Rapidly his employers moved to get rid of him, but at the same time "they feared what he might do without them."[3]

A number of his initiatives after he was released from prison also served to increase the tension between them. He had established the Ghana National College for students who had been expelled from their colleges and secondary schools for going on strike in protest against the arrest of the Big Six in 1948. Some of the teachers who had also been expelled for striking were the first tutors, and within the space of a year the school had grown to 230 students. Nevertheless, the Working Committee complained bitterly about this initiative. Nkrumah also established a newspaper for the movement, which the Working Committee was afraid would embroil them in sedition and libel cases. The paper, the *Accra Evening News*, had become an instant success, and had prompted the Working Committee to establish its own papers, which were inevitably short-lived affairs.

However, what irritated them most of all was Nkrumah's establishing of the CYO, which included a number of youth organizations both from the colony and Ashanti. In the socialist world of the 1940s, youth were praised as being in the vanguard of the revolution. Youth organizations in the Gold Coast sought to link themselves with this tradition, but age was not necessarily the only criteria for membership in such organizations. In addition, youth were likely to be commoners as opposed to being royals, but above all they would have seen themselves as politically progressive and representing the interests of the common man. The Working Committee feared this development, as they recognized that this organization represented potentially a serious political rival to the UGCC.

The CYO adopted the slogan "Full self-government now" in contrast to the UGCC's "Self-government within the shortest possible time." It was more than just a semantic difference. The Working Committee was willing to work within the framework of constitutional procedure. They were members of the Coussey Committee, which was working toward a constitution that would give the colony a semiresponsible government. On the other hand, the youth, who were not represented on the Coussey Committee, wanted self-government immediately and were willing to take unconstitutional actions to achieve this. They were bitterly hostile to the UGCC in the pages of the *Accra Evening News,* and eventually the Convention made membership in the CYO and the UGCC incompatible. Nkrumah, even though he was still the secretary of the UGCC, also published articles in the *Accra Evening News* that were critical of the convention's Working Committee, and finally they decided to expel him from the UGCC. However, Nkrumah preempted this attempt to remove him by breaking way from the UGCC, and on June 12, 1949, at the Arena meeting ground in Accra, before an audience of 60,000 people, he announced the formation of the Convention People's Party (CPP). Kojo Botsio became its secretary, K. A. Gbedemah its vice chairman, and Nkrumah its chairman.

POSITIVE ACTION

The first major challenge to the party was how to react to the recommendations of the Coussey Committee which proposed a semi-responsible form of government with an executive council with three members selected by the colonial government, eight elected ministers, and a nationally elected assembly. Initially Nkrumah dismissed the new constitution proposed as a "Trojan gift horse" that was "bogus and fraudulent," and he began to talk about the need for "Positive Action." This was to consist of civil disobedience that would include agitation, propaganda, and, at the last resort, "the constitutional application of strikes, boycotts and non-cooperation based on the principle of absolute non-violence, as used by Gandhi in India."[4] The goal would be to force the government to call a constituent assembly. The idea of Positive Action created considerable consternation in the colony with the memory of the 1948 riots still fresh in mind. At a meeting of Ghana People's Representative Assembly, held a month after the launching of the CPP, the delegates responded by shifting the emphasis away from confrontation to making amendments to the suggestions that had come out in the Coussey Report. There was little likelihood that the secretary of state or the governor would accept these amendments, and by the end of the year Nkrumah was again threatening Positive Action.

The government responded by prosecuting and jailing several of the party's newspaper editors who had called for Positive Action. Nkrumah himself was fined £400. However, it was the Trades Union Congress (TUC), an umbrella organization of trade unions that had been formed in 1945, that eventually precipitated Positive Action by calling for a general strike in support of the Meteorological Employees' Union, which was locked in a bitter dispute with the government. In a last-ditch attempt to avert Positive Action, the colonial secretary, H. R. Saloway, met with Nkrumah, but eventually the TUC forced the party's hand by declaring a general strike in January 1950. A day later Nkrumah announced at a meeting at the Arena meeting ground that Positive Action would begin at midnight. However, on this occasion the government was much more prepared for disorder than had been the case in 1948. A state of emergency was quickly declared, a curfew was imposed, and a new force of mobile police was used to maintain order in the large towns. The government also decided to take a firm stance, without the need for a commission of inquiry, and rapidly began to arrest TUC and CPP members, prosecuting and convicting them for promoting an illegal strike, attempting to coerce the government, and sedition. Nkrumah, one of the last to be arrested, was convicted on all three charges and sentenced both in Accra and Cape Coast to one year for each of the charges, which were to run consecutively.

The call for Positive Action also generated considerable opposition from Nkrumah's political opponents. At the height of the campaign, the Joint Provincial Council of Chiefs invited him to put the case of the Ghana People's Representative Assembly before them, but the result had been "abusive" speeches. Dr. Danquah, who was in attendance, accused Nkrumah and his followers of going "against constitutional authority" and that they should expect "to pay for it with their necks."[5] There followed several attacks both on the CPP and Nkrumah in the *Gold Coast Weekly Review,* a government-sponsored newspaper. It was as a result of these attacks that shortly afterward Nkrumah, during a speech at the Arena meeting ground, prophesied that for those chiefs "who join[ed] forces with the imperialists . . . there shall come a time when they will run away fast and leave their sandals behind them."[6] In essence he was encouraging the angry young men who chafed under the power of their traditional rulers to destool them. This bitterness between the chiefs and the party was to leave an important legacy.

With most of the radical leadership in prison and the government seemingly in control, the time was ripe for the chiefs and the conservative intelligentsia to once again take control of the movement for self-government. However, they soon began fighting among themselves, with the UGCC attacking "reactionary forces" for "even questioning some of the plans of the progressive and saner groups."[7] In reality both groups remained a small an ineffective minority, which their internecine squabbling indicated. Neither did the "very large body of moderate and responsible people" whom the governor felt existed and would act as a bulwark against the CPP extremists really exist.[8] Nevertheless, the government's major strategy was to see the modified Coussey Constitution put into operation after a general election, with the hope that a period of stability would follow.

Clearly, however, this could not be done without the participation of the CPP and its leader. Indeed the incarceration of the party's leaders had increased the CPP's attractiveness. Indicative of this, the party won all seven seats in the Accra Municipal Council elections in April 1950, and in November was almost as victorious in the Kumasi Town Council elections. Gbedemah, who had been in prison at the time of the declaration of Positive Action and released shortly afterward, was extremely successful in establishing a network of party branches across the southern half of the colony. The party's strategy was to contest all 38 popularly elected seats in the election for the new legislature that was scheduled for February 1951.

THE ELECTION OF 1951

In spite of Nkrumah having dismissed the new constitution as "bogus and fraudulent," the election was to be a watershed in the colony's political life, since it was the first to be held under adult franchise. The CPP also scored an important victory when Kwesi Plange was able to get the Legislative Council to agree to reducing the voting age from 25 to 21. He himself had been under 25 at the time of his election as a CPP candidate to represent Cape Coast on the Legislative Council. It was a decision that benefited the CPP, since youth were far more likely to support the party of "self-government now" than their opponents, whose slogan was the far less appealing "self-government in the shortest possible time."[9] In addition, the CPP developed an important working relationship with officials whose task it was to organize the election itself. Delimiting constituencies in an egalitarian fashion was not always possible since the committee charged with this responsibility did not want to override local interests and arbitrarily divide communities. The result was considerable variation in the size of constituencies. In addition, the north, in spite of its much larger population, was given the same number of representatives as Ashanti.

Nevertheless, the party accepted these violations of the principle of one man–one vote. Even more important was the party's role in the registration of voters. Indeed, in many areas of the colony people registered only when encouraged to do so by CPP representatives. To do so also meant paying the local levy so that the party that government officials had described as a subversive organization was in the forefront of encouraging people to pay their levy so that they could register to vote. This was money that provided Native Treasuries with a regular source of income and consequently supported the chiefs and the indirect rule that the party opposed. Given all the challenges involved, it was not surprising that the final registration figure was only 40 percent of the total electorate.[10]

In addition to working closely with the administration, the CPP enjoyed a number of other important advantages. The party benefited from the cult of martyrdom that developed around its imprisoned leadership. It maintained this momentum with public ceremonies "awarding" these "prison graduates" with "diplomas" as soon as they were released from prison.[11] Also, the party benefited from its association with other organizations. For example, the recently formed Ghana Farmer's Congress gave its support to the CPP when the party supported its opposition to the government's swollen-shoot campaign. Similarly fueling discontent with the colonial administration were a number of immediate complaints that helped the CPP. For example, the government's choice of six Europeans to be the permanent secretaries of the ministries that were to be set up after the elections undermined its claims to be engaged in the Africanization of the civil service.

A poor harvest at the end of 1950 resulted in black marketing that reignited the tensions associated with the Nii Bonne Anti-Inflation Campaign. The entry, at this time, of the London Daily Mirror Group into the colony's newspaper world with the establishment of the *Daily Graphic* fanned tensions even higher. It raised the specter of metropolitan monopoly just like the Association of West African Merchants had done in 1937 and in 1948. The party was able to benefit from a number of local elections that allowed it to fine-tune its electioneering strategies. There were rallies, picnics, dances, and skits, and loudspeaker vans painted in the party's colors (red, white, and green) were first used in the Accra municipal elections with telling effect.

On a more emotional level, the party was masterful in adapting hymns, prayers, and biblical phrases to popularize its message among people for whom Christianity had deep appeal. One of the party's popular songs was an adaptation of Cardinal Newman's hymn "Lead Kindly Light." The party also published in the *Accra Evening News* adaptations of the Lord's Prayer and the Apostle's Creed that scandalized the colony's clergymen. Most memorable of all, Nkrumah, an avowed marxist socialist and nondenominational Christian, called on his followers to "seek ye first the political kingdom, and all things will be added unto it."[12] This call to arms adorned the masthead of the party's newspapers in Accra, Cape Coast, and Sekondi-Takoradi.

The campaign generated a great deal of excitement and enthusiasm, so much so that selecting the party's candidates was often difficult and contentious. Many of the leading members of the party were in prison. There was conflict between the National Executive Committee and local branches of the CPP over the selection of suitable candidates. It was the inevitable byproduct of the highly parochial nature of the colony's political life that indirect rule had done so much to create. In general, loyalty to the party was the most important criteria for selection, but nevertheless in the final list the majority of those selected were local figures. Loyalty to the party played a crucial role in resolving the disputes that did develop. Nkrumah's decision to stand for election also created dissension, since there were those who felt that if he and similarly incarcerated candidates were later disqualified, the party would lose these seats. However, he felt that it was worth the risk since he was convinced that if he and his colleagues won, the government would be forced to release them before their terms of imprisonment expired.

The upcoming election also brought the chiefs and the intelligentsia together since they feared a CPP victory. They realized that they were not likely to win many of the popularly elected seats, but the new constitution reserved 18 territorial seats for the chiefs. Voting in the north was to be for 19 delegates to the Northern Electoral College, and since the CPP had little strength in this part of the colony, there was hope that the opposition could control almost half of the seats for Africans in the proposed assembly. Neither did this mean conceding all other seats, and especially in rural areas, where the CPP was supposed to be weakest, there were a number of local alliances between the intelligentsia and the chiefs. The UGCC also issued an election manifesto entitled *Plan for the Nation* in which they called for "self-government by all legitimate and constitutional means." It also outlined a 10-point program to develop the country within "the framework of the WELFARE STATE."[13] Apart from the more combative language, there was very little difference between this manifesto and the CPP's, entitled *Towards the Goal*. The latter also called for self-government, and promised immediate material benefits for the people.

In addition to the CPP and the UGCC, there were five other parties that entered the electoral contest. They were highly local in their focus and unlikely to have any impact on the election. By the date of the election, only the Accra-based National Democratic Party remained. As it was, the CPP swept the elected positions, winning 29 to the opposition's 4. The UGCC won only two of these seats, both in Akyem Abuakwa, with the other two going to anti-CPP independents in southern Togoland, where there was considerable opposition to unification with the Gold Coast. CPP support was most evident in the towns where the CPP swept all of the five municipal seats. In Accra Nkrumah won one of the two seats contested with over 22,000 votes out of 23,122 that were cast. In the rural areas, where chiefs had more influence, support was less overwhelming, with some areas recording as much as a 20 percent anti-CPP vote. As far as the territorial seats were concerned, only a small minority were sympathetic to the CPP. However, when the 19 northern representatives realized that the CPP was going to form the government, they gave their support to the CPP, since they were accustomed to supporting the government in power. The result was that the CPP ended up with a very comfortable working majority.

The governor, Nobel Arden-Clarke, quickly realized that if the new constitution was to work, Nkrumah and his party would have to be invited to form a government. Similarly, Nkrumah realized that in spite of his criticisms of the Coussey Constitution, he could not pass up this opportunity. As soon as he and his imprisoned colleagues were released from prison, Nkrumah accepted the governor's invitation to become leader of government business. In a spirit of compromise, he prevailed upon his party to select only five of the seven ministers the party was allowed to choose from among its membership. Of the other two, one came from the ranks of the Ashanti territorial representatives and the other was from the Northern Territories. In general, the hopes that members of the intelligentsia had entertained for ministerial positions were disappointed and served to increase the bitterness between them and the upstart CPP.

THE FIRST CPP GOVERNMENT

The new legislature, now named the Gold Coast Assembly, consisted of 84 members. 33 had been elected in rural districts of the colony and Ashanti by electoral colleges; 37 had been elected by territorial councils of chiefs; 5 had been elected from the towns of Accra, Cape Coast, Sekondi-Takoradi, and Kumasi; 3 represented the Chamber of Commerce and 3 the Chamber of Mines; and 3 were nominated by the governor. These nine members were the assembly's only European members. In an important attempt to maintain continuity with the past, Nkrumah proposed that Emmanuel Quist, who had served as the president of the previous Legislative Council, should be the Speaker of the Assembly. He was not a member of the CPP.

Initially there was considerable confusion over how this body should work, since neither the officials nor the newly elected members had much idea about how parliamentary democracy worked. For the CPP it meant moving from Positive Action to what Nkrumah called Tactical Action. In essence this meant compromise rather than confrontation with officials. It was made easier by the "close" and "friendly" relationship Nkrumah developed with Governor Arden-Clarke.[14] Initially Nkrumah's title had been leader of government business, but indicative of his "not unfruitful partnership" with the governor, in 1952 the latter agreed to an amendment to the Coussey Constitution that allowed Nkrumah to acquire the more substantive title of prime minister.[15]

Most important, the 1950s was a period of unparalleled prosperity for the colony, and this also served to reduce friction between the CPP and colonial officials. Between 1948 and 1952 the price for cocoa rose from £139 per ton to over £300 per ton. The colony's other exports also enjoyed boom prices, and government revenue, which was predominantly based on export taxes, increased almost fourfold, from over £11 million to over £42 million. There were resources to alleviate the distress of the postwar era and to pay for reforms. The government increased the daily wage for unskilled workers by over 30 percent. It was also able to pay for considerable expansion in the size of the civil service, with significant Africanization of its upper ranks. By 1954 over 38 percent of what had been European appointments in the civil service were held by Africans, up from 13.8 percent in 1949. Not all of these new appointees were necessarily CPP supporters, but this development reduced one important source of friction between the party and the British government.

On the local level there was a major reform of the native authority system. The old system of native authorities was abolished and replaced with local, district, and urban councils. One-third of their membership continued to be made up of traditional authority figures, with the other two-thirds elected. The CPP swept most of these positions, and even though these new bodies seldom worked well, they did absorb the energies of many party members. With the soaring revenues it was even possible to defuse the contentious issue of dealing with the swollen-shoot epidemic in the cocoa industry. After coming to power, the CPP had suspended the Agricultural Department's very unpopular cutting-out program to control this virulent disease. The government had convened a committee that criticized the compulsory cutting-out program, but eventually returned to a similar program. However, there was no serious opposition as the government was able to offer compensation that muted protest.

In general the first CPP government, from 1951 to 1954, oversaw a period of unprecedented growth. One historian has described it as Nkrumah's finest period.[16] The 10-year development plan that had been drawn up in 1946 and was to involve £11.5 million in expenditure was dramatically expanded to produce a 5-year development plan that was to cost

£120 million. During this period many of the country's existing roads were paved and a number of new roads were begun, like the coastal road between Accra and Takoradi and the main artery of the country between Accra, Kumasi, Tamale, and Bolgatanga. The Adomi Bridge over the Volta River was completed, Takoradi Harbor was expanded, and an entirely new harbor at Tema was started. The Akyease-Kotoku railway, which was to reduce significantly the train journey between Accra and Takoradi, was also started. The government also completed several municipal housing projects, granted loans for housing, and tried to provide prefabricated housing for workers. There was a major effort to provide good drinking water in the rural areas as well as to expand water supplies in the main towns. Kumasi received a new hospital that cost over £1.5 million.

In the field of education, free compulsory primary education was provided for children between the ages of 6 and 12. The government continued subsidies given to mission schools and allowed local councils to establish their own schools. The result was that the number of pupils in elementary schools increased from 212,000 in 1950 to over 270,000 by 1952. The government set up 16 teacher-training colleges that by 1955 more than doubled the number of teachers being annually produced. By 1955 the number of government-assisted secondary schools increased from 13 to 31, while in the area of tertiary education the government contributed £1.5 million toward the establishment of the University College of the Gold Coast at Legon, near Accra, and also for the establishment of the College of Arts, Science, and Technology in Kumasi. Finally, the government awarded a large number of overseas scholarships to students to pursue courses that were not available in the colony, such as in law, medicine, and the applied sciences.[17]

Nevertheless, criticism of the government did begin to develop. The opposition in Parliament asserted that now that the CPP had "landed themselves good jobs they had forsaken their policy of 'self-government now.'"[18] Nkrumah responded by inviting them to join the CPP in another round of Positive Action. He fully realized that there was no likelihood that they would accept this invitation, since they had been critical of the first Positive Action. However, there were members of the party who also began to voice complaints. Some felt that "Nkrumah had succumbed to the flattery of the British press."[19] It was harder to nullify these internal critics, and by 1952 a number of important members of the CPP's national executive either left or were expelled from the party. The party's third annual meeting, in Sekondi in 1952, was dominated by this issue, with Nkrumah, the life chairman, coming under attack from individual delegates. Eventually a committee was appointed to draw up a "tactical plan

. . . to lead the country into Canaan."[20] However, a few months later, when the British government suspended the constitution of British Guiana because of the chaotic manner in which that colony was proceeding to independence, Nkrumah was able to silence his critics and defend the CPP's program of Tactical Action.[21]

There was also criticism of how the government was planning to finance the Volta River Dam. The idea of damming up the Volta River at the Ajena Gorge had been suggested as far back as 1915. More recently the Watson Commission had called upon the government "to harness the waters of the Volta for the production of electrical energy and its utilization, among other things, in the manufacture of aluminum on the spot."[22] Nkrumah considered the scheme to be the key to the country's industrialization.[23] However, to obtain the capital necessary for the scheme meant offering very favorable terms to the British government, which was to contribute over 60 percent of the capital but was to have a 74.8 percent controlling interest in the aluminum smelter. Both in the Legislative Council and in the press, CPP party members and others criticized the "economic enslavement" and the "bartering away our newly won (or almost won) political freedom" that they felt the scheme threatened.[24]

The rate of Africanization at the permanent secretary level was another disputed area. All of these positions were still filled by expatriates. They were in a position to oppose the government, and some undoubtedly did so by procrastinating in their implementation of policies with which they disagreed. In addition, even though there had been considerable Africanization of the civil service, the overall size of the civil service had expanded and the numbers of European appointments had increased. It was inevitable that this would happen as functions of government became more extensive, but the presence of so many Europeans in key positions was something of a lightning rod to those who felt they were still in control of the key ministries.

In addition, with so much money being spent, it was not long before there were rumors of corruption and malpractice. Even Nkrumah was touched. He was supposed to have borrowed £1,800 from the chairman of the Finance Committee of the CPP to pay for the importation of a Cadillac. Eventually these rumors became so rife that the government was forced to set up a commission of inquiry to investigate. There was more than enough information from this investigation to implicate ministers in bribe taking and the abuse of office for personal financial gain. The large houses that many had built and their flamboyant lifestyles indicated just how much the party's leadership was becoming what even Nkrumah conceded was "a new ruling class of self-seeking careerists."[25]

Part of the problem with corruption lay in the party's continual problems with finance. Ironically, as the party grew in size if became harder to generate funds from dues, appeals, the sale of party memorabilia, and social functions. Instead, contributions from Indian and Lebanese businessmen seeking favors from influential party members, or as general donations, came to play an increasingly important role as a source of funds. State companies like the Cocoa Purchasing Company and the Industrial Development Corporation also were even more important sources of funds, equipment, and personnel who could propagandize for the CCP. However, these charges of corruption, which were "generally accepted as valid," did not necessarily undermine support for the CPP.[26] The party was still very much a commoner's party, and indeed, if anything, the trappings of office, the fine bungalows and shiny limousines, enhanced the status of its ruling elite.

International acclaim for the party's leader also enhanced the CCP's standing. In 1951 Nkrumah was invited to the United States to receive an honorary doctor of laws from Lincoln University, his alma mater. His discussions with State Department officials and press conferences in New York and Philadelphia also indicated just how much that Gold Coast's struggle for independence had captured American attention. Most of all was this so for African Americans: as their New York City newspaper, the *New York Amsterdam News,* expressed it, he got a "royal welcome from Harlemites."[27] In 1953 he was the guest of President Tubman of Liberia, where he received "as much encouragement from the enthusiastic crowd as [he] did from [his] own people at the Arena in Accra."[28] Shortly afterward Nkrumah appeared on the front cover of *Time* magazine. To the British newspaper the *Manchester Guardian,* he was "Africa's man of destiny." Even Nkrumah's enemies recognized his significance for the future of the continent. The South African prime minister, Daniel Malan, one of the main framers of the policy of apartheid in that country, maintained in 1954 that the unrest in Africa was due primarily to Nkrumah's movement for self-government in the Gold Coast.

THE ELECTION OF 1954

The Coussey Constitution had stipulated that as the colony received a greater degree of internal self-government, there was to be an increase in the size of the legislative assembly. The Van Lare Commission on Electoral Reform that had been charged with this responsibility divided the country into 104 constituencies. Many thought that the election that followed in 1954 would be the final stage before independence. However, in spite of the CPP's seemingly dominant position in the country, the electoral contest generated both local opposition and bitter struggles within the party itself.

As early as 1952, the remnants of the UGCC and those who had been expelled from the CCP formed the Ghana Congress Party (GCP). The leader was K. A. Busia, who was then a lecturer in sociology at the recently created University College of the Gold Coast. A far more serious challenge to the CCP came from the Northern People's Party (NPP), which was established in 1954. Unlike the GCP, the NPP had significant regional support, which derived from the fear that northerners had of being dominated by radicals from the south. A similar fear of being discriminated against by the new CPP elite stimulated Muslim people of the colony's main towns to transform in 1954 what had been the Muslim Association into the Moslem Association Party (MAP). Finally, there was also considerable opposition to the CPP in the United Nations Trust Territory of Togoland. Rather than joining an independent Ghana, a faction within the area's Ewe population wanted to recreate what had been the former German colony of Togoland. To achieve this goal, in 1949 they had formed the Togoland Congress.

Even more threatening were struggles within the party to win nomination as an official candidate in the upcoming election. There were over 1,000 claimants. It proved impossible to settle all these claims, and eventually there were "rebel candidates" challenging official candidates. Nkrumah finally "expelled" 81 of these "rebels" from the party.[29] Most of them stood as independents, and altogether there were 160 such candidates. The increased number of constituencies, up from 38, and direct election stimulated this splintering. Neither was there an obvious imperialist enemy to stress the need to unite against. It was reflected in the party's cumbersome election slogan: "Vote the Common Man's way to shorten the transition to independence."[30] Instead, local rivalries increased as the benefits of office became more obvious. It was reflected in the fact that, with the exception of the large towns with mixed populations, no nonlocal stood a chance of being elected in rural areas. By the time of the election there were dangerous rifts within constituencies and between them and the national headquarters.

However, the opposition was not able to exploit these weaknesses. The GCP attacked what they considered the CPP's attempt to impose a corrupt dictatorship on the country and their failure to achieve full self-government. Nevertheless, they failed to unite the non-CPP vote. The NPP, with its regional base and skillful linking of chiefly authority and educated leadership, was far more successful. Eventually the NPP ran 15 candidates in the 26 northern constituencies. It allied with MAP, which was able to put up 15 candidates who represented the *zongos,* the Muslim communities in the country's large towns. It was not a particularly effective alliance. The CPP was able to exploit the many rivalries that existed between northern chiefs, and the conflicts among the many different ethnic groups that made up the country's Muslim population to maintain support in the north and in the *zongos.* Much the same situation applied to the Trust Territory, where it was difficult for the Ewe-based Togoland Congress to build support even from all Ewes.

Sixty percent of the registered voters voted, significantly better than the 40 percent in the 1951 election, but still only 31 percent of the colony's adult population. The CPP scored an overwhelming victory, winning 72 out of the 104 constituencies. Independents won 16 seats and the NPP won 12, while the GCP was all but swept away, winning only 1 seat. Nkrumah was able to use this disarray on the part of his opponents as the rationale for denying them the status of an officially recognized opposition in the new government. However, as far as the popular vote was concerned, the result was not as overwhelming as it seemed on the surface. Non-CPP candidates received over 44 percent of the vote. Neither was the success of regional opposition lost on the country, and almost immediately after the election there was to develop a far more dangerous challenge to national unity in the Ashanti Region than that which the NPP represented in the north. This election undermined the unity that the nationalist agitation had initially created. It underscored the importance of regional divisions based on ethnic allegiance, and indicated, as Nkrumah recognized, how the "objectives of the nationalist movement [could be] sacrificed on the altar of tribalism."[31]

THE NLM AND THE STRUGGLE FOR POWER

A spectacular rise in the price of cocoa was the catalyst that was to spark what were already rumblings of discontent. Shortly after winning the election, the CPP tried to stabilize the price paid to cocoa farmers by passing the Cocoa Duty and Development Funds (Amendment) Bill, which fixed the price paid to cocoa farmers at 72 shillings per 60-pound load. Ostensibly this was to prevent inflation, as the price on the world market soared to twice this level. The government also argued that the substantial difference between the world-market price and what it intended to pay Gold Coast cocoa farmers could be used for national development that would benefit all sections of the population. Cocoa farmers all over the country were rapidly up in arms, since CPP election propaganda had promised an increase in prices. Most of all this was so in the Ashanti Region, which produced almost half of the country's cocoa.

There already existed considerable discontent in this region over the very modest increase in the number of seats (two) that the Van Lare Commission had granted Ashanti in the new legislature.[32] However, it was the passage of the Cocoa Bill that "set ablaze the petrol dump of Ashanti nationalism."[33] Initially, opposition to this legislation came from the AYA. The *nkwankwaa,* or youth, who made up this association were typical of their counterparts in other areas of the Gold Coast. They consisted of people, not necessarily young, like small traders, clerks, accountants, teachers, and journalists. Invariably they had attained at least a primary education. Some were involved in cocoa production, but they all appreciated just how much cocoa prices affected the region's economy. Many were CPP supporters, while others had rebelled against the party during the 1954 elections. In general, the CPP had failed to satisfy their aspirations, and the Cocoa Bill gave them an opportunity to express their dissatisfaction with what they felt was an overly centralized and corrupt government.

Indicative of their relative powerlessness, the *nkwankwaa* rapidly turned to the chiefs for support. Eventually they recruited Nana Bafour Osei Akoto, the *asantehene's okyeame* (spokesman) and a wealthy cocoa farmer, to help them build "the bridges they themselves could not."[34] The first public rally in early September 1954 drew thousands of supporters, and rapidly the cry was for the "Ashanti people [to] separate themselves from the rest of the country."[35] Shortly afterward, farmers' representatives, members of the GCP, and members of the old-guard intelligentsia who had supported the UGCC were drawn into supporting the new movement. A few weeks later, over 40,000 Asantes gathered at the source of the Subin River in Kumasi, the traditional meeting ground of the Asante people, to proclaim the establishment of the National Liberation Movement (NLM). There was clearly a powerful ethnic appeal symbolized by the swearing of oaths, the pouring of libation and the singing of Asante war songs, and appeals to the most potent of Asante symbols, Asante Kotoko, the porcupine with a thousand quills. The NLM, Bafour Osei Akoto claimed, was not a party but a movement to save the (Asante) nation from lawlessness, corruption, and dictatorship. The NLM called for a federal form of government so as to give each region an effective voice in the central government.

Rapidly the region's chiefs, including the *asantehene,* sided with the movement. It was not surprising that this was so, as ever since the CPP had come to power the chiefs had watched their power and privileges erode. Chiefs' councils had been replaced by new local authorities that from 1952 had taken over levying local rates. The Asanteman Council and the Joint Provincial Council of Chiefs had petitioned in 1953 for an upper house of the assembly to which chiefs would belong, but this the CPP had refused. Most ominously, Nkrumah seemed to be saying that the future of the chieftaincy was to be determined by the Ministry of Local Government rather than as part of constitutional deliberations.[36] It meant, however, that the NLM was an uneasy alliance. The young men of the AYA, who had taken the lead in forming the movement, had earlier been responsible for upstaging the UGCC, who had been allied with the chiefs. When the *asantehene* finally gave his support to the movement, he was quick to point out how much "vilification, abuse and insults had been leveled against him by the youth when the Self-Government wave started."[37]

The murder of the movement's propaganda secretary, Emmanuel Yaw Baffoe, by the CPP's regional propaganda secretary a few weeks after the NLM's inauguration day provided the movement with a martyr. There were firebombings and assaults on CPP supporters. It brought Asante nationalism to a fever pitch. The Kumasi State Council enthusiastically gave its support to the movement and made available the sum of £20,000 from the *asantehene*'s New Palace Building Fund.[38] The Asanteman Council voted overwhelmingly to give its support to the NLM and sent a request to the queen for a royal commission to investigate the setting up of a federal government for the Gold Coast.

The NLM, though it claimed to be a movement rather than a party, rapidly adopted the techniques of mass political action that the CPP had pioneered, like party flags, propaganda vans, slogans, and salutes. It established a paramilitary organization of Action Groupers to protect its candidates, and also a Women's Section, every bit as passionate in their advocacy of federation as the CPP Women's League had been in championing freedom. By early October 1954, the movement claimed over 20,000 members and had spread outside of Kumasi to other major towns in the region like Sunyani and Obuasi.

First of all, the CPP tried unsuccessfully to defuse "the unrest in Ashanti" by informally trying to meet with the leaders of the NLM. When this failed, Nkrumah publicly condemned the NLM at a rally in Accra as "another attempt by imperialists and reactionary agents to bring together some chiefs and disgruntled opposition politicians to undermine the popular elected government."[39] This and other attempts to undermine the movement only served to inflame passions in Ashanti. It forced Governor Arden-Clarke into assuming an active role in seeking to bring about conciliation, but rapidly the NLM felt that he was too supportive of Nkrumah and the CPP. Eventually he became so unpopular in the Ashanti Region that on a visit to Kumasi he and his entourage were stoned by an unruly mob. Even the secretary of state, Lennox-Boyd, was to question his impartiality. The NLM executive set all sorts of conditions for meeting with their opponents. They realized that time was on their side. As the movement began to gain support outside of Ashanti, the CPP's claim that it was ready to take the colony into independence was undermined.

The violence in Ashanti also continued to escalate, often fueled by the government's actions. In February the CPP-dominated legislative assembly began consideration of a bill to allow for "the establishment of two administrative regions for Ashanti."[40] They took advantage of the previously existing tension between the Kumasi chiefs and those in the Brong region, northwest of Kumasi. Tension between these regions went back to precolonial times, when the Brong had formed a confederation to resist Asante conquest. It had continued during colonial times, fueled by disputes over landownership, and in 1951 the chief of the state of Techiman had formed the Brong-Kyempen Federation.

Fighting the NLM in this fashion was a dangerous game, since it undermined national unity and exposed the CPP to the charge of tribalism, which it was using to discredit the NLM. It was enough to influence three of the CPP's prominent Asante members—J. E. Appiah, R. R. Amponsah, and Victor Owusu—to desert the party and join the NLM. Appiah was a particularly telling loss, since he had been one of Nkrumah's close companions in England and a delegate to the historic fifth Pan-African Conference in Manchester in 1945. Rapidly they assumed leadership roles in the NLM, and they were gradually to steer the movement away from the path to violence that by May of 1955 seemed ominous enough to raise the fear of "another Mau Mau."[41]

A by-election to fill the seat of a CPP member of the legislature from Ashanti who had been killed in a car accident gave those who favored a more constitutional approach to the crisis in Ashanti the opportunity that they needed. Even though the NLM was not a party, it supported a candidate in this contest, and the distinction between being a movement and a party rapidly vanished. In July the NLM's candidate scored a resounding victory over his CPP opponent, which to many in Ashanti seemed to vindicate the constitutional electoral approach. The NLM sent Busia, who had also become a major voice in the movement, and R. R. Amponsah, the general secretary, to London to request that the secretary of state for the colonies, Lennox-Boyd, send a "constitutional expert to the Gold Coast to examine the claims of the various regions."[42] In the colony, the NLM's executive called for a general election and began to gather all opposition parties together to challenge the CPP. It seemed as though the opposition was "on the verge of coalescing into Her Majesty's Loyal Opposition."[43]

However, CPP actions once again inflamed passions in the Ashanti Region, and for a while gave the initiative back to the *nkwankwaa* and those who had made Kumasi and the region in general ungovernable. In August the government began debate over the passage of a bill to amend the State Councils (Ashanti) Ordinance of 1952, which would allow a chief below the status of paramount chief to appeal constitutional decisions of a state council to the governor. Nkrumah defended this legislation on the grounds that the *asantehene* and the Asanteman Council he headed was no longer objective, since the latter had joined a political party. The council's recent destoolment of chiefs in the Ashanti Region who supported the CPP was indication of this situation.[44]

Initially the NLM's leadership took little notice of the bill, even though it threatened to undermine the power of the *asantehene* and the Asanteman Council. It was left to youth associations and local chiefs to oppose this "iniquitous" legislation that threatened to destroy "the Great Ashanti Nation."[45] This opposition was enough to foil the attempt on the part of the constitutional adviser, when he finally arrived in September, to fashion a compromise to the crisis. Shortly before the bill was finally passed into law, Nkrumah's residence in Accra was bombed. The violence in Kumasi escalated dramatically. There was talk of armed resistance and succession. The *Ashanti Pioneer* was filled with announcements about defections of former CPP members in Ashanti to the NLM, and it seemed as if the constitutional road had been undermined.

Significantly, the constitutional adviser, Sir Frederick Bourne, never met officially with the movement's leaders. Neither did they attend the conference that Nkrumah convened to discuss his recommendations. Nevertheless, the constitutionalists, with the support of the *asantehene,* were able to regain the initiative. They did so by turning to the British government and successfully agitating for another general election. This strategy clearly paid off. In early December 1955 the secretary of state announced to Parliament that "Her Majesty's Government, before granting Independence, [had to] be satisfied that the constitution of the country was satisfactory to all."[46] By March 1956 he was informing Nkrumah that "there [would] be no other alternative to the holding of another General Election."[47] On May 11, he made this announcement public. The recently concluded United Nations plebiscite to determine the future of the Togoland Trust Territories had been ambiguous enough in its results to give the NLM hope that a general election would go their way. In the southern area of the territory almost 58 percent had voted for separation from the Gold Coast, which to the NLM represented a rejection of the CPP.

THE ELECTION OF 1956

It was an indication of how much the election was to be a rerun of 1954 that the NLM selected Dr. Kofi Busia to be its leader. To be the majority in the new legislature, the NLM realized that the party and its allies the NPP, MAP, and the Togoland Congress would need to win more than a majority of the constituencies in their respective regions. They would need to win at least a dozen of the constituencies in the colony. It meant that the NLM had to follow a double election strategy of appealing to Asante nationalism in the Ashanti Region while at the same time emphasizing that it wanted to protect the country in general from the CPP's "dictatorship" and "corruption."[48] The question of how the party should divide its resources to appeal to these two regions of the country was to remain a highly debated and divisive issue during the campaign.

The CPP, on the other hand, raised doubts about the NLM's commitment to federation, and how this could work in a small country. At political rallies the CPP's candidates disparaged the NLM and its allies as feudalists, saboteurs, and tribalists. But undoubtedly their most potent counter to the NLM's attempt to canvass in the colony was the fear that this represented another Asante invasion of the south. In the north the CPP won the support of chiefs it elevated to the status of paramount chiefs. It also did a far better job of settling intraparty rivalries than was the case in 1954, and the party was able to contest all 26 of the northern seats. In the Togoland Trust Territories the election came right after the rather inconclusive plebiscite of May 1956, but 42 percent of the overall electorate had voted for union with the Gold Coast, which was an indication of their pro-CPP sympathies.

In spite of the violence that had preceded it, the election was remarkably peaceful. Only 50 percent of the registered voters voted, which represented about 30 percent of the voting population. Low voter turnout usually helps incumbents, and this probably was the case in this election. In this winner-take-all system, the CPP won a resounding victory, winning 71 out of the 104 seats contested. They did so by winning 57 percent of the popular vote. Even in the Ashanti Region they did well, winning 8 of the 21 seats contested with over 43 percent of the popular vote. In the Northern Region they also did well, winning 11 of the 26 seats contested with almost 48 percent of the popular vote. In the Togoland Trust Territories the CPP was able to hold on to its support and won 8 of the 13 seats contested. Undoubtedly, however, it was in the colony that the party did best of all. Here they won all of the 44 seats contested, with almost 81 percent of the popular vote.

The NLM tried to make the best of this defeat by pointing out that they had won 43 percent of the popular vote, but clearly they had badly miscalculated their strength. The CPP, as the incumbent party, had been able to take advantage of disputes in areas where the NLM and the NPP were supposedly strong, while in the colony, fears of an "Asante invasion" had worked so well that even in cocoa-growing areas the NLM had done poorly.[49] Also working to the NLM's disadvantage was the similarity between its candidates and those of the incumbent party. As the constitutional approach to resolving the conflict in Ashanti had developed, there had been a great deal of opportunism with UGCC and GCP people getting on the NLM bandwagon.[50] The result was that very little of the popular feeling that had ignited the NLM carried over. It was not surprising that even after two years of agitation and violence, voter turnout was so low.

With the mandate that this victory gave him, on August 3 Nkrumah introduced a motion in the legislative assembly calling for independence. The CPP had more than met the requirements that the British government had placed on them of winning "a reasonable majority in a newly elected legislature."[51] The leadership of the NLM, still in a state of shock from their defeat in the elections, initially refused to participate in the new assembly. Far more threatening were the young men of the AYA, who once again began to assert themselves. They called for total secession of Ashanti from the Gold Coast. Gradually the more conservative NLM leadership was able to regain control of the movement. They turned to the British government to intervene in what they described as a constitutional crisis. In August 1956 Busia led a four-man delegation to London for this purpose, but they were clearly on the defensive. Rather than talking about federalism, the delegation only argued for "constitutional safeguards." Specifically, they asked for "Regional Assemblies," a "Second Chamber" for the chiefs, the "decentralization of the police," and "security of tenure for the Judiciary."[52]

The colonial office sympathized with these concerns. The debate then going on in the Gold Coast over the report on the affairs of the Cocoa Purchasing Company made these concerns seem particularly relevant. There had clearly been gross misuse of public funds by this semigovernment body that Nkrumah had established in 1952 to provide inexpensive loans to the colony's cocoa farmers. Nevertheless, the colonial office did not shift from its position that the opposition in the Gold Coast had to work within the confines of the colony's legislative assembly rather than expecting the British government to intervene. Ironically, the spirit of compromise that the delegation demonstrated in London indicated to officials in Great Britain that the crisis could be resolved and that it was time to move forward toward independence. Shortly after meeting with the delegation, the secretary of state announced in Parliament that the date for independence would be March 6, 1957. At the same time, he pressured Nkrumah into meeting with the opposition to discuss constitutional affairs before the official debate on the constitution began in the colony's legislative assembly.

In October 1956 two meetings were held in Accra at which all talk of federation was replaced with calls for regional autonomy. Not everyone accepted these concessions, and when in November the government published its *Revised Constitutional Proposals for Gold Coast Independence,* which did not include any of the provisions that the opposition had demanded, there were angry calls, once again, in Ashanti for secession. Most incendiary of all, the government had not abandoned its plan to divide Ashanti into two regions. This unwillingness to compromise forced even the moderates in the NLM, NPP, and Asanteman Council into supporting the call for a separate independence for Ashanti and the Northern Territories. They retained legal counsel in Great Britain to petition for a partition commission. The lawyers applied to the United Nations for membership in that body for Ashanti and the Northern Territories while plans were drawn up for a £500,000 House of Parliament in Ashanti, and work began on a constitution for the nation in the making.

For some while British officials in the colony were concerned that another Cyprus, Kenya, or Malaya might be in the making, since people in Ashanti were very much aware of how small numbers of freedom fighters had been able to challenge British rule in these colonies. However, the moderates who controlled the NLM were not really prepared to take on both the CPP and the British government. They still placed their faith in British intervention, and eventually the leadership was able to convince Secretary of State Lennox-Boyd to visit the Gold Coast before independence. It meant convincing Nkrumah, who was initially hostile to the idea, but eventually, in January 1957, the secretary did arrive. The opposition hailed this as a great victory. In contrast to the debacle that Governor Arden-Clarke's visit to Kumasi in 1955 had been, Lennox-Boyd's visit was a resounding success. More than 70,000 people lined the streets to cheer him as he made his way to the Manhyia Palace.[53] Safeguards in the constitution replaced talk of secession, and the secretary was able to assure the NLM's leadership that regional autonomy and the chieftaincy would be protected in independent Ghana's constitution.

In reality it was the opposition that gave most ground on the constitutional issues. In the final White Paper that the British parliament issued on the colony's future constitution, the National Assembly was to retain most power. A two-thirds majority of this body would be necessary to amend the constitution, and significantly, the question of establishing regional assemblies was to be left until after independence. Nevertheless, the opposition heralded the White Paper as a great victory. Busia, in the legislative assembly, called for all members of the house "to join together for the success and greatness of our nation."[54] For a brief moment the government's issuing of equal numbers of invitations to the Asanteman Council and the Brong-Kyempen Council, which indicated that the Nkrumah government had not given up the idea of separating the Ashanti Region, provoked cries, once again, from the young men for secession. However, the *asantehene* and the moderates who controlled the NLM were resolutely against such a move, and instead were willing to wait until after independence to resolve this contentious issue. Like elsewhere in the colony, the raising of the country's new flag at midnight on March 6, 1957 was greeted in the Ashanti Region with equally enthusiastic cries of "Freedom."

NOTES

1. Quoted in Aiken Watson, A. Dalgleish, and Keith A. Murray, *Report of the Commission of Enquiry into Disturbances in the Gold Coast: 1948* (London: HMSO, 1948), 92.

2. Ibid., 17.

3. Dennis Austin, *Politics in Ghana: 1946–1960* (London: Oxford University Press, 1964), 83.

4. Kwame Nkrumah, *Ghana: The Autobiography of Kwame Nkrumah* (New York: International Publishers, 1957), 112.

5. Ibid., 120.

6. Quoted in an editorial in the *Accra Evening News,* January 5, 1950.

7. Austin, *Politics in Ghana,* 113.

8. Ibid., 90.

9. Nkrumah, *Ghana,* 113.

10. Austin, *Politics in Ghana,* 113.

11. Ibid., 127.

12. This is an adaptation of Jesus' words from the Sermon on the Mount (Matthew 6:33).

13. Austin, *Politics in Ghana,* 137.

14. Sir C. Arden-Clarke, "Eight Years of Transition in Ghana," *African Affairs* (January 1958): 34.

15. Austin, *Politics in Ghana*, 153.

16. Adu Boahen, *Ghana: Evolution and Change in the Nineteenth and Twentieth Centuries* (Accra, Ghana: Sankofa Educational Publishers, 2000), 173.

17. Ibid., 177–78.

18. Nkrumah, *Ghana*, 145.

19. *Daily Graphic*, March 7, 1951.

20. *Accra Evening News*, August 7, 1952.

21. In 1953 the British government sent warships to British Guiana, Britain's only South American colony, to depose its recently elected prime minister, Dr. Cheddi Jagan, who was considered too radical and socialist.

22. Watson, *Report of the Commission of Enquiry*, 55.

23. Boahen, *Ghana: Evolution and Change*, 198.

24. Legislative Assembly Debates, February 23, 1953. Quoted in Austin, *Politics in Ghana*, 166.

25. Kwame Nkrumah, "Dawn Broadcast," *Selected Speeches of Kwame Nkrumah*, vol. 2, comp. S Obeng (Accra, Ghana: Afram Publications 1997), 60.

26. Austin, *Politics in Ghana*, 194.

27. *New York Amsterdam News*, June 16, 1951.

28. Nkrumah, *Ghana*, 184.

29. Ibid., 209.

30. Austin, *Politics in Ghana*, 212.

31. Nhrumah, *Ghana*, 215.

32. W. B. Van Lare was a judge in the supreme court, and in 1953 he had chaired the Commission of Enquiry into Representational and Electoral Reform.

33. *Ashanti Pioneer*, September 4, 1954.

34. Jean Allman, *The Quills of the Porcupine: Asante Nationalism in an Emergent Ghana* (Madison: University of Wisconsin Press, 1993), 42.

35. *Ashanti Pioneer*, September 7, 1954.

36. Richard Rathbone, *Nkrumah and the Chiefs: The Politics of Chieftaincy in Ghana 1951–60* (Athens: Ohio University Press, 2000), 61.

37. *Ashanti Pioneer*, October 22, 1954.

38. Austin, *Politics in Ghana*, 272.

39. *Daily Graphic*, October 25, 1954.

40. Gold Coast Legislative Debates, March 25, 1955.

41. *Daily Graphic*, May 19, 1955. The Mau Mau rebellion was then going on in Kenya. There was very much an ethnic component to this anticolonial struggle, as it involved primarily the Kikuyu people, who had lost land to white settlers.

42. *West Africa*, July 16, 1955.

43. Allman, *Quills of the Porcupine*, 117.

44. Nkrumah, *Ghana*, 219.

45. Allman, *Quills of the Porcupine*, 122.

46. *Daily Graphic*, December 9, 1955.
47. Allman, *Quills of the Porcupine*, 144.
48. D. Austin, *Politics in Ghana*, 324.
49. Allman, *Quills of the Porcupine*, 153.
50. Ibid., 158–59.
51. Austin, *Politics in Ghana*, 353.
52. Allman, *Quills of the Porcupine*, 164.
53. This is the *asantehene*'s palace in Kumasi.
54. Gold Coast, Legislative Assembly, *Debates*, February 12, 1957.

7

Independence:
The Nkrumah Years

In 1957, when the Gold Coast became the first West African colony to become independent, the country had a population of about 6.2 million people, with an annual population growth rate of 2.5 percent. Between 1921, when the Gold Coast attained its modern size with the attachment of the mandated territory from the former German Togoland, and 1960, when the country's most complete census was conducted, the population had nearly tripled. Life expectancy had increased from 39.5 years in 1948, the time of the last official census before independence, to 45.5 years in 1960. Reflective of the high population growth rate, the median age was about 18. Forty-four and a half percent of the population was under 15 years of age. Considerable immigration from surrounding West African countries had added to the country's population growth, but also exceptionally high rates of fertility (over seven births per woman of childbearing age) contributed to what was one of the highest population growth rates in West Africa.[1]

Per-capita income was around $170 per annum, about one-ninth of Great Britain's and about twice Nigeria's, Britain's most important West African colony, which became independent in 1960. Between 1955 and 1962 the average yearly growth rate was 4.8 percent. There was a significant disparity in wealth between the cocoa-growing areas of the south and the northern savanna. This was so both in terms of actual monetary income and for services available to people living in these different areas of the country. In the south, children were more likely to attend school, and villages were more likely to enjoy piped water and be accessible to motor traffic. People in these rural communities could more easily move back and forth between the country's larger towns and cities, most of which were in the south, where there was far more economic opportunity. An important indication of how much more opportunity existed in the south was the considerable migration from the north to the south, much of it to the cocoa-growing areas of Ashanti, but also to the urban areas of this region.

Not surprisingly, it was these urban centers that registered the most significant population increase. Between 1948 and 1960 the population of Accra, the nation's capital, increased from 133,200 to 337,800. The populations of Kumasi and Sekondi-Takoradi, the two other largest towns, increased from 58,600 and 43,700 in 1948 to 180,600 and 75,400 in 1960. Significantly, in 1960 23.7 percent of the population lived in towns of over 5,000 inhabitants, in contrast to only 9 percent in 1948. Here there was also considerable disparity in income. A successful member of the professional elite in Accra with an income of over $16,000 per annum could live in a house "built on the pattern of an English country mansion having spacious and well-kept gardens and all the modern comforts and conveniences available."[2] In contrast, unskilled laborers making 63 cents a day and living in Ussher Town, a particularly congested part of Accra, did so in tumble-down houses made of *swish* (sun-dried mud), 82 percent of which the Accra Town Council considered "ought to be demolished as soon as possible." One room 10 by 15 feet could house "from ten to thirteen women and children . . . and had one double bed on which four grown women slept."[3] Water had to be fetched from public standpipes, and the only sanitary conveniences were public latrines.

Enormous variations in living standards had characterized colonial society, and the rapid urban growth of the 1950s accentuated these differences. Nkrumah had promised in 1949 that with self-government the CPP would transform the country "into a paradise in ten years."[4] The CPP's first development plan had been designed to achieve this goal. The favorable economic conditions of the 1950s had made it possible to make important strides in this direction, though even by the end of the decade, paradise was still a considerable distance away. In spite of fluctuations in the world price of cocoa, the country's main export, the trend in prices had been dramatically upward. Over 80 percent of this development had been funded from cocoa revenue.[5] In addition, since the Second World

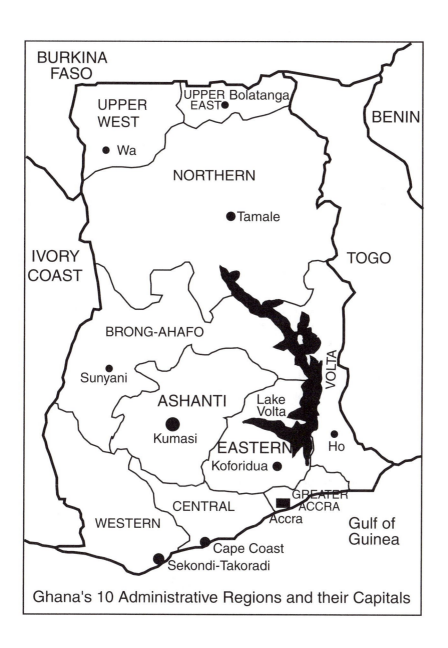

Ghana's 10 Administrative Regions and their Capitals

War extensive reserves had been accumulating, and only a very small part of these reserves had been used to fund development. They derived from the difference between what the Cocoa Marketing Board paid to the colony's cocoa producers and the world price for this commodity. In 1956, when cocoa was selling at $850 a ton, the Gold Coast's cocoa farmers were receiving only 44 percent of the world price. The result was that in 1957 Ghana also enjoyed substantial reserves in Great Britain of over $470 million.

DEVELOPMENT PLANNING AND ECONOMIC PERFORMANCE: 1957–61

Unfortunately, the coming of independence coincided with a fall in the world cocoa price to what was considered the catastrophic level of $490 a ton. At independence, Nkrumah could only promise a period of financial and economic consolidation. The first independence budget the leader of the opposition, Dr. Kofi Busia, scathingly described as a "Matchstick Budget."[6] To help make up the shortfall in revenue, there were modest increases in income tax and the cost of government services and selected increases in import duties. None of this had much effect on overall revenue, and the far more important decision was to fund all development out of the country's reserves. Undoubtedly the most important lesson from this change in economic fortune was the realization that Ghana would have to turn to the world's financial markets to fund its ambitious development plans. Most of all this was apparent for the Volta River hydroelectric scheme. Nkrumah considered this his "baby and his ambition." He believed that the project could be the nucleus around which the industrialization of the country would take place, but he realized that to finance this massive project was going to require capital and technology beyond Ghana's ability to provide.[7]

Initially, Ghana turned to the British government and British and Canadian aluminum companies to provide the financing and expertise for the project. Unfortunately for Ghana, there were several dam projects in the offing that were competing for capital. The most important was the massive Kariba Dam on the Zambezi River, to which the British government was already heavily committed. In addition, the oversupply of aluminum on the world market made both British and Canadian companies unwilling to commit to investment in new facilities. By 1956 there was no longer any interest on the part of the British government or British or Canadian aluminum companies. However, in 1958, when he was visiting the United States, Nkrumah met Edgar Kaiser, the president of Kaiser

Aluminum Company of America, and interested him in the project. With-out some major consumer of electricity, like an aluminum smelter, limited domestic demand in Ghana or even in neighboring countries made the project unviable.

In 1959 Kaiser's engineers reassessed the project. Apart from picking a site at Akosombo, about a mile downstream from the original site at Ajena, they also scaled back the cost of the project, even though the dam was going to produce 25 percent more electrical energy. The public-utilities aspect of the project was to be separated from the aluminum in-dustry, with the former financed with public money and the latter by the aluminum companies. It was not to be an integrated aluminum industry but only a smelting plant using imported alumina.[8] President Kennedy was afraid that the Russians might take a leading role in the construction of the dam, as they were doing with the Aswan High Dam in Egypt, and he put pressure on the World Bank to finance the project. The result was that 50 percent of the funds for construction of the dam came from the World Bank or from U.S. government agencies. The Ghana government funded the remaining $98 million that the project was to cost, and work finally began in 1961.

In general a more systematic approach to development planning seemed necessary, and in September 1957 West Indian economist Profes-sor Arthur Lewis was appointed economic adviser to the Ghana govern-ment. In 1953 he had prepared a report on industrialization in the Gold Coast in which he had recommended increasing agricultural productivity and expanding the country's infrastructure. The Second Five-Year Devel-opment Plan, which Nkrumah announced in 1959, was far more ambi-tious. Nevertheless, the plan itself was not much different from the shopping-list style of earlier plans in that it set targets for government investment in various areas of the economy without showing how this would contribute to the overall growth of the economy.[9] Neither was there any attempt to integrate the private sector into the overall development plan, and the actual amount of funds to be spent was uncertain.

In reality there were two plans, which in parliamentary debate were referred to as the "small coat" and the "large coat." The $370 million allocated for the small-coat plan was designed to cover the cost of "pro-jects for immediate implementation." Supposedly when funds became available a further $330 million was to be spent on more prestige-type projects. This was the large-coat plan. A further $280 million was seen as necessary to carry out the complete Volta River Project, which apart from dam construction was going to include such items as resettlement of the 70,000 people the dam would displace, the construction of a low-head dam further downriver, electricity transmission lines, fishing, and irrigation projects.

Professor Lewis played an important role in the formulation of these plans. He introduced the idea of foreign public and private investment in the Ghanaian economy.[10] He believed that the government should have a limited role in industrialization, which should be spurred by foreign investment. Nkrumah, in his autobiography, had criticized capitalism as too complicated a system for a newly independent nation and had advocated the need for a "socialistic society."[11] Not surprisingly, he maintained an ambivalence toward foreign capitalist investment. However, if Ghana was going to attract such investment to fund its development, his government had to make the economy attractive to foreign capital. In the early years of independence, the CPP government went out of its way to do this. It hired American consultants, who assured potential investors that Ghana, even though it was "socialist," was "pragmatic" so that "foreign enterprise . . . would probably be safe from nationalization."[12] Foreign companies investing in the Ghanaian economy were granted tax holidays, company tax was reduced from 45 to 40 percent, and there were very liberal provisions for the repatriation of profits.

Contributing to the climate of economic optimism was a brief rebound in cocoa prices. By 1958 a ton was selling for over $850, and government revenue increased significantly. Nevertheless, it was not sufficient to offset the high expenditure on development projects. This increased dramatically from around $47 million in 1957–58 to $72.8 million in 1958–59, and almost doubled to $126 million between 1960 and 1962.[13] Even if cocoa prices remained above $670 per ton, which was the government's assumption, this rate of expenditure was going to deplete the country's reserves in two years. One response was increases in taxation that made Ghanaians highly taxed by the standards of developing countries. The falling price of cocoa on the world market, beginning in 1958, also made it imperative to reduce the price paid to cocoa farmers from $11.20 a load in 1957 to eventually $7 a load in 1961. However, this producer price reduction did little to offset the budget imbalance as the world price of cocoa, after peaking in 1958, began to decline, until in 1961 it had once again reached the catastrophic level of under $500 per ton.

The reduction in prices paid to farmers did not keep pace with the fall in the price on the world market, which meant that the government's share of cocoa revenue also began to decline. At the same time, the cost of marketing cocoa increased. In 1959 the UAC, which had dominated the cocoa purchasing market in Ghana, withdrew from this activity as a result of pressure from the Ghana government, and the United Ghana Farmers'

Council (UGFC) took over all cocoa buying in the country. As the UGFC became a monopoly, its costs began to increase dramatically, and by 1960–61 the government's share of the cocoa revenue had become negative.[14] The revenue generated from cocoa was also being squeezed from the considerable expenditure that the government was undertaking to rehabilitate the industry. Government statistics, not the most reliable, claimed that in 1960 the Cocoa Marketing Board spent over $75 million on cocoa replanting, about half of which went into the swollen-shoot control program. The year before, more than $33 million had been spent on spraying against capsid pests.[15]

The stimulus of high prices earlier in the decade, the government's replanting program with faster-maturing hybrids, and aggressive use of pesticides to control cocoa diseases all contributed to a dramatic expansion in the amount of cocoa Ghanaian farmers were able to produce. By 1961 Ghana was producing well over 400,000 tons of cocoa, 50 percent more than what had been produced in 1957. Not only in Ghana was this happening. World cocoa supplies were increasing at a time when demand for chocolate was weakening, with the inevitable result of a collapse in prices. Ironically, in spite of the vastly increased amount of cocoa Ghana sold during the 1960s, the country's revenue from cocoa exports remained more or less the same. Ghana took a leading role in trying to form a Cocoa Producers Alliance to stabilize world cocoa prices, but lack of capital and the cost of production varying as much as it did between African and South American producers made this initiative unsuccessful. Neither did attempts to store cocoa, a basically perishable item, meet with any more success.

In the country's development planning, industrialization had been seen as the long-term solution to reliance on a one-crop economy. But neither did the government's attempts to attract foreign investment to fund such development work out particularly well. Professor Lewis had anticipated that about 100 new factories would be started in Ghana during the period of the Five-Year Plan. The Industrial Development Corporation had inflated this number to 600, but in reality the number of industries established was even less than the more modest figure. They included factories to make cigarettes, insecticide, bricks, and tiles as well as tomato and milk-products processing plants, a steel mill, and vehicle-assembly plants. To facilitate Ghana's entry into the world of commerce, a shipping line, the Black Star Line, was also established in 1957. Initially it was joint shipping venture with the Zim Israeli Navigation Company, but two years later, when the Ghana government decided to expand the line, the partnership came to an end. Already a new harbor was being constructed for Accra at Tema that was to play an important role in the country's expanded trade. With all of these projects underway, it was hardly surprising that the size of the country's working class increased almost seven times, from 45,000 in 1948 to over 304,000 in 1960.

CURBING THE OPPOSITION IN THE POLITICAL KINGDOM: 1957–60

The CPP's ambitious and often controversial plans for development placed the heaviest economic burden on the cocoa-growing areas of the country and benefited most of all the country's large urban populations. They inevitably sparked opposition. Independence ushered in only a brief period of euphoria. Indeed, at that time the people of southern Togoland were in open rebellion and had boycotted the independence celebrations. Shortly afterward, the government was forced to send troops and police into the area, and three people were killed in the town of Kpandu. In Nkrumah's own Accra constituency, discontent also developed. Local Gas felt that they had been discriminated against in terms of access to public housing and jobs in favor of Akan outsiders. In July 1957 this discontent erupted into a full-blown political movement known as the Ga Shifimo Kpee (Ga Standfast Association). In an unsuccessful attempt to head off this movement, the government had suspended the Accra Town Council in April, but obviously this had not been enough of a warning. Shortly afterward the Kumasi Municipal Council, controlled by the NLM, was also suspended.

Nkrumah realized that local opposition of this nature could easily undermine the CPP's rather tenuous hold on power, and it was this fear that lay behind the introduction of the highly controversial Ghana Nationality and Citizenship Bill. The legislation gave the minister of the interior the right to determine who was a citizen without subject to appeal in the country's courts. Shortly after, in July 1957, the government passed the Deportation Act and immediately used this legislation to deport two leaders of MAP in Kumasi as well as a number of anti-CPP Syrians and Lebanese in the country.[16] A month later the same legislation was used to deport Bankole Timothy, originally from Sierra Leone, and the deputy editor of the country's main daily newspaper, the *Daily Graphic*. He had provoked Nkrumah's ire by questioning his decision to have his head rather than that of the queen on Ghana's new currency as well as to have his statue erected in Accra.[17] At that time Nkrumah was under attack both in Ghana and in Great Britain for being "power drunk" and a dictator in the making.[18]

In December 1957 the government passed the Avoidance of Discrimination Act, which forbade the existence of parties on regional, tribal, or
religious bases. It was designed to thwart the efforts of the opposition,
which had come together shortly before to form the United Party (UP).
The astonishing speed with which this new party spread eventually
prompted the government to pass the most draconian of all legislation,
the Preventive Detention Act, in July 1958. This legislation made it possible to keep someone in detention for up to five years, without the right
of appeal to the courts, for conduct considered prejudicial to the defense
and security of the state and its foreign relations. By November of that
year 39 people had been arrested under this law, all of whom were members of either the Ga Shifimo Kpee or the UP. Nine of the 12 arrested in
1959 were prominent members of the UP in the Ashanti Region, and all
16 arrested in 1960 were members of the UP in the Volta Region.[19] Reports
of plots against the government and well-publicized trials of suspects
fanned this fear of the opposition.

The government also moved to consolidate its power in the rural areas.
Soon after independence, regional commissioners took over from regional
officers who had been civil servants and all expatriates. The latter became
the secretaries of the regional commissioners, who were drawn from the
ranks of the elected CPP members in the legislative assembly and were
to be of cabinet rank.[20] The CPP-sponsored UGFC became the only recognized farmer's association, and a concerted effort was made to eliminate chiefly opposition. In Ashanti a number of pro-NLM paramount
chiefs were downgraded and pro-CPP chiefs upgraded. Pro-CPP factions
that sought to destool pro-NLM chiefs quickly won government approval.
Both the *okyenhene* of Akyem Abuakwa and the *asantehene* were publicly
forced to disassociate themselves from politics. Indeed, the former was
"derecognized" while a government commission undertook an investigation into charges that his state had "imped[ed] the Government in the
execution of its lawful duties."[21] Eventually he was found to have abused
his powers and officially destooled.

In 1958 regional assemblies, as the independence constitution had
promised to the opposition, were established, but only as advisory bodies.
The opposition boycotted the elections to these bodies and the CPP won
an overwhelming majority. Quickly these members agreed to a constitutional change that would abolish these bodies, and in 1959 the National
Assembly passed such legislation. All that was left were regional houses
of chiefs, which could only concern themselves with chiefly matters. Neither was the government under any obligation to consult them on legislation affecting chieftaincy itself.[22] Finally Nkrumah made good on his

threat to divide the Ashanti Region by first creating eight new Brong states, and then in 1959 his government created the new Brong-Ahafo Region, which consisted of 62 percent of the former Ashanti Region.

By this time Ghana's chiefs had lost their control of stool revenue, they no longer had a voice on local councils, and their "independent political influence . . . had been virtually extinguished."[23] However, it did not mean the demise of the chieftaincy, but the emergence of one that was sanctioned and dependent on government support and creating yet another drain on government revenue. It created bitter disputes over destoolments and enstoolments that were contested as being contrary to custom. Eventually the government passed even more legislation to regulate the institution and its officeholders. The Chiefs (Recognition) Bill of 1959 made government recognition of enstoolment or destoolment necessary. Even more important, it gave the government the power to legally depose chiefs without recourse to customary law. With the passage of this legislation, in reality, "tenure of chiefly office" became dependent "on political party affiliation."[24]

The government also moved to control civic organizations in the country, the most important of which was the TUC. The Industrial Relations Act of 1958 established a centralized structure of a limited number of national unions under CPP control. In addition the government created a National Co-operative Council in place of the independent Alliance of Co-operatives. One of the more controversial of these party-affiliated organizations was the Builders Brigade, established in 1957, which was designed to reduce urban unemployment. It was an important source of patronage, but opponents accused it of being like a Nazi labor camp. Organizations like the Ex-Servicemen, the Women's Organization, the National Association of Socialist Students, and the League of Ghana Patriots were all brought under the party's control. Nkrumah likened them to the many branches of a mighty tree. At the 10th anniversary of the CPP, in 1959, he proclaimed that "the Convention People's Party is Ghana, and that the party [was] the state and the state [was] the party."[25]

As the CPP gathered power into its hands, the opposition began to lose even its strongholds. In 1959 it suffered the indignity of losing a by-election in Kumasi. The leader of the opposition, Dr. Kofi Busia, went into exile in 1959, and by 1960, of the 31 other opposition members at independence, 3 were being held in detention and 12 had crossed to the government's side.[26] Nevertheless, opposition still existed, and there were institutions, like the judiciary, the post of governor general, and the civil service, that were still outside the party's direct control. Nkrumah clearly wanted more control. He had been impressed by the authoritarian manner in which President Tubman ran Liberia and was to introduce many of his procedures in Ghana after his visit to Liberia in 1958.[27] In 1960 his government conducted a plebiscite to determine whether Ghana should also become a republic, with a president far more powerful than the prime minister had been. It was more like a general election than a plebiscite. Even though the opposition opposed the idea of a republic, they ran Dr. Danquah as their presidential candidate, and the election had more to do with party programs than with the proposed republican constitution.[28]

It was a highly unequal contest, as the opposition could offer little to counter the CPP's promises. Instead, they attacked, as they had in the past, the "dictatorial" nature of the CPP, and especially the deportation and detention acts. If the UP's candidate won the election, the party promised to call a constitutional commission "to give the nation a constitution worthy of our country."[29] In major urban areas of the country, there was considerable voter apathy. Only 45 percent of the registered voters voted in Accra, and there was a significant minority (35 percent) who voted against the republican constitution and for Danquah. Here it seemed the vote was free. The CPP was clearly alarmed by this outcome, and in up-country rural constituencies resorted to massive vote rigging to insure high turnouts and overwhelming support for the constitutional changes. The republican constitution abolished the post of governor general, held by an Englishman (the Earl of Listowel), and was probably acceptable enough to many Ghanaians, but aspects of the new constitution, like the president's power to appoint and dismiss the chief justice and to dismiss members of the judicial service and the police force, were definitely unsettling, particularly to public servants. Nkrumah did use these powers, and this created "an atmosphere of insecurity which grew with the years as more and more public servants were summarily dismissed."[30]

FOREIGN POLICY: 1957–65

Nkrumah always had a passionate interest in African unity, and his pursuit of this goal contributed to his increasing ideological radicalization. The political struggles with the NLM had forced this dream to take a back seat, but soon after independence he was proclaiming that the "independence of Ghana [was] meaningless unless it was linked up with the total liberation of the African continent."[31] He quickly set out to realize this goal and to put Ghana in the forefront of this struggle. In 1957 he appointed his West Indian friend from London days, George Padmore, his adviser on African affairs. The first major pan-African activity took place in 1958, when the first conference of independent African states was held in Accra. The conference issued a joint declaration on the need to assert "the African Personality" and established an informal secretariat of the independent African States (IAS) at the United Nations.[32] However, not far beneath the surface there were significant tensions between the five North African Arab nations and the three sub-Saharan nations that attended.

The far more electrifying gathering that took place at the end of that year was the All-African Peoples Conference, once again held in Accra. It was meant for Africans still under colonial rule and brought together more than 200 delegates from 62 nationalist organizations and parties in 28 African countries. The leading national figures from all over the continent discovered one another, and like the young Patrice Lumumba of the Belgium Congo and Holden Roberto of Angola, they went back to their home countries determined to intensify the struggle against colonial rule. The conference resolved to establish a permanent secretariat in Ghana and to hold a similar conference each year, the purpose of which would be to "accelerate the liberation of Africa from imperialism and colonialism."[33]

In the meantime, Nkrumah had found an important ally in Sékou Touré, who in September 1958 had been responsible for the people of French Guinea voting against membership in the French Community.[34] He too had preferred "poverty in freedom to opulence in slavery," which had become one of Nkrumah's most electrifying slogans during the early years of the independent struggles, and in November he joined his newly independent Republic of Guinea with Ghana to form the Ghana-Guinea Union. The French had withdrawn all support from Guinea after their no vote, and in addition to exchanging ministers, Ghana offered its poorer partner a $28 million grant. At the end of 1960 the union was joined by the Mali Republic, which had broken from its union with Senegal. Eventually the three countries issued a charter outlining 14 articles of a Union of African States, which was to be the nucleus of the United States of Africa. Nkrumah was elected the president, and at this point Ghana was very much in "the forefront of a new pan-Africanism firmly placed in Africa itself."[35]

Nevertheless, paralleling these pan-Africanist initiatives was a much more conservative set of foreign policies designed to maintain good relations with the former colonial power and the West in general. It was from these countries that Nkrumah believed that the economic aid that Ghana needed for industrialization would come, and he felt could not afford to antagonize them. He attended all the Commonwealth Conferences even after Ghana became a republic. At his first conference in 1957, as the head of state he had called for a guaranteed cocoa price and for an aid plan for Africa similar to the Colombo Plan that the richer Commonwealth nations had offered Asian members of the Commonwealth. Ghana even retained a friendly relationship with South Africa. In 1959 Nkrumah invited South Africa's foreign minister, Eric Louw, to visit Ghana. It was more the implications of a reciprocal visit of the Ghanaian foreign minister to apartheid South Africa than anything else that prevented the visit from taking place. In keeping with his search for aid, Nkrumah made important visits to Canada, the United Kingdom, and the United States, where in 1958 he enjoyed a triumphant motorcade through the streets of Harlem.

Officially Ghana's foreign policy was one of nonalignment, but there was great ambiguity in how this policy was publicly expressed. Until the early 1960s most of Ghana's contact was with Western countries. Even such an anticolonial meeting as the Positive Action Conference held in Accra in 1960 was attended by American and British left-wing organizations. There were no delegates from Eastern counties with the exception of Yugoslavia.[36] Not until 1959 was the Soviet embassy opened in Ghana, and in the following year Ghana's embassy was opened in Moscow. In the same year relations were established with Czechoslovakia, Poland, and communist China. Most controversially, in the early years of independence Ghana established close relationships with Israel. Even young CPP radicals were impressed by the Jewish state. Apart by being impressed with Israel's dynamism, some observers felt that this link gave Nkrumah the ability to counter Egyptian influence in black Africa.[37]

In the early 1960s Ghana's role as the leader of the pan-Africanist movement was challenged as the anticolonial floodgates opened up and other African countries became independent. There was a major about-face on the part of both France and Belgium toward the independence of their colonies. In 1960 France gave up the idea of the French Community, and its colonies in West Africa became independent nations. Ghana acquired three independent francophone neighbors: the Ivory Coast, Upper Volta (now Burkina Faso), and Togo. Rapidly, relations with the Ivory Coast soured after the expulsion of 4,000 Ghanaians in 1958 and Ghana's claims to Ivorian territory. Also, the Ivory Coast's prime minister, Houphouet-Boigny, retained close links with France, even to the point of supporting French atomic testing in the Sahara. He was bitterly attacked in the CPP's newspaper as a "puppet dancing savagely to the tunes of the French imperialist shampoolah."[38] Neither were relations with Togo any better. Nkrumah wanted Togo's unification with Ghana, but there was little interest on the part of Togo's new leader, Sylvanus Olympio, in such an arrangement. So much hostility developed between the two countries that when Olympio was assassinated in 1963 there was considerable suspicion that the Ghanaian government had been involved.

Most important in challenging Ghana's leadership role in Africa was Nigeria, which became independent in 1960. Nigeria, the much larger and potentially wealthier colony, had always considered itself to be the leader of anglophone West Africa. Indeed, with the largest population in Africa, many in Nigeria felt it was their birthright to be the leader of the entire continent. Ghana's earlier attainment of independence had temporarily upset this ambition. As an indication of how intense the rivalry between these two countries was, Nkrumah did not attend Nigeria's independence celebrations in 1960. Tension between the two countries increased also as disputes developed over the fate of the large number of institutions that they shared in common. As early as the 1920s, the British had established a number of West African institutions like the West African Currency Board (1921) and the West African Court of Appeal (1929). After the Second World War, this organizational pan–West Africanism had accelerated, so that by the 1950s there were interterritorial organizations that also dealt with administration, education, marketing, the military, agricultural and academic research, and transport. Some of these organizations clearly benefited one territory more than another, and it was this feeling that contributed to Ghana withdrawing from membership in the West African Airways Corporation a month after independence in 1957.

By 1962, of these interterritorial organizations, only the West African Examination Council remained. Nkrumah defended Ghana's withdrawal from these organizations on the grounds that it was "a demonstration of our sovereignty."[39] He feared the influence of the many British civil servants still in Nigeria on that country's leaders, and he felt that by remaining part of these interterritorial organizations, Ghana would be exposed to dangerous "neo-colonialist influences."[40] Nationalist rivalries and ideological differences between socialist Ghana and the more conservative Nigeria did much to make this breakup of interregional cooperation inevitable. As Nigeria became more and more politically divided along regional and ethnic lines Ghana took advantage of these divisions to interfere directly in Nigerian affairs. In 1959, when the Action Group that dominated the Western Region of Nigeria "became more vigorous in presenting a socialist ideology," it turned to Ghana for support.[41] This included sending men to subversion-training camps in Ghana, and forced the Nigerian federal government to realize "that it had to assume greater leadership in pan-African movements."[42] By this time the two countries were publicly trading insults. According to the CPP's paper, the *Evening*

News, Sir Abubakar Tafawa Balewa, Nigeria's prime minister, was a "dark-skinned Englishman," while to the Lagos newspaper, the *West African Pilot*, Nkrumah was a "black Hitler."[43]

The political crisis that followed the Congo's independence in 1960 did much to increase Ghana's differences with its African rivals. Ghana was one of the first African countries to send troops to the Congo when public order broke down and secessionist movements emerged. Nkrumah was determined to show that Africans could deal with their own crises and prevent the former colonial power, Belgium, from taking advantage of the situation to de facto reimpose colonial rule. He supported the Congo's prime minister, Patrice Lumumba, even to the point of signing a secret Ghana-Congo unity agreement, but most of the francophone countries of West and Central Africa supported his more conservative rival, President Joseph Kasavubu. In December 1960 these states met in Brazzaville and demanded that no state intervene either militarily or diplomatically in the internal affairs of the Congo. It was a not-so-thinly-veiled attack on Ghana, which had continued to keep troops in the Congo even after Kasavubu had demanded their withdrawal. The latter also wanted the recall of Nkrumah's representative, Nathaniel Welbeck, who had been involved in a gun battle in Leopoldville in which people had been killed. Indeed, even Ghana's supporters were unenthusiastic about that country's military contingent, commanded as it was by white officers.

Early the following year the radical states that supported Lumumba met in Casablanca. Nkrumah felt that there should be immediate political union, and it was at this meeting that the creation of the Ghana-Guinea-Mali Union was announced. However, the other states wanted no more than a common market, a common military high command, a cultural committee, and an economic-development bank. Nkrumah was also the odd man out when his suggestion that the United Nations be given a last chance to support Lumumba was turned down. Shortly after, Lumumba was captured by his Congolese enemies and murdered in the secessionist Katanga province. This crime had the effect of increasing the division between African states. The Casablanca group, in contrast to the Brazzaville group, looked increasingly toward the Soviet Union to counter the effects of what they felt were the neocolonial policies of Western countries. The death in a suspicious plane crash of the UN secretary-general, Dag Hammarskjold, in September 1961 contributed even further to this sentiment. To Nkrumah it was "a terrible example of the iniquity of colonialism which [was willing] to go to any lengths to achieve its criminal aims."[44]

In May 1961 the conservative group met in Monrovia and at this meeting was joined by Liberia, Nigeria, and other countries that rejected Nkrumah's call for an immediate political union. The Nkrumanhist press in Ghana bitterly attacked this diluted version of pan-African union, but eventually it was out of this grouping that an all-African organization of independent states, the Organization of African Unity (OAU), was to emerge in 1963. By this time the Casablanca group had collapsed, and Ghana's attempts at political union with Guinea and Mali had failed as well. At the Addis Ababa conference in May 1963, where the OAU was founded, Ghana was without the support of even its erstwhile union members.

Nkrumah's third book, *Africa Must Unite,* had appeared shortly before the Addis conference, and in it he had stressed the dangers of neocolonialism and the need for a continental union. However, it was the view of Nigeria's prime minister, Sir Abubakar Tafawa Balewa, that prevailed at this meeting. He argued that "African unity must be based on the sovereignty of all African countries, whatever their size, population, and social level."[45] On the other hand, there were some victories for Ghana. The OAU members were unanimously agreed that all African people should be free. A special coordinating committee was set up to aid liberation struggles in South Africa and in Portuguese Africa. Significantly, Ghana was not a member of this group. It was an indication of just how diplomatically isolated Ghana had become that "the first of the pan-Africanists was ignored."[46] Also, the major battles for African liberation had moved far away from Ghana, mostly to southern Africa, and countries closer to the region were the more obvious bases for freedom fighters.

Even though Nkrumah signed the OAU charter, he never gave up his determination to achieve pan-African unity, and after the OAU established a secretariat, his diplomats worked toward transforming this body into continental union government. To other African countries this was a dead issue, and they preferred to focus on practical considerations like political and diplomatic cooperation. Nkrumah also bitterly opposed regional unions, like the proposed East African Federation between Kenya, Tanzania, and Uganda, since he felt that this federation could be used as a "tool of British imperialism" in a similar fashion to how he felt the French-linked associations worked in West Africa.[47] Serious troop mutinies in Tanzania in 1964 also underscored the need for union government, particularly when that country's president, Julius Nyerere, requested British troops to restore order. But most disturbing to his fellow OAU members was the way in which Nkrumah allowed political refugees from other African countries to use Ghana as a base of subversion. These activities directly contravened the provisions of the OAU charter. The presence of these politically active refugees in Ghana was to be a continual source of friction with Ghana's West African neighbors, like the Ivory Coast, Togo, and Nigeria.

The outbreak of conflict once again in the Congo in 1964 allowed Nkrumah to stress the need for union government rather than depending "on disinterested help from Western powers."[48] He did so at the Cairo OAU summit of heads of state in 1964, but he was no more successful than he had been before. However, he was able to get Accra accepted as the site for the 1965 OAU meeting. Lavish plans were drawn up for a conference center that would cost almost $30 million at a time when Ghana was basically bankrupt. To many it seemed as if Nkrumah was anticipating that Accra would become the new African capital. To make sure that African heads of state did not boycott the meeting, Nkrumah had to adopt more conciliatory policies toward his neighbors and reign in the activities of foreign dissidents operating from Ghana. But even this was not enough to satisfy eight African states led by Ivory Coast, and they boycotted the summit. By this time Nkrumah had begun to recognize the divisiveness of continental union and agreed to compromise by agreeing to the establishment of an executive committee to revise the OAU's charter, but for even this he could not get the necessary two-thirds support. Nkrumah was so angry at this outcome that he threatened to pull Ghana out of the OAU, but Emperor Haile Selassie of Ethiopia and Sir Albert Margai of Sierra Leone prevailed on him not to do this.

MOVING LEFTWARD: 1961–66

The failure to affect policy in the Congo contributed to Nkrumah moving away from his previous position of nonalignment to a more active identification with the communist bloc. Even before Lumumba's murder, Ghana had been tilting in an eastward direction. Kojo Botsio, the minister of trade and labor, had visited Russia with a large delegation in 1960. He had come back with exciting promises of financial aid and technical cooperation with apparently no strings attached. Early in 1961 President Leonid Brezhnev visited Ghana, and by that time other East-bloc countries, like Czechoslovakia and Poland, had established diplomatic relations as well as China.

However, most visibly indicating this shift in political orientation was Nkrumah's extensive trip to the East-bloc countries in 1961. It was a great success for the Soviets as Nkrumah's speeches became more and more sympathetic to the Soviet Union. He applauded their welding together so many republics and nationalities into one union and saw this as a model that Africa could follow. Nkrumah had always been an avowed socialist, but his concern with obtaining Western funding for the Volta River Project had forced him to be ideologically circumspect. By 1961 he had secured American support for the project and could afford to be more open about his socialist convictions.

This increasing identification with socialism created a major division within the party's ranks between the old guard (represented by such long-time stalwarts as Krobo Edusei, minister of the interior, and Komla Gbed-emah, minister of finance) and a typically younger generation of socialists. For the old guard, their links and sympathies remained with the West. The socialists were themselves divided between the African socialists and the scientific socialists. The former group, led by Kofi Baako, minister of information, wanted to adapt socialism to African conditions, while the latter, led by Tawia Adamafio, the general secretary of the CPP and later minister of presidential affairs, were opposed to any such adaptation. Crisis situations like the Congo's independence tended to strengthen the position of the socialists in general as Nkrumah attributed his failures to affect the outcome of such situations "to the evil maneuvers of the western and capitalist powers."[49] In 1961 Nkrumah established the Kwame Nkrumah Ideological Institute in Winneba to train dedicated socialists and African freedom fighters. It never was particularly successful, since it was not able to attract students of high caliber, and many of its faculty from East-bloc countries could hardly make themselves understood in English, the language of instruction. Nevertheless, by 1961 socialists were in key positions in Ghanaian society. They either dominated or held commanding positions in such bodies as the TUC, the newspapers (the *Evening News* and the *Ghanaian Times*), the party, the Bank of Ghana, Ghana Commercial Bank, and, of course, the Ideological Institute.

Arthur Lewis was later on to describe the CPP as "torn in two, between Marxist and non-Marxist factions, who hate each other and alternate in Nkrumah's favor."[50] Nkrumah sought to deal with this increasingly dangerous rift in party unity in his "Dawn Broadcast to the Nation" in April 1961. He used this opportunity to attack the corruption that was then endemic in Ghanaian society. Much of this involved party members and important members of his government. The old guard were particularly easy scapegoats. For example, Krobo Edusei's wife had gone to the extreme of importing a gold-plated bed from Great Britain. The CPP had become "a very profitable source of wealth for those who held power within" the organization, and in recognition of this, Nkrumah laid down rules on what party members could own.[51] Far more meaningfully, the speech was an opportunity to acquire new followers who shared Nkrumah's socialist convictions. Old comrades who had "lost the early spirit of zeal and self-sacrifice" were demoted or dismissed, with the most important casualty being Komla Gbedemah, who had made himself unpopular by asking whether the Soviet Union would help to pay off the rapidly escalating Western debts.[52] He was removed from being the minister of finance and for a short while was demoted to being the minister of health. A few months later, along with many of the old guard, he was forced to resign, and after condemning the Preventive Detention Act in the National Assembly, he quickly left Ghana and joined other Ghanaian political refugees abroad.

The new followers embraced "Nkrumahism" and a cult of personality that assumed that Nkrumah would become the first president of Africa. They referred to him with "such ridiculous and nauseating appellations as 'Showboy,' 'His Messianic Dedication,' 'Fount of Honor,' and [most typical of all] 'Osagyefo.'"[53] In 1961 Nkrumah also established a youth organization named the Ghana Young Pioneers that was to substitute for the Boy Scout movement, which was condemned as imperialist and neo-colonialist. The hero worship of Nkrumah that its youthful members practiced, to the point of deifying him and proclaiming him their messiah, scandalized large segments of Ghana's Christian and religious population. As a result of playing a major role in leading opposition on the part of Ghana's Christian churches to this "incipient atheism," the Anglican Bishop of Ghana, Reverend R. R. Roseveare, an Englishman, was deported in 1962.[54] The Young Pioneers were encouraged to report anti-Nkrumahist sentiment on the part of their parents and teachers and "aroused more private opposition to Nkrumah and his regime than possibly any other of his quixotic activities."[55]

Contributing to Nkrumah's shift leftward was the balance-of-payments crisis that Ghana faced in 1961. By the end of that year the world price of cocoa had plummeted to under $500 a ton. The country was forced to draw heavily on its rapidly diminishing reserves. In addition, rather than cutting expenditure, the government introduced a harsh budget that expanded and increased consumer taxes, a new purchase tax, and, most unpopular of all, a compulsory five percent levy on all incomes over $330 per annum. The latter affected predominantly skilled and semiskilled workers, and the first attempt to collect the levy in September 1961 precipitated a major strike among transport workers in Accra and Kumasi and primarily among the dock and railway workers in Sekondi-Takoradi. At the time, Nkrumah was out of the country attending the Conference of Nonaligned Nations in Belgrade, but on his return he quickly came to see the strike as politically motivated. There was a wave of arrests of workers and leading members of the opposition, like J. B. Danquah and

Joe Appiah, for their alleged role in what the government considered an illegal strike. Even more indicative of the state's authoritarian lurch leftward was the arrest at this time of CPP MPs whose loyalties were also suspect.

The collapsing economy also inspired an economic shift leftward. In 1961 the Second Development Plan, which was to run until 1964, was publicly abandoned. Instead, in 1961 the drafting of a new Seven-Year Development Plan began, which was to result in the "'socialist transformation' of the economy and the complete eradication of its colonial structure."[56] Two new foreign socialist economic experts were recruited for this purpose: Professor Nicholas Kaldor, who had taught economics at the London School of Economics, and Hungarian economist Joszef Bognor. Kaldor especially believed in the need to increase compulsory saving, and a massive increase in taxation was included in the 1961 budget. Finally, this new socialist advice was presented in the CPP's 1962 *Programme for Work and Happiness* and in the 1963 Seven-Year Development Plan.

In this new economic order, the state was to dominate the economy. The Ghanaian National Trading Corporation, established in 1961, became the main importer and distributor of goods in the country. Most of the gold and diamond mining in the country was nationalized. Construction was taken over by the State Construction Corporation. The state also took over the banking and insurance industries. Industrial development was also taken over by the state, and by 1965 there were 22 wholly owned state industries with a further 20 in the process of construction. State farms were set up that relied on mechanized technology, most of which was imported from the East-bloc countries. The Builders Brigade was renamed the Workers Brigade and operated primarily on the state farms. Neither did the state permit competition from private entrepreneurs. To eliminate one particularly effective rival to the State Fishing Corporation, Nkrumah offered to put the young businessman in charge of the state operation, which would then have absorbed his company. When he declined to accept this position, knowing full well the corruption and nepotism he would face, it became impossible for him to obtain import licenses for equipment he needed for his business.[57] The only major activity to remain outside the control of the state was the Volta River Project, which was completed in September 1965.

These new economic polices did succeed in breaking the powerful grip that foreign capital had exerted in Ghana, as well as preventing the rise of a local entrepreneurial class. However, the consequences for the country's economy were disastrous. The inefficiency of the National Trading Cooperation and Nkrumah's insistence that goods from East-bloc countries should be imported resulted in terrible shortages of imports on which Ghanaians depended. Essential goods like sugar, rice, milk, flour, soap, drugs, and motor-vehicle spare parts could not be obtained in the country. Hoarding and dramatic increases in prices followed. People had to line up in the Sports Stadium in Accra to "purchase single packets of sugar."[58] The state farms functioned so inefficiently that the Workers Brigades that farmed them were unable to feed even themselves. The poorly planned, often unworkable industries faltered, and Ghana had to resort to fantastically expensive short-term loans from financial institutions in Europe to make it possible to import the basic items that the country needed. By 1965 external reserves that had been close to $500 million in 1957 had sunk to less than $1.5 million.

Compounding Ghana's economic problems was the continuing slide in the world price of cocoa. By 1964–65 it had declined to $347 a ton, and increasing marketing costs made the public share of revenue generated from the sale of cocoa negative.[59] Ironically, Ghanaian cocoa farmers produced a bumper crop that year of 572,000 tons, which was more than twice what had been produced in 1957–58. The East-bloc countries, increasingly more important as Ghana's trading partners, were only marginally helpful. They increased their consumption of Ghanaian cocoa but proved to be hard bargainers, and bought it at world-market prices while they wanted Ghana to pay for their products in Western currency. Even their aid programs turned out to have hidden strings attached. Inevitably Ghana was expected to make large contributions of hard currency to complete East-bloc projects, which by 1962 Ghanaian officials had come to see as primarily designed to help the socialist countries "meet export drives in machinery and equipment."[60] Even student-exchange programs turned out to be suspect. The quality of education available in the socialist countries was low and living conditions for African students in general were poor, with significant amounts of racial discrimination to make matters worse.

In these difficult times, widespread corruption was rife and made the mismanagement of the economy even worse. It stretched all the way from the very top to the lowest echelons of the society. In A. K. Armah's depressing characterization of Nkrumahist Ghana, in his novel *The Beautiful Ones Are Not Yet Born,* it is the few honest individuals who have become the criminals in their society, despised even by their families for not being able to cheat and steal their way to riches. Opposition was dangerous, and assassinating Nkrumah seemed the only way to effect change. In August 1962, in the border town of Kulungugu, after returning from the Upper Volta, where he had met with President Maurice Yameogo to iron out trade difficulties between the two countries, an assassin threw a grenade at Nkrumah that killed one person and wounded 55 others. Nkrumah himself received fragmentation wounds. In the following weeks there were several bomb explosions in and around Accra. Nkrumah used these attacks to strike out at those he felt had too much power. Tawia Adamafio, the minister of presidential affairs and often spoken of as Nkrumah's potential heir, and Ako Adjei, the foreign minister, who had been one of the Big Six arrested in 1948, were detained along with several hundred others suspected of involvement in the assassination attempt.

Eventually 12 people were brought to trial before a special court presided over by the country's chief justice, Sir Aku Korsah, and two judges of the supreme court, W. B. Van Lare and Akufo Addo. Five of the accused were found guilty and sentenced to death, but the evidence linking Adamafio, Adjei, and Coffie Crabbe, the executive secretary of the CPP, to the attempt was weak, and in December 1963 they were acquitted. Nkrumah was incensed, and he dismissed the chief justice. Shortly after, the National Assembly passed the Law of Criminal Procedure, which allowed the president to nullify decisions of the supreme court, which Nkrumah did for the recently completed trial. To the editor of the party-controlled newspaper, the *Ghanaian Times,* the chief justice's dismissal was well deserved, since he had "not [told] Nkrumah before hand what the verdict would be."[61] Nkrumah also used the assassination attempt to strengthen further his political power by holding a referendum to make two amendments to the constitution. One was to give the president the power to dismiss judges for reasons that appeared sufficient, and the other was to de facto make Ghana a one-party state. According to the government, a 93 percent voter turnout in this farcical referendum overwhelmingly supported these changes. At this time, most opponents of the CPP had fled the country or were in detention. Officially, in 1963 there were 586 people in preventive detention.

Nevertheless, opposition still existed, and shortly before the referendum, in January 1964, a police constable on duty at Flagstaff House in Accra, where Nkrumah had his office, fired five shots at him that missed their target but killed another security guard. Nkrumah used this attempt on his life to purge the upper echelons of the police and security forces, and from then onward the police were not allowed to carry firearms. Instead, an elite presidential unit with Russian officers took over the task of guarding the president, who had become extremely paranoid about his safety. There was once again a spate of arrests, with J. B. Danquah the most prominent victim. It was to be his last such experience, for a year later he died while still in detention in the notorious Nsawam Prison, where the other prominent Nkrumah opponent, the Ga lawyer and politician Obetsebi Lampety, had died in 1963. Faculty at the University of Ghana were also seen as disloyal, and Dr. De Graft Johnson, the director of the Institute of Public Education, was arrested and a number of foreign staff members were deported. There were rowdy demonstrations at the university with party loyalists shouting abuse at the students and breaking windows. The party's hostility was not surprising, since at that time the University of Ghana, particularly the Legon campus, was resisting Nkrumah's attempts to control admissions, appointments, and the location of programs.[62]

The regime had become so unpopular that the elections scheduled for 1965 were canceled. They were to be based on new constituencies that were to increase the size of the legislature from 104 to 198 members. Instead, the CPP's Central Committee filled these seats, which in essence meant that Nkrumah picked these members himself. Ghana was no longer even a one-party state, but directly under the personal rule of its president. A few members of Parliament were still courageous enough to speak out against the government and criticize the blatant corruption of party members, or the lack of drugs in the nation's hospitals, but inevitably such opponents were expelled from the legislative assembly. To many at the time it seemed as if the greatest danger came from the "dogmatists," who "were more Marxist than Marx and more Nkrumah than Nkrumah." It seemed as though they were "actively preparing the ground to take over the leadership."[63]

Through all of these changes, Ghana nevertheless retained ties to its former mother country. In spite of strained relationships with the British, Nkrumah had been able to get Queen Elizabeth II to visit Ghana in 1961. As late as 1964, Lord Mountbatten, a hero of the First and Second World Wars and then Britain's chief of defense staff, visited Ghana, which was an indication of how important British military training remained to the erstwhile colony. Ghana also remained a member of the Commonwealth, but in 1965, when the white Rhodesians unilaterally declared themselves independent from Great Britain, this link to the West also began to weaken. Ghana took a leading role in criticizing Britain for not preventing this seizure of power by the white minority. Nkrumah called for military intervention, and with the example of the Congo in 1960 still fresh, he hoped that Ghanaian forces would play a prominent role. Eventually, under pressure from other OAU members, Ghana was forced to break diplomatic relations with Great Britain. However, even after the latter's diplomats left, a military mission remained that included a British brigadier.

The possibility of military involvement in Rhodesia was most unwelcome to the demoralized Ghanaian military. It seemed as if the President's Own Guard Regiment (POGR) was going to succeed the regular military, which was suspect and being starved for funds. Even as Nkrumah was holding out the possibility of offensive operations in Rhodesia, he was forcing into retirement the army's most senior officers. It was this action more than any other, according to then Major A. A. Afrifa, that led to the military-police coup that overthrew Nkrumah on February 24, 1966. Nkrumah had welcomed the military coup that took place in Nigeria a few weeks before and had tried to strengthen the position of the more radical members of the military government that took power. Little did he realize how soon his own demise was to come at the hands of his own military. When this happened, Nkrumah was out of the country in China, where he had gone on a mission initiated by Ghana's fellow Commonwealth nations to end the war in Vietnam. As was the case for so many of Nkrumah's projects, it was totally unrealistic mission, since neither the Americans nor the North Vietnamese were interested in following the lead of a bankrupt African nation. The Americans were convinced that Nkrumah's collapse was imminent. They had refused to supply badly needed food aid. The North Vietnamese felt the tide of war was going their way and there was no need to negotiate. Nkrumah's own staff was dead set against the mission, but his determination to go ahead with it was an indication of how desperate the Osagyefo had become for a diplomatic triumph.

The coup itself was welcomed in Ghana with far more enthusiasm than had been the case for independence. Only the Presidential Guard put up a brief resistance, and within 24 hours the coup was over. Nkrumah's statue outside Parliament House, which proclaimed him the founder of the nation, was battered to the ground and smashed into pieces. The bars were jammed with celebrants the night after the coup. There were demonstrations of support for the new rulers, who styled themselves the National Liberation Council (NLC). Even members of the 74-man delegation that had accompanied Nkrumah to China deserted their former leader. Foreign Minister Quaison-Sackey, who Nkrumah had sent to protest the seating of the new Ghanaian government's mission at the OAU meeting in Addis Ababa, flew instead to Accra, where he pledged his loyalty to the new government.[64] The prisons emptied of Nkrumah's detainees and began to fill with new political prisoners. The CPP, with its 2-million-strong membership and 500,000 militants, offered no resistance, and the party allowed itself to be disbanded by a single radio announcement. As for Nkrumah, his friend and sometimes rival President Sékou Touré offered him refuge and made him the honorary copresident of Guinea. He was to spend five years in his new home engaged in writing projects and cultivating roses while waiting for the people of Ghana to call him back. Eventually, stricken with cancer, he was flown to a clinic in Bucharest, where he died on April 27, 1972.

APPRAISAL

The lack of any real opposition to Nkrumah's overthrow and the obvious enthusiasm with which it was greeted by Ghanaians has prompted a wide range of explanations as to why 15 years of CPP rule came to an end so easily. To die-hard Nkrumahists, echoing the words of Nkrumah, Ghana had been "captured by traitors among the army and the police who were inspired and helped by neo-colonialists and certain reactionary elements among [the] population."[65] The coup had been far from bloodless, as its defenders asserted. According to Nkrumah, around 1,600 people had been killed in the fighting and "in the looting and robbery that followed."[66] In keeping with the cold-war mentality of the 1960s, it was easy for him to single out Western intelligence sources led by the U.S. Central Intelligence Agency (CIA) as one of the main forces behind the coup. Indeed, there was a history of such subversion. As early as 1961 CIA agents had been in touch with Komla Gbedemah in Togo after Nkrumah had ousted him from power and had offered the former financial minister help in seizing power. The agency had also offered financial assistance to J. B. Danquah in 1962. Revelations about the CIA's subversive activities in Africa in general had become common knowledge, and in 1962 Nkrumah, according to the U.S. embassy officials in Ghana, "was 'pathologically obsessed' with the CIA and was passing out copies of Andrew Tully's expose, *CIA: The Inside Story,* on an indiscriminate basis."[67] The Kulungugu assassination attempt and the obvious connection of the plotters to Togo reinforced these feelings. In the last years of the regime an "atmosphere of intrigue and distrust . . . increased in intensity."[68] In 1965 even his long-serving British secretary, Erica Powell, who had transcribed Nkrumah's autobiography, was suspected of being a foreign agent.

However, there was obviously too much local support for the coup for even those on the left to accept totally this CIA-engendered explanation of events. Instead, the coup stimulated a historical materialist analysis of Nkrumah's Ghanaian socialism that criticized the superficial nature of the socialist transformation that had taken place in Ghana. Socialism had peacefully tried to coexist with capitalism with disastrous consequences.

In one of the most influential of these analyses, reliance on Arthur Lewis's conventional recommendations, in which Ghana was to rely on foreign capital for development, was seen as having been the major misstep. Very little foreign capital had been invested in Ghana. Indeed, there had been a net outflow of capital. The switch in 1961 to socialist development planning had come too late and had not resulted in a clean enough break with the capitalist past. The economy's collapse that followed had made the masses "realize that the bargains struck by the political elite were worthless to them."[69] It was not surprising that workers and peasants, who had seen their standard of living nose-dive in the latter years of Nkrumah's rule, had failed to come to the support of a regime that had so dismally failed them.

More conventional explanations have pointed to how little Ghana actually followed either capitalist or socialist development plans. Arthur Lewis left Ghana in 1958 to return to the academic world as the vice-chancellor of the University of the West Indies a scant few months after taking up his position in Ghana.[70] He had quickly become exasperated at the lack of adherence to any planning that characterized Nkrumah's government. The elaborate plan drawn up in 1963 for the socialist transformation of the economy was little more than a "piece of paper with an operational impact close to zero."[71] Nkrumah never had the patience or the discipline to follow plans, particularly those that saw agricultural development as necessary for industrial development. Neither was he constrained by the availability of funds. One economist, in describing how the 1963 development plan was implemented, observed that

> new projects appeared which had never been envisaged in the Plan but were now being pushed by contractors willing to pay commissions to the persons who accepted them. Projects were begun without feasibility studies and without competitive tendering. New enterprises were distributed among party functionaries as private fiefs, enabling them to give patronage to relatives, friends and supporters. By the middle of 1965, the development program, as far as the central government was concerned, was effectively reduced to the completion of the new conference hall in Accra in time for the meeting in November of the heads of state of the Organization of African Unity.[72]

Many commentators also focused on "the volatile, unpredictable nature of Nkrumah himself" as important in contributing to his downfall.[73] Some even believed that there was a change in his "character and personality

... during the second period of his rule." From being frugal and morally upright he had become "obsessed with his own power and ambition" as well as "superstitious, corrupt and immoral."[74] Several investigations into corruption in Ghana after the fall of Nkrumah's regime help to fuel this belief that the Osagyefo had succumbed to the culture of corruption around him. Lurid tales about his reliance on *jujumen,* traditional priests, and soothsayers, completed this portrait of the flawed leader. Unable to accept the advice of potential rivals, he had surrounded himself with syco-phants, and eventually "he had alienated nearly all classes of Ghanaian society," and "had become completely out of touch with Ghanaian realities."[75]

Others saw this political isolation as also derived from the colonial leg-acy, which "had blocked the development of a spirit of citizenship."[76] The colonialists had forced a highly centralized and authoritarian regime on people whose "heritage had very little that was of practical relevance ... in the solution of Ghana's pressing social and economic-development problems."[77] Nkrumah had filled this void by superimposing himself upon a "politically paralyzed and disoriented people."[78] His personal rule had survived as long as it did in Ghana because there had been nothing to challenge it, but neither did this system of rulership strike deep roots, and eventually the shaky facade had collapsed.

Clearly, however, there was much more to Nkrumah than the sum of his many failures. He was the towering figure of the independence era in Africa south of the Sahara. It was not surprising that he was wooed both by the East and by the West. In a visionary fashion he confronted many of Africa's fundamental problems that have yet to be solved. He did so at a particularly difficult time, when newly independent nations could not escape the rivalries of the cold war. One of the most important indications of his appeal was the way in which he attracted a host of anticolonial activists to Ghana from the many areas of the African diaspora, like George Padmore from the West Indies and W.E.B. Du Bois from the United States. Many of these outsiders wrote highly supportive accounts of the Gold Coast revolution, while both Padmore and Du Bois sought to make Ghana their new home.[79] Significantly, both men are buried in Ghana. There were many others who also spent years in Ghana contributing pro-fessional and academic skills to the cause of the new nation. African American author Maya Angelou, who was one of these expatriates, has described this as opening the "hallowed portals" to "come home at last."[80]

Undoubtedly the most important indication of Nkrumah's enduring stature is how much better he has done in retrospect than those who overthrew and succeeded him. He left a stamp on Ghanaian history that continues, long after his death, to fascinate and inspire many of his countrymen as well as people all over the world of African descent. In the following chapters we shall see just how much his countrymen continue to "render homage" to his "immortal memory," even to the point that his weakness and failures have been largely forgotten.[81] Ghana pioneered the road to independence for much of Africa. Nkrumah's violent removal from office also unfortunately brought Ghana into line with what was emerging as the dominant trend in much of the continent—the military intervention into politics.

NOTES

1. W. Birmingham, I. Neustadt, and E. N. Omaboe, eds., *A Study of Contemporary Ghana*, vol. 2 (London: Allen and Unwin, 1967), 88–89.

2. I. Acquah, *Accra Survey: A Social Survey of the Capital of Ghana, Formerly Called the Gold Coast, 1953–1956* (London: University of London, 1958), 46.

3. Ibid., 47–48.

4. *Ashanti Pioneer*, March 5, 1949.

5. G. B. Kay, ed., *The Political Economy of Colonialism in Ghana: A Collection of Documents and Statistics, 1900–1960* (Cambridge: Cambridge University Press, 1972), 94.

6. *Daily Graphic*, June 8, 1957.

7. *West Africa*, March 16, 1957.

8. T. Killick, "The Volta River Project," in *A Study of Contemporary Ghana*, vol. 2, ed. W. Birmingham, I. Neustadt, and E. N. Omaboe (London: Allen and Unwin, 1967), 393.

9. D. Rimmer, *Staying Poor: Ghana's Political Economy 1950–1990* (Oxford: Pergamon Press, 1992), 86–87.

10. A. P. Osei, *Ghana: Recurrence and Change in a Post-Independence African State* (New York: Peter Lang, 1999), 59.

11. Kwame Nkrumah, *Ghana: The Autobiography of Kwame Nkrumah* (New York: International Publishers, 1957), x.

12. G. H. Whittman, Inc., *The Ghana Report: Economic Development Opportunities, Legal Problems Relative to Investment, Sociological Factors Relative to General Development* (New York: G. H. Whitman, 1959), 167.

13. Rimmer, *Staying Poor*, 79.

14. Ibid., 77–78.

15. Francis Danquah, *Cocoa Diseases and Politics in Ghana, 1909–1966* (New York: Peter Lang, 1995), 123. Capsids are small insects that feed on cocoa pods and young plant shoots.

16. Adu Boahen, *Ghana: Evolution and Change in the Nineteenth and Twen-

tieth Centuries (Accra, Ghana: Sankofa Educational Publishers, 2000), 193–94.

17. "What Next, Kwame . . . ?" *Daily Graphic*, June 22, 1957.

18. "Nkrumah: I Am No Dictator," *Daily Graphic*, June 21, 1957.

19. Boahen, *Ghana: Evolution and Change*, 194–95.

20. Richard Rathbone, *Nkrumah and the Chiefs: The Politics of Chieftaincy in Ghana 1951–60* (Athens: Ohio University Press, 2000), 100.

21. Ibid., 113.

22. Ibid., 132.

23. Ibid., 150.

24. J. Dunn and A. Robertson, *Dependence and Opportunity: Political Change in Ahafo* (London: Cambridge University Press, 1973), 204.

25. "10th Anniversary Address," *Evening News*, June 14, 1959.

26. Dennis Austin, *Politics in Ghana: 1946–1960* (London: Oxford University Press, 1964), 386.

27. W. Scott Thompson, *Ghana's Foreign Policy 1957–1966* (Princeton, N.J.: Princeton University Press, 1969), 41.

28. Ibid., 387.

29. *West Africa*, April 30, 1960.

30. Boahen, *Ghana: Evolution and Change*, 211.

31. Kwame Nkrumah, "Africa Must Be Free," *Selected Speeches of Kwame Nkrumah* vol. 2, comp. S. Obeng (Accra, Ghana: Afram Publications, 1997), 67.

32. Thompson, *Ghana's Foreign Policy*, 32.

33. *West Africa*, December 20, 1958.

34. In 1958 France offered its colonies internal self-government within the "French Community." Guinea was the only French colony to reject this offer, and voted instead for total independence.

35. Austin, *Politics in Ghana*, 396.

36. Thompson, *Ghana's Foreign Policy*, 111.

37. A. Rivkin, "Israel and the Afro-Asian World," *Foreign Affairs*, 37, no. 3 (1959): 486.

38. *Evening News*, September 5, 1959.

39. Kwame Nkrumah, *Hands Off Africa! Some Famous Speeches by Kwame Nkrumah. With a Tribute by George Padmore written by Tawia Adamafio* (Accra, Ghana: K. Owusu-Akyem, 1960), 36.

40. Ibid.

41. T. Falola, *The History of Nigeria* (Westport, Conn.: Greenwood Press, 1999), 100.

42. Thompson, *Ghana's Foreign Policy*, 239.

43. Ibid., 240.

44. *Ghana Today*, September 27, 1961.

45. *West Africa*, June 1, 1963.

46. Austin, *Politics in Ghana*, 399.

47. Thompson, *Ghana's Foreign Policy*, 331.

48. K. Nkrumah, *Challenge of the Congo* (London: Nelson, 1967), 228.

49. Boahen, *Ghana: Evolution and Change*, 208.

50. A. Lewis, *Politics in West Africa* (Toronto and New York: Oxford University Press, 1965), 40.

51. Austin, *Politics in Ghana*, 404.

52. D. Rooney, *Kwame Nkrumah: The Political Kingdom in the Third World* (New York: St. Martin's Press, 1988), 176.

53. Boahen, *Ghana: Evolution and Change*, 209.

54. J. S. Phobee, *Kwame Nkrumah and the Church in Ghana, 1949–1966* (Accra, Ghana: Asempa Publishers, 1988), 173. He was allowed back in the country a few months later when the Anglican Church gave him a vote of confidence.

55. Boahen, *Ghana: Evolution and Change*, 219.

56. Rimmer, *Staying Poor*, 87.

57. Rooney, *Kwame Nkrumah*, 190–91.

58. Boahen, *Ghana: Evolution and Change*, 215.

59. Rimmer, *Staying Poor*, 77.

60. Thompson, *Ghana's Foreign Policy*, 275.

61. *Ghanaian Times*, December 12, 1963.

62. F. Agbodeka, *A History of the University of Ghana* (Accra, Ghana: Woeli Publishing Services, 1998), 139–48.

63. Rooney, *Kwame Nkrumah*, 239.

64. B. Fitch and M. Oppenheimer, *Ghana: End of an Illusion* (New York: Monthly Review Press, 1966), 2.

65. K. Nkrumah, *Dark Days in Ghana* (London: Lawrence and Wishart, 1968), 9.

66. Ibid., 27.

67. R. Mahoney, *JFK: Ordeal in Africa* (New York: Oxford University Press, 1983), 185.

68. Rooney, *Kwame Nkrumah*, 240.

69. Fitch and Oppenheimer, *Ghana: End of an Illusion*, 129.

70. His contract had been for two years. F.M. Bourret, *Ghana: Road to Independence 1919–1957* (Stanford, Calif.: Stanford University Press, 1960), 209.

71. T. Killick, *Development Economics in Action: A Study of Economic Policies in Ghana* (London: Heinemann, 1978), 140.

72. D. Rimmer, "The Abstraction from Politics: A Critique of Economic Theory and Design with Reference to West Africa," *Journal of Development Studies* 4, no. 1 (1969): 195.

73. Austin, *Politics in Ghana*, 416.

74. Boahen, *Ghana: Evolution and Change*, 209.

75. Ibid., 221.

76. H. Bretton, *The Rise and Fall of Kwame Nkrumah: A Study of Personal Rule in Africa* (New York: Praeger Publishers, 1966), 11.

77. Ibid., 11.

78. Ibid., 172.

79. For example, Padmore published *The Gold Coast Revolution* (London: D. Robson, 1953). Fellow West Indian C.L.R. James published *Nkrumah and the Ghana Revolution* (Westport, Conn.: Lawrence Hill, 1977).

80. Maya Angelou, *All God's Children Need Traveling Shoes* (New York: Random House, 1986), 23.

81. Rooney, *Kwame Nkrumah*, 257, quoting a speech by Amilcar Cabral, leader of the anti-Portuguese liberation struggle in Guinea Bissau on the occasion of Nkrumah's funeral in Conakry.

Logging in the rain forest of the Central Region. *Source:* Author's photograph, 1974.

Cocoa pods, not yet ripe, growing in the Eastern Region.
Source: Author's photograph, 2004.

A small village in the savanna woodland, in the rainy season, near the town of Wa in the Upper West Region. *Source:* Author's photograph, 2001.

Cape Coast Castle with the governor's residence in the background. Underneath the parade ground in the forefront are the slave dungeons. *Source:* Author's photograph, 1997.

Women porters leaving Cape Coast Castle with supplies for the British troops fighting the Asante in the war of 1874. Human porterage was necessary in the rain forest region because of the absence of beasts of burden. They cannot live in this tsetse-fly infested region. *Source:* From the *Illustrated London News*, January 31, 1874.

Stringing telegraph wires from Cape Coast to the interior during the Asante War of 1874. *Source:* From the *Illustrated London News*, February 7, 1874.

Shipping out invalids from Cape Coast Castle during the Asante War of 1874. Tropical diseases like malaria and yellow fever, along with dysentery from contaminated water, claimed more victims than the actual fighting. *Source:* From the *Illustrated London News*, February 21, 1874.

Contemporary statue of Tetteh Quashie who went to work in the island of Fernando Poo and brought back cocoa to the Gold Coast in 1878. He is credited with being the founder of Ghana's cocoa industry. The statue stands outside one of the halls of residence at the University of Ghana at Legon. *Source:* Author's photograph, 1994.

First class of S.P.G. Grammar School. This school was set up by the Church of England's missionaries in Cape Coast in 1910. It is now known as Adisadel College. The headmaster, Rev. George B. Brown (an Englishman), was a firm believer in Africans retaining their customs. Indicative of this a number of the boys in the picture are wearing African cloths. *Source:* Mr. L. Phillips, Cape Coast, 1974.

The Central National Committee delegation to London in 1934 to protest the "Obnoxious Ordinances." *Left to right sitting:* Akilagpa Sawyerr (BL), Dr. F. V. Nanka Bruce, the Hon. Nana Sir Ofori Atta (*okyenhene* of Akyem Abuakwa), Hon. K. A. Korsah (BL), James Mercer. *Back standing:* Yao Boaffo (state umbrella holder for Nana Sir Ofori Atta), K. Minta (*okyeame* or linguist, for Nana Sir Ofori Atta), W.E.A. Ofori Atta (son of Nana Sir Ofori Atta), Dr. J. B. Danquah (BL). Seated in front is Jones Osare, Nana Sir Ofori Atta's *awoso*, or soul bearer. Missing from the picture are E. O Asafu-Adjaye (BL) and H. K. Agyeman (secretary to the Kumasihene) They represented the Asantes and joined the delegation later. *Source:* Mrs. E. Armah, Cape Coast, 1974.

The Central Province Provincial Council of Chiefs meeting with colonial officials in the 1930s. *Source:* Public Records & Archives Administration, Accra.

Ghana Young Pioneers with Adowa Drums, 1962. Photo by K. Boateng. *Source:* Ghana Information Services Department.

President Nkrumah and HM Queen Elizabeth II being cheered by enthusiastic crowds in Cape Coast, November 17, 1961. *Source:* Ghana Information Services Department.

Dr. W.E.B. DuBois (with cane) and Dr. Alpheaus Hunton, his secretary on the Encyclopedia Africana project, Accra, ca. 1963. *Source:* Ghana Information Services Department.

Colonel I. Acheampong arriving at the Cape Coast Fetu Afahye Festival (the town's annual thanksgiving festival) in 1974. *Source:* Author's photograph.

Dr. Kofi Busia, Prime Minister of the Second Republic, 1969.
Photo by J. T. Ocansey. *Source:* Ghana Information Services Department.

President Rawlings, President Clinton, Hillary Rodham Clinton, and Nana Konadu Rawlings at Independence Square, Accra, March 24, 1998. Over 500,000 people filled this vast square to welcome the first U.S. president to visit Ghana. *Source:* Ghana Information Services Department.

HM Queen Elizabeth II greeting Ghana chiefs on the occasion of her visit to Ghana November 7–9, 1999. Behind her is her husband, Prince Philip and to the right is President Rawlings. An estimated 1.5 million people thronged the streets of Accra to welcome the British monarch on her second visit to Ghana. *Source:* Ghana Information Services Department.

President J. A. Kufuor with Prime Minister Tony Blair visiting a cocoa farm in the Eastern Region during Blair's visit to Ghana in February 2002. *Source:* Ghana Information Services Department.

View of Kumasi, Ghana's second city, from Maxwell Road looking down onto the central market in the distance. *Source:* Author's photograph, 2001.

Central Accra looking north up Kojo Thompson Road in the center. *Source:* Author's photograph, 2004.

Accra with Supreme Court buildings in the foreground. All the high-rise buildings in the distance have been constructed since the 1990s. *Source:* Author's photograph, 2004.

8

From Military Coup to Second Republic

THE NATIONAL LIBERATION COUNCIL IN OFFICE

The military officers who planned "Operation Cold Chop," the coup against Nkrumah's government, were able to move troops to Accra without causing suspicion. Troop movements could be disguised as part of what many believed were preparations for a Rhodesian expedition. The plotters brought in troops from Kumasi and from as far north as Tamale. They quickly took command of key points in Accra, like the radio station and the airport, while the police, who were also involved in the coup, arrested members of the government and the CPP. Only at Flagstaff House was there about six hours of resistance from the POGR. Fewer than 20 people died in this fighting, but among them was Major General Charles Barwah, the officer commanding the Ghanaian army, who resisted the attempt to place him under arrest.

The soldiers and police who staged the coup defended their actions on the grounds that Nkrumah's autocratic use of power had led to the abuse of individual rights and liberty, he had ruled in a capricious manner, the rule of law had been violated to the advantage of favorites, and he had been running the country "as his own personal property."[1] Undoubtedly of most immediate concern to the soldiers who staged the coup was the way in which they saw Nkrumah's actions threatening the army itself, the largest in West Africa. Some were long-term complaints. Major A. A. Afrifa, one of the main plotters, felt that 43 Ghanaian soldiers had lost their lives in the Congo because of Nkrumah's disastrous policies in that conflict.[2] Afrifa had contemplated using force against the regime as early as 1962, when he had returned from the Congo. He had again considered this in 1964. Nkrumah's creation of his own guard regiment, his proposal to create a people's militia, and his dismissal of the army's commanders in 1965 all seemed to point to his determination to bring the military under his direct control, as was the case of most of the state's institutions.

Two days after the coup, the army and the police established the NLC, which consisted of eight members. Its chairman was Lieutenant General J. A. Ankrah, whom Nkrumah had removed as commander of the army in 1965, and the deputy chairman was J.W.K. Harlley, the commissioner of police. The other six members of the council were divided between the army and the police, with the two most important being Major Afrifa and Colonel Kotoka, who had played major roles in planning the coup. The NLC established four committees to deal with the economy, foreign relations, administration, and relief for those who had suffered under the CPP government. The economy was the most immediate problem, and to insure that foreign nations would come to Ghana's aid, they agreed, very controversially, to honor nearly all the debts that the former government had incurred. However, the swing was to the West, and relationships with the socialist countries were discontinued. Western nations did provide immediate assistance with food and basic medical supplies. Later on, the IMF provided over $36 million in credit to pay short-term trade bills. The NLC was also able to reschedule medium-term loans with Western and socialist creditor nations.

The new government also followed a policy of economic austerity. Apart from abandoning the Seven-Year Development Plan, it canceled work on prestige projects like the Accra-Tema Motorway and the projected Nkrumah Tower, which was to be the centerpiece of the planned Trade Fair site in Accra. Ministries and administrative districts were also reorganized, so that the latter declined in number from 167 to 47 and the former from 32 to 17. The number of foreign missions were also reduced by about 40 percent.[3] An attempt was also made to place state corporations under more competent management, even to the point of bringing in foreign companies to run them. However, at the same time, the government wanted to make sure that small business was reserved for Ghanaians. Eventually, in 1968, the NLC introduced the Ghanaian Enterprises Decree, which sought to achieve this goal by restricting small retail, wholesale, extracting, processing, manufacturing, and transport enterprises to Ghanaians. To support this aim the government sought to impose stricter controls over immigration. In general, the first budget was popular. It reduced duties on essential food imports as well as on petroleum products. There was an income-tax exemption to those earning less than $468 per annum. Most risky of all, the NLC increased the price paid to cocoa farmers from $4.68 to $5.62 per load of cocoa at a time when cocoa was selling on the world market at the rock-bottom price of $306 per ton.

In the field of foreign relations the NLC also moved to defuse the near state of war that existed between Ghana and many other African countries. In 1966 a goodwill mission visited states all over Africa to mend fences, and most importantly, the NLC expelled from Ghana the refugee groups that had been living in Ghana and using the country as a base for subversion against their home countries, particularly Nigeria, Togo, and the Ivory Coast. Those refugees who were considered genuine and agreed to abide by OAU resolutions on such status were allowed to remain. Eventually, in 1967, Ghana opened its borders with its neighbors, Togo, Upper Volta, and the Ivory Coast. The NLC reaffirmed Ghana's commitment to nonalignment and pledged support for the United Nations, where Ghana supported Western initiatives. Very rapidly Ghana reestablished diplomatic relations with Great Britain, but relations with socialist countries were either ended or severely curtailed. With the United States relations were more complicated due to the war going on in Vietnam. At first Ghana supported the United States, but then, under pressure from the OAU, the NLC was forced to reverse this stand.

There were numerous commissions of inquiry set up to probe the corruption of the Nkrumah years. They dealt with the mismanagement of national corporations as well as official corruption. According to the Apaloo Commission, Nkrumah himself was guilty. At the time of his overthrow he possessed cash and other properties valued at over $6.5 million.[4] How much of this was actually his or belonged to the state, without a clear demarcation, is open to debate. Nkrumah made little distinction between the state's resources and his own, but obviously he did not spirit this wealth out of his country, like later generations of African autocrats, as his frugal lifestyle in his Guinea exile indicated. In addition, the corruption investigations were rather selective in their focus. They never undertook "a root and branch examination [that] would have discredited just about anyone [in] public office and many of them were vital to the NLC's maintenance."[5] Nearly 200 of the pro-CPP chiefs were destooled and others were elected "by popular assent and government pressure," but the regional houses of chiefs that the CPP had created were allowed to remain.[6] In general, organizations and associations of the Nkrumahist era continued to function, but were quick "to take on the color of the new regime."[7]

Soon after the coup the NLC also established the National Relief Committee to help the ex-detainees with food and clothing as well as to reintegrate them into society. The government also appealed to political exiles to return home. There were no wholesale dismissals, and instead the new government went out of its way to prevent government and municipal departments from dismissing any of their staff without NLC approval. Eventually, in 1968, the Preventive Detention Act was abolished, and those who had been detained by the former regime and were still in prison were released along with many who had been arrested in the early days of the coup.

ROLLING BACK SOCIALIST POLICIES

Publicly, the NLC government was committed to rolling back the socialist policies of the CPP. Many of the state enterprises were sold to private individuals. There was an extensive opening up of the economy to external influence, and in general the new government opted for a return to the Arthur Lewis economic strategy. However, in reality the NLC government was far more interested in correcting what it saw as the abuses in Ghanaian society than in a complete restructuring. Very quickly the inexperienced soldiers and policemen turned to the senior bureaucrats for guidance. The two most important policymaking bodies became the Economic Advisory Committee (EAC) and the Political Advisory Committee (PAC). All six members of the former were senior civil servants, while the latter was filled with politicians who had opposed Nkrumah and the CPP. So much did it seem that bureaucrats were in control that late in 1966 the NLC had to appoint commissioners to head government departments. In spite of their pro-free-market pronouncements, the reality was that the new rulers acted on the premise "that politicians and officials could pursue the common interest better than private actors in the economy."[8]

However, the mixture of state control and the polices that the IMF suggested had a limited impact on improving economic conditions in Ghana. There was some expansion in manufacturing, fishing, and the amount of locally produced foodstuffs.[9] Nevertheless, during the three and a half years the NLC ruled, it became increasingly unpopular, as it failed to accomplish what it had claimed was its most important goal. The devaluation of the cedi in 1967, which the IMF advised, did not lead to a decline in imports and higher exports. The balance-of-payments problem the country was facing continued, and inflation rose even higher.[10] The external debt increased, which put more strain on debt servicing. Ironically, this financially strapped nation became "a net exporter of capital to the developed countries."[11] Those hit hardest by these policies were workers and peasants. The IMF had suggested retrenchment in the overstaffed state enterprises, with the result that unemployment skyrocketed at a time when the cost of living was also shooting upward. Not surprisingly, there was a wave of strikes. In 1966 there were 32; in 1967, 27; in 1968, 36; and in 1969, the last year of NLC rule, 51.[12] One of the largest began late in 1966 when 5,000 workers at the Obuasi gold fields went on strike. In 1968 there was also a paralyzing strike of 8,000 railway workers in Sekondi. Shortly after, the Takoradi dockworkers followed suit. In 1969 the most violent of these strikes took place, once again in the Obuasi gold fields, and several miners were killed when the police opened fire.

Conditions for rural dwellers were also affected by the austerity polices the government followed. There were periodic attempts to improve conditions in cocoa-growing areas by increasing the price paid to farmers. It was possible to do this, as the price of cocoa on the world market steadily increased during this period. But overall there was a steady decrease in state aid to agriculture and development in general in the rural areas. One of the most significant indications of this was the overall decline in cocoa production, which went from a high of 410,000 tons in 1966 to 334,000 tons in 1969. Increased smuggling to Togo and the Ivory Coast may have contributed to this decline, in addition to the fact that even before the 1966 coup, government support for cocoa-disease control had begun to decline. This continued to be the case during the NLC period. It was most obviously seen in the dramatic decline in the availability of insecticide. Most disastrous of all for cocoa farmers, their share of the export price fell from 71 percent before the coup to 36 percent in 1969. In the new order, "cocoa continued to be treated as the milch cow of the Ghanaian state."[13] In general, the economy stagnated. In 1966 the gross national product (GNP) grew by a mere 0.6 percent, and it remained at this level during the period of NLC rule. At the same time, the population was growing at the rate of around 2.4 percent per annum.

Nevertheless, the NLC seemed inordinately generous to the military and the civil service. The country's defense budget more than doubled from 1965 to 1966. The salary difference between senior civil servants and lower-paid workers increased dramatically, so that by 1969 it was 39:1. There was talk once again of corruption in high places, and by 1967 the NLC found itself under intense criticism. Nkrumah, in Conakry, was fiercely attacking on all fronts and obviously still had supporters in

Ghana. This so upset the NLC that they posted a reward of $28,000 for bringing him and his three closest associates back to Ghana, dead or alive. In reality it was elements in the army that were much more to be feared. Once shown the way by their senior commanders, disgruntled junior officers were quick to follow with coup plans of their own. The most serious took place in April 1967, when a group of radical lieutenants tried to overthrow the government. In the fighting General Kotoka was killed, and for a while it seemed that the coup had been successful. The NLC was so badly shaken by this event that the two coup leaders were eventually publicly executed by firing squad.[14]

In a similar fashion to Nkrumah, the new rulers saw the media in general as a tool for propagating their political and ideological objectives. Significantly, when they seized power they had not denationalized the daily press. Nevertheless, a much greater degree of press freedom was allowed. New independent publications were established, like the *Legon Observer*, a fortnightly published by faculty members at the University of Ghana, and the *Evening Standard*, which was to become the mouthpiece of one of the emerging political parties. However, as the regime's popularity began to decline and criticism increased, relations between the press and the government became more strained. In October 1966 the NLC passed what it described as an antisubversion decree (Prohibition of Rumors Decree), which was designed to prevent the press from being highly critical of the new government. It became "a crime to air any statement, even if true, that might cause 'disaffection' against the NLC, the police or the armed forces."[15] On the basis of this law, in 1967, an editor of the *Evening News* was jailed for three years for reporting on dissension within the military. Shortly after, four editors of the three national dailies were fired for criticizing the government's plan to have an American company take over the financially troubled state-owned drug company.[16] In 1968 the *Legon Observer* also came under attack for criticizing the country's courts for their tardiness. The editors were forced to apologize publicly and were also fined.[17]

THE RETURN TO PARTY POLITICS

The new rulers had anticipated only a short stay in power while they looked for honest people to whom they could turn over the country, but the NLC's declining popularity resulted in accelerating this process. In September 1966, even before its popularity had begun to wane, the NLC established the 16-member constitutional commission under the chairmanship of Chief Justice Akufo Addo to draft a new constitution for the country. Most of its members were leading figures of the nationalist period and had either opposed Nkrumah or had become disillusioned with him and the CPP.[18] They were the people the military approved of, and the constitution they drafted the NLC was likely to accept. Also, the commission sought public input that was often contradictory and "indigestible."[19] In the end it was the commission and particularly its standing committee that was primarily responsible for a constitution that they hoped would "span generations, even centuries."[20] Reflective of the commissioners' backgrounds, the inspiration for this constitution came primarily from Westminster-type constitutions, like those of Great Britain and the United States, though it did contain a provision for an ombudsman based on the Scandinavian example. The language was that of the philosophers of the Western liberal tradition, like J. S. Mill and John Locke. There were only two references to socialism, and they were both pejorative.[21]

The constitution, as was to be expected, protected the interests of the military and the civil service. In trying to balance the powers of different arms of the government, it also created a very unwieldy system in which there was considerable ambiguity between the powers of the executive and those of the judiciary. This confusion was not surprising, as the constitution attempted to blend British parliamentary democracy with American constitutionalism. More immediately, the commission did not resolve the highly contentious issue of who would be barred from running for election in the upcoming elections. Instead, this was left to the NLC to determine by decree, though the committee did create a procedure whereby those disqualified could appeal for exemption. However, the question of who should be excluded became caught up in ethnic rivalries, which had quickly come to undermine the solidarity of the NLC. The feeling that the Ewe were on the offensive, even though they were hardly disproportionately represented in either the government or on its advisory committees, had created animosity between the police and the military, many of whose senior officers were Akans. The alleged coup attempt by Air Vice-Marshal Michael Otu, a Ga, who was chief of defense staff of the Ghana Armed Forces in 1968, had compounded these divisions. So too did the political activities of the NLC's chairman, Lieutenant General Ankrah, another Ga, who was forced to resign when it became known he was encouraging a political party that would support him for president in the upcoming elections.

However, it was the return to political prominence of Komla Gbedemah, Nkrumah's former minister of finance, that did more than anything else to bring the issue of ethnicity to the fore. He was seen as potentially able to rally the support of those who had brought the CPP to power, and consequently feared as a populist. In addition, he had allies in the NLC in its vice chairman, J.W.K. Harlley, and another policeman who had been added to this body, A. K. Deku, who were also both Ewes. In November 1968 Gbedemah was successful in his application to the Exemptions Commission, the chairman of which was Mr. Justice Apaloo, also an Ewe, but the NLC issued a decree that nullified this and similar actions. However, shortly after, the NLC issued yet another decree that rescinded Gbedemah's banning. Nevertheless, his troubles we not yet over. A few months before the election in 1969, he was found guilty of financial malfeasance when he had been a minister in the CPP government. The Constituent Assembly, which was then sitting, decided to include an article in the constitution banning such persons from public office, but Gbedemah was able to appeal his case. He was able to run for office while he was awaiting a judgment from the country's supreme court, which eventually ruled against him. These ups and downs fueled intense speculation about ethnic alliances and divisively thrust the issue of ethnicity into the limelight.

In addition to wrestling with the issue of who should be barred from public office, the Constituent Assembly, which was established in January 1969, also had to wrestle with other contentious issues like balancing the power of the prime minister and the president, and how much central power should be given to the regions. In general, the assembly, which consisted of 150 members elected from local bodies and organizations, consisted of men and women of prominence who were supportive of Westminster parliamentary government. Their deliberations, though at times quite heated, resulted in only modest adjustments to what the Constitutional Commission had proposed. For example, they decided that there should be no salaries for ministers, reduced the power of the judiciary, and made it very difficult to amend the constitution. The most important feature of this assembly was that it allowed the emerging political parties to pick up support from a wide spectrum of those who shared similar positions. Indeed, so rapidly did this happen that in May 1969, long before it had anticipated doing so, the NLC was forced to lift its ban on political parties. The result was that even before the assembly completed its work in August, the leading members of the assembly, like Dr. Kofi Busia and Joe Appiah, were already campaigning for support in the upcoming election.

The machinery for holding an election had already been put in place with the establishment of the Electoral Commission (EC) in 1968. This organization had been responsible for conducting the elections to the Constituent Assembly. After the lifting of the ban on political parties, the commission was given the authority to determine which should be registered. Most of all, this was an attempt to prevent the formation of parties that were ethnically based. Over 20 organizations sought registration, but by the time of the election, on August 29, 1969, they had become five political parties. There was some dissatisfaction on the part of all the parties at the speed at which the NLC had moved toward elections. Particularly was this so for the smaller parties, which had less resources and were slower in gearing up for the campaign. As an indication of how important Ghanaians recognized this election to be, over 75 percent of the potential electorate registered to vote, which was almost twice what it had been in the country's first general election in 1951 (40.5 percent). Only 47 percent of those registered had voted in 1951, but in 1969 the figure was a much more impressive 63.5 percent. Of the 140 seats contested, the Progress Party (PP), led by Dr. Kofi Busia, won 105 with almost 57 percent of the vote; Komla Gbedemah's National Alliance of Liberals (NAL) won 29 seats with slightly over 30 percent of the vote; and the rest went to the three other parties and an independent candidate.

In general, the election proceeded smoothly and with limited complaints, but very much along ethnic lines, with the Akan regions of Ghana voting overwhelmingly for their fellow Akan, Dr. Kofi Busia. The Volta Region voted almost as overwhelmingly for its fellow Ewe, Komla Gbedemah, with non-Akan-Ewe regions somewhat more divided but with the PP doing better than their NAL rivals. Neither of the two main parties, nor any of the other parties, had really significantly different election platforms. They all basically supported the NLC's vision of what Ghanaian society should be, one in which the private sector should dominate the economy, and with the immediate task of promoting "a rural renaissance . . . encouraging Ghanaian business enterprise . . . building more roads and hospitals, overhauling food marketing systems, expanding educational opportunities, and creating a favorable climate for foreign investment."[22]

Consequently, apart from ethnic considerations, the PP's overwhelming victory was also influenced by how the Ghanaian electorate viewed the main candidates. Gbedemah was at a major disadvantage because of his close association with the CPP past. He had been intimately involved in Nkrumah's strikebreaking tactics in the Railwaymen's strike of 1961, while Busia's UP, which was then in opposition to the CPP, had offered support. The memory of the CPP's heavy-handed taxation of cocoa farmers also worked to the former minister of finance's disadvantage in cocoa-growing areas. Gbedemah was not able to function as a populist as some had feared. He had never been a member of the Constituent Assembly.

The NLC was particularly suspicious of him, and there were rumors that if he did win the election he would be disqualified. Indeed, this did happen, and the NAL eventually had to find a new leader in Erasmus Madjitey, who had been Nkrumah's chief of police, but had spent two years in preventive detention.

In contrast, Busia was able to use his presence on the Constituent Assembly to win over many of its members, so that by the time of the election about two-thirds of them were in the PP camp. Many of these assembly members were associated with the organizations that had sprung up after the coup to represent local and regional interests. They were a reaction to the autocratic centralization that the CPP had practiced, and contained people who had a long history of opposition to the CPP as well as younger newcomers who had less reason to be bitter toward the CPP. In this sense they were the brightest and the best of the new political order, and Busia's being able to recruit the lion's share of their number meant that the PP's candidates had an edge over those of the NAL. Undoubtedly the most attractive of all was Busia himself. His opponents accused him of having deserted Ghana when, in 1959, he had left the country to take up a professorship in sociology in Holland. However, by this decision he had avoided certain detention and he had been able "to stay alive."[23] To his friends and supporters, the boyish-looking professor, with his long career in Ghanaian politics, had acquired the reputation of being a prophet.[24]

THE PROGRESS PARTY IN OFFICE: 1969–72

On September 3, 1969, a scant three days after the election, Busia took over as the prime minister of what was officially known as Ghana's Second Republic. His government obviously intended to follow the policies of the previous government, and indicative of this, many of the NLC's appointees remained in their positions. Victor Owusu became first the minister of external affairs but later reverted to his position in the NLC government as attorney general and minister of justice, while J. H. Mensah, who had been the NLC's commissioner for finance and economic planning, became the minister of finance. Indeed, when it came to such important initiatives, like increasing the Ghanaianization of the economy, Busia's government considerably accelerated the NLC's timetable for achieving this result. Two months after coming to office, Busia's government introduced the Aliens Compliance Order, which required aliens who lacked work permits get them within a period of two weeks or leave the country. Most of these people were West Africans, predominantly Nigerians, and between December and April 1970 about 150,000 of them were forced to leave Ghana.[25] They were mostly traders, artisans, and laborers and their families.

In June 1970 the government went one step further in promoting Ghanaianization with the passage of the Ghanaian Business (Promotion) Act. This superseded the NLC's Ghanaian Enterprises Decree, which had stipulated that within five years many small businesses in Ghana should be reserved for nationals. Instead, the new act expanded the range of small businesses that were to be off-limits to aliens and made this effective within two months. The act also specified seven categories of business that were to be reserved exclusively for Ghanaians. As was the case with the Aliens Compliance Order, implementing this act was fairly strictly enforced. However, there were not enough Ghanaians with either the capital or the expertise to take over all the business that were vacated, even with government help, and particularly for the larger businesses, the state-owned enterprises had to step in. Unlike the CPP, the PP government wanted to assist private businesses to expand their role in the Ghanaian economy. It had scaled back on the activities of the Black Star Line, Ghana Airways, and the State Fishing Corporation, and the Ghana National Construction Corporation had lost its monopoly on public-works contracts. However, the lack of local Ghanaian entrepreneurs limited how much of this large-scale business activity could be taken over by individuals, and in practice the government was forced to permit the expansion of the state's role as well.

Nevertheless, the modest expansion in production that had begun under the NLC continued. The value of manufactured goods increased, and by mid-1971 nearly all of the state-owned companies were making a profit. Food production also increased, as the country was lucky to enjoy good harvests as well as increased fish production as the Volta Lake fishing schemes became more established. The new government also made loans available to farmers, constructed feeder roads to help in marketing, and even guaranteed prices for some commodities.[26] Indeed, the government made a concerted effort to improve conditions in the rural areas, from which the country's wealth came, and consciously sought to reverse the emphasis on industrialization that had been the focus during the Nkrumah period.

However, economic growth did not keep pace with the expansion of the labor force, and by 1970 there was more than 50 percent unemployment. The Busia government was particularly concerned by this, as it realized that large numbers of these unemployed were urban dwellers who stood to gain little from what was going on in the countryside, but historically had been far more politically conscious than their rural counterparts. It was hardly surprising that there was so much unemployment, since during the 1960s the country's population grew at a rate of 2.3 percent per annum, while for much of this period the economy grew at less than 2 percent per annum. The main beneficiaries of the PP's economic polices were a relatively small number of businessmen who were able to step into the vacuum created by the removal of their foreign competitors.

Like previous governments, the PP struggled with dependence on a single export, cocoa, the price of which they could not control. The price did continue its upward trend from the rock-bottom level of 1965–66, so that by 1971 it had climbed back to over $300 per ton. Cocoa production also began a modest expansion from the particularly lean year of 1968–69, when only 334,000 tons were sold, and total sales increased to 457,000 tons in 1971–72.[27] To increase production the government doubled the price paid to cocoa farmers, from four to eight cedis per load. It was a two-edged sword, for if the price of cocoa went down on the world market, there was little likelihood that the government could pay this rate, and there would be little foreign exchange left to pay for the foreign materials that were needed if the economy was really to expand. As the price for cocoa did begin to decline, the government was not able to even pay farmers, and the highly unpopular chit system of payment developed, where the farmer had to be content with what was basically an IOU.

In addition, the earlier years of hardship had created a pent-up demand for foreign consumer goods, and in response to this situation the new government substantially relaxed the NLC's import-control policies by getting rid of most import licensing. The result was that spending on imports soared, which further limited the amount of capital available for funding development projects. At the same time, the new government continued with the NLC's policy of honoring the debts contracted in the Nkrumah era. In 1969–70 the country was actually paying out more for debt servicing than it was receiving in foreign aid. In 1971 the government was able to renegotiate the country's debt obligations. Only 10 percent of the amount originally due had to be paid, and capital inflow was then somewhat more than what was being paid out.[28]

The new government's struggles with the economy were matched by equally contentious disputes over domestic policies. Soon after taking power, the Busia government sought to amend the constitution to make it possible to fire, after six months, any official appointed by the NLC, and between March and April 1970 it fired 568 officials. Most were Ewes and Gas whose support for the new government was considered questionable.[29] One of the officials, E. K. Sallah, who was the manager of the Ghana National Trading Corporation, took his case to court, since his appointment predated the NLC. The court of appeals decided in his favor and ruled that the government should reinstate him and pay damages. Many of those fired had also filed suits, and the ruling obviously had serious implications, since Ghanaian law, like common law, is based on precedent. Busia was incensed. He accused the court of playing politics and went on radio and television to announce that "no court can enforce any decision that seeks to compel the Government to employ or re-employ anyone."[30] His actions set the government and the judiciary on a collision course, especially after the acting chief justice, Azu Crabbe, reacting to criticisms in the press about the way the Sallah case had been handled, announced that the "judiciary did not intend to share power with anyone."[31]

Busia promised that his government was "irrevocably committed to the establishment of a free press in Ghana."[32] Even though he made no attempt to surrender government control of the country's main dailies, the press was undoubtedly far freer than it had been during the Nkrumah period, and perhaps freer than it had been under the NLC, but inevitably there were conflicts. One of the first involved the editor of the *Daily Graphic*, Cameron Duodu, who disagreed with Busia's call for dialogue with the apartheid government of South Africa. In contrast, Duodu called for revolutionary action and condemned the talk of dialogue as aiding the minority racist white government. He kept up a string of highly critical editorials of Busia's dialogue approach, and eventually he was fired and replaced by someone who was far less combative. Around this time the government also arrested Kofi Badu, the editor of the opposition's bi-weekly newspaper, the *Spokesman*, for "communicating a false statement likely to injure the administration's reputation."[33] His paper had carried a story about inappropriate government spending in Colonel Afrifa's hometown, but later the charges were withdrawn.

While these confrontations were going on there was considerable debate over how to ensure the freedom of the country's press. Professor Adu Boahen of the University of Ghana, at a symposium organized by the Ghana Academy of Arts and Sciences, suggested that the government-owned dailies—the *Daily Graphic* and the *Ghanaian Times*—should be turned over to an independent press trust to run. But shortly before, attempts to do so had been defeated in the country's parliament.[34] However, the government did make one concession when it replaced the *Graphic*'s chairman, George Ofusu-Amaah, who most inappropriately was also the head of the police special branch.[35] Even though the government monopolized the daily press, nevertheless there still remained a number of lively weeklies—the NAL's *Spectator*, the Kumasi-based *Pioneer* and the Accra *Echo* (which were aligned respectively with the two minor opposition parties), and the *Legon Observer*—that were not afraid to challenge the government on such emotional issues as the expulsion of aliens and call for dialogue with apartheid South Africa.

LOSING CONTROL OF THE POLITICAL KINGDOM

Not surprisingly, as Busia struggled to control the political kingdom, Nkrumah's presence, not far away in Guinea, began to haunt him. Socialism once again began to seem more attractive than the bungling market-oriented policies of the PP, which depended so much on the unpopular advice of organizations like the World Bank and the IMF. Early in 1971, the People's Popular Party, with the radical Accra lawyer Johnny Hansen as its leader and secretary-general, was inaugurated in Kumasi "amid the singing of old CPP songs."[36] The paranoid government quickly responded by banning this party. Shortly afterward, the National Union of Ghana Students (NUGS) publicly called for an amnesty for Dr. Nkrumah, who should be "treated as an elder statesman, honored for his past achievements . . . and encouraged to live in retirement at home."[37] Busia felt threatened enough by these developments to warn publicly the pro-Nkrumahists against seeking to revive the CPP, and shortly afterward his government passed legislation making it a crime for anyone to promote by any means the restoration of the former president.

More seriously, there were a series of major strikes by civil servants, workers at the Kaiser-owned engineering company, timber-mill workers, and train drivers that indicated how much discontent there was among the country's workers. The TUC, the umbrella organization of Ghanaian trade unions, had initially called for patience as the new government wrestled with the country's economy, but by 1971 workers were no longer willing to wait. A precipitous fall in the price of cocoa during the middle of the year forced the government to introduce an austerity budget for 1971–72 that fueled even more worker discontent. There were steep increases in prices for such basic items as petroleum products, and as a result of import restrictions, goods that Ghanaians had become accustomed to having were no longer available. The highly unpopular National Development Levy of between one and five percent on all incomes above $980 brought back memories of the CPP's compulsory-savings scheme. The decision to make university students pay for their upkeep or take out government loans for this purpose stimulated students to make common cause with the country's workers and terrified the government with visions of paralyzing student-worker strikes similar to those in France in 1968. The government responded to the worker threat by passing legislation to ban the TUC on the grounds that it was a holdover from the CPP era. Shortly afterward, the government claimed that union leaders were plotting a nationwide strike to topple the PP government.[38]

The country was in a state of crisis. The austerity budget had gambled on increasing government spending to stimulate exports and also that cocoa prices would rise. Instead, in spite of price increases, imports continued to outrun exports, and by the end of 1971 the country's short-term debt, due within less than a year, amounted to the import bill for half a year.[39] With hardly any reserves, Ghana was on the brink of bankruptcy. Repayment of medium-term debts, those that the Busia government had agreed to honor from the Nkrumah era, also posed a drain on the economy, and by the end of the year both Busia and his finance minister, J. H. Mensah, were in Great Britain soliciting loans to tide Ghana through this time of crisis. However, the really significant decisions were being made in Accra, where a team from the IMF had arrived to "report on the economy and suggest remedial measures."[40] When the price of cocoa had begun to decline earlier in the year, there had been talk of the country's need to devalue its currency as the most effective way of making imports expensive. At the end of the year the government finally had to accept this unpopular measure and devalued Ghana's currency by more than 40 percent. In the space of less than four years the Ghanaian cedi had been devalued twice. The claims of those who had replaced Nkrumah with promises of improving the country's standard of living rang increasingly hollow.

The result was that less than a month after this devaluation, on January 13, 1972, when Busia was abroad in London seeking medical treatment, the Ghana army intervened to overthrow his government in a bloodless coup. The coup leader, Colonel Ignatius Acheampong, commander of the Fifth Battalion in Accra, defended what he called the "13th January Revolution" in very much the same manner that the NLC putschists had done in 1966 when they had overthrown Nkrumah.[41] He claimed that the "mal-practices, bribery, corruption, tribalism, arbitrary dismissals, economic mismanagement, dissipation of public funds, inference in judicial affairs, and a host of other malpractices that characterized the Nkrumah regime [had] come back to stay with [Ghanaians]."[42] Busia's opponents had even taken to describing him as another dictator. Nevertheless, there was less euphoria than that which greeted Nkrumah's downfall, but still there were many people "who sang 'hosanna, hosanna' when Acheampong seized power."[43] During his short stay in power, Busia had managed to alienate most of his erstwhile supporters and had proven hypersensitive to criticism, but he never came close to exercising Nkrumah's capricious power. He did try to bully his critics, whether they were civil servants, judges, or students, into silence, but he placed no one in preventive detention. Indeed, in mid-1972 his government was planning on holding local government elections, and as the influential news weekly *West Africa* speculated at the time of his coup, in a "freely conducted general election in Ghana ... the Busia government would again have been returned to power."[44]

NOTES

1. Radio Ghana announcement by the army, February 24, 1966. Quoted in Robert Dowse, "Military and Police Rule" in *Politicians and Soldiers in Ghana 1966–1972*, ed. D. Austin and R. Luckham (London: Frank Cass, 1975), 17.

2. A. A. Afrifa, *The Ghana Coup* (London: Frank Cass, 1966), 66.

3. Adu Boahen, *Ghana: Evolution and Change in the Nineteenth and Twentieth Centuries* (Accra, Ghana: Sankofa Educational Publishers, 2000), 228.

4. V. T. Le Vine, *Political Corruption: The Ghana Case* (Stanford, Calif.: Hoover Institution, 1975), 135.

5. R. Rathbone, "Ghana," in *West African States: Failure and Promise: A Study in Comparative Politics*, ed. J. Dunn (Cambridge: Cambridge University Press, 1978), 25.

6. D. Austin, *Ghana Observed: Essays on the Politics of a West African Republic* (New York: Holmes and Meier, 1976), 107.

7. Ibid.

8. D. Rimmer, *Staying Poor: Ghana's Political Economy 1950–1990* (Oxford: Pergamon Press, 1992), 106.

9. J. D. Esseks, "Economic Policies," in *Politicians and Soldiers in Ghana 1966–1972*, ed. D. Austin and R. Luckham (London: Frank Cass, 1975), 51.

10. A. P. Osei, *Ghana: Recurrence and Change in a Post-Independence African State* (New York: Peter Lang, 1999), 81.

11. Ibid., 81.

12. Y. Petchenkine, *Ghana: In Search of Stability, 1957–1992* (New York: Praeger Publishers, 1993), 40.

13. Rimmer, *Staying Poor*, 113.

14. K. Nkrumah, *Dark Days in Ghana* (London: Lawrence and Wishart, 1968), 127.

15. C. Asante, *The Press in Ghana: Problems and Prospects* (Lanham, Md.: University Press of America, 1996), 43.

16. Ibid., 47.

17. Ibid., 48.

18. R. Luckham, "The Constitutional Commission 1966–69," in *Politicians and Soldiers in Ghana 1966–1972*, ed. D. Austin and R. Luckham (London: Frank Cass, 1975), 63.

19. Ibid., 66.

20. *Memorandum on the Proposals for a Constitution of Ghana* (Accra, Ghana: Government Printer, 1968), 16.

21. Luckham, "The Constitutional Commission 1966–69," 69.

22. From a radio broadcast talk by the NLC national chairman, March 2, 1966. Quoted in Y. Twumasi, "The 1969 Election," in *Politicians and Soldiers in Ghana 1966–1972,* ed. D. Austin and R. Luckham (London: Frank Cass, 1975), 142.

23. *West Africa,* September 13, 1969.

24. Ibid., 160.

25. *Ghanaian Times,* August 5, 1970.

26. Esseks, "Economic Policies," 51.

27. Rimmer, *Staying Poor,* 112.

28. *West Africa,* August 27, 1971.

29. Petchenkine, *Ghana: In Search of Stability,* 49.

30. *Daily Graphic,* April 21, 1970.

31. Asante, *The Press in Ghana,* 54.

32. Ibid., 51.

33. Ibid, 55.

34. *Daily Graphic,* November 19, 1970.

35. *West Africa,* May 14, 1971.

36. Ibid., January 23–29, 1971.

37. Ibid., April 30, 1971.

38. Ibid., October 22, 1971.

39. Esseks, "Economic Policies," 55.

40. *West Africa,* November 26, 1971.

41. Asante, *The Press in Ghana,* 59.

42. Mike Oquaye, *Politics in Ghana: 1972–1979* (Accra, Ghana: Tornado Publications, 1980), 7.

43. Ibid., 11.

44. *West Africa,* January 21, 1972.

9

Return of the Soldiers

THE NATIONAL REDEMPTION COUNCIL

In a similar fashion to the soldiers who overthrew Nkrumah's government in 1966, Colonel Acheampong and his fellow coup leaders also had specific grievances against how Busia's government had treated the Ghanaian military. The austerity budget of 1971 had significantly reduced expenditure for the country's armed forces, by almost 25 percent. The military was expected to pay taxes on items ordered from overseas, which made it impossible to order replacement parts and supplies in general. Much of their equipment was unserviceable, and there was very little money for training and exercises. In addition, the Busia government had sought to redefine the military's role away from strictly defense of the nation to much less glamorous activities like helping the Border Guards in antismuggling campaigns, aiding the police to combat crime, and assisting with anticholera drives, and there had been talk of them assisting in development projects like road construction and the building of sanitary facilities. On an even more immediate level to the military's officers was the loss of many of their privileges, which led Acheampong to complain that "the few amenities and facilities which the army enjoyed even under the Nkrumah regime were taken away." The petty nature of many of these losses was enough for Busia to describe Acheampong's intervention as "an officers amenities coup arising from my efforts to save money."[1]

Acheampong and the middle-ranking officers who supported him were also able to take advantage of the considerable disruption in the leadership of the Ghanaian armed forces that had begun in the Nkrumah period and had continued through the NLC and PP government periods. It had resulted in a command structure that was weak, inexperienced, and, as the history of earlier attempted coups indicated, not able to control the actions of its members. Many of the middle-ranking officers felt that they had been unfairly passed over for promotion either because of their non-political nature or because of their ethnicity.[2] From as early as 1970 Acheampong had been preparing his coup, which indicated that more than the protection of amenities lay behind the coup. However, by 1972 the PP government had alienated even those who had initially supported it, and the coup reflected what was then a strong anti-Busia mood in the country. Significantly, unlike the coup against Nkrumah, which many felt had been actively supported by the CIA, no such allegations were made in the case of Acheampong's coup. The general opinion at the time was that Busia's government, which had started with high ideals, had "nothing to its credit," and that the "professor" would do better going back to "teach in the university."[3]

The new government, the National Redemption Council (NRC), was initially made up of the seven military coup leaders (majors and lieutenant colonels) and one civilian, E. N. Moore, who had been a defense counsel in the trial arising out of the 1962 Kulungugu attempt on Nkrumah's life. He became the attorney general. However, indicative of the jockeying for positions that was going on, a day later a number of more senior officers replaced all but three of the original officers. Eventually, by the end of January, 9 of the 13 NRC members were given ministerial portfolios, and the new government, in essence, represented "a coalition of the 'outs' of the NLC and Busia period."[4] The new government did not consist of a single senior officer from the NLC period. Indeed, Lieutenant General Akwasi Afrifa, who had been NLC chairman and head of state, was a Busia supporter, and he was arrested and held in detention for more than a year. Significantly, these new military rulers were all relatively young, with an average age of 40, and came from a wide diversity of ethnic backgrounds, but with an overrepresentation of Ewes. Indicative of Acheampong's dominant role in this government, he put himself in charge of the two most important ministries: the Ministry of Finance and Economic Planning and the Ministry of Defense.

The government's religious-sounding name indicated its high sense of moral purpose. It obviously intended to achieve its "revolutionary" agenda by shifting to the left. A vague kind of socialism was once more in vogue. It was not surprising that this was so, since the younger generation of officers on the NRC were "not impressed with the anti-Nkrumah posture of the older and more 'colonial officers' of the sixties." Instead, they were "irked" by what they saw as the "antics of the nakedly neo-colonial Busia administration."[5] Apart from reversing Busia's devaluation of the cedi, one of the first things that they did was to repudiate Ghana's foreign debts that they considered dishonestly incurred. In reality this turned out to be only about $84 million of the country's medium-term debts, estimated at about $268 million, and represented about half of what was owed to Britain as a result of contracts drawn up during the Nkrumah period. To many students and workers who shouted *"yentua, yentua"* ("we won't pay, we won't pay"), this was still not enough. They wanted to see all foreign debt repudiated. The revaluation of the cedi was also only partial. The 44 percent devaluation of the PP government was scaled back to 20 percent, which made the cedi worth 78 cents to the U.S. dollar.

In general, the government promised to "capture the commanding heights of the economy." As part of this "war on the economy," the NRC "compulsorily acquired majority shareholdings in four large foreign-owned timber companies and in Ashanti Goldfields, the country's principal gold-mining company."[6] Initially, the government banned the importation of items that to many Ghanaians had become essential imports, like corned beef, sardines, milk, and sugar. Shortly after Acheampong seized power, he had warned Ghanaians that the "country ha[d] been living beyond its means."[7] Eventually, however, the government set up a central organization to purchase these essential commodities, and ordered that their prices be reduced to pre-devaluation levels, and a subsidy of 23 million cedis was provided for this purpose.

To fill the gap created by restricting imports, the NRC initiated a program of self-reliance and "Operation Feed Yourself" (OFY). Initially there was considerable support for this effort, encouraged in no small part by one of the NRC's most enthusiastic commissioners, Colonel Frank Bernasko, who was the commissioner for agriculture. For a while even urban professionals were drawn into backyard farming, while university students volunteered to harvest sugar cane for the Komenda Sugar Factory in the Central Region. The government also gave generous loans to encourage farming and provided seeds and seedlings as well as fertilizer, pesticides, and expert agricultural advice.[8] The NRC also embarked on a number of irrigation projects, the most important of which were the Tono irrigation project in the Upper Region and the Dawhenya project to irrigate an area of the Accra Plains.[9]

OFY was undoubtedly the NRC's most successful program. Contributing to this success were two years of good rains in 1972–73. During this period the country was able to produce a large proportion of its food needs. Indeed, in 1973 the country was even able to export rice and in general enjoyed an unprecedented trade surplus. From a trade deficit of $56 million in 1971, the country was able to achieve a trade surplus of $204 million in 1973. OFY was later supplemented with Operation Haul the Food to Markets. Encouraged by the success of OFY, in 1975 the government introduced the second phase of this program—Operation Feed Your Industries—which was aimed at producing cash crops either for local industries or for export. Here also there were initially gains in production. To critics, however, all these gains were more the result of factors over which the NRC had no control, like increase in world prices, or they were benefits that derived from the agricultural initiatives that had been put in place by the Busia government.

Of more long-term importance, the emphasis on food-crop production affected cash-crop production, particularly cocoa, which remained the country's main source of revenue. The return on growing cocoa had been decreasing ever since the 1960s, and yields were declining because of lack of maintenance and aging trees. Busia's expulsion of aliens, many of whom had worked in cocoa farming, had been merely one more strike against this industry and had made labor more expensive. Instead, labor was switched to growing food crops like maize, cassava, and yams, which were more profitable. It was ironic that this was so, as shortly after Acheampong seized power, cocoa and many of the country's other exports experienced a significant rise in world-market prices. By 1973 cocoa was selling at over $900 a ton. Consequently, the government increased the price paid to cocoa farmers by 25 percent. It was not enough to make up for even the official devaluation of the country's currency, which, in addition, was depreciating in real value. Not surprisingly, those cocoa-growing areas close to Ghana's neighbors, Togo and the Ivory Coast, witnessed an increase in cocoa smuggling. In these francophone countries the price was higher and payment was in CFA francs, a hard currency that could be used to buy commodities that were not easily available in Ghana.[10] The NRC railed against this "subversive offence" and quickly passed a decree that made it a capital crime.[11]

Initially, however, the NRC enjoyed something of a honeymoon period with Ghanaians. Many of the government's first actions were popular. The NRC abolished the unpopular National Development Levy, workers' wages were raised by 30 percent, the TUC was once again recognized, fringe benefits for civil servants were restored, and the government promised to abolish the loan plan for university students. The military discipline that the soldiers brought to the business of government contrasted with the corruption and ostentatious display that had characterized their predecessors. Instead of traveling in Mercedes-Benzes, they were content to use more modest military jeeps. They were on time for work, and some of the more zealous officers tried to instill discipline in the notoriously lackadaisical civil service by subjecting them to military drills. For a while military members of the NRC publicly refused to accept increases in their salaries to compensate them for their additional responsibilities, and only did so when urged by the national press on the grounds that "no army moves successfully on an empty stomach."[12]

THE DEATH OF NKRUMAH AND ITS IMPACT ON FOREIGN RELATIONS

Nkrumah's death on April 27, 1972, shortly after Acheampong seized power, also presented the NRC with an opportunity to be conciliatory and statesmanlike. After the former president died in Bucharest, his body was taken to Guinea, and President Sékou Touré held a state funeral for his copresident. At first Sékou Touré refused to allow the body to be returned to Ghana unless Nkrumah was given all the honors of a head of state. Eventually, however, the NRC, which had already been taking some tentative steps toward normalizing relations with Guinea, was able to convince the Guinean president that Nkrumah should be buried in his own country without preconditions. Other African heads of state, most importantly General Gowon of Nigeria, also argued that Nkrumah's body should not end up in a mausoleum in Guinea, but should be returned for final burial in Ghana.

Sékou Touré hardly had to be worried about a fitting burial for this "true son of Africa" in his homeland. There was an outpouring of sympathy for the fallen leader, which combined a sense of "loss and at the same time guilt that he had died in a far away country."[13] Even those who had suffered at Nkrumah's hands were affected. Joe Appiah, who had spent over a year in preventive detention, and Komla Gbedemah, whom Nkrumah had fired in 1961 and who had escaped into exile, were members of the delegation that the NRC sent to Guinea to negotiate for the return of the body to Ghana. As soon as the death had been known, the NRC had sent a delegation to Nkroful, Nkrumah's birthplace, to offer condolences to his octogenarian mother, Madam Nyaniba, and preparations were begun for holding a state funeral in this out-of-the-way village almost 200 miles to the west of Accra. In Ghanaian religious belief it was unthinkable that Nkrumah's body would not be interred in his place of birth.

In general, the death stimulated the already sympathetic reexamination of the Nkrumah past that had begun in the Busia period. The NRC, at Guinea's urging, agreed to end the anti-Nkrumah campaign and allow his followers in Guinea to return home. Nevertheless, the full recognition for the former president that Sékou Touré initially demanded placed the NRC in a difficult position. Acheampong and his fellow soldiers were members of the same military that had overthrown the Osagyefo in 1966, and publicly Acheampong acknowledged that this coup had been necessary because of the "mistakes that [Nkrumah] had made."[14] At the same time, his government was moving in the direction of far more state control of the economy, which had been one of the hallmarks of the Nkrumah period. It also intended to follow a nonaligned foreign policy and was critical of the West. Acheampong described his government as revolutionary. It seemed to be Nkrumahism without Nkrumah, but by telling Ghanaians to revere Nkrumah and also those who had overthrown him, the NRC struggled with a major contradiction. Indicative of how disquieting this could be, the *Pioneer* (formerly the *Ashanti Pioneer*), which had been less than enthusiastic in its editorial on Nkrumah's death, had begun campaigning for a fitting recognition also for Nkrumah's archenemy, Dr. J. B. Danquah. He had died while Nkrumah had held him in preventive detention.

It took more than two months of negotiations before Nkrumah's body was finally returned to Ghana, as there was substantial opposition in Guinea to this decision. The body lay in state for 10 hours in Accra, and thousands, including Colonel Acheampong, paid their respects. Following this lying in state, there was then a burial service in Nkroful attended by over 20,000 people. Attending the church service conducted by the Roman Catholic bishop of Sekondi-Takoradi that preceded the burial was Nkrumah's Egyptian wife, Madam Fathia Nkrumah, and a who's who of politicians from the Nkrumah era. To the *Ghanaian Times*, the burial was a victory "for matured reasoning." It would have been "unthinkable . . . that the man who more than anyone else fought so hard to bring unity should, in death, provide the occasion for a drawn-out conflict between two African states."[15] Resolving this conflict clearly enhanced the NRC's public image. Several official delegations attended the funeral, and for a while there was even the bizarre rumor circulating in Kumasi that Chairman Mao himself would come.[16]

Negotiations with Guinea over the return of Nkrumah's body also set the tone for more harmonious relations with Ghana's West African neighbors, who had been upset by the Busia government's deportation of aliens. Shortly after the funeral the NRC undertook a review of the Aliens Compliance Order, and shortly afterward annulled this decree. The NRC sent delegations to neighboring African states to foster better relations with them. Acheampong himself visited Togo, where he spoke about the need to develop the West African Economic Community. Shortly afterward, Ghana began to export electricity to Togo and Benin. Beginning in 1973, Ghana was visited by the heads of state from a number of West African countries, and in 1973 signed a treaty of friendship with the Ivory Coast. Ghana abandoned the policy of dialogue with South Africa, and in 1973 the Organization of African Unity's Liberation Committee met in Ghana for the first time. In addition, Ghana also renewed relations with East-bloc countries, which had been disrupted in 1966. There was no attempt to revive economic projects that had been abandoned, but the government publicly recognized that Ghanaians who had been trained in the USSR and East-bloc countries were to be considered every bit as qualified as their Western-trained counterparts.

However, relations with the West were strained. Acheampong had come to power by overthrowing Busia's democratically elected government. The latter had taken sanctuary in the United Kingdom, which refused the NRC's demand that he be repatriated to Ghana to appear before the Taylor Assets Committee, which had been set up to investigate how PP ministers had acquired their assets. The issue of debt repayment remained a sensitive issue, and the nationalization of foreign companies exacerbated suspicion in the West that Ghana was again going socialist. At the end of 1973, after the Arab-Israeli conflict of that year, Ghana broke diplomatic relations with Israel. To a large extent this was determined by Ghana's dependence on Arab oil, but it reinforced the feeling that Ghana had returned to the anti-imperialist camp.

OPPOSITION DEVELOPS

In spite of the NRC's initial successes, there still remained considerable opposition to military rule. One of the NRC's first actions was to detain over 1,000 PP officials, and many former ministers remained in custody until the middle of 1973. In July 1972 the NRC reported that it had foiled the first of what were to be a series of attempted coups. Allegedly Busia supporters had tried to take advantage of "dissatisfaction among lower-ranking armed forces personnel" to "subvert the NRC" and bring back

Dr. Busia.[17] Indicative of how insecure the government felt in the face of this challenge, it passed a subversion decree that made any attempt to overthrow the government punishable by death. Both Kojo Botsio and John Tettegah, who were supposedly leaders of the second attempted coup in August 1973, were initially sentenced to death, but like the previous coup plotters, their sentences were committed to life imprisonment.[18] However, this draconian response to coup plotting had little effect. By 1977 there had been six coup attempts, and by the time the regime was overthrown in 1979, there were 20 people on death row for subversion.[19] Not surprisingly, the NRC's record on trials and punishment had come under severe criticism from Amnesty International, which felt that "fundamental human rights were being violated in Ghana."[20]

On assuming office, the NRC also moved against the country's press. The editors of three state-owned papers were briefly detained. To make sure that the press in general supported the revolution, the NRC issued in May 1972 the Defamation by Newspapers Decree, and at the same time Acheampong reshuffled his government to take charge of the Ministry of Information and Public Relations. Immediately upon seizing power, Acheampong had passed a decree indemnifying the NRC against any action undertaken in connection with the overthrow of the Busia government. The decree prevented any court from hearing cases against the state and included the state-controlled press. Members of the Busia government who felt they had been libeled in this press were barred from seeking legal recourse.

The private press was even more severely repressed. After the second attempted coup, the government passed the National Redemption Council Control of Publications Decree, which banned the publication of the *Pioneer* and the *Echo*. Eventually the banning order was lifted, and the papers resumed publication later in 1973. However, the *Pioneer* changed editors, and when it reappeared it did so as a staunch supporter of the NRC.[21] In March 1973, as the NRC began to come under more unfavorable criticism, it passed legislation similar to Nkrumah's Newspaper Licensing Act of 1963, which made it illegal to publish or circulate printed material without a license issued by the Ministry of Information. Members of the press who felt threatened by these developments began to call for the establishment of a press trust. However, to the NRC freedom of the press was far less important than using the mass media to promote the revolution. It was hardly surprising that under these circumstances those publications that were critical of the NRC were gradually forced to close. This was the fate of the *Legon Observer*, which had supported students at the three University of Ghana campuses who had protested against government policies early in 1974. Shortly afterward, the fortnightly was forced to shut down, as it could not find a printer willing to risk its printing.

By 1974 deteriorating economic conditions played a major role in increasing discontent with the NRC. Some of these factors were beyond the government's control, like the Organization of Petroleum Exporting Countries' (OPEC) dramatic increase in oil prices in 1973. The good rains of 1972 and 1973 were followed by drought conditions, even in the rainforest region of the country, and cocoa production declined. Even though between 1975 and 1979 prices almost tripled on the world market, by 1979 production had sunk to 250,000 tons. Undoubtedly, however, it was the government's poor economic policies that compounded the country's problems, and by 1975 Ghana was at the point of economic collapse. The decision to keep the price of petroleum products down, in the face of rising costs, contributed to a rapid deterioration in the balance of payments. The government's response to rising prices in general was to subsidize basic commodities at the wholesale level and introduce price controls. Inevitably this gave rise to hoarding and profiteering and a thriving black market for increasingly scarce basic commodities like sugar, flour, rice, and tinned goods. Waiting in long lines for scarce supplies of these items became a hallmark of Ghanaian life in those times. To meet its bills, the government responded by printing more money, which fueled a rampant inflation that by 1977 had reached 116.4 percent.[22] Ghana enjoyed the dubious distinction of having the highest inflation rate in the world after Argentina.

Initially the NRC made major concessions to the country's workers. One of its first decrees had canceled the development tax that the Busia government had imposed. It also introduced a five-day work week, improved the social security system, introduced an unemployment-insurance scheme, and, most popular of all, raised the minimum wage from 1.29 to 2 cedis a day. However, by 1974 the country's rampant inflation had negated these gains, and the relatively quiescent work force began to become increasingly more restless. By that time strike activity had increased beyond what it had been in the last year of PP rule.[23] It might have been a lot worse, but there had been a mass exodus of trained workers for other countries. 14,000 qualified teachers were reported to have left the Ghana Education Service between 1975 and 1981. Nigeria, which was benefiting from the boom in oil prices, was the most important destination and attracted not just teachers but workers and skilled professionals. Particularly those in public employment who were on fixed incomes were affected by the dramatic drop in their standard of living and left in droves for greener pastures.

As the economy began to unravel, corruption developed to such un-precedented levels that a new word, *kalabule,* came into use at this time to describe the "hoarding, profiteering and the unbridled cheating meted out against the majority by the few."[24] By centralizing the economy, the NRC undoubtedly made it inevitable that such abuses would develop as the experience of the 1960s had indicated. Runaway inflation meant that there was no correlation between official prices and market value and offered infinite opportunities for graft, while finally the increasing venal-ity of the members of the NRC set the standard for the rest of the society. The granting of chits to their favorites, often young women, to import scarce goods was one of the more scandalous aspects of this corruption. A thriving black market developed for Ghana's overvalued cedi. Vast amounts of cocoa money ended up in private accounts overseas. Cocoa smuggling to Togo and the Ivory Coast increased dramatically, and it was not surprising that it was during this time that the Ivory Coast surged ahead of Ghana as the world's leading exporter of the crop.

THE SMC REPLACES THE NRC: THE STRUGGLE FOR UNIGOV

Initially the NRC had been made up of the largely middle-ranking of-ficers who had staged the coup. In 1975 the service commanders, fearing that the emerging economic crisis would discredit the army as a whole, forced a change in the structure of the NRC that almost removed Acheam-pong himself. The Supreme Military Council (SMC), which replaced the NRC, contained the commanders of all the military services as well as the inspector general of police. To keep in step with this upgrading of the revolution's command structure, Acheampong was promoted from colo-nel to general. It made very little difference, and the government found itself turning to foreign moneylenders for expensive short-term loans, as had been the case in the last years of the CPP. By 1977 "it had run up debts as large as any of its predecessors."[25] Unable to solve the country's problems, the top military officers were drawn into the rampant corrup-tion around them, which alienated the lower ranks from their command-ers and was to have serious consequences four years later. Further discrediting the military, those officers who were "retired," even if they had been involved in corruption, were inevitably "rehabilitated" by being given import licenses for their personal utilization.[26]

In 1976, in a desperate attempt to regain some legitimacy, Acheampong tried to devise a new constitution that would give the military a perma-nent place in the country's government, but would bring in civilians who would not belong to parties. He called this "Union Government," or UNI-GOV. He argued that "party politics" had "brought in division, tribalism, victimization and various forms of social evil," and that instead he wanted a government "of the people, for the people" to which "everybody must belong."[27] He pointed to the bitter struggles between the CPP and the NLM in 1954–56 as an indication of how divisive political parties had been in Ghana. Party allegiance promoted tribalism, which he argued had bedeviled Busia's government. Military participation in the country's government, Acheampong felt, would ensure stability. In 1977 he set up the Ad Hoc Committee on Union Government to sound out public opinion and draw up specific proposals for how this system of government would work. Unlike the "transplant[ed] foreign systems" of government that had been accepted with no "modification or adaptation," this new form of government was to "suit Ghanaian political demands."[28]

Ironically, the effort to promote UNIGOV served to crystallize opposition to the SMC. In 1976 the Ghana Bar Association (GBA), at its annual conference, called for the return to civilian government not later than 1978. The association demanded the abolition of military tribunals and asked their members not to appear before these bodies, which gave them the "semblance of legitimacy."[29] In addition, the association demanded that a committee should be set up to draft a new constitution for the country. Shortly afterward, the Association of Recognized Professional Bodies (ARPB) also called upon the government to resign. Not surprisingly, university students also added their voice to this protest. Ever since the collapse of Nkrumah, university students in Ghana had become more and more politicized. The Oxbridge system that the University of Ghana had initially been patterned on, with student control within autonomous halls but with close links between student and hall tutor, had broken down with the rise of NUGS. Successive governments had furthered this development by dealing directly with NUGS instead of through university authorities.[30] Initially, students had supported the NRC's coup, but as the economy began to collapse, inevitably friction had developed. As early as 1974, students had demonstrated against the government, which had responded by shutting down all three of the country's universities for several weeks. In 1977, as conflict over UNIGOV intensified, students demonstrated in Accra, and the irate government again responded by closing down the country's universities for almost a month. Shortly afterward the ARPB withdrew their services, and social services in Ghana were thrown into chaos.

The SMC responded vigorously against its critics. It used its control of the media to push UNIGOV without giving its critics an opportunity to respond. The editor of the government-owned daily the *Ghanaian Times* was particularly active in defending the idea of UNIGOV, and in his editorials mounted a series of attacks on the country's professionals. Several organizations sprung up to support UNIGOV and even staged demonstrations in support of the government. There was also important support from well-known politicians like Joe Appiah and Krobo Edusei. The former was appointed "commissioner and special advisor to the head of state" and was sent abroad to win international support for the idea of UNIGOV. In response to the ARPB's strike, the government banned the organization and froze the organization's assets and its leaders' bank accounts. In a effort to intimidate medical doctors, who were influential members of this organization, armed soldiers stormed Korle Bu Hospital and forcibly ejected doctors and their families from their houses.[31]

Nevertheless, in the face of so much opposition the SMC was forced to concede that there would be a return to constitutional, but not civilian, rule on July 1, 1979. Of even more immediate significance, the government agreed to hold a referendum on the issue of UNIGOV on March 30, 1978. Inevitably, the referendum became a vote of confidence in the SMC, and served to create the very political parties that the government opposed. The largest and most prominent was the People's Movement for Freedom and Justice (PMFJ), which was formed in January 1978. Among its leaders were General A. A. Afrifa, the final chairman of the NLC; William Ofori Atta (Paa Willie), the last of the Big Six; Komla Gbedemah, the leader of the parliamentary opposition in the Second Republic; and Professor Adu Boahen of the University of Ghana. Dr. Kwame Safo-Adu, who had been the minister of agriculture under Busia, and Victor Owusu, a prominent member of the PP, formed the Front for the Prevention of Dictatorship, while G. W. Amartefio, who had vigorously opposed UNIGOV on television and had been dubbed "Mr. No," was instrumental in establishing the "Third Force."[32]

UNIGOV also had its civilian supporters. Many of them identified with the former CPP and were attracted by Acheampong's earlier Nkrumahist leanings. They formed organizations like the Society of Friends and the Peace and Solidarity Council, which functioned very much like political parties in embryo. Indeed, leading figures in these organizations were later to establish the People's National Party (PNP), which was to win the elections of 1979. Ironically, the anti-UNIGOV campaign reflected Ghana's traditional party alignments, and it was an important indication of why campaigning was so vigorous. The government enjoyed great advantages over its opposition. It liberally helped itself to funds from the Cocoa Marketing Board to fund its campaign and promised to repeal oppressive legislation like the Disqualification Decree. It returned assets seized from discredited CPP politicians, like Krobo Edusei, A. E. Inkumsah, and J. E. Hagan in exchange for their support. On the other hand, military personnel who were opposed to UNIGOV, or were at best lukewarm, were retired. Civilian officials who opposed UNIGOV or seemed unreliable were also retired. This was the fate of the country's chief justice, Samuel Azu Crabbe, who opposed UNIGOV, and Dr. Amon Nkoi, governor of the Bank of Ghana, who questioned the dubious ways in which the government was financing its campaign.

There was also considerable physical intimidation of UNIGOV opponents, who could expect very little police protection. Nevertheless, in spite of all the advantages that the government enjoyed, it was obvious, as March 30 drew near, that the UNIGOV campaign was faltering. The Ad Hoc Committee on Union Government failed to resolve just how the military would participate in the UNIGOV trinity. There was considerable confusion over whether soldiers should retire from the military or could remain on active duty. Against the background of increasingly chaotic social and economic conditions, this uncertainty added to the feeling that it was time for all soldiers to return to barracks. Neither did Acheampong's penchant for blaming Ghanaians for being a "problematic people" help him to convince those who were skeptical about his government's ability to lead the nation to prosperity.

Recognizing that he was probably going to lose, Acheampong intervened on referendum day and demanded that all polling boxes be taken to regional centers for counting, rather than being counted at individual polling stations. The electoral commissioner, Justice I. K. Abban, tried to challenge this directive, which he knew would allow for tampering with the vote. He was fired and had to go into hiding. Initial results had showed a defeat for UNIGOV, but the next day the new electoral commissioner announced that UNIGOV had won with 55.6 percent of the vote. Anticipating opposition from his opponents, Acheampong quickly banned their organizations and warned that "the days of leniency [were] past."[33] Almost immediately, the SMC arrested prominent UNIGOV opponents like Komla Gbedemah, Victor Owusu, and William Ofori Atta, as well as several university lecturers and students. By June 1978 most of these opponents were either in jail or in hiding.

SMC II REPLACES SMC I

At this time the country was in the grip of a terrible fuel crisis, and it seemed as if some kind of violent revolt was inevitable if the SMC was not removed. On July 5, a small group of officers were able to isolate Acheampong from his bodyguards and force him to sign his own resignation. The driving force behind this coup were middle-level officers, but they turned to Lieutenant General Fred Akuffo, who was chief of defense staff and second in command to General Acheampong and a member of the SMC. The latter was accused of running a "one man show" and spurning "the advice of members of the Supreme Military Command."[34] Some senior members of the SMC were also retired and some civilians were brought into the new government, which was to be a reformed version of its predecessor and came to be known as SMC II. Those who had been arrested for their opposition to UNIGOV were released and Acheampong-support organizations were disbanded, but there was no attempt to prosecute those who were responsible for corruption or mismanagement. Acheampong himself was stripped of his military rank and suffered a brief period of arrest, but eventually was allowed to retire to his hometown in the Ashanti Region. Most indicative of how little change there had actually been, Akuffo announced that he intended to retain the UNIGOV constitution for return to civilian rule in 1979.

The new government did make an effort to get control of the economy by following more conservative policies than those of its more socialist predecessor. One of its first acts was to devalue the almost worthless cedi. It was allowed to float, and by early 1979 it had been devalued by 58 percent. In addition, SMC II decided to change the country's currency by replacing what became known as "Acheampong cedis" with new notes. Currency in bank accounts was exchanged on a one-to-one basis, but there was a sliding scale for currency in circulation. The exercise was an attempt to combat the rampant inflation, but given the widespread corruption, it was obviously open to manipulation and seemed designed to benefit the rich, who had bank accounts, at the expense of the poor, who did not. In general, SMC II seemed incapable of instilling the discipline in Ghanaian life that Akuffo claimed was its most important goal. Instead, there were a number of high-profile scandals that were dealt with inconclusively and suggested that senior members of the government were at least as incompetent as their predecessors and also had something to hide. To the man on the street, the new government seemed like "the same car with a different driver."[35]

Opposition to SMC II quickly began to mount. Radicals opposed the devaluation and the government's promotion of private enterprise. Akuffo's unpopular health program and austerity cuts introduced in September 1978 unleashed a wave of strikes. The most disruptive was that by the workers at the state-owned electricity corporation. In response, Akuffo imposed a state of emergency in November and fired workers. Even the state-owned press was critical, with the *Ghanaian Times* describing the poorly patronized local elections, held during the emergency, as "elections for the rich."[36] By the end of the year it was obvious that SMC II was losing control, and Akuffo was forced to lift the ban on political parties. Indicative of how pent-up political life was in the country, within the space of two months 29 parties had been formed. Only 16 managed to get registered, and by the time electioneering began in earnest in April 1979, there were only 6 parties left. The two most important were the PNP, which presented itself as the Nkrumahist successor, and the Popular Front Party (PFP) which identified with the UP and Busia's PP. However, the vagueness of their platforms was indicative of how much they both attempted to offer all things to all people.

THE ARMED FORCES REVOLUTIONARY COUNCIL

On May 15, about a month before the election was to take place, there was yet another coup attempt. The leader was a young flight lieutenant, Jerry John Rawlings, who with fellow conspirators from the lower ranks of the army and the air force tried to seize the military headquarters in Accra. Rawlings had become disgusted with the SMC's inability to prosecute senior military officers for embezzlement of state funds. Initially his primary interest seems to have been "to force a dialogue with the senior military command."[37] But after the coup failed Rawlings was placed on trial, and rapidly he became a hero to the military's rank and file. Eventually, on June 4, some of them released him from prison, and from the radio station nearby Rawlings called for a revolutionary council to replace the SMC. For a while there was considerable uncertainty as to what would happen as elements of the army remained loyal to the SMC, and there was fighting between them and those who had released Rawlings. Eventually, the leader of this resistance, Army Commander Major General Odartey Wellington, was killed in action, and the resistance collapsed.

The coup plotters quickly established the Armed Forces Revolutionary Council (AFRC), which was made up of middle-ranking and junior officers with representatives from the lower ranks. Rawlings was elected chairman. Meanwhile, an explosive situation existed in the country. Soldiers were ransacking shops and redistributing wealth, particularly at the expense of Lebanese businessmen. Hoarded goods were confiscated and sold to the public at controlled prices. Market women who were judged guilty of hoarding and price gouging were stripped naked, beaten, and in some cases shot. In a furious response to what was seen as the entrenched *kalabule* in the country's markets, soldiers blew up Makola Market in Accra. They arrested senior officers and humiliated them. The Cocoa Marketing Board, which was riddled with corruption and which the Acheampong government had used to fund its campaign for UNIGOV, was summarily abolished. The mood was for vengeance, with university students adding to the hysteria by demonstrating with posters calling for the "firing squad for nation wreckers" and to "let the blood flow."[38] Eventually, Acheampong was brought to Accra, and on national television he was confronted with his wrongdoings. He was recklessly unrepentant, and on June 6 he and the former commander of the Border Guards, General Utuka, were executed by firing squad in full view of the public.

In spite of this bloodletting, the presidential elections that were scheduled for June 22 did take place calmly and fairly. The PNP won a narrow victory over the PFP, and their candidate, Dr. Hilla Limann, had to face a runoff against the PFP's candidate, Victor Owusu. The PNP's victory was an indication of how alive the Nkrumahist tradition remained. The party's organization was better preserved than that of the PFP, which drew its inspiration from Busia's PP. The Nkrumahists could point to the CPP's achievements and promised to restore Ghana to its earlier position of prominence in African affairs. Busia's three years in office seemed threadbare in comparison. During the elections, popular interest was diverted from the thirst for "people's justice," but as soon as it was over it was clear that there was going to be another round of executions. Rawlings, who realized that not all of the senior officers "were part of the problem," and would be needed "to assist us save and restore the integrity of [the] country" was unable to combat this mood.[39] For a while there were even rumors that he would be removed if he tried to stop the flow of blood. Only Elizabeth Ohene, an editor of the *Daily Graphic*, publicly spoke out against the mood. University students invaded her office and painted slogans on its walls calling for her death. Fortunately, she was not there.

Eventually, six former members of the SMC were quickly tried before special secret courts, and Rawlings was forced to sign their death warrants. He made attempts to delay the execution, but eventually the ranks took matters into their own hands, and on July 26, 1979, the six were executed by firing squad to enthusiastic cheers from a large crowd that had gathered on the road beside the firing range. The six consisted of two former heads of state, General A. A. Afrifa (1969) and General Fred Akuffo (1978–79), and Air Vice Marshal G. Y. Boakye, Rear Admiral Joy Amedume, former chief of defense staff General R.E.A. Kotei, and former commissioner for foreign affairs Colonel Roger Felli.

Ohene returned to the fray and called upon the churches and the professional bodies to condemn the executions and the arbitrary floggings that were taking place in marketplaces. They did with some degree of caution, but along with Rawlings's announcement that there would be no more executions, the most turbulent month in Ghana's history came to an end. There was also a new enemy to attack. Nigeria, which was also going through a transition from military to civilian rule, reacted harshly against the executions by cutting oil exports to Ghana. Eighty percent of Ghana's oil came from Nigeria, and the economy ground to a halt. But rather than undermining support for what the AFRC had described as a house-cleaning exercise, there was a tremendous outpouring of national support for the revolution. People walked to work, university students demonstrated with placards that said "Nigeria hoard your oil—we shall clean our house," and more secret trials continued.[40] However, on this occasion there were no executions, only mammoth prison sentences of up to 150 years.

The AFRC was determined that these sentences would stick. It added a set of special clauses to the new constitution known as the Transitional Provisions, which indemnified the coup makers and made it unconstitutional to undo any of the official actions that the AFRC had taken. Indeed, Rawlings was so confident that his house-cleaning actions would continue that he was willing to hand over the government, a week early, to Dr. Hilla Limann, who had won the presidential runoff. In general, the AFRC was proud of its three and a half months in office. Food was scarce, but its draconian measures had brought prices down dramatically and had slashed inflation. The price paid to cocoa farmers had been increased by 50 percent. In the last days of AFRC rule, Rawlings had abolished the Cocoa Marketing Board, which had been used by a small number of people to make vast amounts of money illegally. Also, adding to the AFRC's popularity, it had been able to collect an enormous amount of unpaid taxes. Most impressively, it had been able to awaken a spirit of enthusiasm in the Ghanaian people. Rawlings himself was wildly popular. He was obviously going to be standing by in the wings to see how the new civilian government performed. The low voter turnout in the elections, only 36 percent of the registered electorate, indicated that Ghanaians in general were not too optimistic about the PNP's ability to steer the ship of state into calmer waters.

NOTES

1. *New York Times*, January 22, 1972. For example, they lost their vehicle-maintenance allowances, they had to pay for water and electricity,

their telephone allowance was reduced, their rent payment was increased, and there were rumors of an impending salary cut.

2. V. P. Bennett, "Malcontents in Uniform—The 1972 Coup D'etat," in *Politicians and Soldiers in Ghana 1966–1972*, ed. D. Austin and R. Luckham (London: Frank Cass, 1975), 304–5.

3. Letter to the editor, *West Africa*, January 28, 1972. He did return to teaching and took a position as a professor of sociology at Oxford University in Great Britain.

4. Bennett, "Malcontents in Uniform," 308.

5. Kofi N. Awoonor, *Ghana: A Political History from Pre-European to Modern Times* (Accra, Ghana: Sedco Publishing, 1990), 225.

6. D. Rimmer, *Staying Poor: Ghana's Political Economy 1950–1990* (Oxford: Pergamon Press, 1992), 134.

7. "How Can Ghana Recover?" *West Africa*, February, 4 1972.

8. Mike Oquaye, *Politics in Ghana: 1972–1979* (Accra, Ghana: Tornado Publications, 1980), 13.

9. In 1983 the Upper Region was divided into the Upper West and the Upper East Region. The Tono irrigation project is in the Upper East Region near the town of Navrongo.

10. The CFA franc (Franc de la Communautè Financière d'Afrique) is the currency of the 14 African countries that were formerly French colonies. It was directly convertible into French francs.

11. *West Africa*, August 4, 1973.

12. "Dateline Africa," *West Africa*, April 28, 1972.

13. "All Eyes on Nkroful," *West Africa*, May 12, 1972.

14. "Acheampong's Revolution," *West Africa*, May 19, 1972.

15. "Nkrumah Laid to Rest," *West Africa*, July 21, 1972.

16. *Ghanaian Times*, May 12, 1972.

17. Ibid., July 28, 1972.

18. Ibid., April 22, 1974

19. Awoonor, *Ghana: A Political History*, 230.

20. "Amnesty and the Detainees," *West Africa*, November 13, 1972.

21. C. Asante, *The Press in Ghana: Problems and Prospects* (Lanham, Md.: University Press of America, 1996), 60–61.

22. Y. Petchenkine, *Ghana: In Search of Stability, 1957–1992* (New York: Praeger Publishers, 1993), 70.

23. Ibid., 67.

24. Oquaye, *Politics in Ghana*, 17. The word probably came from the Hausa expression *kerekabure*, which means "keep it quiet." The Hausa, often used to refer to Nigerians in general in Ghana, are predominantly from northern Nigeria.

25. Kevin Shillington, *Ghana and the Rawlings Factor* (London and Basingstoke: Macmillan, 1992), 22.

26. Ibid., 31.

27. Interview with a British Broadcasting Corporation (BBC) correspondent broadcast on January 14, 1977. Quoted in Oquaye, *Politics in Ghana*, 68.

28. Ibid., 92.

29. Ibid., 57.

30. F. Agbodeka, *A History of the University of Ghana* (Accra, Ghana: Woeli Publishing Services, 1998), 224.

31. Oquaye, *Politics in Ghana*, 59.

32. Ibid., 84.

33. Ibid., 108.

34. Ibid., 113.

35. Ibid., 132.

36. Shillington, *Ghana and the Rawlings Factor,* 40.

37. *Ghanaian Times,* October 14, 1978.

38. Shillington, *Ghana and the Rawlings Factor*, 52.

39. Ibid., 48.

40. B. Okeke, *4 June: A Revolution Betrayed* (Enugu, Nigeria: Ikenga Publishers, 1982), 57.

10

The Third Republic and the PNDC

THE THIRD REPUBLIC

On September 24, 1979, Dr. Hilla Limann was inaugurated as the president of Ghana's Third Republic. He faced a daunting task. The country's economy was still in shambles. Production had declined steadily, to the point where the country's industry operated at only 10 to 15 percent of capacity. In 1979 the cocoa exports had sunk to 189,000 tons, their lowest since independence. Timber exports registered a similar decline, as did gold, diamonds, and the country's other mineral exports. Between 1971 and 1982 the GDP fell by 12 percent, while the population grew by more than 30 percent.[1] In 1979 cocoa prices, which had been rising earlier in the decade, began to fall, and this coincided with a major increase in the world price of oil, which made it difficult to buy petroleum products on the world market. Compounding the problems of transportation, the country's road system had deteriorated so badly that it was extremely difficult to transport the country's products to market. Lack of spare parts for road transport meant that perhaps as much as 70 percent of what farmers sent to domestic markets had to be head-loaded.[2] The country's rail system was also badly deteriorated. For example, the railway lines of the Western Region that were vital for the transport of cocoa to the port of Takoradi were no longer in operation.

Drastic economic policies were obviously needed. Most of all, a devaluation of the cedi was required to combat the inflation that rapidly soared once the draconian measures that the AFRC had imposed were lifted. However, the Limann administration was terrified to do this, since similar action had brought down the Busia government. Instead, the PNP government was characterized by an inability to formulate polices. It took several months just to make ministerial appointments, and the government seemed to be waiting for foreign investors to come to Ghana's assistance. In the meantime, the PNP used the tax receipts that the AFRC had collected to pay for an import splurge that it hoped would satisfy the electorate. In an attempt to satisfy workers, the minimum wage was raised from 4 cedis to 10, and eventually, by the end of 1980, to 12. By 1981, inflation had soared to over 70 percent, and 12 cedis could only buy one loaf of bread. The state-owned factories tried to buy off worker discontent by paying them with goods that they had made and expecting them to be sold at above the controlled price. Not surprisingly, there were bitter strikes, which the government dealt with in a very heavy-handed fashion. It was not until the end of 1981 that the price paid to cocoa farmers was also tripled, but by that time the real price was less than half what it had been when SMC II had doubled prices in 1979.

Trying to meet increased expenditures resulted in massive budget deficits, which fueled even more inflation, so that by the end of 1981 it was over 100 percent. In 1980 revenue was less than half of public expenditure. So bad did the situation become in 1981 that Parliament voted down the government's draft budget, and the opposition took advantage of this situation to declare a vote of no confidence. To the people of Ghana, what this economic chaos meant was that the parallel economy that had developed during the Acheampong years continued unabated. Prices in the official economy bore no relationship to market prices. It was obviously advantageous to buy in the official economy and sell in the parallel economy, where the cedi was worth one-eighth of its official value. For example, a farmer who could buy a bag of fertilizer in Ghana at the official rate could then smuggle it across the border and sell it at a fantastic profit. He could then sell the empty bag in Ghana for more than he had paid for the bag and the fertilizer in the first instance.[3] Those who could not take advantage of such dealings tended to withdraw into subsistence farming, reducing the government's revenue base even further. *Kalabule* came back with a vengeance and was at least as bad as it had been in the Acheampong years. Inevitably there were scandals involving members of the government and their supporters. One of the most damaging involved the leadership of the PNP, who were accused of taking £2.7 million in "fees" from a British company that had received a large order for printing the nation's currency.[4]

Part of the reason for Limann's inability to stem this continuing descent into the political abyss lay in the nature of the Third Republic's constitution. It was patterned after the U.S. Constitution with its separation of powers, but with a strong presidency. Unfortunately, there was little likelihood that Limann could live up to this expectation. He was a northerner and a political newcomer, which were advantages since he was untarnished by political scandals like many of the PNP's more established leadership. However, this meant that he had no real base of his own, and he was dependent on those who had engineered his election. They expected favors in return, which meant that there was always considerable behind-the-scenes machinations.

Ethnic tensions also existed between the Ewes, who saw themselves as excluded from the government, which they felt was dominated by northerners like Limann. On the other hand, Akans held aloof, waiting for an opportunity to challenge the administration.[5] By 1981, scandals and in-feuding resulted in a purging of the party's leadership. Limann was powerless to restore order. The United National Congress (UNC), which had formed an alliance with the PNP, broke away to join the opposition (the PFP), which then had almost as many votes as the government (71 to 69). As it was, the PNP was divided between its left wing, which wanted to follow socialist principles, and the conservatives, who were more pragmatic. By the end of 1981 the opposition was also in disarray. They did not offer an attractive alternative to the PNP.[6] Rather than governing, MPs seemed far more interested in jockeying for positions as elections became imminent.

It was difficult to hush up this chaotic state of affairs, since with the birth of the Third Republic the press became freer than it had ever been since independence. There was far more coverage of the views of the minority parties than had been the case previously. Their leaders were able to use the press to berate the government for its poor performance. The government tried to counter by appointing more sympathetic editors for the *Daily Graphic*, the country's number-one daily. The constitution provided for the establishment of the Press Commission to manage the state-owned mass media and to insure its independence, and these appointments rapidly became a bone of contention. The Press Commission tried to settle what became known as the "*Graphic* rumpus" by creating new boards of directors for the state-owned media. However, in 1981 the *Daily Graphic*'s new board demanded more control over editorials, which produced yet another confrontation. Underlying these conflicts was the factionalism that had existed in the paper's editorial department ever since the 1979 political campaign, when some members had supported the PNP and others the PFP. The Press Commission was never able to resolve the disputes that roiled the newspaper, and some of them ended up in the Accra high court.[7]

Overshadowing all these considerable challenges was the even more contentious question of how to deal with the AFRC's legacy, and most of all with the still extremely popular Flight Lieutenant Jerry Rawlings. To prevent what Limann feared might be another military coup, his government tried to separate AFRC leaders from direct contact with the military. Many of the officers who had been involved with the AFRC were either encouraged to retire from the military or sent on long courses abroad. Rawlings rejected these enticements. Eventually the government forcefully retired him from the military on the grounds that his "continued presence in the Armed Forces as a serving officer [was] incompatible with his former status."[8] At the same time, the government retired key AFRC appointees: Brigadier Joseph Nunoo-Mensah, the chief of defense staff; Brigadier Arnold Quainoo, the army commander; and C. O. Lamptey, the inspector general of police.[9] There was also a well-orchestrated attempt to discredit the achievements of the AFRC government. It was claimed that the tax they had collected had not been handed over to the PNP government. The government's Military Intelligence circulated reports and rumors of plots and coups that Rawlings and his associates were allegedly planning. Even after he was retired they continued to watch him, and prevented his friends within the ranks from visiting him. Captain Kojo Tsikata, who had offered left-wing advice to the AFRC, was also watched, and at one point it seemed as if Military Intelligence wanted to kill him.[10]

There were also legal attacks on decisions that the AFRC's courts had handed down. Limann realized that this was playing with fire, but he was incapable of getting his legal friends to leave the testing of the legality of the Transitional Provisions to the next elections. In spite of a ruling by the supreme court in June 1981 that the Transitional Provisions made it impossible for Ghana's courts to review AFRC judgments, by the end of the year most of the AFRC convicts had been released by high-court judges on technical grounds. To many in the country, and especially AFRC supporters, this seemed like a deliberate attempt to undermine the June 4th Revolution.[11] The result was that left-wing organizations began to coalesce and became an increasingly important challenge to the parliamentary parties. The most important were the June Fourth Movement (JFM) and the New Democratic Movement (NDM). Initially established by left-wing students and academics, these organizations had a marxist interpretation of the Ghanaian situation.[12] They wanted to uphold what they felt had been the gains of the AFRC period and to continue the house-cleaning exercise that the AFRC had begun.

As an indication of how disillusioned Rawlings was becoming with the Limann government, in 1980 he accepted the chairmanship of the JFM. He was an ideal figure as the leader of a popular revolution. He also brought in radical members of the military who could be the foot soldiers in any future seizure of state power. Chairmanship of the JFM gave Rawlings a platform from which to attack the Limann government and its failings. The movement's members could be the cadre to implement the programs of a new revolutionary government. As Military Intelligence continued to harass members of the military and the country's economic condition worsened, it became increasingly more likely that these highly politicized soldiers would indeed enact the scenario the PNP government feared most, another military coup.

THE SECOND COMING: DECEMBER 31, 1981, AND THE PNDC

Toward the end of 1981, as the PNP continued to self-destruct, there were rumors of both left-wing and right-wing military plots to overthrow the government. On December 23, troops in Takoradi organized a coup that failed, but as was the case in 1979, the trial of the junior officers involved prompted other members of the military to act. Shortly afterward, while Ghanaians were celebrating the New Year's holiday, Rawlings and his military followers struck once again. This time it was not a mutiny, and the military side of the coup was over very quickly. The politicians were taken by surprise. Many were celebrating the new year when the military acted, and in a matter of a few days President Limann and his ministers were arrested. However, Rawlings resisted attempts to have fast trials and executions of the PNP leadership, even though he described them as a "pack of criminals."[13] He realized that such actions against SMC II had damaged the AFRC's reputation. It was enough to announce the suspension of the Third Republic's constitution and the dissolution of Parliament as well as the banning of all political parties.

At the same time, Rawlings indicated on national radio that he was asking for "nothing less than a revolution," which at the same time was to be a "holy war" against corruption.[14] He promised to continue the house-cleaning that he accused the PNP of reneging on doing, and as a strong indication of the links with the AFRC, he reinstated Brigadier

Nunoo-Mensah as chief of defense staff and Brigadier Arnold Quainoo as army commander. The new government was to be known as the Provisional National Defense Council (PNDC). Rawlings became the chairman of this body. The six other members were Nunoo-Mensah and Quainoo as well as two junior members of the military, one labor leader, the secretary of the JFM, and a Catholic priest with a strong record of service to the poor. There were provisions for expanding the council to a maximum of 11 members. There was also to be a National Defense Committee to advise the council, and the EC, which had been responsible for registering voters in the 1979 election, became the National Commission for Democracy (NCD). Its role was to see that the central government addressed the needs of the people.

Apart from including civilians as members of the PNDC, Rawlings sought to distinguish this coup from previous ones by also creating new institutions that would involve the "active participation of the people in the decision-making process."[15] The PNDC established Workers' Defense Committees (WDCs) to monitor activities in factories and workplaces. People's Defense Committees (PDCs) were to function in the same way in urban and rural communities and protect local interests and organize communal labor when necessary. These institutions were based on Cuban and Libyan models. The Interim National Co-ordinating Committee (INCC) had the task of coordinating their activities. The National Investigations Committee (NIC) investigated corruption on the part of businesses and individuals, while the Citizens Vetting Committee (CVC) did much the same, but sat in public and acted more like a judicial body that could hand out punishment. Rawlings also promised to establish People's Tribunals that would act on "evidence properly assembled," but were not to be "fettered by technical rules that in the past [had] perverted the course of justice and had enabled criminals to go free."[16] These instruments of revolutionary justice were to be the counterparts of the AFRC's People's Revolutionary Courts. However, they were to be more structured and were to exist together with the regular criminal courts. According to Rawlings, it would be left "for the people to decide the correctness or otherwise of the judgment of the two systems."[17]

THE MURDER OF THE JUDGES

Initially, the revolution meet with limited enthusiasm, but as it became clearer how much the PNDC intended to involve the people in the decision-making process, this changed. A massive demonstration took place in Accra on January 8 with placards proclaiming "JJ" to be "Our

Moses" and embracing "the Holy War."[18] There were smaller demonstrations in other cities. Students volunteered to help bring the cocoa harvest locked up in the rural areas to Tema Harbor, and defense committees sprang up so rapidly that the PNDC had to establish regional coordinating committees to insure unanimity of action. There was, however, a conscious effort to exclude the middle classes, who were described as citizens to distinguish them from the people. Rapidly, the former came to be seen as enemies of the revolution, as they indicated their displeasure at the overthrow of a legitimate civilian government. Not surprisingly, they were targeted by the defense committees, members of the armed forces, and the police. Reporters were too afraid to report these brutalities, and the media, which had been taken over by the PNDC, wanted to downplay what was obviously a dark side of the revolution. According to the ARPB, by July 1982 180 people had been killed since December 31, 1981, without any prosecution taking place.

The most heinous example of these excesses was the kidnapping and brutal murder on the night of the June 30, 1982, of three high-court judges, Justices F. P. Sarkodee, K. A. Agyepong, and Cecilia Koranteng Addow, and a retired army major, Sam Acquah, who was the director of personnel at Ghana Industrial Holding Corporation (GIHOC). They were seized from their homes and taken to a military firing range not far from Accra, where they were shot, and their bodies were partially burned in an attempt to cover up this crime. When their corpses were discovered a few days later, a visibly shaken Chairman Rawlings appeared on national television to denounce "these hideous acts of terrorism" committed by "enemies of the revolution."[19] However, there were immediately rumors that members of the PNDC were involved in the killings, as these judges had been responsible for overturning rulings handed down by the AFRC's People's Revolutionary Courts. Father Vincent Dumah, the clergyman member of the PNDC, called for an investigation of all the extrajudicial killings that had been taking place, and soon afterward he resigned from the council. The PNDC was very much on the defensive, and Rawlings was forced to proclaim publicly his innocence and that of the PNDC.

The Special Investigations Board (SIB), which was set up after the bodies were discovered, soon uncovered evidence that members of the PNDC were indeed involved in these murders. Implicated were PNDC members Joachim Amartey Kwei and Sergeant Alolga Akata-Pore. Amartey Kwei was the former secretary-general of the GIHOC Workers' Union and harbored bitter resentment against Major Sam Acquah over the way that GIHOC workers had been fired for holding rowdy demonstrations in Accra in 1981. Supposedly this was why the latter was included along with the three judges, who were seen as "enemies of the revolution." According to the SIB, Amartey Kwei was "the hub around which the wheel of conspiracy revolved." The board also recommended that Captain Kojo Tsikata, the special security adviser to the PNDC, be prosecuted as the alleged "architect of the plot."[20] The attorney general decided not to accept the latter recommendation. He felt that the evidence against Tsikata was too contradictory. Eventually, only Amartey Kwei and four killers, soldiers and former soldiers, were brought before the Accra Public Tribunal in 1983 and charged with the murders. They were eventually found guilty and sentenced to death on August 15, and shortly afterward three of the five were executed by firing squad.[21]

However, the trial left too many questions unanswered to put the rumors to rest about Tsikata's involvement and other leaders of the PNDC. What the chairman of the SIB, Justice Samuel Azu Crabbe, described as the "most outrageous crime in the annals of this country" continued to have reverberations.[22] Shortly after the trial was completed, the chief of the Defense Staff, Joseph Nunoo-Mensah, resigned, claiming that "he rejected the goals and methods of Rawlings's leadership."[23] To critics, in spite of the thoroughness of the SIB's investigations, it seemed like the PNDC was more concerned with its own survival than really getting to the bottom of this crime. Invariably, at the time of the annual memorial service for the judges and the retired army officer, suspicion about the PNDC's role in these killings resurfaces, and discussion of this case inevitably brings up other trials from the PNDC era where the fast-track justice of the Public Tribunals seemed less than blind. Most of all, suspicion continues to be focused on Tsikata's role in the affair. Indicative of how contentious this issue continues to be, in 1992 Tsikata brought an unsuccessful libel suit against the British daily the *Independent* for publishing the SIB's report that claimed that he had "masterminded" the kidnapping and subsequent murders.[24]

More immediately, what the case indicated was how much the PNDC needed to control the military and the police, who had been taking the law into their own hands. For this purpose a military tribunal was set up to try soldiers and policemen who terrorized civilians. There was also a thorough reorganization of the military to restore discipline, which had broken down badly ever since the general mutiny against the officer corps in 1979. A number of plots that were uncovered before they could be implemented and two major coup attempts, on November 23, 1982, and June 19, 1983, were indications of how much the military was out of control. Both conservatively minded and radical officers and soldiers were involved in these coups. Ethnic tensions also contributed to this disaffection, which was fueled by what was seen as the excessive control that the Ewes, Rawlings's ethnic group, were coming to have in the government. After the first coup attempt, two of the original members of the council, Sergeant Akata-Pore and Chris Atim, were dismissed from their positions, as there were well-founded suspicions that they had known about what was planned but did not inform the PNDC.[25] Indicative of how much disagreement remained even after this, the council's membership was reshuffled numerous times.

ECONOMIC RECOVERY PROGRAM I

Dealing with the country's mounting economic crisis exacerbated the divisions within the ranks of the PNDC. Initially there had been a call for "a fundamental break from the existing neo-colonial relations, and from the existing foreign monopoly control over the economy and social life."[26] This seemed to indicate that the regime was going to be pro-socialist, and as an indication of this, early in 1982 the PNDC sent two aid-seeking delegations to socialist countries. One went to Libya and the other went to Cuba, Eastern Europe, and the Soviet Union. Libya was able to supply a considerable amount of oil at concessional prices, but in general Ghana did not get the kind of financial support that it needed. There were already members of the PNDC, like Brigadier Nunoo-Mensah, who believed that Ghana should "make friends with everyone regardless of their ideological thinking or political persuasion."[27]

The inability of the socialist bloc to offer substantial help contributed to converting Rawlings and his secretary of finance and economic planning, Dr. Kwesi Botchwey, to a similarly pragmatic position. By default they realized that to get major assistance Ghana would have to turn to the donors of the capitalist world and specifically to the IMF and World Bank. This had been the advice from the Soviet Union. Nevertheless, it was a decision that was anathema to the hardcore socialist revolutionaries within the ranks of the PNDC, who "argued that even to negotiate with the IMF and the World Bank signified that the revolution had been betrayed."[28] To the radical socialists in the JFM, Rawlings became the enemy of the revolution, and removing him forcefully was the driving force behind many of the plots and coup attempts of 1982 and 1983. Botchwey's conversion to being an "apostle and evangelist" for seeking financial assistance from the West also came as a shock to those who had known him in his earlier days as a lecturer in economics at the University of Ghana.

At that time he had been an avowed marxist and "a 'born critic' of governments whether right or left . . . and an extreme hater of the World Bank and the IMF."[29]

The essential element of any IMF intervention meant devaluing Ghana's overvalued currency to stimulate exports. In the Economic Recovery Program (ERP), which the PNDC announced in December 1982, the politically explosive issue of devaluation was disguised as a subsidy to be paid on exports like timber, cocoa, coffee, minerals, and manufactured items. Important imports, with the exception of oil, were to be surcharged. The focus of the ERP was to stimulate exports, cut government subsidies on imports, reduce the deficit, and collect revenue more efficiently. Rather than waiting for the IMF to lay down conditions, the PNDC drew up a program of financial reform that closely followed standard IMF austerity programs but was tailored to Ghanaian reality.[30] To the PNDC leadership, it was the only way to get the IMF to provide the loans that the country so desperately needed.

In October 1983 the country finally accepted a clean devaluation, with the cedi going from 2.75 to 30 cedis to the U.S. dollar. In 1983 prices to agricultural producers were also increased and continued to be adjusted upward. By 1989 the price paid for cocoa had increased 14-fold from what it had been in 1982. This made cocoa farmers more willing to replant with higher-yielding hybrid cocoa. The result was a significant increase in the size of the country's cocoa crop. From an all-time post–Second World War low of 160,000 tons in 1983–84, it rose to a steady 300,000 tons by the end of the decade. The Ghana Cocoa Board also set up a system of direct payments to cocoa farmers, eliminating the highly unpopular chit system that had characterized the operations of the past and had contributed to the high rate of smuggling. Prices for local foodstuff were also increased so as to benefit farmers at the expense of urban populations. The PNDC also created a new investment code that encouraged foreign investment if it was likely to earn foreign currency. Between 1984 and 1986, 70 percent of the available new capital went toward aiding the recovery of the private sector.[31] There was also a considerable effort to collect taxes and at the same time make them more equitable and less regressive.

Western investors were impressed enough with these changes to invest in the country. The timber industry, which had earned less than $15 million in 1982, achieved earnings of $132 million in 1990. The gold industry also rebounded as a result of this investment, and by 1990 it had nearly doubled its output from a low of 283,000 ounces in 1983. There had also been some progress made in the export of nontraditional products like mangoes, watermelons, and smoked fish, which earned the country over

$60,000 in 1990. Western countries were impressed by these changes, and their annual aid commitments, which had been over $400 million in 1984, by 1989 reached almost a billion dollars.[32] Ghana was able to convince these countries that it would deal "faithfully" with its creditors, and a number of these nations wrote off some of the debts owed them.[33] Inflation fell from 120 percent in 1983 to 10.4 percent in 1985.[34] GNP growth, which had been a negligible 0.7 percent in 1983, rose to 5.5 percent in 1984, and it was to remain at this level for the rest of the decade. By 1985 Ghana had become the model for other African countries that were seeking to follow the IMF and the World Bank's prescriptions for overcoming economic decline.

This turnaround was a considerable achievement, as it came in the face of major challenges over which the PNDC had no control. In January 1983 the Nigerian government, in response to the downturn in that country's economy, decided to expel all undocumented aliens, who allegedly were taking jobs away from Nigerians. Over a million Ghanaians, who had gone to Nigeria during the years of that country's oil boom, were affected. Within the space of the two-week deadline that the Nigerian government provided for this repatriation, the PNDC and private organizations and individuals succeeded in getting these returnees back to Ghana. Most returned to their home villages, and in an amazing show of communal spirit, within the space of a few months most were reabsorbed back into national life. This reabsorption was made even more difficult by the drought conditions that prevailed in 1983. Bushfires raged even in the rain-forest region of the country, destroying cocoa farms where there is usually far too much rainfall for this to happen. The country's main source of power, the Volta Dam, was so low that by the middle of 1983 only one out of the five units at the Akosombo generating station was in operation. In June 1983 power to the Valco aluminum smelter had to be suspended and exports of power to Togo and Benin reduced by 60 percent, all with a tremendous loss of revenue to the state.

Consequently, the huge increases in prices that followed the introduction of the ERP could not have come at a worse time for Ghanaians. As government subsidies were removed and surcharges were levied on most imports, prices of even basic goods increased by as much as 100 to 300 percent. After the introduction of the new budget in April 1983, there were several antigovernment demonstrations. University students, who were already up in arms over how the PNDC had restructured university councils, took to the streets in Kumasi and Accra to protest the budget. In response the government eventually shut down the country's three universities. To suppress protest at the Legon campus, the most important center of student dissent, the government sent a group of "Revolutionary Cadres" to the campus for a "course."[35] The shutdown was to last until March 1984 and was to be followed by three other such closures or early recesses during the rest of the decade.

The budget had raised the minimum daily wage from 12 to over 21 cedis, which contributed to muting protest from the country's main trade union, the TUC, which the PNDC had already weakened by the creation of the WDCs. Far more serious than student or worker protest was an attempted coup on June 19. Eight soldiers from the failed coup of November 23, 1982, infiltrated from Togo and released prisoners who were standing trial for previous coup attempts from three of the country's prisons. For a short while the insurgents were able to hold the Ghana Broadcasting Corporation's headquarters in Accra, and proclaimed that they were "revolutionary fighters with the support of the suffering masses."[36] However, soldiers loyal to the PNDC were quickly able to regain control of the building, and the coup collapsed.

In an attempt to win support from socialists, the secretary of finance and economic planning, Dr. Kwesi Botchwey, compared the ERP to Lenin's New Economic Policy of the 1920s.[37] At that time the Soviet Union had turned to capitalists to help rebuild the economy, which had been shattered by the First World War and the civil war that had followed. It was an argument that could win over moderate socialists who were willing to be pragmatic, but there still remained considerable opposition from those the PNDC described as "infantile super-revolutionaries" to getting loans from the IMF, who, they pointed out, had "never invested in revolutions."[38] However, indicative of how much the PNDC was moving away from radical socialist solutions, earlier policies like a state monopoly of the import trade, people's shops to distribute commodities at controlled prices, and more government control of banking were quietly discarded. Membership in the PNDC also underwent significant changes. Four of the first generation of PNDC members had been military men. By 1983 only Rawlings and Warrant Officer Joseph Adjei Buadi had a military background. Significantly, one of the newcomers was a woman manager of the State Fishing Corporation, one was a trade-union official, and another was a chief from the Upper West Region. As an indication of how much the PNDC was seeking to be more socially inclusive, in 1984 a retired judge, Justice D. F. Annan, was also added to the council.

ECONOMIC RECOVERY PROGRAM II

In 1985 Rawlings decided that more than just a stabilization of the Ghanaian economy was necessary, and that a major restructuring was also needed. Officially introduced in 1986, it was known as ERP II. A start was made in restructuring the country's banking system. In 1986 the value of the cedi was determined by a weekly auction, and the rate quickly went from 90 cedis to the U.S. dollar to 150 to the U.S. dollar. Two years later the government allowed the establishment of foreign-exchange bureaus (forex bureaus) licensed by the Bank of Ghana, where individuals could buy foreign exchange at the market rate. The cedi became a fully convertible currency, and this brought to an end much of the black-market activities that had played an important role in undermining economic stability in the past. Nearly all price controls were eliminated. With an increase in the tax base it was possible to reduce the exemption level and also reduce corporate and sales taxes. The government also indicated its intention to divest itself of many of the state enterprises that were a drain on its resources. Thirty-two companies in agriculture, fishing, manufacturing, and services were affected by this decision. Undoubtedly the most controversial aspect of ERP II was the intention to reduce the staffing in the civil and the public services. The civil service was to lose 12,000 workers per year and public enterprises about 40,000–50,000 workers, with the Cocobod to lose 20,000 of its employees.[39]

There was also a major attempt to rehabilitate the country's infrastructure. Work began on the modernization of the country's two ports, Tema and Takoradi. There were major investments in repairing roads and upgrading others. New irrigation projects were begun, and there was a concerted attempt to extend potable water and electricity to every district capital. The PNDC also initiated major reforms in the country's educational system. The most important change was the introduction in 1987 of junior secondary schools, which were designed to widen the opportunities for secondary education and shift the focus from the liberal arts to more practical and cultural subjects in the curriculum. The qualifications for entry into the country's universities were also changed. The government also proposed a reduction in subsidies to secondary and tertiary education, which meant that students were going to have to fund some of the cost of their education. In 1986 the government created a new autonomous Internal Revenue Service, and there were concerted attempts to restructure the tax-collecting system. Self-employed people, who in the past had avoided paying income tax, were brought onto the tax rolls and given the responsibility of collecting this money.

In reality, the difference between ERP I and ERP II was not as sharp as it seemed on the surface. There was considerable overlap between what was described in official circles as the stabilization phase and the structural-adjustment and development phase. At times there could be conflict between the short-term needs of stabilization and the more long-

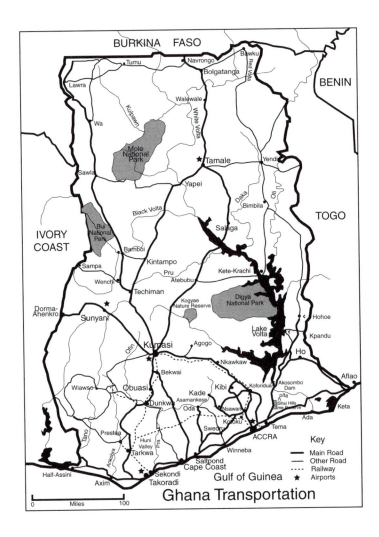

Ghana Transportation

term needs of development. Nevertheless, by the end of the 1980s even the PNDC's critics were willing to concede that the government had brought about a significant overall improvement in the country's economy. There had been a reversal of economic decline and the resumption of growth. Chronic budget crises had ended, and a significant rehabilitation of the country's infrastructure was underway. However, critics could point to the lack of any real structural change in how the economy functioned, as the country was still as dependent as ever on a few export crops. Indeed, during the 1980s the prices for these exports declined. By 1987 the price of cocoa had sunk to $1,500 per metric ton, which was lower than what the World Bank had projected, and it was eventually to fall to $600 per metric ton in 1989.

Nevertheless, the country did not face a balance-of-payments problem, as had been the case in the past when prices for exports declined. The substantial inflows of capital meant that it was possible to increase imports and still maintain an overall balance-of-payments surplus. The cost, however, was a ballooning national debt. By 1987 the long-term debt had doubled from what it had been in 1983 and was continuing to grow at an alarming rate. To critics it also seemed as if Ghana had lost control over its own economic polices to the IMF and World Bank, and hordes of foreign consultants had taken over the day-to-day operation of the economy.

Undoubtedly the most serious criticism of the ERPs was that whatever their macroeconomic successes, they had done very little for average Ghanaians. For most Ghanaians there was a hollow ring to the government's claim in 1986 that the growth in real income was increasing by two percent per annum. There were more goods available in the stores, but with the removal of subsidies they were beyond the reach of most people. Fertilizers and insecticides were too expensive for farmers to afford, which undermined the PNDC's stated goal of increasing agricultural productivity. User fees for education, health services, and public utilities meant that many people could no longer benefit from these services. As the government cut back on its expenditure and reduced employment, there had been significant job losses that were not compensated for by increased employment opportunities in the private sector. The PNDC had come to power claiming that it intended to champion the interests of the "toiling and sweating masses," but neither ERP I nor II really tackled the issue of chronic unemployment or underemployment.

The Program of Action to Mitigate the Social Cost of Adjustment (PAM-SCAD), which the government introduced in 1989, was an indication that it did recognize that the lot of the underprivileged had not improved. Rawlings maintained that one of his government's main aims was to improve conditions among "Ghanaians toiling away in rural areas."[40] However, in spite of increases in the producer price paid for cocoa, farmers remained among the poorer Ghanaians. Compounding this inequality, as a 1989 report indicated, there remained major divisions among this population, with 32 percent of them receiving 94 percent of the total income and 68 percent receiving only 6 percent.[41] Inflation, which had declined to 10 percent in 1985, had climbed back to 25 percent in 1986, reached 40 percent in 1987, and hovered somewhat below this for the rest of the decade.

According to a U.S. House of Representatives mission that visited Ghana in 1988, particularly urban Ghanaians did not believe that they were benefiting from the ERPs. Government officials conceded that the programs were unpopular, and if put to a vote would have lost in urban areas. Even Captain Kojo Tsikata, a leading member of the PNDC, recognized that there was a vast divergence between what the international financial institutions were saying in praise about the "economic recovery" and how "life was tough for the common man who deserve[d] to enjoy more and more fruits of [the] recovery."[42] However, not all Ghanaians were affected in the same negative manner by the ERPs' policies. For those on fixed incomes, the statistics do indicate that they suffered a decline in their standard of living after 1985, when inflation had overtaken the wage increases they had initially received from the PNDC.[43] Among the self-employed the situation was more varied. For example, with the rehabilitation of the country's roads, the number of vehicles had increased dramatically, and roadside mechanics were one group that had done quite well.[44] However, in general even supporters conceded that "the government [had] saved the country at the expense of the people."[45] In his December 31, 1986, broadcast to the nation, Rawlings promised "a free and frank debate on the direction of the economy." However, he was obviously afraid to allow this to happen fearing that it would degenerate into what he envisaged would be "rival gangs tearing at each other's throats."[46]

MAINTAINING CONTROL

Coupled with attempts to be more inclusive, the PNDC also sought to exercise control over the institutions of the state and to use them, if necessary, to eliminate opposition. From the start of PNDC rule Rawlings made changes in the administration of the Ghanaian news media. There was a reshuffling of editors and directors of the public media to ensure that the aims of the revolution were better promoted. To reflect this new emphasis, at the beginning of 1983 the *Daily Graphic* became the *People's Daily Graphic*. Like previous governments, the PNDC established a series of newspaper laws that made it necessary to get a license before setting up a newspaper. Initially some independent publications ignored this requirement, but after a number of such papers were attacked by PNDC supporters for trying to subvert the revolution, they came into line with this requirement, and most importantly refrained from being critical of the government's policies.

Preventing the independent press from obtaining newsprint was a subtle method of forcing these publications out of business. More directly, the

PNDC banned a number of independent newspapers that were accused of "distorting the news," "fabricating stories," or, in the case of the *Catholic Standard* in 1985, for "unpatriotic reporting."[47] Even the government press could incur the PNDC's displeasure, which inevitably meant the removal of offending editors. It was a state of affairs that contributed to what even Rawlings acknowledged was leading to the return of the "culture of silence."[48] Not surprisingly, by 1990 there were more sports and lotto papers being published in the country than those that covered political and economic issues.

Even religious organizations were subjected to state control. In the 1980s something of a Christian revivalist movement swept the southern half of the country, partly inspired by American gospel churches, which discovered Ghana, and indeed much of Africa, as a fertile ground for missionary activity. Foreign faith healers from the United States and Europe were regular visitors to Ghana, and their videos and cassette recordings did much to popularize the appeal of what, to many critics in Ghana, were seen as "spiritually fraudulent . . . money-making machines" that took "advantage of the naivety of their followers."[49]

In 1989 the PNDC government "ordered a freeze" on two of the foreign churches operating in Ghana, the Church of Jesus Christ of Latter-day Saints (the Mormons) and the Jehovah's Witnesses. Two local sects were also banned, and the government passed a law making it necessary for all churches in Ghana, which at that time included over 600 Gospel/Pentecostal churches and sects, to apply for official approval to operate.[50] The mainstream religious bodies belonging to the Christian Council of Churches and the Conference of Catholic Bishops protested this Religious Bodies (Registration) Law on the grounds that it was "uncalled for" and represented the greatest affront to religious freedom in the country.[51] However, the government insisted that the law was only intended to protect the interests of all citizens.

The "immorality" of many of the country's self-styled prophets and their avaricious search for wealth did trigger considerable public concern.[52] Exchanges in the state-controlled media also insinuated that foreign missionaries were inherently racist, potentially CIA spies, and unpatriotic.[53] By controlling their activities, the PNDC maintained its revolutionary anti-imperialist credentials and took advantage of the belief in Ghana that Christian churches should maintain high standards of conduct. For similar reasons, the PNDC's passage of family laws in 1985 also received considerable support, since they were designed to protect the disadvantaged, primarily women and children. The Head of Family (Accountability) Law made heads of families accountable to all other members, so as to prevent these often illiterate persons from being cheated in the distribution of family property. The Intestate Succession Law sought to resolve the contentious issue of the inheritance of the self-acquired property of an intestate by guaranteeing that surviving spouses and children would inherit the bulk of this property rather than the lineage.

The PNDC also used its various investigative bodies to intimidate its opponents, primarily members of the "bourgeoisie." Nearly "every professional or business person known to the public appeared before [the CVC] in Accra or in its Regional Offices."[54] Lawyers were particularly singled out, with the *People's Daily Graphic* publishing the "shocking figures unearthed" for their nonpayment of taxes.[55] The WDCs and PDCs also assumed judicial roles that included rent cases, land disputes, family matters, and worker versus management disputes. These bodies operated independently of the regular courts. They invariably sided with the poor and the underprivileged in an attempt to redress the imbalance in the regular courts, which were seen as biased in favor of the wealthy and influential. In the early stages of PNDC rule, the government-controlled press made every effort to discredit these courts, which were seen as having contributed to upholding for so long the "malevolent dictatorship of Acheampong/Akuffo."[56] It was an effective way of undermining some of the regime's most articulate critics, who, either as lawyers or judges, were intimately associated with the regular courts.

The murder of the high-court judges increased the hostility between the revolutionary and the regular courts, but also underscored the need to bring order to the chaotic and overlapping systems of popular justice that then existed. The PNDC's establishment of a Public Tribunal in Accra in September 1982 was undoubtedly the most important response to this situation. This tribunal, and the others that were to follow, were designed to calm fears that they were going to "use unorthodox methods," as had been the case for the Revolutionary Courts of the AFRC period.[57] Panel chairmen did not have to be lawyers, but in practice all were. The three to five panel members, who assisted the chairman in making judgments, were laymen, but they were usually people who had some familiarity with criminal law, like retired policemen and law clerks.

Initially the tribunals were designed to take over the roles of PDC and WDC courts, but still allow for lay participation. However, as counter-coups developed, the trial of subversives, with the possibility of death sentences, was added to their responsibilities. Those who were involved in the November 23, 1982, coup were tried and convicted by the Accra Public Tribunal, but no one was sentenced to death. Punishment for the far more threatening June 23, 1983, coup was much harsher. Nineteen people were sentenced to death by the tribunal, and many were executed right after the trial was over, at about the same time that the judges' murderers were also executed.[58]

By 1984 there were regional tribunals in all of the country's 10 regions, and the PNDC also promised subordinate district and community tribunals. For a while it even seemed as if the tribunal system was going to replace the regular courts both for criminal and civil justice. In June 1983, WDCs of Accra and Tema invaded the supreme court in Accra and claimed that the Judicial Council had been "dissolved," the position of the chief justice had been "abolished," and the law school was to be "closed down." They wanted to replace the old judicial system with a "people's court of justice."[59] This did not happen, and the tribunals remained exclusively criminal courts. Indeed, for criminal cases, both systems continued to exist, with some degree of confusion over whether criminal cases should be prosecuted in the regular courts or the tribunals.

In general the Public Tribunals prosecuted what were described as crimes against the state. Coup plotting was high on this list. Not far behind was "economic sabotage," which included embezzlement and black-market trafficking, and for serious bank fraud the death sentence was possible. In 1983 the chairman of the Board of Public Tribunals, George Agyekum, also suggested that cocoa smugglers should receive the same treatment. Very soon after their inception, the tribunals were also used for prosecuting common criminals. Armed robberies seemed to have increased after hundreds of thousands of young Ghanaians began returning from Nigeria with little in the way of work prospects. Armed robbers often committed homicide, but even if this was not the case, those convicted could expect to be sentenced to death. In contrast to the regular criminal courts, which continued to exist and had a well-deserved reputation for procrastination and delay, the Public Tribunals were known for their speed and dispatch.

With the stakes so high, and with so many people involved in the administration of justice, inevitably there were scandals involving the operation of the Public Tribunals. Poorly paid tribunal personnel were open to bribery. In one particularly notorious case, the chairman of the Ashanti Public Tribunal, Kwame Arhin, was convicted of taking bribes. On a number of occasions the head of state forced tribunals to reconsider their verdicts. More than anything else, the establishment of the Public Tribunal system put the revolution and its critics on a collision course. The GBA publicly condemned this "misguided attempt to supplant the machinery of the ordinary criminal courts of Ghana," and called on its members to boycott the Tribunals."[60] The association pointed to the absence of an appeal system, the lack of experience in conducting criminal trials, and the decision in advance to decide what technicalities to ignore.

Nevertheless, by 1984 most of the criminal adjudication in Ghana was taking place in the tribunals, and even senior members of the bar felt that by boycotting the tribunals they were violating their code of ethics. In addition, the PNDC did respond to criticisms of how the Public Tribunals worked, and created an appeal system with the National Public Tribunal in Accra the final court of appeal. But the rejection of any oversight from the regular courts, the liberal and swift recourse to the death penalty, and that capital convictions were seldom ever overturned on appeal continued to raise both local and international objections as to how the tribunal system worked.

A more draconian way of maintaining control was through the passage of legislation that allowed for preventive custody and denied the courts the right to inquire into the grounds for such detention. With this legislation the PNDC was able to use "arrest and imprisonment [as] major instruments of subjugation."[61] To the PNDC's critics, the regime more systematically undermined the civil rights of Ghanaians than had been the case in the Nkrumah era. By 1984 over 1,000 people were in prison, and torture was regularly used by the Bureau of National Investigations (BNI) to secure confessions. Along with the operation of the Public Tribunals, this use of torture kept a continual focus on the issue of human rights in Ghana. International organizations like Human Rights Watch/Africa and Amnesty International were particularly concerned with what they saw as the political nature of many of the crimes the tribunals prosecuted. They were strongly opposed to the use of the death penalty and the manner in which the PNDC deprived its opponents of legal protections.

Rawlings maintained that "the majority of the Ghanaian people" had carried his government "and thus ensured [its] survival."[62] At least as important, the PNDC's "strength lay in the goodwill of the armed forces."[63] The command structure had been rebuilt, and in 1985 two senior officers were added to the PNDC. Equally important, in the same year, Captain Kojo Tsikata, who had previously been the special adviser to the PNDC, became the PNDC member responsible for foreign affairs and national security. A fellow Ewe and a long-term associate of Rawlings, he was credited with being primarily responsible for creating the Rawlings security network that ensured the survival of the PNDC. Skillfully, the PNDC also gave many of its initiatives a reformist character that appealed to Ghanaians who were critical of how poorly the country's established institutions functioned. Even feared institutions like the Public Tribunals enjoyed considerable popular support, since they seemed to be so much harder on criminals than the regular courts. They played an important role in preventing Ghana from slipping into the violence and anarchy that characterized many of the military interventions in Africa, even though their excesses and failures were all too apparent in a country with a long-established legal tradition.

OPPOSITION AND THE LOOSENING OF CONTROL

The suppression of civil liberties and Ghana's support for "progressive regimes" in Africa and elsewhere were enough to give the impression that Ghana in the early years of PNDC rule was anti-West. There was considerable fear on the part of Western governments that other African people would follow Ghana's revolutionary example. In 1983 Ghana's northern neighbor, then known as Upper Volta (now Burkina Faso), did indeed do this, and its military government announced objectives very similar to those of the PNDC. Shortly after, the civilian government of Shehu Shagari in Nigeria was overthrown, also by the military, who promised draconian reforms. Ghana's links with Libya and support for Cuba and Nicaragua inevitably incurred the displeasure of the United States, and the CIA clandestinely supported counterrevolutionary groups operating in neighboring countries like Togo, the Ivory Coast, and Nigeria. According to the *People's Daily Graphic* and the *Ghanaian Times,* Western embassies had advance knowledge of the November 23, 1982, coup attempt.

Similarly to the last years of the Nkrumah period, there was great paranoia in Ghana over the role of the CIA in supporting and arming coup plotters. Tension reached a high point in 1985 when a network of local CIA agents was uncovered in Accra and eight Ghanaians were "denationalized" and exchanged for a Ghanaian agent who had been arrested in Washington. Shortly afterward, four U.S. diplomats were expelled from Ghana for activities that "were wholly unacceptable and not conducive to good relations between Ghana and the U.S."[64] The United States responded by terminating aid to Ghana and announcing that Ghana was no longer a serious candidate for further U.S. aid. These confrontations allowed the state-controlled media to keep up a strident anti-imperialist rhetoric that appealed to militant urban workers, students, and the East-bloc countries. In conjunction with Ghana's support for the antiapartheid struggle going on in South Africa and the attempt to restore relationships with the socialist East-bloc countries, anti-American pronouncements sustained the PNDC's anti-West posture.

Undoubtedly the PNDC did have good reason to fear coup plotters.

Between 1982 and 1989 there were more than 20 coup plots and attempted coups.[65] Many of them were aimed at assassinating Rawlings. Dissident groups were able to operate in the Ivory Coast, Nigeria, and most of all Togo. Considerable amounts of Ghanaian cocoa were also smuggled through Togo and contributed to making relations between the two countries especially sour, with coup recriminations being traded back and forth. Dissidents outside of Africa were also engaged in plotting. One of the most spectacular plots involved a ship, the MV *Nobistor,* that was stopped off the coast of Brazil with $1 million worth of arms on board that had been loaded in Argentina. The eight American Vietnam veterans on board intended to join with 80 Ghanaians on another ship and sail for Ghana to stage a coup against the PNDC. The international nature of the plot convinced the PNDC that Ghanaian dissidents were "working in close collaboration with certain foreign intelligence agencies and powers."[66] There were also bitter recriminations from the Ghanaian government that the Western media, "especially the BBC and the Voice of America," had been collaborating with Western intelligence agencies.[67]

In reality Ghana was following what its foreign secretary, Obed Asamoah, described as a two-track policy. On one hand, the PNDC was trying to maintain its revolutionary credentials with left-wing factions in Ghana and the East-bloc countries while at the same time accepting IMF and World Bank advice and loans. Even in the PNDC's dealings with non-Western states, its links were much more with conservative than radical nations. Most of the loans that came into the country from the Middle East came predominantly from conservative countries like Saudi Arabia and Kuwait. By 1987 even the relationship with the United States began to improve. This was helped considerably when three Ghanaians, including J. H. Mensah, who had been the finance minister in the Busia government, were arrested and brought to trial in the United States for attempting to purchase military equipment that included machine guns and grenade launches. It helped also that by this time the Soviet Union was so mired in its own problems that it no longer offered the same ideological attraction that it had during the height of the cold war.

Instead, the winds of change were also blowing through the African continent, stimulated by Mikhail Gorbachev's policy of *glasnost* in the Soviet Union.[68] In 1986 and 1987 the PNDC's NCD reflected this concern for greater openness and democratization by holding a number of political seminars in regional capitals to discuss the kind of democracy that should evolve in Ghana.[69] In 1987 the commission issued its report and proposed a system for electing local assemblies. These district assemblies were to be the highest political and administrative bodies in the 110 assembly districts that the NCD drew up. They were to guide, supervise, administer, and control all other political and administrative authorities in the district. They had the power to raise taxes from specified sources. They could initiate development, and eventually they were going to have control over departments like health and education. One-third of their members were to be "appointed representatives of traditional authorities and of other organizations involved in the productive life of the district."[70]

What most of all distinguished this attempt to decentralize power was that it was to be done on a nonpartisan basis. The number of candidates per district was limited to five. Campaigning was limited to three weeks, and wealthy candidates were allowed no advantages over their poorer opponents. All had to appear on the same platform on the same day to answer questions put to them by the electorate. The result was that the candidates came from all walks of life, which contributed to generating considerable interest in the exercise, particularly in the rural areas.

The turnout in the elections that began in November 1988 was much larger than it had been in 1979, when elections had last been held in Ghana. Fifty-nine percent of those registered voted, in contrast to the 35 percent who voted in 1979. The 31st December Women's Movement (DWM), which Chairman Rawlings's wife, Nana Konadu Rawlings, had played the pivotal role in organizing, contributed to women becoming much more politicized than had been the case in the past, and they made up a disproportionate percentage of the electorate. There was also far more support for the election in rural areas than in the urban areas, where many former politicians criticized the exercise as a ploy on the part of the PNDC to legitimize its rule and a replay of the Acheampong government's UNIGOV proposals.

However, district assemblies immediately raised the possibility of regional assemblies, and the NCD began to hold regional seminars to discuss this next step. Here it seemed that the PNDC was indeed seriously considering its own provisional nature. Nevertheless, there were still vocal critics like the GBA, who felt that the whole affair was a farce, but the seminars became an opportunity for opponents to call for the PNDC's resignation and for an immediate lifting of the ban on political parties. On the other hand, district assembly delegates, who had a vested interest in preserving the system they were part of, advocated that elections to a national assembly should be conducted on the same nonparty basis that had allowed people like themselves to be elected at the local level.

THE ELECTIONS OF 1992

By the end of the 1980s the winds of change were blowing irresistibly in the direction of political pluralism. The most important indication of this was a public lecture delivered by well-known University of Ghana historian Professor Adu Boahen at the Ghana Academy of Arts and Sciences in 1988, in which he placed the blame for the "culture of silence" squarely on Rawlings and the PNDC. It was a courageous standing-room-only performance with Ghanaians lining up for many hours to listen to the professor.[71] Eventually a loose alliance of political groups came together in 1990 to form a pressure group that called itself the Movement for Freedom and Justice (MFJ). Appropriately, it was chaired by Professor Adu Boahen, and other members of its executive were people who were affiliated with the political parties of the First, Second, and Third Republics. It united opponents across the UP-CCP divide and was an important marriage of political convenience. The MFJ clearly felt that it was poised to steal the initiative from the PNDC. It criticized the idea of a nonparty national assembly, which Rawlings favored, comparing it to the "much-reviled Acheampong's UNIGOV proposal of 1977–78."[72] In general, criticisms of the PNDC government became much more outspoken, and the culture of silence was broken.

Nevertheless, unlike Acheampong in 1979, Rawlings did not lose the initiative. The PNDC, in contrast to the SMC, had eight and a half years of fairly effective government that had been free of major corruption to its credit. It could count on military support and considerable rural support, and even in the urban areas, where the MFJ had its greatest support, the PNDC was still a considerable opponent. Much of the PNDC's leadership had been active in the anti-UNIGOV campaign and were well aware of the mistakes that Acheampong had made. They refused the MFJ official recognition and gave the NCD considerable leeway. Eventually they enhanced its credibility by accepting its recommendation that there should be a return to a multiparty system, but with regulations that would check the undesirable features of multiparty politics in the past. In May 1991 a special committee of constitutional experts was set up under the chairmanship of Dr. S.K.B. Asante, a former solicitor general, with the task of making recommendations for a consultative assembly.

Even though the PNDC had deprived the MFJ "of the oxygen of publicity," it did allow for a considerable loosening of government control and consequently was able to maintain the moral high ground.[73] The *Catholic Standard* was allowed to resume publication, and a number of independent publications, the most important of which was the *Ghanaian Chronicle,* also came into existence. Most of them were bitterly opposed to the PNDC and engaged in "muckraking and mudslinging" that could well have been considered libelous.[74] Nevertheless, only on a few occasions did the government seek to bring actions against this press. Instead, members of the government who were attacked had to defend themselves in the government-owned press. The PNDC also released most detainees and political prisoners (around 70) by October 1992 and repealed most of is draconian legislation relating to habeas corpus, newspaper registration, and detention without trial.[75]

Eventually, in November 1991, a Consultative Assembly did begin deliberations on a new constitution. The MFJ and GBA both criticized its composition and modus operandi, but the PNDC was able to point out that it was far more representative of all sections of Ghanaian society than what they suggested. Ironically, it also demonstrated its independence by recommending the 1979 American-style constitution. The PNDC's only interference in this process was steamrolling through a blanket indemnity clause as part of the Transitional Provisions. The constitution was then presented to the people of Ghana in April 1992 and overwhelmingly accepted.[76] Shortly afterward, the ban on political parties was lifted. No symbols were allowed that would link the contesting parties with those of the past, and there were strict limits established as to where funding could come from and its amount. Presidential and parliamentary elections were set for November and December 1992.

In May 1992 the ban on political parties was lifted, but it was not until September that parties were finally officially registered. Undoubtedly this gave Rawlings an advantage over his opponents. He did not formerly announce his presidential candidacy until September 30, but he had obviously been campaigning for several months before and very effectively using the advantage of incumbency. He was also able to distance himself from the PNDC's failings and retained considerable popularity. He was very visible touring the country, officially opening PNDC projects, where he took the opportunity to stress his government's achievements while at the same time attacking intellectuals and their attempts to mislead the masses. In addition, he made a major effort to win the support of chiefs and church leaders. He even addressed the Pentecostal Association of Ghana, where he apologized for mistakes that had been made during the AFRC period and in the early 1980s. Even though the PNDC had lost much of its earlier support, Rawlings himself remained easily the most popular Ghanaian. There was some opposition within the ranks of the party to his candidacy, but eventually centrist and pragmatic PNDC secretaries led by Dr. Obed Asamoah, the foreign secretary, established the National Democratic Congress (NDC) with Rawlings as its presidential candidate. The NDC also took over the EGLE (Every Ghanaian Living Everywhere) Party, which had begun as a grassroots organization but with most of its support coming from the Committees for the Defense of the

Revolution (CDRs). In 1984, when the PDC and the WDCs had been brought under greater control, this organization had eventually taken their place.

Ranged against the NDC were six other parties that were closely allied with the political groupings of the past. Many of them had been making preparations even before the ban on parties had been lifted. Out of the Nkrumahist tradition, four main parties emerged. The largest concentration of old-guard Nkrumahist politicians formed the National Independence Party (NIP), ex-President Dr. Hilla Limann established the People's National Convention (PNC), a younger group of Nkrumahists formed the People's Heritage Party (PHP), and finally a former minister in the Nkrumah government formed the National Convention Party (NCP). The latter party eventually was to ally with the NDC. The Danquah-Busia political group were determined not to make the mistake they had made in 1979 when they had split into two parties, and they agreed to remain united as the New Patriotic Party (NPP).

The clear favorite to lead the party was Professor Adu Boahen, who had been Rawlings's chief public critic, but there were challengers. The most important of them was John Agyekum Kufour, a lawyer with a degree in political philosophy from Oxford University who had been executive chairman of the Kumasi-based Asante Kotoko, one of Ghana's most prominent soccer clubs. Like Boahen, he too was an Akan and would have been able to link together Ashanti Region political movements from the NLM of 1954–57 and the PFP of 1979–81. However, his major disadvantage was that he had served for a brief while, 10 years before, in the PNDC administration as the minister of local government, and to many he seemed to lack the "bravery" of "a warrior people."[77] This clearly worked against him, and he eventually came third behind Professor Boahen in the voting at the party's congress in August 1992.[78] In spite of this division it was obvious that the NPP was going to be the NDC's main opposition. It was the best financed of all of the NDC's opponents.

The NPP claimed that they would be better able to implement the market reforms that the country's economy needed. Its leadership claimed that the PNDC had stolen from them its ERP. They had the support of business, professional people, and senior civil servants, which would make it easier for them to negotiate more successfully with the IMF and the World Bank. Rawlings, they claimed, was not really in support of the market economy, since he was temperamentally opposed to successful entrepreneurs. However, they were never really able to make this an election issue, and the main contest came down to one between personalities, and specifically whether Ghanaians felt that 11 years of Jerry Rawlings was enough. Rawlings, on the other hand, ran on what the PNDC had been able to achieve and made no promises. Instead, he maintained that the future would not be easy and that hard work would have to continue.

Much to the surprise of the opposition, in the remarkably peaceful election held in December, Rawlings won a substantial victory with 58.3 percent of the vote to 30.4 percent for his nearest rival, Adu Boahen. The official voter turnout figure was 48 percent, but it seems as if this figure was based on an inflated estimate of the potential voting population. A closer estimate of the turnout was more around 60 percent, which would have made this election almost as contested as that of 1969. The Commonwealth Observer Group and a team from the Carter Center from the United States both noted that there had been irregularities in the conduct of the election, but that they were not enough to disqualify the results.[79] Nevertheless, the NPP challenged the validity of the election in a publication entitled *The Stolen Verdict*. They argued that the electoral roll had left out anti-PNDC sympathizers who had refused to register for the 1988 district-assembly elections, and that the roll had been inflated in size, which had given opportunities for double voting. They also cited cases of more blatant intimidation and ballot rigging. Along with the other anti-NDC parties, they called upon the Interim National Electoral Commission (INEC) to withhold the results until all irregularities had been investigated.[80]

The INEC rejected this request, and for a while it seemed as if there would be a major eruption of violence, particularly in the Ashanti Region. Fortunately, the *asantehene* took the initiative of bringing all the parties together to form a "Peace Committee," and the demonstrations, riots, and bombings that had been taking place in the Ashanti Region and elsewhere in Ghana came to an end. Instead, the opposition parties announced that they would withdraw from the upcoming parliamentary elections unless there was a new voters list and voters' identity cards. The PNDC rejected this suggestion on the grounds of cost and time involved to accomplish these changes, with the result that the opposition parties boycotted the elections. The NDC won 189 of the 200 seats available, with eight going to the NCP and one to the EGLE Party. Officially only 29 percent of the electorate voted, which to the opposition was further proof that the presidential election had been rigged. In reality the turnout was somewhat larger, around 35 percent, and since many parliamentary seats were not being contested this was a fairly respectable figure that coincided fairly closely with the percentage of votes cast for Rawlings in the presidential election.[81]

Their humiliating loss in the presidential election clearly came as a major surprise to the NPP and the other opposition parties. They had assumed that electoral politics would mean the end of the Rawlings era. Not only did they fail to appreciate the advantages of incumbency, but they had obviously underestimated Rawlings's continuing popularity. By 1992 the PNDC had lost much of its earlier popularity and appeal, but especially in rural areas Rawlings's personal reputation for hard work and integrity remained intact. Even the Brong-Ahafo Region, which the NPP had assumed would side with its fellow Asantes, had instead voted for Rawlings in spite of the supposed Ewe domination that his government represented. Higher cocoa prices for farmers and rural electrification programs had obviously counted more than attacks on the PNDC's human-rights record. Even in urban areas, where there was a more educated population that resented the PNDC's intolerance of criticism and closed style of governance, Rawlings had run close to the NPP. Wealthier suburbs had voted for the NPP, but poorer areas had voted for Rawlings. He proved to be a far more effective public speaker than Adu Boahen, the university professor, who often lost his audience by being excessively intellectual. Rawlings was also able to nullify the impact of the Nkrumahist parties by adopting the chants and slogans of the CPP era and cultivating an image of reverence for Nkrumah.[82]

NOTES

1. D. Rimmer, *Staying Poor: Ghana's Political Economy 1950–1990* (Oxford: Pergamon Press, 1992), 143.

2. J. D. Stryker, *Trade, Exchange Rate, and Agricultural Pricing Policies in Ghana* (Washington, D.C.: World Bank, 1990), 112.

3. Naomi Chazan, *An Anatomy of Ghanaian Politics: Managing Political Recession 1969–1982* (Boulder, Colo.: Westview Press, 1983), 197.

4. Y. Petchenkine, *Ghana: In Search of Stability, 1957–1992* (New York: Praeger Publishers, 1993), 115.

5. Chazan, *Anatomy of Ghanaian Politics*, 316.

6. Ibid., 319.

7. C. Asante, *The Press in Ghana: Problems and Prospects* (Lanham, Md.: University Press of America, 1996), 87.

8. This was a radio broadcast. Quoted in Kevin Shillington, *Ghana and the Rawlings Factor* (London and Basingstoke: Macmillan, 1992), 68.

9. Ibid., 68.

10. Ibid., 69.

11. The June 4th Revolution took its name from the day on which Rawlings had been released from prison by members of the military's rank and file on June 4, 1979.

12. Ibid., 76.

13. Ibid., 80.

14. Radio broadcast, December 31, 1981. Quoted in ibid., 80.

15. Ibid., 82.

16. *Daily Graphic*, January 7, 1982.

17. Ibid.

18. Shillington, *Ghana and the Rawlings Factor*, 85. Rawlings's full name was Jerry John Rawlings. He became publicly known as "JJ," and as "Junior Jesus."

19. Ibid., 91.

20. "SIB Murder Investigations," *West Africa*, June 13, 1983.

21. Two of the killers, Corporals S. K. Amedeka and H. E. Tekpor, escaped from prison during the June 19, 1983, coup attempt.

22. "SIB Murder Investigations," *West Africa*, June 13, 1983.

23. Petchenkine, *Ghana: In Search of Stability*, 127.

24. *Independent*, June 18, 1992. Tsikata subsequently won his libel suit, and on September 29 the *Independent* publicly expressed its regrets at the harm the allegation had done to him.

25. Akata-Pore was arrested, but Atim managed to escape to London.

26. Rimmer, *Staying Poor*, 180..

27. *West Africa*, January 25, 1982.

28. Donald Ray, *Ghana: Politics, Economics, and Society* (Boulder, Colo.: Lynne Rienner, 1986), 37.

29. "Botchwey's Volte-Face," *West Africa*, September 4–10, 1995.

30. Ray, *Ghana: Politics, Economics, and Society*, 130.

31. Ibid., 131.

32. Rimmer, *Staying Poor*, 190.

33. Kwame Boafo-Arthur, "Ghana's External Relations since December 31, 1981," in *Ghana Under PNDC Rule*, ed. E. Gyimah-Boadi (Chippenham, England: Anthony Rowe, 1993), 150.

34. Shillington, *Ghana and the Rawlings Factor*, 116.

35. Francis Agbodeka, *A History of the University of Ghana: Half a Century of Higher Education (1948–1998)* (Accra: Woeli Publishing Services, 1998), 230.

36. "How the PNDC Won June 19," *West Africa*, June 27, 1983.

37. Ray, *Ghana: Politics, Economics, and Society*, 63.

38. *Workers' Banner* (the JFM's paper), September 16–23, 1982.

39. Kwasi Anyemedu, "The Economic Policies of the PNDC," in *Ghana Under PNDC Rule*, ed. E. Gyimah-Boadi (Chippenham, England: Anthony Rowe, 1993), 22.

40. "Forward Ever: Davina Doughan Interviews Flt-Lt Jerry Rawlings, PNDC Chairman," *West Africa*, February 9, 1987.

41. Anyemedu, "The Economic Policies of the PNDC," 37.

42. *People's Daily Graphic*, October 21, 1989.

43. Richard Jeffries, "Urban Popular Attitudes towards the Economic Recovery Programme and the PNDC Government in Ghana," *African Affairs* 91 (1992): 211.

44. Ibid., 214.

45. Ibid., 214.

46. "Forward Ever," *West Africa,* February 9, 1987.

47. Asante, *The Press in Ghana,* 108.

48. *People's Daily Graphic,* April 6, 1987.

49. "Spiritual Onslaught," *West Africa,* April 17–23, 1989.

50. "Crackdown on Religious Sects," *West Africa,* June 26–July 3, 1989.

51. Mike Oquaye, "Law, Justice, and the Revolution," in *Ghana Under PNDC Rule,* ed. E. Gyimah-Boadi (Chippenham, England: Anthony Rowe, 1993), 173.

52. "Spiritual Onslaught," *West Africa,* April 17–23, 1989.

53. "Crackdown on Religious Sects," *West Africa,* June 26–July 3, 1989.

54. Oquaye, "Law, Justice, and the Revolution," 161.

55. "Lawyers and their Taxes," *West Africa,* May 30, 1983.

56. Oquaye, "Law, Justice and the Revolution," 156.

57. *Daily Graphic,* September 1, 1982.

58. Roger Gocking, "Ghana's Public Tribunals: An Experiment in Revolutionary Justice," *African Affairs* 95 (1996): 207.

59. *People's Daily Graphic,* June 25, 1983.

60. *Daily Graphic,* September 28, 1982.

61. Oquaye, "Law, Justice, and the Revolution," 171.

62. "Forward Ever," *West Africa,* February 9, 1987.

63. Rimmer, *Staying Poor,* 197.

64. "Ghana/US Expel Four Diplomats," *West Africa,* December 9, 1985.

65. J. Haynes, "Ghana: Indebtedness, Recovery, and the IMF, 1977–1987," in *The African Debt Crisis,* ed. T. W. Pafitt and S. P. Riley (London: Routledge, 1989), 115. There were over 20 by 1987. There was another assassination plot in 1989 that involved senior members of the military.

66. "Osei Recruited U.S. Mercenaries," *West Africa,* April 7, 1986.

67. Ibid.

68. Mikhail Gorbachev became the First Secretary of the Communist Party of the Soviet Union in 1985, and introduced policies of *perestroika* (restructuring) and *glasnost* (openness).

69. The NCD had been established in 1982, but it was not until 1986 that political consensus had emerged over what its role should be.

70. "Timetable for Districts," *West Africa,* July 13, 1987.

71. Paul Nugent, *Big Men, Small Boys, and Politics in Ghana: Power, Ideology, and the Burden of History, 1982–1994* (London: Printer Publishing, 1995), 164.

72. Richard Jeffries and Clare Thomas, "The Ghanaian Elections of 1992," *African Affairs* 92 (1993): 335.

73. Shillington, *Ghana and the Rawlings Factor,* 171.

74. Jeffries and Thomas, "The Ghanaian Elections of 1992," 336.

75. Amnesty International, "Ghana: Releases of Political Prisoners and New Arrests," *Amnesty International,* December 16, 1992.

76. It was 92 percent in favor out of 3,608,973 votes. *West Africa,* May 11–17, 1992.

77. Ivor Agyeman-Duah, *Between Faith and History: A Biography of J. A. Kufour* (Trenton: N.J.: African World Press, 2003), 60.

78. Boahen got 56.6 percent of the vote, Dr. Kofi Dsane Selby (a Kumasi-based medical doctor) got 17.3 percent, and Kufour got 16.5 percent.

79. The Carter Center sent a team of 18 international observers and the Commonwealth Observer Group sent 15. There were also teams from the OAU and the European Community.

80. This body had been established in November 1991 for conducting the referendum on the constitution and then the presidential and parliamentary elections.

81. Jeffries and Thomas, "The Ghanaian Elections of 1992," 363.

82. A few months before the election, the late president's remains had been reinterred in an impressive new mausoleum in a newly created Kwame Nkrumah Memorial Park in Accra. *West Africa,* July 20–26, 1992.

11

The First NDC
Administration: 1993–97

PARLIAMENTARY GOVERNMENT AND ITS CHALLENGES

The opposition parties' refusal to participate in the parliamentary elections meant that when the first elected Parliament of the country's Fourth Republic convened in January 1993, the NDC had no significant opposition. Even for many who had voted for the NDC this was disappointing, as an effective opposition offered the real possibility that Rawlings would have been forced to "adopt a more conciliatory style of rule" than had been the case during the PNDC era.[1] However, there were some significant changes. For the first time in Ghana's history there were 16 women in Parliament, two of whom had won as independents. Nevertheless, Adu Boahen, the NPP's leader, felt that the poor turn out for the parliamentary elections was indicative of the "fraudulent nature of the whole election exercise—both presidential and parliamentary." He was convinced that the "political group that enjoyed real majority support was not J. J. Rawlings and his NDC," and there had been no need to absorb another electoral humiliation.[2]

Not all NPP members agreed with this position. The pro–J. A. Kufuor faction, though they believed that the elections had been fraudulent, still felt that even as a minority in Parliament the NPP would have been able to act as a check on the government. Kufuor would clearly have gained more from this situation than Adu Boahen. He had made an arrangement to stand for election as the MP from his home constituency of Atwima in the Ashanti Region after he lost the contest with Adu Boahen to lead the party. Undoubtedly, he would have won this seat and very likely would have emerged as leader of the opposition in Parliament.[3] In contrast, as the defeated presidential candidate, Adu Boahen would have had no position in this body, and would have been upstaged by his rival. Kufuor's supporters believed that the decision to boycott the parliamentary elections was as much inspired by this fear as anything else.

Instead of participating in Parliament, the four major opposition parties formed a "shadow cabinet" to play the role of an effective opposition. They "called for a truly independent electoral commission and a new voter's register, as well as for unconditional amnesty for all Ghanaians in exile." As an indication of their willingness to be "conciliatory," they called on their supporters to "give the NDC-led government a chance to prove that it [was] genuinely interested in the institution and restoration of genuine democracy."[4] However, for a while after the election, as unrest continued, confrontation rather than conciliation was more the norm. Adu Boahen refused to appear as a witness before the Accra Public Tribunal that tried the "Farighan" bombers. They were accused of being responsible for five bombings in the Accra/Tema area and belonging to an anti-NDC group that wanted to "overthrow the Rawlings government."[5] Eventually four people were brought before the Accra Public Tribunal and Adu Boahen was ordered to appear as a witness in the proceedings. He refused to do so, but indicated his willingness to testify if the case was brought before a traditional court.

No one had been seriously hurt in the explosions and Boahen did not risk alienating the public by refusing to cooperate with institutions that for many seemed to epitomize the worst excesses of the PNDC era. Eventually he was charged with contempt, but he was successfully able to challenge the tribunal's right to try this case, since their authority expired on January 7, 1993.[6] This legal wrangling was undoubtedly an embarrassment to the new government, which at the time was already having to deal with scandals that the independent press had been publicizing regarding the operation of the Public Tribunals.

The NPP also challenged in the supreme court a number of existing laws and decrees that it considered were in violation of the 1992 constitution. The party scored notable victories in forcing the Ghana Broadcasting Corporation to grant it equal access to its facilities and challenging as unconstitutional the arrest of some of its members for demonstrating against the 1993 budget. It also scored an important symbolic victory by getting the court to rule against the continued celebration of December 31, the anniversary of the PNDC's seizure of state power, as a public holiday. In one of the NPP's other constitutional suits against the government, the supreme court even demanded that Rawlings appear as a witness, which was also an important symbolic victory for the opposition.

The unpopular nature of the NDC's first budget, which the NPP described as a "Killer Budget," also provided ammunition for attacking the government. Most unpopular was the 60 percent rise in fuel prices, which inevitably affected the cost of transportation and food. The NPP was quick to point out that this increase came at a time when world prices for petroleum were declining. The party also kept the issue of "rigged" presidential elections alive by a public launching of its compilation of the evidence of how this had happened in a work entitled *The Stolen Verdict*.[7] However, at an official price of 2,500 cedis, the work was affordable only by people of middle class means, who, judging from the election results, were anyway likely to have voted for the NPP.[8]

With the absence of a formal opposition in Parliament, the independent press also saw itself as the watchdog of the new constitution. Most of these publications were "no more than four-page weekly scandal sheets so hastily put together [to be] almost incomprehensible."[9] Nevertheless, they kept up a series of blistering attacks on the government that varied from denouncing the "satanic," "wicked," and "insensitive" budget proposals to attacking the NDC's celebration of PNDC holidays like June 4 and December 31.[10] There were also bitter personal attacks on members of the NDC government, including Nana Konadu Rawlings, the president's wife. Not surprisingly, there were complaints from government officials, unfamiliar with this level of attack, that by "publishing half-truths" this press was "creating unnecessary tension among political parties."[11] Neither were threats of libel actions able to stem this flow of scandal. In spite of considerable pressure behind the scenes, the *Ghanaian Chronicle* published details about Dr. Kwesi Botchwey's affair with a former Canadian high commissioner that had resulted in a "love child."[12] The *Free Press* accused Vice President K. N. Arkaah of having had sex with a schoolgirl.

On the international level, the situation for the NDC government was more encouraging. The essential smoothness of the transition from military to elected government impressed foreign donors, so that promises of assistance for 1993–94 significantly exceeded the $1.7 billion that the NDC government had anticipated.[13] Maintaining this level of support required that Ghana live up to its new democratic ideals as well as meet donor demands for financial responsibility. It was a difficult tightrope to walk. Significantly, in the election year of 1992 the government's expenditure had increased by more than 13 percent, largely due to substantial salary increases to civil servants. The result had been a budgetary deficit of 4.8 percent of the GDP.[14] Donor assistance in 1993–94 was conditional on achieving a small surplus for that budget year in spite of the fact that world prices for Ghana's main products were declining. The 1993 budget, announced two days before the formal transfer of government to the NDC, was an attempt to meet this condition. However, in a society where the culture of silence had been replaced by vociferous demands for openness, confrontation was inevitable. One of the most publicized was police action at Legon, site of the country's main university campus, where students demanded that government loans to students be more than doubled. Their protests had been curbed by violent police action reminiscent of the dark days of military rule.[15]

The coming of NDC rule unleashed a struggle in the party over controlling the direction that the country's ERP should take. Technocrats like Dr. Kwesi Botchwey, the minister of finance and economic planning, wanted tight fiscal and monetary policies to prevent deficits. On the other hand, elected politicians, with an eye on upcoming elections, were far more interested in projects that would win the support of the electorate. Reflective of this important divide was the long time it took for the NDC government to select its ministers, which was reminiscent of similar problems that the Limann government had faced in 1979. The size of the executive, 110 ministers and deputy ministers, was further indication of the unwieldy nature of this government. Not surprisingly, corruption, which had bedeviled previous governments that had failed to be fiscally responsible, began to reappear as a far more serious problem than it had been in the PNDC era.

Even more important, during its first four years in office, the NDC government failed to meet the conditions for fiscal responsibility established by the IMF and the World Bank. In 1993 few of the targets set for the economy were met. In the government's Accelerated Growth Program, introduced in that year, GDP had been slated to increase by 5 percent but registered a far more anemic 3.9 percent in spite of good harvests and strong performances from the mining sector. Inflation had been 27.4 percent rather than the estimated 8.5 percent. There had been a budget deficit rather than the intended surplus, and not surprisingly, the cedi had continued to depreciate, so that by the end of the year it had lost almost 50 percent of its value. Troubling also was that government expenditure had outpaced revenue, with the tax component of revenue declining in comparison to what it had been during the PNDC era.

The 1994 budget was an attempt to be more realistic about what the economy could achieve, but once again there were serious shortfalls. To deal with growing deficits, the government resorted to borrowing from local banks, which reduced the amount of capital for private investment and fueled an inflation that by December 1995 had reached 79 percent. The cedi continued its depreciation, so that by this time it was worth only half of its value at the beginning of 1993. Growth continued at around 3.9 percent per annum and barely kept ahead of the country's annual population growth rate of close to 3 percent. External indebtedness also increased significantly. It had risen from $3.5 billion in 1990 to over $5 billion by 1994. A major reason for this increase lay in the tailing-off of foreign aid as Ghana failed to meet conditions that the IMF had established.[16] There was some success in restructuring this debt to long-term rather than short-term loans, but this still meant that the government's largest expenditure became paying the interest on this debt. In 1994 the government was also able to achieve a modest budget surplus, but even this was illusory, as it was due largely to the sale of 25 percent of the government-owned Ashanti Goldfields Corporation (AGC). Indeed, overall tax revenue was 14 percent lower than it had been in the three previous years.[17] The government's critics were quick to point out that Ghana fell within the category of the heavily indebted poor country (HIPC) as defined by the World Bank.

In 1995, along with more price increases in the cost of fuel, the NDC government introduced a value-added tax (VAT) of 17.5 percent that was to be levied on service and retail transactions excluding education, health, foodstuffs, financial services, and some categories of equipment. The aim was to create a broader indirect tax base, which previously had been dependent on duties imposed on cocoa exports, taxes levied on the sale of petroleum products, duties on many imported items, and corporate and individual income taxes. It had been a very volatile system, as world-market prices for cocoa and crude oil could vary enormously. In addition, as the economy had been made more market-oriented, many import and export duties had been abolished to stimulate the local economy. It was hardly surprising that revenue had declined, and as the government's expenses increased it was obvious that a more efficient and equitable system of tax generation was necessary. This was undoubtedly how the IMF felt about the situation not just in Ghana but elsewhere in Africa, where VATs were being made an important revenue-generating component of structural-adjustment programs.[18]

There was considerable discussion about the implementation of this tax among academics, businessmen, and senior government officials prior to 1995, but very little attempt was made to make the general public aware of what the government was planning. Not surprisingly, as soon as the government sought to introduce the new system, there was immediate opposition. In Accra between 50,000 and 100,000 demonstrators, organized by an opposition grouping called the Alliance for Change (AFC), took to the streets and eventually clashed with the pro-government Association of Communities for the Defense of the Revolution (ACDR). In the melee that followed four people were killed.[19] The AFC's slogan for the demonstration had been *"kume preko,"* an Akan expression meaning "you might as well kill me now." This had indeed come to pass for some of the protesters, and it was a serious embarrassment for the NDC government. President Rawlings quickly convened Parliament, and by June 1995 the VAT law and regulations were repealed and the previous system of indirect taxation restored.

In retrospect, the attempt to introduce a VAT was botched in several critical ways. There had been too much delay in the passing of the bill in Parliament, and then, in an attempt to keep the legislation on schedule, it had been implemented far too quickly. This had meant little public debate, and the legislation had been introduced at a time of the year when food production is most difficult in Ghana. The hasty attempt to register retailers and service providers had inevitably created considerable apprehension, and the attempt to cram too many activities into too short a time undermined public confidence in the program.[20] What was perceived as the excessively high rate of taxation, initially to be 15 percent, also hurt the government's credibility. In Great Britain, the former mother country, the rate was also 17.5 percent, but when this tax had been first introduced in 1973, it had been at the far more modest rate of 8 percent. During the struggle over the introduction of the tax, far more exemptions from taxation had been conceded than had originally been intended, which had made the higher rate necessary. Business that failed to get such waivers inevitably felt that the system was arbitrary and unfair. Not surprisingly, VAT's opponents blamed it for an acceleration in the increase in prices, which was all too constant a feature of life in Ghana.

By the middle of 1995 it was clear that the economy was not going to meet the targets that had been set and that a revenue shortfall was certain. The cedi was depreciating at a faster rate than had been anticipated, and inflation was also increasing. In December 1995 it was over 70 percent. The government continued to borrow heavily from local banks, which effectively crowded out local businesses from the financial markets. Ironi-cally, though private saving had increased during the 1990s, government saving had become negative. The anticipated expenses for conducting the 1996 election were inevitably going to compound this situation. In restor-ing the old tax system, the government had left the door open for an expansion of the tax system, which the AFC had been quick to point out was an attempt to bring VAT "back through the back door."[21] In reality, however, with elections a year and a half away, the NDC government was resigned to wait until after these elections before revisiting the issue of VAT's reintroduction.

In the short term the most important casualty of the failure to imple-ment VAT was the minister of finance and economic planning, Dr. Kwesi Botchwey. Some of his opponents felt that he should have resigned right after the government withdrew its VAT legislation, but instead he waited several months to do so. In his registration letter he focused more on his frustration over bringing the runaway losses of the Ghana Petroleum Cor-poration under control than the failure to introduce VAT. More so than any other institution in the country, this state corporation's excessive bor-rowing from the Bank of Ghana had contributed to the deficit the country had faced in 1994. This inability to control this borrowing was symptom-atic of what Botchwey felt was the government's failure to implement its own decisions. After 13 years of directing Ghana's economic recovery, he felt that he was being marginalized by others who had more influence on Rawlings. Indicative of this fall from favor, Botchwey had not accompa-nied the president on investment-seeking trips to Great Britain and the United States shortly before he resigned. While in Britain, Rawlings had even criticized those members of his government "who [were] beginning to lose touch with the reality of our people," which to many in the press was seen as an oblique criticism of the man who was seen as the main architect of the economic recovery.[22]

Neither was Botchwey the only casualty among the old guard. In 1996 P. V. Obeng, who had been the presidential adviser on governmental af-fairs, left or was ousted from his position. Almost at the same time, Kojo Tsikata retired as chief of security, and there were further resignations from the Ministry of Finance and also from the diplomatic service of peo-ple who had long been associated with the PNDC. Some were to become critics of the new team style of management, but probably even more unsettling to many of this old guard was the alarming increase in corrup-tion, which seemed to be "eroding the ascetic image that had served the regime so well in the difficult days of adjustment."[23]

ETHNIC AND REGIONAL CHALLENGES

Along with the challenge that administering the country's economy offered, the NDC government was also faced with serious ethnic unrest shortly after taking office. Toward the end of 1993 there were reports that the Konkombas living in the Dagomba Traditional Area were restive, and that clashes between them and the Dagombas, Gonjas, and Nanumbas were imminent. Such conflict was not new. In 1981 there had been bitter fighting between the Konkombas and their traditional enemies, the Nanumbas, in which perhaps as many as 2,000 people had died.[24] In 1993 the main source of conflict was over the Konkomba demand that their main chief at Saboba be elevated to paramount status. A core group of Konkombas had been living in the region around Yendri as far back as the seventeenth century, but many had migrated into this area and others in northern Ghana from Togo during colonial times.[25] Originally these Konkombas were a stateless people, but in many instances they had become successful farmers, often better off than the local chiefs to whom they were subject and into whose area they had migrated.

There was also a religious dimension to this conflict, as many Konkombas had converted to Christianity while the Dagombas and many of the other ethnic groups around the Konkombas were predominantly Muslim. Indicative of the Konkombas' increasing dissatisfaction with their subordination, they had formed the Konkomba Youth Association and had petitioned the Dagomba Traditional Council for the right to have a paramount chief. To the other ethnic groups this seemed like a "back-door move towards landownership by 'outsiders.'"[26] It seemed this way since land in the north, as is most of Ghana, is held in trust by paramount chiefs who can distribute it to those in need. With so much at stake, it was not surprising that the council had denied the Konkombas' request.

According to the *Ghanaian Chronicle*, passions had risen even higher when the NDC, which the Konkombas had supported in the 1992 elections in the hopes of getting help with their claim, had provided little assistance. Northern Regional Minister Lieutenant Colonel Abdulai Ibrahim had done no more than plead with the Dagomba Traditional Council to deal "dispassionately" and "objectively" with the Konkombas' request, and when it had been rejected he had urged the "protagonists to resort to the courts for redress."[27] However, given the level of hostility between the government and the independent press, the *Ghanaian Chronicle*'s report of an impending explosion was discounted. Eventually, in February 1994, a relatively trivial dispute between a Konkomba and Nanumba man provided the spark that resulted in widespread fighting between these two groups in which officially over 1,000 people lost their lives and 144 villages were destroyed.[28]

The government sent 3,000 soldiers and police to restore order, and seven districts on the border with Togo were closed. In spite of this, there was a stream of refugees into Togo, which upset the already inflamed relationship with that neighbor. Konkombas had migrated into many areas in the north, and even the capital of the Northern Region was not spared serious disturbances. On one occasion soldiers fired into a group of predominantly Dagomba youths who were bent on attacking a group of Konkomba men transacting business at a local bank, and 12 people were killed.[29] The government had allocated funds for 20,000 dislocated people, but with violence so widespread the number rapidly shot up to well over 150,000. Supplies of foodstuffs from the north were reduced to a trickle, as in many areas farming activities were impossible.

Immediately the opposition blamed the government for the catastrophe by "stoking the flames of the conflict."[30] Rawlings was accused of having made promises to the Konkombas to win their support in the 1992 election. The militant faction among those who had opposed the Konkombas readily agreed with this position. The Konkomba Youth Association, on the other hand, accused the MP for Bimbilla, Dr. Mohammed Ibn Chambas, who was also the First Deputy Speaker of Parliament, of having armed the other side. They also complained that the task force had been less than even-handed in dealing with the warring sides.[31] In general the feeling was that the government had been too slow to react and that it would pay the price in the next elections by losing the support of voters in the Northern Region.

On an even wider level, the strife graphically underscored how quickly an otherwise peaceful country could rapidly experience a breakdown in law and order. A year before there had been a breakdown in law and order in the neighboring country of Togo when the army had gone on a rampage, shooting members of that government's opposition. Here too ethnic rivalries had played an important role, with the Togolese Ewes suspected of seeking some sort of linkage with their Ghanaian counterparts. Over 90,000 refuges streamed into Ghana, and for a while there was a tense standoff between the two counties, with the Ghana armed forces on a "Third Degree Alert," and Togo threatening to bomb Ghana's Akosombo Dam if Ghanaian soldiers were "involved in any acts of sabotage."[32] Eventually Ghana and Togo were able to defuse this situation, but the bitter civil wars then going in Liberia and Sierra Leone, also inflamed by ethnic rivalries, were prime examples of how such internal conflicts could expand to endanger the overall security of the region. The genocidal explosion in Rwanda, which coincided with the ethnic conflict in Ghana but vastly overshadowed it, was an indication of how such conflict could come close to destroying an African nation.[33]

However, even though the NDC government came in for a great deal of criticism for its handling of the ethnic conflict in the north, Rawlings was able to establish a reputation for himself as a mediator in regional conflicts of this nature. As an indication of Ghana's return to a position of influence in West Africa, in 1994 he was elected president of the Economic Community of West African States (ECOWAS). Rapidly he became involved in trying to negotiate an end to the civil wars in Liberia and Sierra Leone. Parties to these conflicts meet in Ghana in 1994. In 1995, on the 20th anniversary of ECOWAS's founding, the organization met in Accra, and restoring peace to Liberia and Sierra Leone were the main issues on the agenda. Closer to home, President Rawlings was mending fences with his counterpart in Togo, President Gnassingbe Eyadema, and shortly before the ECOWAS meeting the two had met in Togo. There was enough of a reconciliation between them for Eyadema to attend the Accra ECOWAS summit.

LEAD UP TO ELECTIONS IN 1996

The struggling economy and ethnic strife in the north were not the only headaches that the NDC government faced. High inflation and the declining cedi inevitably caused considerable discontent even among the better-paid members of the country's workforce. A well-publicized and controversial strike by junior doctors in 1994 provided fertile ground for criticizing the government's plans for privatizing the country's health-care system. Even MPs were dissatisfied with their salaries, and they used this as an excuse for their high rate of absenteeism from parliamentary debates. Indicative, however, of their legislative advantage, at the end of 1994 they received a new and far more generous salary. University lecturers who were on strike for much of 1995 were not so successful, and eventually returned to work at their original salaries.[34] Industrial workers and civil servants, with less visibility than their professional counterparts, nevertheless succeeded in embarrassing the government on a number of occasions in 1995 when they laid siege to the Ministry of Finance and sealed off the building.

Poor examination results for students who took the Senior Secondary School (SSS) examinations in December 1993 were also seen as a reflection on the failure of government's attempt to reform secondary education in the country. Out of the over 42,000 students who took the examination, only 1,656 passed.[35] In 1987 the PNDC government had shortened the period of preuniversity education from 17 to 12 years in an attempt to cut the cost of education and make it available to a broader cross-section of the population. There had been many critics at the time who had felt that the program was too hastily implemented, and the dismal performance of the first batch of students to graduate from this new system seemed graphic proof of these concerns. The failure of the government schools to educate successfully their students seemed likely to increase the numbers of private schools, which would work to the disadvantage of those who could not pay school fees. Once again, a supposedly revolutionary government seemed to be favoring the interests of the privileged over the underprivileged.

There was also a bruising struggle over the appointment of I. K. Abban as the new chief justice. In 1995 the GBA tried to have the supreme court nullify his appointment on the grounds that "he was not a person of high moral character and proven integrity."[36] He was accused of altering the wording in a judgment he had given without acknowledging that he had done so. It was a highly political case involving the NPP, one of the independent newspapers, the *Free Press*, and the attorney general. The conflict served to continue the well-established hostility between members of the legal profession and the government.

Even more troubling to the NDC was the loss they suffered in a by-election in the Upper East Region in 1995. It was the NDC's first such loss and was an indication of weakening support in the north of the country as a result of the government's handling of the ethnic conflict there in 1994. Even more ominous, the four major opposition parties had combined to offer one candidate, and in spite of massive state support he had defeated his NDC opponent. The implications were obvious for the upcoming presidential and parliamentary elections.

Neither did the NDC enjoy the same degree of control over state media as had been the case in 1992. In 1994 the government's monopoly on the airwaves was challenged by an independent FM station, Radio Eye. Initially the government had tried to ban this station as illegal and took court action against the directors. However, after almost 60 years of monopolizing the country's airwaves, it was obvious that the end was in sight, and early in 1995 the government was forced to open up broadcasting in the country. There were over 60 applications for permits, and by 1996, when the election campaigns really got underway, the Ghana Broadcasting Corporation no longer enjoyed its earlier monopoly. Many of these stations were critical of the NDC to varying degrees. They played an important role in publicizing the revelations of corruption on the part of

NDC MPs that had been revealed during hearings undertaken by the Commission on Human Rights and Administrative Justice. They also played an important role in defeating the government's attempts to have the constitution amended during the election year.

Rawlings had always been critical of many aspects of the 1992 constitution, but he had become even more so when his vice president, K. N. Arkaah, had refused to resign even after his party, the NCP, had terminated its alliance with the NDC and joined the opposition. The constitution stipulated that if an MP crossed the floor he or she had to resign, but it said nothing about a vice president. Eventually relations between Rawlings and Arkaah had become so stained that they came to blows at a cabinet meeting in December 1995. In addition to amending the constitution to make it mandatory for a vice president who was not a member of the ruling party or in an alliance with it to resign, the NDC also wanted to make it possible for Ghanaians to have dual citizenship, allow the chiefs to participate in politics, and to remove paramilitary services, like the police and customs officers, from the public service. With the election so close, the opposition parties inevitably saw these proposed amendments as politically inspired. Attacking them became yet another way of putting the NDC on the defensive.

However, taking full advantage of all the NDC's weaknesses proved to be no easy task for the opposition. Even picking a leader for the NPP proved extremely divisive. Initially Professor Adu Boahen's supporters argued that since the 1992 election had been stolen, there was no reason to convene another party congress to elect a new candidate. Other potential candidates felt that this contradicted the party's own constitution, which stipulated an election not later than 24 months before the election. Eventually, in 1994, Boahen conceded the need for a party congress. Questions about his ability to campaign vigorously (he was then 62) as well as complaints about his "dictatorial" and "sentimental" tendencies worked against him.[37] Immediately there developed a major struggle between seven contestants to lead the party in the 1996 elections.

Many NPP supporters favored Kwame Pianim, a Yale University–trained economist who had worked for the United Nations. He had been particularly effective on both radio and TV in attacking the NDC's economic policies, and had more charisma than his two main opponents, Boahen and J. A. Kufuor. Eventually, however, the supreme court ruled against his right to contest the election on the grounds that he had been convicted of participating in an attempt to overthrow the PNDC in 1983.[38] It was a highly controversial ruling, since it seemed as if he was being punished twice for the same crime. Indicative of how bitter rivalries were in the NPP, the challenge to Pianim's right to run had been initiated by an NPP party member. Kufuor, who was not as popular with the media as Pianim or as popular with the electorate as Boahen, undoubtedly benefited most of all from Pianim's disqualification. He had to overcome the suspicion that surrounded him for having served briefly as a secretary for local government during the early years of the PNDC government. He did so by carefully cultivating the support of the 2,000 delegates who were to vote at the party's convention. Eventually he won 52 percent of their vote to Professor Boahen's 35.7 percent, with the rest going to the four other candidates.

It was not until April 1996, a scant seven months before the election, that the NPP was finally able to settle the question of who would be their flag-bearer. Neither was alliance making with other parties any easier to accomplish. Not until June did negotiations begin for what was to be called the Great Alliance. In spite of its name it was hardly inclusive. Three months later, after much now-it's-on now-it's-off negotiations, former vice president Arkaah of the People's Convention Party (PCP), agreed to run as Kufuor's running mate.[39] This attempt to forge an alliance between a Nkrumahist party (the PCP) and one that belonged to the Danquah/Busia tradition (the NPP) was never entirely successful. The NDC was easily able to point to the opportunism of the arrangement, and the NDC only had "to replay the TV footage and radio commentaries of Arkaah to confirm his double standards."[40] Selecting candidates from the ranks of the two parties resulted in equally damaging squabbles with no final agreement on the alliance's official list. The other Nkrumahist parties failed even to unite among themselves, and the only one that stood much of a chance in winning seats in the new Parliament, the PNC, decided to run on its own. Its leader, Dr. Hilla Limann, who had led the party to victory in 1979, was in ailing health and eventually handed over to the rather unknown Dr. Edward Mahama, who practiced in Accra but like Limann was originally from the north.

In the face of this less than perfect alliance among the opposition parties, the NDC nevertheless decided to form its own alliance, the Progressive Alliance. It included the EGLE Party and the Democratic People's Party (DPP); neither was electorally significant, but with them on board it was easier to claim that the alliance was the true Nkrumahist party. Rawlings had never been a great fan of the Osagyefo, and obviously the NDC's economic policies were radically different from the policies that the CPP had followed. Instead, the alliance stressed that it too had a concern for "the common man," supposedly one of the hallmarks of the CPP.[41] Some defections from the PNC also helped these claims, as did the alliance's choice of Professor J. E. Atta Mills as its vice president. He had spent some time at the Winneba Ideological Institute, the Nkrumahist training center, in the 1960s.

However, the Progressive Alliance was not without its damaging internal squabbles. Seventy-five NDC MPs were "deselected partly as a result of internal factional competition and partly because the NDC was seeking to raise the quality of its parliamentary representatives whom the party felt would be better able to stand up in the next Parliament to the "heavyweights" that the Great Alliance was running.[42] Apart from including people of often dubious reputations, it seemed poor reward for those who had served the party loyally. In retaliation, many of the deselected incumbents boycotted parliamentary sittings, which further served to publicize the discontent within the ranks of the NDC. They publicly demanded 20 million cedis as "end-of-term-benefits" and wanted to be appointed to boards of government institutions and to jobs in the civil service.[43] Unlike the Great Alliance, the Progressive Alliance had far more resources and was able to buy off and suppress this protest and present a single slate of candidates.

The Progressive Alliance also enjoyed other advantages against its opponent. Not all of the economic news was bad. During the 1990s tourism had expanded significantly from a paltry figure of about 50,000 in the early 1980s to close to 300,000 visitors by 1995. In that year it had earned the country $237 million.[44] Events like PANAFEST (the Pan-African Historical Theater Festival), which was begun in 1992 and held biennially, had helped to put Ghana on the tourist map, particularly for people of African descent in the diaspora.[45] There had also been a significant increase in value of nontraditional exports from a minuscule $2 million in 1984 to over $200 million by 1996.[46] This represented only about one-fifteenth of the country's total exports, but nevertheless it signified an important breaking away from dependence on a few products that had characterized the export economy in the past. Significantly, the Great Alliance did not really have an economic policy that differed from that of the NDC. The NPP, the senior partner in the alliance, basically agreed with the government's SAP. Its claim was that it would be able to administer this program more effectively, as it "possessed greater expertise in how to help private business and attract foreign investment."[47]

Neither was its attack on the NDC for a lack of a commitment to democracy that convincing. The NDC government had often backed down, though not always gracefully, when challenged by the courts and in the face of hostile criticism from the independent press. Preparations for the election were the best indication of how receptive it had been to criticism from an opposition that held no seats in Parliament. The NDC-appointed chairman of the EC, Dr. K. Afari-Gyan, even though the opposition suspected him of being a Rawlings sympathizer, made a major effort to bring all the political parties together to let them have input into the conduct of the elections. In 1994 he had established the Inter-Party Advisory Committee, which had met monthly with party representatives. In spite of some initial government opposition, the EC had compiled a new voters' register in 1995. It had also satisfied another request of the opposition by issuing registered voters with identity cards, a substantial number with photographs. Shortly before the election the EC had conducted a supplementary registration to include those who had just turned 18. Finally, there had been many concessions to the opposition in regards to how the ballots would be counted to prevent any attempt to rig the election.

Ghana's good standing with the international donor community helped enormously in making these concessions possible. Even though the country's economic performance had not always been that stellar, they wanted the upcoming elections to be a model of openness, and an example for other African countries that were also trying to consolidate their democracies. Five European countries, the United States, and Canada contributed over $23 million for computer equipment and software, ballots, transparent ballot boxes, security bags, and training for electoral workers. The election was to be monitored by observers from the Commonwealth Secretariat, the European Union, the OAU, and the National Democratic Institute of the United States, as well a number of local human-rights organizations. Claiming, as had been done in 1992, a "stolen verdict" was not likely to be convincing.

THE ELECTION OF 1996

On December 7 both the presidential and the parliamentary elections were held. There was a record turnout, with 77.9 percent of the registered electorate of 9.27 million voting for a president as well as electing 200 members of Parliament. Rawlings received 57.4 percent of the vote to Kufuor's 39.6 percent and Mahama's 3 percent. The NDC won 134 seats; the NPP, 60; its ally the PCP, 5; and the PNC, 1. Voting patterns were remarkably similar to what they had been in 1992, and the NDC was quick to use this as vindication of the fairness of its earlier victory. Like Boahen in 1992, Kufuor had swept the Ashanti Region, but Rawlings had won in all the other nine administrative regions of the country. The latter had once again scored an overwhelming victory in the Volta Region, sweeping 94.5 percent of the vote, but more than just the ethnic loyalty of fellow

Ewes was involved. A sizeable non-Ewe population had voted for Rawlings, while even in the Akan region of Brong-Ahafo he had easily outperformed his Akan rival, Kufuor. In spite of fears about the fallout from the ethnic tensions in the north, Rawlings did surprisingly well there also. In only three constituencies did the NPP win a majority.

In a similar fashion to 1992, Rawlings and his NDC parliamentary candidates did better in the rural rather than the urban areas, while the NPP did best in large urban areas. It was in these areas that the impact of the

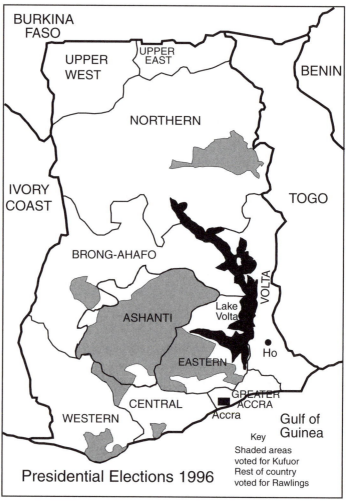

The 1996 Presidential election. *Source*: Paul Nugent, "Winners, Losers and Also Rans: Money, Moral Authority and Voting Patterns in the Ghana 2000 Election," *African Affairs* 100 (2001): 412, figure 2. By permission of Oxford University Press.

SAP had been most acute. Ironically, in the wealthier upper-class constituencies, where people had benefited most from economic liberalization, the NDC did worst off all. Educational levels undoubtedly played an important role in shaping perceptions of Rawlings as an upstart with blood on his hands. However, the poorer constituencies, where living standards had suffered significantly, still continued to support the NDC. Rawlings had clearly been able to play on the fear that the big men of the Busia/Danquah tradition lacked a real concern for the people. Neither had they attempted to seek out northerners or people from the Volta Region for positions of party leadership. In the country in general, as well as in multi-ethnic communities like those of Accra and Takoradi, this only "confirmed a well-entrenched stereotype of Ashanti arrogance."[48] The NDC's record of road building, electrification, and provision of potable water in rural areas was largely responsible for the party's success in these constituencies. How much this had improved living standards is hard to determine. More important, what the opposition described as "project politics" had been undertaken with little regional discrimination, and sent the message that Rawlings was "a firm, strong leader who delivered on his promises."[49]

Given the amount of effort taken to make the election free, it was difficult for the opposition to claim a stolen verdict. Nevertheless, they did dispute how fair it had been and the manner in which the NDC had exploited the advantages of incumbency. They complained that the state-owned media had basically ignored the opposition, the NDC had used government vehicles to travel all over the country, and by making sure that only NDC supporters were awarded state contracts, they had made businessmen, potentially NPP supporters, very hesitant to support the opposition. As a result, the Great Alliance had far less in the way of financial resources. This had been particularly to their disadvantage in the rural areas, where the NDC had done best, as they had been unable to canvass effectively and counter what they claimed had been intimidation and vote buying by their opponents. The Great Alliance accepted the election results but with considerable disgruntlement. They made "threatening noises as to what would happen if the government refused to implement measures such as public funding for opposition parties to ensure a more level playing-field in 2000."[50]

However, in contrast to the disputed 1992 elections, when Kumasi had been placed under a five-day curfew and an NDC ward chairman in the Takoradi/Sekondi area had been abducted from his home by political opponents, beaten up, and set on fire, and eventually died, there was very little violence during the 1996 elections or afterward. Businesses in Accra had closed down for three days before and after the polling. There was a ban on political activities in Kumasi to stop election victory celebrations from becoming violent, but this was soon lifted. Also in contrast to 1992, Kufuor attended Rawlings's inauguration as the second president of the Fourth Republic, as he did the swearing in of the elected MPs. Nevertheless, to many observers the opposition's convincing defeat raised the question of whether Ghana had de facto become a one-party state.

NOTES

1. R. Jeffries and C. Thomas, "The Ghanaian Elections of 1992," *African Affairs* 92 (1993): 331.

2. "Predictable Landslide," *West Africa*, January 11–17, 1993.

3. Ivor Agyeman-Duah, *Between Faith and History: A Biography of J. A. Kufuor* (Trenton: N.J.: African World Press, 2003), 69.

4. "Shadow Role for Opposition," *West Africa*, January 18–24, 1993.

5. *Daily Graphic*, November 9 and December 8, 1992. This group called itself "Farighan" in the note it sent to the Ghana News Agency.

6. Eventually Boahen's contempt case came before the Ghana supreme court, but by the time this court ruled the Public Tribunals had passed out of existence and the case ended up in the Accra high court. *Ghanaian Times*, July 13, 1993.

7. "The Stolen Verdict," *West Africa*, April 26–May 2, 1993.

8. This would have been a little more than $4 at current rates of exchange. It does not seem much, but per-capita income in Ghana was then around $400 per annum.

9. "The Press as Opposition," *West Africa*, January 25–31, 1993.

10. June 4 was the day of the AFRC coup in 1979.

11. "Uneasy Calm Prevails," *West Africa*, May 15–22, 1994.

12. "Kwesi Botchwey has Child with Canadian High Commissioner," *Ghanaian Chronicle*, August 1–3, 1994. He was already married and according to the *Ghanaian Chronicle* had a reputation for such extramarital affairs.

13. "High Expectations," *West Africa*, July 18–26, 1993. Ghana was promised $2.1 billion.

14. Eboe Hutchful, *Ghana's Adjustment Experience: The Paradox of Reform* (Oxford: James Currey, 2002), 215.

15. "Furore over Legon Brutality," *West Africa*, April 12–18, 1993.

16. Hutchful, *Ghana's Adjustment Experience*, 216.

17. "Is Ghana the Success Story?" *West Africa*, May 15–21, 1995.

18. For example, in 1995 Togo introduced a VAT (18 percent), and in 1996 Uganda did likewise (17 percent).

19. "VAT Rising Shakes Capital," *West Africa*, May 29–June 4, 1995.

20. Seth Terker, "VAT in Ghana: Why It Failed," *Tax Notes International* 12, no. 23 (1996): 1806.

21. "Ghana: Revenue Shortfall Certain," *West Africa,* July 24–30, 1995.

22. "Where was Dr. Botch?" *West Africa,* July 24–30, 1995.

23. Hutchful, *Ghana's Adjustment Experience,* 223.

24. Artur Bogner, "The 1994 Civil War in Northern Ghana: The Genesis and Escalation of a 'Tribal' Conflict," in *Ethnicity in Ghana: The Limits of Invention,* ed. Carola Lentz and Paul Nugent (London: Macmillan Press, 2000), 185.

25. Ibid., 196.

26. "Fatal Miscalculation," *West Africa,* February 28–March 6, 1994.

27. Ibid.

28. This was often referred to in the country's press as the "Fowl War," since the precipitating event had been a dispute over payment for a guinea fowl. Unofficial estimates of fatalities were much higher. Estimates varied from 5,000 to 10,000 killed.

29. "Tension Remains," *West Africa,* March 14–20, 1994.

30. "Opposition Throws Down the Gauntlet," *West Africa,* March 28–April 3, 1994.

31. Paul Nugent, *Big Men, Small Boys, and Politics in Ghana: Power, Ideology, and the Burden of History, 1982–1994* (London: Printer Publishing, 1995), 278.

32. "Togo Squares Up?" *West Africa,* February 8–14, 1993.

33. Ghana sent 700 soldiers to act as peacekeepers in Rwanda.

34. "Lecturers Call off Strike," *West Africa,* January 22–28, 1996.

35. "Poor Exam Results Raise Hackles," *West Africa,* June 6–12.

36. "Lawyers Sue Chief Justice," *West Africa,* April 3–9, 1995.

37. Agyeman-Duah, *Between Faith and History,* 73.

38. He had served 12 years of an 18-year sentence when he was released in 1992 as part of an unconditional PNDC amnesty leading up to the return of civilian rule. "The Pianim Precedent," *West Africa,* April 22–28, 1996.

39. "The Great Alliance," *West Africa,* September 2–8, 1996.

40. Agyeman-Duah, *Between Faith and History,* 88.

41. *Daily Graphic,* September 21, 1996.

42. R. Jeffries, "The Ghanaian Elections of 1996: Towards the Consolidation of Democracy?" *African Affairs* 97 (1998): 196.

43. "MPs Demand Pay Off," *West Africa,* July 22–28, 1996. This would have been equivalent to $11,940, a considerable sum by Ghanaian standards.

44. ISSER. *The State of the Ghanaian Economy in 1997* (Accra, Ghana: Institute of Statistical, Social, and Economic Research, 1998), 138.

45. In 1999 Emancipation Day was added to the PANAFEST itinerary as a day of atonement for African participation in the transatlantic slave trade.

46. Among these nontraditional exports were fruits, like pineapples and mangoes; yams; cashew nuts; and various kinds of seafood.

47. Richard Jeffries, "The Ghanaian Elections of 1996: Towards the Consolation of Democracy?" *African Affairs* 97 (1998): 194.

48. Paul Nugent, "Living in the Past: Urban, Rural, and Ethnic Themes in the 1992 and 1966 Elections in Ghana," *Journal of Modern Studies* 37, no. 2 (1999): 308.

49. Ibid., 205.

50. Jeffries, "Ghanaian Elections of 1996," 207.

12

The Second NDC
Administration: 1997–2001

A STRUGGLING ECONOMY AND A
PARLIAMENTARY OPPOSITION

When Jerry John Rawlings was sworn in on January 7, 1997, as the second president of the Fourth Republic, it was the first time in Ghana's history that an elected government had completed a term in office. He was also the longest-serving head of state, having served in this position six years longer than his closest rival, Kwame Nkrumah. According to the 1992 constitution, which stipulated only two terms for a president, this was to be his last. At the time Rawlings was only 50 and very much at the height of his power. He was very much the bedrock upon which the NDC depended, and without him as the party's flag-bearer, winning again in 2000 was uncertain. Soon after his victory there was a move on the part of the NDC faithful to change the constitution and extend the presidential term to seven years to "allow who ever was in power to carry out his party's policies effectively." They also argued that this would "save costs" and "not put Ghanians through regular periods of anxiety caused by elections."[1] There was little likelihood that such an amendment would have been accepted in a country where heated public debate had long since replaced the earlier culture of silence.

From the first parliamentary sessions it was obvious that the opposition intended to challenge what it saw as similarly dangerous threats to constitutional government. They demanded that the minister of finance, Kwame Peprah, be screened by the Parliamentary Appointments Committee before he could act as a minister. Since they lacked a majority in Parliament to win this demand, they resorted to the courts, as they had done in the past. When this failed to prevent the minister from presenting the annual budget, they staged yet another walkout. They had already resorted to this technique twice before to protest what their leader, J. H. Mensah, had described as "the introduction of procedures that would lead to Parliament abandoning its constitutional obligation." Eventually, after having made what in essence was a symbolic protest, the opposition decided to take part in the debate on the budget "to ensure that the good people of Ghana [had] the best deal."[2]

There was good reason for this, as there was controversial legislation to challenge. In his budget speech, Kwame Peprah announced that the government intended to reintroduce VAT. However, on this occasion there was to be a full year's preparation to provide "adequate public education." Also, the tax rate was to be much lower at 10 percent, as opposed to the 17.5 that had been proposed in 1995. This "more equitable, fair and broad-based tax" was designed to redress the imbalance between revenue and expenditure.[3] Election-year spending had compounded this situation, and inflation in 1996 had been significantly higher than it had been in the previous year. Peprah's promise to reduce it to 15 percent by the end of 1997 met with considerable skepticism even from independent economic analysts. According to the Center for Policy Analysis, an Accra-based nongovernmental research organization, it was highly unlikely that the government would do any better at balancing its budget than it had done in the past.[4] J. H. Mensah, who had been the minister of finance in the Busia administration (1969–72), was easily able to criticize what the opposition felt was the lack of openness on the part of government ministries that would not submit reports.

The most obvious indication of this inability to control the economy was the "cedi on roller skates," which continued to depreciate. In June 1997 it crossed something of a watershed when it sank to 2,000 to the U.S. dollar. Contributing to the imbalance between revenue and expenditure that fueled this depreciation was the roller-coaster ride on which Ghana's main exports careened. The world price for cocoa, the country's second-most-important export, gained slightly in 1997, but the price for gold, the number-one export, slipped from almost $390 to under $350 per ounce, while the cost of crude oil, which had climbed to over $20 a barrel in 1996,

remained almost this high. During the course of the year the cedi continued its downward slide. Eventually, at the end of the year, the minister of
finance was removed from his chairmanship of the SAP and replaced by
the "fiscally hawkish" governor of the Bank of Ghana, Dr. Kwabena Duf-
fuor.[5] His strategy for dealing with the country's high rate of inflation and
the depreciation of the cedi was to refuse to honor checks that were going
to contribute to government deficits.

The year 1998 was a particularly difficult one, as there was a serious
drought that reduced the country's ability to generate electricity from the
Akosombo Dam by more than 10 percent. Luckily for Ghana, the cost of
petroleum declined substantially, to around $12 a barrel, while cocoa con-
tinued to rise on the world market. These factors, coupled with the Bank
of Ghana's strict monetary policies, did contribute to bringing inflation
down to under 20 percent per annum, and the cedi only depreciated by
4 percent during the year. But even here there was a cost involved, as in
effect the government shifted the burden of the deficit to private contrac-
tors, who were not being paid. The result was a decline in economic activity, increased bankruptcies, and rising unemployment.[6] At the same
time, the reduction in subsidies to agriculture had contributed to sky-
rocketing food prices, which gave the opposition plenty of ammunition
for criticizing these policies.

In 1999 even the small gains that strict monetary policies had achieved
were undermined as the price of oil began to rise dramatically while cocoa
and gold began to fall. Contributions from donor nations also lagged, and
the government's attempt to maintain tight spending policies collapsed.
The government resorted to heavy borrowing from the Central Bank, with
the result that there was a sharp decrease in the value of the cedi. Between
November 1999 and April 2000, the cedi went from 2,700 to well over
5,000 to the dollar. It was the worst rate of depreciation for the cedi since
it had been allowed to float in 1991 and contributed to the return of a
currency black market. The year 2000 was an election year, and the government's increased spending to win votes exacerbated this situation. By
the end of 2000, before the elections, the cedi was exchanging at over 7,000
to the dollar. Inflation had roared back, and by this time it was over 40
percent per annum.

Coinciding with this bleak economic picture were the shock waves then
coursing through the gold industry, the country's most important source
of foreign exchange. AGC, which produced over 60 percent of Ghana's
gold exports, almost overnight found itself in a state of near bankruptcy
on account of its excessively aggressive hedging strategies. In the previous
decade AGC had been able to protect is earnings in a market that was

notorious for its ups and downs by agreeing to sell gold to its buyers at what seemed to be the average long-term price. As the price of gold had declined from over $500 an ounce in 1987 to well under $300 by 1997, hedging in this fashion had been extremely successful. However, in June 1999 leaders of the Western industrialized world decided to sell their gold reserves, ostensibly to raise funds to help Third World countries. The world price for gold plunged to $250 an ounce, and there was a chorus of complaints from African countries like Ghana and South Africa, both heavily dependent on gold mining. Heeding these complaints, European central banks quickly decided to end these gold sales. The result was an unanticipated rapid rise in the price of gold, and AGC found itself having to fulfill "forward contracts" by buying gold on the world market that was substantially above the value of these contracts. In September AGC found itself owing over $570 million to U.S. financial institutions with which it had signed forward contracts.[7]

Two divestment exercises in the 1990s had reduced the government's share in the company from 55 percent to 20 percent. Nevertheless, the government still remained a major shareholder, and AGC's financial crisis became a major political issue. It was compounded by poor relations between the company's Ghanaian chief executive, Sam Jonah, and President Rawlings. They had disagreed over the selection of a new *asantehene* earlier in 1999, and it was easy enough for Rawlings to blame Jonah for the company's "extreme indebtedness," which had been the "result of mismanagement."[8] The options available for saving the company were also controversial. The value of AGC's shares had plummeted, and the company was vulnerable to a takeover bid. A merger of this nature was what Lonmin, the majority shareholder in the company, favored. On the other hand, the Ghana government felt that this would compromise the company's Ghanaian identity, and that it should sell some of its non-Ghanaian holdings to raise funds to meet its debts. Eventually the government used its veto power to block a takeover and sacked its own representatives on the AGC's executive board who had sided with Lonmin. This included the minister for lands and mineral resources as well as the finance minister, Kwame Peprah, who was then the chairman of the board. Jonah barely managed to survive as chief executive officer. To raise cash, AGC finally decided to sell 50 percent of its holdings in one of its potentially most profitable mines in Tanzania.

POLITICAL ALIGNMENTS

With the economy in so much turmoil, the field was open for a great deal of soul-searching about what had gone wrong with the country's

SAP. The 40th anniversary of Ghana's independence was in 1997, and there was considerable interest in reexamining the Nkrumah past to see what lessons it had to offer. One of Nkrumah's sons, Gamal Gorkeh Nkrumah, was a guest of honor at the country's independence celebrations. There were also a number of African heads of state as well many visitors from the African diaspora, which gave the celebrations a highly pan-African dimension. The pan-Africanist vision of Ghana's first president seemed particularly appropriate, and former Tanzanian president Julius Nyerere "reiterated Nkrumah's warning that Africa's economic salvation lay in political unification."[9] In a similar vein, the country's newspapers, both government and independent, were full of praise for Nkrumah and what he had achieved. Symbolically, the University of Science and Technology in Kumasi reverted back to its original name, the Kwame Nkrumah University of Science and Technology.

However, this resurgence in interest in Nkrumahism did not necessarily transfer into greater unity and sense of purpose among the Nkrumahist family. The movement to unban the CPP resulted in bitter wrangling over who could claim the name. One of the parties trying to claim the Nkrumah mantle, the Convention Party, was brought before the high court in Accra and prevented for a while from holding its national congress. The PNP, the party of former president Hilla Limann, refused to join any alliance of Nkrumahists. The NDC continued to maintain that it was natural home for true Nkrumahists. Even though Rawlings was well known for his coolness toward the Osagyefo, some of the party's most dynamic leaders tried to use the Verandah Boys and Girls Club (VBGC), which had been formed before the 1996 election, to attract young people who were inspired by the Nkrumah legacy. The organization took its name from the unemployed young men who hung around and often slept on the verandahs of the stores in the main streets of Ghana's larger towns in the 1950s. The term *verandah boys* came to be applied to these malcontents who became enthusiastic supporters of Nkrumah. From their ranks had come the CPP's shock troops.

Within the NDC there was also a grassroots reaction to what was seen as the increasing corruption among government officials and the party's lack of internal democracy. Rank-and-file NDC organizers also complained about the economic hardships that ordinary Ghanaians were experiencing, which was a not-so-veiled criticism of the highly unpopular revenue measures that the government had introduced in 1997. The result was the emergence of the Reform Movement within the NDC, made up of members of the former PNDC defense committees, who represented the left wing of the party. They were particularly critical of what they saw as the numerous power centers outside of the party executive organs.

According to the issues-oriented weekly the *Public Agenda,* "what was looming was a showdown between the two pillars of Rawlings' power base. On one side [were] the foot soldiers who for years have taken orders and worked to keep him in power. On the other side [were] the heavyweights of the regime."[10] The leader of this movement, Goosie Tanoh, was too young to have been active in the heady days of the CPP, but much of his populist rhetoric had a distinctly Nkrumahist flavor.

Even more important in contributing to this division within the ranks of the NDC was the question of who would succeed Rawlings as the party's flag-bearer in the 2000 elections. Amending the constitution to allow him to continue as president was out of the question. It would have produced a maelstrom of protest and would have damaged the country's standing with donor nations. On the other hand, the struggle to succeed him was almost as contentious. It was an open secret that the president's wife, Nana Konadu Rawlings, wanted the party's nomination. Apart from raising questions about the propriety of establishing such a precedent, she had a reputation for abrasiveness that had been very much on display in her numerous confrontations with the independent media. Nevertheless, as the president of the 31st December Women's Movement (DWM), which had played an important role in securing NDC support among women in the 1992 election, she possessed an important power base. The DWM also obtained funds as a nongovernmental organization (NGO) and later on she was to be accused of using this money to fund political activities. She also used the VBGC as another important power base, and had the support of some of this organization's most important organizers, among whom was Dr. Obed Asamoah, the justice minister and attorney general. There was considerable speculation that he would be her running mate, or together they might even split off from the NDC to form a new party that would unite the left wing of the NDC with others who were not traditional party supporters.[11]

However, it was soon apparent that Rawlings did not support his wife's presidential ambitions, and instead he began to groom his vice president, Professor Atta Mills, to be his successor. At an NDC political rally in the Central Region town of Swedru in June 1998 he praised Mills's "diligent work and competence," which to many in the party represented an endorsement of the vice president as the NDC's presidential choice for the 2000 election.[12] This "Swedru Declaration," which it came to be known as, was obviously an attempt to settle the question of succession, but the undemocratic manner in which it had been done rankled particularly members of the Reform Movement, and finally in 1999 they broke away from the NDC and formed their own party, the National Reform Party (NRP), with Goosie Tanoh as its presidential candidate.

Even before this, the Konadu-Asamoah alliance had begun to fall apart, when in December 1997 Asamoah had vast amounts of money stolen from his home. Supposedly the culprits were his aides, but the fact that he had bags and bags of cedis stashed in his home raised all sorts of embarrassing questions about the source of this money and its intended use. Senior NDC officials began to question Asamoah's activities with the VBGC, an organization whose members were not NDC members. He claimed that this was part of a master plan to draw in pro-Nkrumahists to the Progressive Alliance, but in making this claim he began to distance himself from Mrs. Rawlings, who eventually stopped providing him with funding from the DWM. As Asamoah's star began to wane, she realized that there was little likelihood of her being Mills's running mate, as together they would be an all-Akan ticket. She as an Asante and Mills as a Fante would have upset Ewes in the Volta Region, which Rawlings had characterized as the "World Bank" of his regime.

Asamoah still entertained hopes that he would be the NDC's vice presidential candidate, and with his great familiarity with the NDC's internal workings he must have thought that the position was his for the taking. However, indicative of how contentious this selection was, it was not until September 2000, a scant three months before the election, that the choice was made. When Mills finally announced who this would be, he picked instead of Asamoah the latter's deputy, Martin Amidu. Apart from obviously not wanting to be overshadowed by Asamoah, who had a far better base in the NDC, Amidu offered the important advantage of being a northerner, which would give the ticket important regional and ethnic balance. Mills and Asamoah as Fantes and Ewes would have done so also, but there was insistent pressure within the party for a northerner. Advocates for a northerner could argue that the size of the northern voting block was large enough to overshadow in importance that of the Volta Region, which would undoubtedly continue to vote overwhelmingly for the NDC as it had in the past.

There were serious implications for the NDC as a result of all these political machinations. After he had been dumped, Asamoah did publicly come out in support of the NDC ticket, but from then onward he stepped back from being actively involved in the campaign. This was particularly damaging as he was he was chairman of the NDC Finance Committee. Neither was Mills in any position to remove him. When the campaign did begin, Mills was forced to rely on "commissioning public projects to gain some of the spotlight."[13] However, with the economy struggling and already sizable budget deficits looming, there was far less of such projects than there had been in 1996. Once again the party styled itself the Progressive Alliance, which included the EGLE and DPP Parties, as had been the case in 1996, but neither party possessed funds nor significant support in areas where the NDC was weak.

The NDC also sought to avoid the heated contests at the constituency level that had characterized the 1996 election. There were no primaries where wealthier aspirants for office bought off members of the selection committees and displaced sitting MPs. Instead, the NDC decided not to hold primaries, and most sitting MPs were confirmed and others were selected by the party to "avoid the unseemly scramble of 1996."[14] However, it confirmed the impression of the NDC as lacking in internal democracy, and there were "vociferous complaints ... about unpopular candidates being foisted on the local party."[15] It did not necessarily mean that such candidates would be rejected by the NDC electorate, but that the turnout to support them was likely to be far lower than in 1996. This lack of enthusiasm for candidates who in many instances had seldom been seen in their constituencies and had done little for them was to have serious implications for the NDC's ability to maintain a majority in Parliament.

THE OPPOSITION'S CHALLENGE

The NDC's disarray did not necessarily translate into an advantage for the NPP. Within the latter's ranks there was also considerable struggle over who would be the party's standard-bearer in the 2000 election. The 1996 presidential candidate, J. A. Kufuor, was not an MP, and was consequently overshadowed by those who were in a position to challenge directly the NDC's legislative initiatives. A number of them emerged as his major challengers. The two most important were the NPP minority leader, J. H. Mensah, and another NPP parliamentarian, Nana Akuffo-Addo, who rapidly became the most serious challenger. He was almost 20 years younger than Mensah and came from a distinguished Ghanaian family.[16] His father was once the chief justice of Ghana, while he himself had an impressive record of having campaigned against military dictatorship since his late 20s. He was easily the most articulate of the three, appealed to younger party supporters, and was the clear favorite of the country's independent media.

In addition to these rivals, Kufuor also had to deal with the hostility of the party chairman, Peter Ala Adjetey, who was an Adu Boahen supporter. Even though the latter was in poor health and not in a position to run again, this did not stop Adjetey from making scathing public remarks about what he described as Kufuor's incompetence. To counter these attacks, Kufuor made every effort to maintain control of the party's electoral college, where he recognized that the decision on the NPP's flag-bearer would finally be made. At the same time, he tried to remain as much above the fray as possible, unlike Adu Boahen, who had often gotten involved in controversial questions. His main strategy for maintaining his good standing in the party was to attend the funerals of the party faithful and to appear presidential by attending international conferences as the leader of the opposition. Most importantly, he wanted the selection of the party's flag-bearer to be made long before the election, and with the help of his supporters he was able to have the party agree to having this done at the 1998 party congress.[17]

Akuffo-Addo countered these moves by methodically traveling all over the country and getting great amounts of publicity from the independent press and many of the country's now over 30 radio stations. However, unfortunately for his campaign, he did come across as rather arrogant and snobbish in contrast to Kufuor, who was far more approachable, even to the point of being what his opponents considered too much a gentleman.[18] Nevertheless, most of the independent newspapers were convinced that Akuffo-Addo would win. Instead, Kufuor proved to be an easy winner at the party's congress in August, getting 1,286 of the 2,000 votes at stake to Akuffo-Addo's 628.[19] There were four other candidates in the race, and ironically, the initial front-runner, J. H. Mensah, ended up last, with only three votes. In his address to the congress, he had made the mistake of bitterly attacking Kufuor, describing him as an "expired cassava," which had alienated those who might have wanted to support him.[20]

By settling the issue of who would be the party's presidential candidate so early, the NPP was able to avoid the mistakes that had been made in 1996, when the selection had been made far too late in the campaign. On the other hand, the contest had been a bruising enough to alienate those who had lost. There were public expressions of support for Kufuor, but little in the way of financial support. Large debts remained from the 1996 campaign, and Kufuor's attempts to raise money from Ghanaian communities in the United Kingdom and the United States were not particularly successful. Shortly after the congress there were a number of major high-level resignations and defections from the party. The first was that of Dr. Jones Ofori, who had been one of the founders of the NPP and one of the party's main spokesman. At least as damaging was the resignation of Dr. Kwame Pianim, who did so with huge publicity. He claimed he had done so to commit himself to working for political reconciliation, but the NDC interpreted this to mean a vote of no confidence in Kufuor's leadership. Even more damaging was the defection of Kufuor's own campaign manager, Alhaji Issaka Inusah, to the NDC. Supposedly this arose out of his inability to secure nomination as an NPP parliamentary candidate, but it was a major coup for the NDC, who used it to show how much disarray there was in the ranks of NPP.

Selecting a vice president was as challenging as it was for the NDC. To many NPP supporters a Kufuor–Akuffo-Addo ticket appeared to be the most attractive, as it would have combined Kufuor's "urbane maturity" with Akuffo-Addo's "refreshing appeal to the youth."[21] There was also talk of paring Kufuor with Ama Busia, the NPP's vice chairperson and the daughter of the Second Republic's president, Dr. Kofi Busia. Apart from achieving gender balance, which would have been a first in the country's history, there would also have been enormous "inspirational" dividends by creating this link with the man acknowledged "as the spiritual father of the so called Danquah-Busia tradition [then] represented by the NPP."[22] However, neither ticket was practical, as they ran afoul of the more important need to maintain ethnic and regional balance. Both Busia and Akuffo-Addo were Akans, like Kufuor, and eventually, in September 2000, he formally presented a northerner as his running mate. The man he picked, Alhaji Aliu Mahama, a graduate in engineering from the Kwame Nkrumah University of Science and Technology, was relatively unknown but was reputed to have money, which the Kufuor campaign needed badly.[23]

THE ELECTION

In the previous two elections, incumbency had been an important advantage for the ruling party, but in 2000 the advantages were not nearly as obvious. When the election campaign began in earnest in September, world cocoa prices had sunk to record lows of under $900 per ton, while at the same time oil prices were climbing to record highs of around $30 per barrel. Three times during the year the NDC government had been forced to raise the price of petroleum products. VAT had finally come into existence in 1999 and shortly afterward was raised by 25 percent. The cedi seemed to be in free fall, and inevitably this had increased the price of the imported goods on which Ghanaians depended. In the face of these increases in the cost of living, workers had become increasingly restive. In July the TUC had gone on a three-hour demonstration to protest the government's refusal to negotiate what it considered an acceptable minimum wage. The situation was serious enough for the minister of finance, Kwame Peprah, to reject publicly the TUC's demands even as the election campaign gathered steam in September.[24] These were hardly conditions that favored the ruling party, which could only claim that the economy was the victim of unfavorable terms of trade. Their campaign slogan was "progressive change," and they sought to emphasize their hands-on experience with government as opposed to the inexperience of the opposition. The struggling economy did not seem to support this claim.

Very effectively, the NPP selected as its slogan the need for "positive change." By doing so they "invited the electorate to focus on all the things that they disliked about the NDC regime and then to imagine the opposite."[25] It meant that the NPP did not have to be specific about the changes it would introduce, but instead claimed to be the party of ideas and experts as opposed to the NDC, a party of nobodies who had run out of ideas. This was also very much the theme at a presidential forum organized by the Ghana Journalists Association, the Ghana Broadcasting Corporation, and an American foundation, the Freedom Forum, that scored a first in the country's history by bringing together six of the seven parties contesting the election to debate with one another. Only the NDC flagbearer, Professor Atta Mills, was absent, claiming misgivings about the "foreign orientation" of the program and his busy schedule as vice president.[26] The smaller parties were most specific about their remedies for the economy and generally critical of what they felt was the NDC's overreliance on foreign assistance. With little likelihood of displacing the NDC in power and having to deal with international financial organizations, they could afford to voice this populist position. Significantly, Kufuor focused more on issues of good governance.

Corruption in high places had once again become a major issue. At the opening of Parliament in 1998, Rawlings had recognized how much *kalabule* had returned in a new guise.[27] He himself had been subjected to allegations about his probity. At a party rally at the end of the year he had been forced to announce that he was not bribable, to put to rest rumors that he had received a $5 million bribe from the then deceased Nigerian head of state, General Sani Abacha. It was much harder to put to rest other stories of corruption on the part of state officials. The *Ghanaian Chronicle* ran an exposé of malpractice within the Social Security and National Insurance Trust (SSNIT) that threatened pension contributions.[28] Atta Mills, who like Rawlings had presented himself as not bribable, was a personal friend of many of the SSNIT board members. Even more damaging were the activities of Kwamena Ahwoi, who was then minister of planning, regional cooperation, and integration. Along with his brother he had been able to use his government contacts to secure a very lucrative contract from the Cocoa Board to rehabilitate cocoa farms. The independent press was quick to remind Ghanaians that Rawlings's PNDC government had executed eight members of the SMC for conduct that seemed no different.

In general, people who had formerly styled themselves revolutionaries had become entrepreneurs, and many were living beyond their official means. The case of J. H. Owusu Acheampong, the majority leader, who had sent three of his children to American universities at a cost of over $75,000 dollars while his official salary was less than $6,000 per annum, received extensive media coverage. Neither were the Rawlingses able to escape similar attention. They had also sent their daughters to study abroad, which Mrs. Rawlings had been forced to defend publicly on an Accra FM radio station.[29] It was at a time when children could not pass basic level examinations due to the unavailability of textbooks and other basic educational necessities. Symbolizing best of all how revolutionary ideals had been replaced by bourgeois conduct was the transformation in the outward appearance of the president himself. The slim, almost gaunt flight lieutenant of the AFRC and early PNDC days had long since metamorphosed into a well-fleshed politician who was very sensitive to any mention of this physical change.

The NPP also made a calculated pitch to win the youth vote. More than half the population had been born after the December 31 revolution. The difficulty of obtaining education and jobs was of much more concern to them than the revolutionary past that the NDC invoked. The NPP was much better able to tap into this discontent, and was able to overcome the rather stuffy image it had projected in past elections. The NPP keep-fit clubs that sprung up in many parts of the country was a good indication of this appeal to the youth. Club members self-consciously jogged through town "to the bemusement of NDC supporters," and attracted other young voters to their ranks.[30] To these NPP supporters, the NDC did "not pay attention to the youth."[31]

Also, in contrast to the 1996 election, the NPP did not seek to enter into an alliance with any of the other parties contesting the elections, even though there were more of them than had been the case in 1996. As was the case in other African countries, increasing democratization had resulted in the proliferation of parties, one of which, the United Ghana Movement (UGM), had resulted from a break-off from the NPP. Its leader, Dr. Charles Wereko-Brobby, had been the first to challenge the government's broadcasting monopoly when he had established Radio Eye, an FM radio station, in 1994. He had gone on to play a major role in the opposition to VAT, but he had clashed with Akuffo-Addo, as both had presidential ambitions. It was similar to how the NRP had emerged, where younger, more radical NDC members had split off to form their party. Neither the UGM nor the NRP were given much chance in the election, but they obviously were not likely to enter into alliances with either parent party.

The Nkrumahist wing of the Ghanaian political establishment had also gone through considerable soul-searching after its dismal showing in the 1996 election. One faction had finally been able to win the right to call itself the CPP. Their standard-bearer was Professor George Hagan, formerly director of the African Studies Institute at the University of Ghana at Legon and a long-term Nkrumahist who had been a member of Gbedemah's NAL. Not all Nkrumahists had come together under the wing of the CPP, and another member of the NAL, Daniel Lartey, had gone on to form the Great Consolidated Popular Party (GCPP). Neither had the PNC been willing to join with other Nkrumahists, and once again, as had been the case in 1996, its standard-bearer was Dr. Edward Mahama. These parties benefited the NDC more so than the NPP, as they could potentially divide the opposition vote. Nevertheless, with the memory of how unwieldy the Great Alliance had been when the NPP had tried to link itself with the Nkrumahist PCP, there was no incentive to repeat this mistake.

In the 2000 election the ruling party also lost the monopoly over the media that it had enjoyed in the past. There were well over 30 FM radio stations with call-in programs that provided outlets for all kinds of opinions. In addition, the Ghana Broadcasting Corporation had lost its monopoly over television broadcasting, as there were then two independent TV stations. Along with the private newspapers like the *Ghanaian Chronicle*, the *Crusading Guide,* and the *Public Agenda,* this independent media played an important role in leveling the political playing field. The opposition had also been able to get access to the state-owned media. There was daily free time on both the state radio and television for all registered parties, as well as guidelines for equal and objective reporting in the state-owned *Daily Graphic,* the daily paper with the largest circulation in the country.

The bitter struggle over voter registration was one indication of this greater equality. The NDC wanted thumbprint IDs to be acceptable proof of voter registration, but the opposition, fearing that this would open the door to voting by those with fake IDs, wanted only photo IDs. According to the NDC, barring those with thumbprint IDs would hurt rural voters, who were less likely to be literate and able to master the more complex process of obtaining a photo ID. About 1.5 million voters were potentially affected by this decision, and many were rural voters, with whom the NDC had traditionally done well. Initially, however, the EC sided with the opposition, but the NDC appealed to the supreme court, which ruled in favor of the NDC. Even though the opposition lost in the long run, the extensive coverage of the struggle in the press gave them every opportunity to revisit all of the previous examples of what were cited as the NDC's misuse of state resources for electoral purposes. Passions ran high enough for calls for an election boycott.

As had been the case in 1996, the international community also saw this election as crucial for the development of democratic regimes in Africa, and contributed over $17 million in funding. It was significantly less than what was contributed in 1996, but much had been learned from the conduct of previous elections, and the money was better targeted.[32] For example, the United Kingdom played an important role in providing funding for converting thumbprinted voter-identification cards to photo IDs, which more than anything else contributed to defusing the acrimony over this issue. A number of other donors contributed to funding election-monitoring projects that, in contrast to 1996, were carried out primarily by local organizations. In conjunction with the presence of TV cameras and reporters, these observers played an important role in guaranteeing the honesty of the election. Prior to the actual voting there were all kinds of rumors about plots to thwart the outcome of the elections if they went against the NDC. Many were directed toward Rawlings, who remained something of a lightning rod by making a number of controversial speeches that attacked the EC or suggested that an opposition victory would threaten the peace and stability of the country.

THE RESULTS

In spite of all of the fears and a few violent incidents leading up to voting, election day, December 7, proved to be calm and orderly, with the exception of the Bawku Central constituency in the Upper East Region. There a bitter chieftaincy dispute had inflamed electoral politics, and seven people were killed in fighting.[33] In general, the role of civic and religious organizations was pivotal in helping to maintain a peaceful election. The voter turnout was significantly lower than it had been in 1996: 61.7 as opposed to 77.9 percent. Significantly, the decline was highest in the areas that had traditionally supported the NDC. The NPP argued that this was conclusive proof that there had been both double and underage voting in these areas in 1996. Probably a more realistic interpretation of this phenomenon was that many NDC supporters who were not enthusiastic about their party's candidates just abstained from voting. The urban-rural divide that had marked previous elections was even more evident, with the NPP winning all the seats in major urban areas with the exception of Ho in the Volta Region and Wa in the Upper West Region. Like previous contests, the election was a two-way contest between the NDC and the NPP, with the other parties gathering minuscule numbers of votes, mostly in the Greater Accra area with the exception of the PNC, which received almost 200,000 votes, mostly in the north. On what turned out to be the first round of voting for a presidential candidate, J. A. Kufuor won 48.2 percent of the vote to J. E. Atta Mills's 44.5 percent. The NPP won 100 seats in Parliament to the NDC's 92, with 3 seats going to the PNC and 1 to the CPP.

The 1992 constitution stipulated that the presidential candidate had to secure at least 50 percent of the vote to be elected, which meant that there had to be a runoff between Kufuor and Mills. The six opposition parties formed an electoral alliance against the NDC, and in retaliation the NDC sought to appeal to ethnic loyalty. They "exhorted the chiefs and people" in the Western and Central Regions "to 'wizen up' and vote for one of their own," Atta Mills, a fellow Fante, rather than vote for Kufuor, an Asante.[34] In general, the NDC played on the traditional fear on the part of Ewes and Gas of Asante domination, while the NPP appealed to the Ewes in the Volta Region, 88 percent of whom had voted for Mills, to come out of their isolation and join the rest of the country. The three weeks of this campaign were also marked by a distinct increase in personal attacks, with both candidates seeking to discredit the other's competence and that of their running mates. For the first time in the country's history, TV "polimercials" played a major role in what became "a fierce battle of media wits."[35]

In spite of the heated campaigning, the outcome of the runoff election was never really in doubt. Kufuor emerged as a relatively easy winner with 56.73 percent of the votes to Atta Mills's 43.27 percent. It was evident that those who had supported the smaller opposition parties in the first election did indeed give their support to Kufuor in the runoff. Also, there was a small decline in the voter turnout, down to 59.8 percent of the electorate, which once again probably affected Mills more than his opponent. In general, however, there was surprisingly little vote switching, giving the lie to those who believe that Ghanaians simply vote for those who are in a position to reward them. There obviously remained considerable distrust of Akan politicians even though the NPP tried hard to dispel this fear.

All over the country, the results were accepted with good grace, and the dire predictions of violence never materialized. Indeed, the election was a watershed in Ghanaian history. It was the first time that an incum-

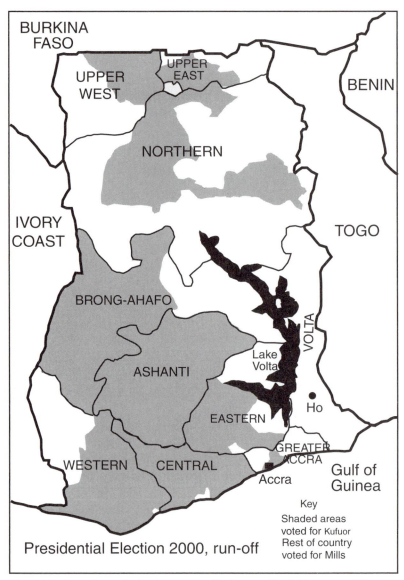

The 2000 Presidential election, run-off. *Source*: Paul Nugent, "Winners, Losers and Also Rans: Money, Moral Authority and Voting Patterns in the Ghana 2000 Selection," *African Affairs* 100 (2001): 426, figure 5. By permission of Oxford University Press.

bent regime had been replaced through constitutional means. The second round of the election was also unique in that it was the first time that the entire opposition had been able to get together and overcome the disunity that has been one of the major weaknesses of opposition movements in general in the continent. This unity carried over even after the election, with the NPP giving ministerial appointments to the leaders of its supporting parties. The campaign was also noteworthy for the degree of transparency and accountability it forced upon the competing parties. They were forced to hold press conferences and issue press statements to rebut or explain positions. Even officials who in the past had treated official information like state secrets were forced to divulge information about who had benefited from state-sponsored overseas medical treatment, or who had bought state-owned enterprises and at what prices.

The campaign and the NPP victory also had a liberalizing effect on Ghanaian society, and "it was celebrated locally as Ghana's 'second independence.'" It was "a powerful demonstration of the power of the thumb as opposed to the power of the gun."[36] This "liberation" was most noticeable on the airwaves, where large numbers of people who in the past had been excluded from the state media were able to participate as analysts and commentators. Previous NDC governments and the PNDC had been able to ignore critical opinions. It was obviously going to be much more difficult for the new NPP government to do so in the future.

For the NDC, the defeat was a terrible blow to party morale, and there was much self-criticism. The lack of internal debate, corruption within the ranks of the party with regards to campaign funds, and most of all the question of leadership were some of the main issues raised. For a while there even seemed to be some danger that internal rivalries might contribute to a split in the party. The party had obviously lost the advantage of incumbency, and it seemed as though it had also lost the support of the DWM, which had provided vitally important financing in the past.[37] On the other hand, the party did enjoy substantial representation in Parliament, which made it potentially a much more potent opposition than had been the case for the NPP. But even here there were uncharted waters. The NPP's strategy of challenging NDC legislative initiatives through court actions and walkouts was not going to be enough if the NDC was going to win reelection in 2004.

Undoubtedly the most challenging question of all was what would be the role of the former president. Rawlings was still a very vigorous 53 and very much at the height of his power. He had twice been the chairman of ECOWAS. In his last term in office he had become a world-recognized leader, welcoming to Ghana Bill Clinton, the first American president to visit Africa, and shortly afterward Elizabeth II, the queen of Great Britain. He had so dominated the election that the NDC's flag-bearer, Atta Mills, had been made to look like the "driver's mate."[38] The latter had even made the damaging confession that, if elected, he intended to consult Rawlings 24 hours a day. His administration would only differ in style but "not in the fundamentals."[39]

The international community had tried to smooth Rawlings' passage from the scene by appealing to his own sense of statesmanship to leave behind a positive legacy. Kofi Annan, the Ghanaian secretary-general of the United Nations, had named him an "eminent person" and charged him with spreading the spirit of volunteerism throughout the world in 2001.[40] Indeed, after the election he was an extremely active participant in forums dealing with the HIV/AIDS pandemic, which has begun to affect Ghana. Nevertheless, the fear of his links to the Ghanaian military still remained. On a few occasions during the election, heavily armed soldiers had appeared at polling stations as election security agents and brought back disturbing memories of past coups.[41] Potentially most unsettling of all was the inevitable reexamining of old abuses that had taken place in the AFRC and PNDC past, in which Rawlings was undoubtedly going to be a major target. Kufuor had promised during the election campaign that he would institute a Truth and Reconciliation Commission (TRC), very similar to the South African Truth and Reconciliation Commission that was then concluding its investigation of abuses under apartheid. Rawlings, in anticipation of such an initiative, had offered an "apology of sorts" in his last address to Parliament in January 2000. This was obviously not going to be enough to satisfy those who felt that they had not simply been "wrongdoers" or persons, as Rawlings maintained, who "deserved to be punished."[42]

NOTES

1. "Constitutional Challenge," *West Africa,* January 27–February 2, 1997.
2. "Walk-outs Galore," *West Africa,* March 3–9, 1997.
3. "VAT to Return," *West Africa,* March 3–9, 1997.
4. "Is Ghana's Economy Shaky?" *West Africa,* June 23–29, 1997.
5. Eboe Hutchful, *Ghana's Adjustment Experience: The Paradox of Reform* (Oxford: James Currey, 2002), 217.
6. Ibid., 217.
7. Ibid., 85.
8. "AGC Crisis Not Over," *Daily Graphic,* February 23, 2000.

9. "Who Will Claim the Mantle?" *West Africa,* July 7–13, 1997.

10. *Public Agenda,* August 11–16, 1997.

11. P. Nugent, "Winners, Losers, and Also Rans: Money, Moral Authority, and Voting Patterns in the Ghana 2000 Election," *African Affairs* 100 (2001): 414.

12. "Gospel According to Rawlings," *West Africa,* January 18–31, 1999.

13. Nugent, "Winners, Losers, and Also Rans," 415.

14. Interview with party activist Tony Aidoo, quoted in ibid., 416.

15. Ibid.

16. Mensah was 72 and Akuffo-Addo was 53.

17. Ivor Agyeman-Duah, *Between Faith and History: A Biography of J. A. Kufour* (Trenton: N.J.: African World Press, 2003), 94.

18. Ibid., 97.

19. "It's Kufuor Again," *West Africa,* November 9–22, 1998.

20. Agyeman-Duah, *Between Faith and History,* 99.

21. "NPP—Search for Fitting Running Mate," *West Africa,* November 29–December 4, 1999.

22. Ibid.

23. Agyeman-Duah, *Between Faith and History,* 111.

24. "Govt Can't Afford ¢5,500," *Daily Graphic,* September 8, 2000.

25. Nugent, "Winners, Losers, and Also Rans," 418.

26. "We'll Tackle Economy," *Daily Graphic,* September 28, 2000.

27. "The Gospel According to Rawlings," *West Africa,* January 18–31, 1999.

28. *Ghanaian Chronicle,* October 4–5, 2000.

29. *Ghanaian Chronicle,* June 26–27, 2000.

30. Nugent, "Winners, Losers, and Also Rans," 420.

31. E. Gyimah-Boadi, "A Peaceful Turnover in Ghana," *Journal of Democracy* 12, no. 2 (2001): 104.

32. Ibid., 111.

33. "Power to the People," *West Africa,* December 18, 2000–January 14, 2001.

34. Gyimah-Boadi, "A Peaceful Turnover in Ghana," 108.

35. "It's Been a Fierce War on the Airwaves," *Daily Graphic,* December 27, 2000.

36. Gyimah-Boadi, "A Peaceful Turnover in Ghana," 112.

37. Nugent, "Winners, Losers, and Also Rans," 428.

38. Ibid., 415.

39. "High Office is No Personal Prize—Mills," *West Africa,* May 15–21, 2000.

40. Gyimah-Boadi, "A Peaceful Turnover in Ghana," 111.

41. Ibid., 109.

42. "Rawlings Qualifies Apologies," *West Africa,* January 31–February 6, 2000.

13

The NPP in Power: 2001–4

DAUNTING TASKS

Coinciding with the NPP's success in the 2000 general election was the victory that the Accra-based soccer club Accra Hearts of Oak secured in the CAF African Champions League. It was only the third time that a Ghanaian soccer club had been able to do this, and the victory added to the sense of euphoria that pervaded a "soccer crazy nation."[1] President Kufuor in his inauguration address took advantage of this "spontaneous joy and feeling of goodwill" to outline what he felt would be his administration's main goals. He promised to forge "ahead in unity." The "turbulent times of the past would not be forgotten," but he also pleaded "that we try to forgive." He also promised "zero tolerance for corruption" and indicated that he intended to set a personal example. He appealed for "continued support and help [from] foreign friends," emphasizing the need for debt relief so that more of the country's revenue could be used to build the economy. He called upon Ghana's business people to lead an economic transformation of the country. To achieve this, he promised "to launch a golden age of business and enterprise" that would transform the lives of Ghanaians within the next decade.[2]

Indicative of the new government's determination to create unity, it offered positions to leaders of opposing parties. Professor George Hagan, the flag-bearer of the CPP, was appointed to the chairmanship of the National Commission on Culture (NCC); Dr. Wereko-Brobby, the presidential candidate for the UGM, was appointed the chief executive of the Volta River Authority, the agency that had been established in 1961 to manage the Volta River hydroelectric project; and Dr. Paa Kwesi Nduom, who had been a driving force in the CPP and had a Ph.D. from the University of Wisconsin in systems management, was appointed minister of energy. He was later on to move up in the ministerial hierarchy to become the minister of economic planning and regional integration.

Much more controversial was Kufuor's decision to visit Togo a scant six days after he had been inaugurated. The rationale behind this visit to Ghana's eastern neighbor was regional unity, by "extend[ing] an olive branch" to his veteran colleague, President Gnassingbe Eyadema, who had often been at loggerheads with the NDC administration.[3] It seemed particularly appropriate at this time, as conditions in Ghana's western neighbor, the Ivory Coast, were getting increasingly chaotic. On the day of Kufuor's inauguration there had been an attempted coup in what was once one of the most stable countries in West Africa. The violence that had engulfed Liberia and Sierra Leone was spreading, and maintaining good relations with Togo seemed very much in Ghana's national interest. Nevertheless, there was considerable protest, both in Ghana and Togo. To opposition parties in both countries it seemed "puzzling" that the leader of West Africa's most shining example of democracy should embrace the ruler of longest-lasting military dictatorship in the region.[4]

Shortly afterward, Kufuor visited Nigeria to cement relations with West Africa's most important country, with whom Rawlings had worked extensively to bring peace to the war-torn areas of the region. Apart from moving ahead with a greater degree of economic integration for ECOWAS, like introducing a common currency for the region, Kufuor also discussed with his Nigerian counterpart, President Olusegun Obasanjo, the contentious issue of Ghana's huge debts to Nigeria for petroleum. There were suggestions that Ghana should reduce the large subsidy it provided to its people for petroleum products, which had contributed to the massive debts the country's refining plant had incurred over the years and also fueled extensive smuggling to neighboring countries, where gasoline was more than double its cost in Ghana. Kufuor obviously felt that resolving such difficult issues required face-to-face discussions between leaders. In general, he felt he should often travel abroad to represent the interests of his country. The seemingly never-ending and expensive nature of these travels was to become a bone of contention between his government and the opposition.

To deal with the turbulent past he quickly moved to have the attorney general draw up guidelines for the rapid release of property that had been seized by the state dating back to the AFRC period. The NDC government had already returned a considerable amount of such property, particularly smaller assets like houses, but there still remained privately owned enterprises, and they had been seized by the state and later on liquidated or turned over to multinational companies. In many cases the original owners had been Indians or Lebanese nationals. In other instances the properties in question were in a poor state of repair, and the question of who should bear the cost of refurbishing them was crucial. Resolving these issues was obviously not going to be easy.

Kufuor also promised a National Reconciliation Commission (NRC) "to provide a forum for those who [were] aggrieved [to] have the opportunity to air their grievances in order to promote the goal of national reconciliation."[5] How this body would function and what the time period would be that it would investigate rapidly became heatedly debated issues. Limiting the investigation to the Rawlings era was obviously seen as politically motivated by NDC supporters. Whether confession would mean amnesty or be self-incrimination was also heatedly debated. Eventually there was an international conference held in Accra in June to examine some of these "vexed" issues.[6]

As a further attempt to achieve some reconciliation with the past, the Kufuor government also allowed the bodies of the three former heads of state and the five military officers the AFRC had executed in 1979 to be exhumed and handed over to their families for more fitting burials than had been performed in 1979. He hoped that this would "bring down the curtain on one of the many sad events of the country's history."[7] Later in the year there was a joint religious service for the eight men.[8] Not everyone agreed with this act of reconciliation, as supporters of the AFRC government felt that the decision set a bad precedent and would spark agitation for similar action from the families of those who had been executed during earlier coups. Most upsetting, they recognized that this gesture could lead to more serious concessions, like a revoking of the indemnity clauses in the Transitional Provisions of the 1992 constitution, which protected from prosecution those who had carried out the orders of the AFRC and PNDC.

The NPP government also moved to deal with the question of high-level corruption. Ironically, it was one of their own ministers who provided them with their first opportunity to demonstrate "zero tolerance for corruption." Barely two weeks after his appointment as the minister of youth and sports, Mallam Yusif Isa was fired for "losing" $46,000 that was to paid as a bonus to the Black Stars, the national soccer team, after a qualifying match for the World Cup against Sudan. Eventually he was prosecuted for "causing financial loss to the state," found guilty, and sentenced to four years imprisonment.[9] Shortly afterward and more importantly, as it had political implications, the government brought charges against the former deputy finance minister, Victor Selormey, for causing financial loss to the state of more than $1 million. The case arose over a project to computerize Ghana's court records. Over $1 million had been paid to a private consultant who had failed to deliver any services. Eventually Selormey was tried, found guilty, and sentenced to eight years imprisonment.[10] To the opposition, this conviction was particularly galling. The law under which Selormey had been convicted had been passed by the NDC government in 1993.

Shortly after the Selormey case, the government brought similar charges against the former finance minister, Dr. Kwame Peprah; the former minister of agriculture, Alhaji Ibrahim Adam; the chief of staff at the presidency, Nana Ato Dadzie; and two other officials of the Rawlings administration for engaging in a conspiracy to cause a loss of $20 million to the state. This scandal, which came to be known as the "Quality Grains Affair," grew out of a project to grow rice in the Volta Region to reduce the country's rice-import bill. The officials charged had committed the Ghana government to guaranteeing approximately $20 million in loans without Parliament's approval. At least $6 million of this money was never invested in the rice scheme.[11] The scandal involved an attractive African American businesswoman who was eventually convicted of fraud in a U.S. district court and sentenced to 15 years. The case gave rise to all sorts of rumors in the press about romantic attachments that drew in President Rawlings himself. Like the previous corruption trials, this one was also conducted in a "fast-track court." These courts had been created to speed up the wheels of the notoriously slow Ghanaian justice system.[12]

Early in 2002 the former chief executive of the Ghana National Petroleum Corporation, Tsatsu Tsikata, who was then also before a fast-track court for causing financial loss to the state, did temporarily halt the activities of these courts when he won a ruling from the supreme court that such courts were illegal. However, it was easy enough for the government to switch his case over into a regular court. In addition, on review the original supreme court's decision on the legality of the fast-track courts was overturned, and by 2003 many more former NDC officials found themselves before fast-track courts facing charges of causing financial loss to the state. As far as the Quality Grains Scandal was concerned, Peprah was eventually found guilty and received a four-year sentence, while his fellow minister, Ibrahim Adam, received a two-year sentence, as did one of the other officials in the case.[13]

In general, the nature of these trials created a great deal of resentment on the part of the NDC, who felt that they were being used as part of a "political vendetta . . . to punish the opposition." Other observers wondered about the legality of the law, and whether the convictions would "criminalize administrative discretion and stifle initiative in the civil service."[14] To these critics, the NPP supporters answered that the prosecutions would "make public servants more careful in handling state property."[15] However, the cases also seemed likely to establish a precedent with incoming administrations seeking to bring charges against previous ministers and officials who had been involved in projects that were financially unsuccessful.

Shortly after coming to power, the NPP government also began to suggest equally controversial economic measures. A number of foreign countries, as a gesture of goodwill toward the new government, canceled the debts Ghana owed them. In exchange, the Kufuor government had to indicate that it was willing to tackle the daunting economic legacy it had inherited. The most immediate was the indebtedness of the Tema Oil Refinery for imported petroleum. More than any other factor, the huge subsidy that the government provided for fuel contributed to its inability to keep revenue and expenditure in line. Much of the borrowing from the domestic banking industry went toward making up this difference, which in turn fueled high interest rates and inflation and resulted in the ever-depreciating cedi. To reverse this situation, the government increased fuel prices by 60 percent in February. Shortly afterward it sought to soften this blow to the public by raising the minimum wage from 4,200 to 5,500 cedis a day.[16]

However, the most momentous decision was over whether Ghana should join the IMF/World Bank HIPC. The HIPC Initiative was launched in 1996 in response to the increasing indebtedness of many poor countries and their inability to service their debts. In exchange for meeting stringent conditions in the management of their economies, they were offered a significant reduction of this debt to what the World Bank and the IMF determined was a sustainable debt level. Eighteen African countries had already joined the initiative, which promised Ghana over $200 million in annual debt relief. At that time Ghana was spending one-fourth of its revenue on debt servicing and was under considerable pressure from Britain and the United States to join the HIPC Initiative to release funds for needed infrastructure development.[17]

A World Bank/IMF program inevitably had its critics. There were those who wondered what naming the country "poor and heavily indebted" would mean to potential investors. Indeed, Japan, one of Ghana's major creditors, quickly indicated its displeasure with the initiative. The Ghana TUC pointed out that Ghana already had a long list of structural-adjustment conditions to meet, "most of which were behind schedule owing to their social implications."[18] There were those who took an even more radical position, that the "so-called debt" was illegal anyway and should be canceled. Doing so would be a just reparation for the atrocities of the slave trade.[19] There were a number of organizations in the United States and Africa that had already been making this connection, and it was not surprising that it surfaced during this HIPC debate in Ghana.

To the government, struggling with a debt of around $6 billion, an inflation rate of over 40 percent when it assumed power in 2001, and a cedi that had depreciated by over 100 percent the previous year, the HIPC Initiative was too much to turn down. Almost immediately there were improvements in the country's overall economic standing. The cedi's rate of depreciation slowed down considerably, to around two and a half to three percent per annum, which was the lowest level achieved since the cedi had been allowed to float in 1988. By the middle of the year inflation had come down to 37 percent, and President Kufuor anticipated that it would be as low as 20 percent by the end of the year. The government had managed to open credit lines with Nigeria for adequate supplies of crude oil, in contrast to when it came to power and there had been only six days of supply left.[20] These achievements came in spite of continuing weak world prices for Ghana's two most important exports, cocoa and gold.

THE NDC IN OPPOSITION

With so many controversial initiatives underway, there were no lack of issues for the opposition. However, among the first were two lawsuits before the supreme court that challenged President Kufuor's right to appoint ministers without parliamentary approval and that of the Council of State. They were very similar to the challenge that the NPP had initiated against the NDC in 1997, and were more of a constitutional legal issue than really substantive. However, by issuing this challenge the NDC indicated that it wanted to ensure that "democratic culture was entrenched," and that no one should "act outside the purview of the constitution."[21]

The impact of NPP policies, like the major increase in the price of fuel, also provided NDC MPs with opportunities to criticize the government.

The increase had come just before the harvest season, when traditionally food supplies are low in Ghana and prices reflect this. The hike in fuel prices had obviously not helped, and the NDC was quick to point out how exorbitant the cost of living had become for the average Ghanaian with the advent of NPP government. The opposition also criticized the new government for its inability to reduce what to many Ghanaians seemed to be an alarming increase in violent crime. Much of this impression stemmed from a brutal series of killings of women in the Accra area. Eventually the new government enlisted the assistance of the U.S. Federal Bureau of Investigation (FBI). A suspect was finally taken into custody, but many questions remained, as he confessed to only 8 of the over 30 killings that had taken place.

The spate of murders fed a rumor mill that had NPP and NDC adherents publicly trading accusations about responsibility for what had happened. Similarly, it was difficult for the political parties to resist politicizing the terrible stadium disaster that occurred during a match in Accra between Accra Hearts of Oak and Asante Kotoko, Ghana's two most successful soccer clubs, which also took place around this time. It had been precipitated by poor police handling of an unruly crowd, and 126 people had died. There were riots in Accra, with youths "chanting for the return of Rawlings."[22]

Much of this skirmishing indicated a healthy give and take between two evenly matched political parties that both had access to a lively press, television coverage, and call-in radio programs. Significantly, in a rare bipartisan display, they came together later in the year to repeal the Criminal Libel and Sedition Laws, which made it possible to claim criminal libel under some circumstances even if the matter reported was true. Ghana had obviously moved a long way forward from the confrontational relationship between the independent press and government in the early years of NDC rule. Unlike during the Rawlings era, journalists from the independent press now followed the president on his official trips. A hundred days into his administration, President Kufuor established a new tradition of holding a press conference to answer questions from reporters from all of the country's newspapers. At the same time, the "unfettered" nature of the press could be disconcerting. According to the acting chief justice, E. K. Wiredu, the repeal of the criminal libel law had allowed unscrupulous journalists to go around "talking rubbish."[23] To many it seemed as if battle lines between the two parties had been drawn aided and abetted by a overly shrill and intemperate press.

The numerous trials of former NDC ministers and, as former president Rawlings expressed it, "the attempt to criminalize everything [the NDC] did" was a major contributing factor to this situation.[24] They seemed to be part of an orchestrated attempt to destroy the NDC and its achievements. Shortly after taking power, the new attorney general, Nana Akuffo-Addo, announced that the government intended to abolish the Public Tribunals, which had been one of the PNDC's major judicial innovations. Indicative of the state of disarray into which these once feared instruments of revolutionary justice had fallen, there was only muted protest. The difficulty of finding lay panel members had increasingly limited the activities of these courts, and in some parts of the country they been idle "for as long as a year."[25] It was hard to justify the expense involved, and to the regular judiciary, which had always been suspicious of this experiment in revolutionary justice, it was yet another powerful reason to do away with the system. However, as a concession, Regional Tribunals were left with the task of adjudicating crimes involving drug offenses.

Similarly, there was a great deal of heated discussion about the future of the BNI, which was also a PNDC creation. There were those who even went to the extreme of suggesting that the bureau should be abolished altogether.[26] Even more emotional was the new government's decision to remove June 4, the day the AFRC had staged its coup in 1979, as a national holiday on the grounds that it had been a military mutiny and therefore "contrary to the principles of a democratic and constitutional order."[27]

However, most contentious of all was the question of Rawlings's resettlement." The first salvo in what was to be an ongoing battle over this issue had to do with the former president's security. While he had been in power, soldiers from an elite army unit had been responsible for his security. On his retirement he had continued with a retinue of 21 bodyguards from this unit, but to many of his enemies, given his coup record and the small number of soldiers such coups had needed, this seemed to be a potential threat to national security. Eventually, after a number of hostile exchanges with the ex-president, during one of which Rawlings claimed his house was under siege, the new government replaced the soldiers with a detachment from the police.

Hostility between the ex-president and the government increased as a result of the address he gave at his party's celebration of the June 4 uprising. He made comparisons between what he saw happening in Ghana and what had been happening in 1979, with the obvious implication that there could be a similar result. Obviously Rawlings did not intend to fade away into his UN-appointed role as an eminent person and be content to turn his attention to the fight against HIV/AIDS in the African continent. He was still the chairman of the NDC and very much wanted to remain in control of its destiny. However, at the party's congress in December, there were many delegates who wanted him replaced. There was considerable resentment over what was seen as his determination to maintain the status quo. This lack of internal democracy was seen as primarily responsible for the electoral defeat in 2000. Reflective of this dissatisfaction, the Congress elected Dr. Obed Asamoah as the new party chairman. It also did away with the previous position of cochairman "to avoid conflicts."[28] This prevented Rawlings from formally sharing the leadership of the party.

This change in leadership was a bruising experience for the NDC, and it seemed as though the party was in danger of falling apart. Neither were there any really substantive areas of disagreement between it and the government to hold the party together. Asamoah criticized the NPP for too closely following IMF polices and its failure to subsidize Ghanaian agriculture. It was not very convincing, since this was what the NDC had done when it had been in power. It was a frustrating situation, which provided Rawlings with opportunities to take up the slack in what seemed like the party's ineffectiveness. At the celebration of June 4 in 2002 he attacked the government's policy on recruitment and retirement in the military.[29] Far more inflammatorily, a few weeks afterward, in a speech to the newly inaugurated Women's Wing of the NDC in Kumasi, he described the NPP government as the worst in the country's history. He called for "positive defiance" against what he described as an "unlawful order," and suggested that Ghanaians did not "have to wait for the next election to prevent the rot."[30]

His remarks unleashed some equally "rash statements from some senior government ministers," and three days after the speech Rawlings was "invited" to the BNI's headquarters in Accra to explain just what he meant.[31] His supporters invaded the BNI's premises, singing NDC songs and calling for an end to the "harassment."[32] Police reinforcements had to be called to restore order. At the same time, Rawlings was involved in importing four Toyota Land Cruisers into the country, two of which were supposedly bulletproof, and this contributed to a flurry of rumors about potential coup plans. There were even suggestions that he should be moved out of Accra to make it more difficult for him to plan a coup. Rawlings obviously relished the attention, which indicated just how much of a force in Ghanaian politics he remained.

At the same time, the results of the party's congress indicated that even within the NDC there were many people who felt that the time had come for him to retire from the active leadership of the party. At the end of the year this became even more evident, when the party convened its special delegates congress to select a flag-bearer for the 2004 election. Significantly, it was to be an open and transparent contest, and it soon became evident that there were a number of contestants. Eventually it came down to a two-man contest between the former vice president, John Atta Mills, and the former finance minister, Kwesi Botchwey. The former had the support of Rawlings and the party's council of elders, while the latter was supported by the party chairman, Dr. Obed Asamoah. There was considerable tension and uncertainty as to the outcome of this contest, but indicative of the support Rawlings and the old guard still enjoyed in the party, Mills overwhelmed Botchwey, collecting 1,116 votes to the latter's paltry 194.[33] Two weeks later the NPP selected President Kufuor again to be the party's flag-bearer. Indicative of his standing in the party and its much greater unity, there were no other contestants and he was accepted by unanimous acclamation without the need for a vote.[34]

NEW INITIATIVES AND CHALLENGES

At the end of its first year in government the NPP government could claim some important successes in the overall performance of the country's economy. This was so in spite of the low prices for Ghana's two most important exports, gold and cocoa. Much of this was due to a reduction in government expenditure and less borrowing from domestic money sources. The result was lower interest rates and a slower depreciation rate for the cedi than had been the case in years before. Nevertheless, the economy still remained highly susceptible to external factors. Apart from export prices, the most important was the cost of petroleum. In 2002 the government discovered that the Tema Oil Refinery's (TOR) debts were even higher than anticipated. Any attempt to privatize this operation, which had been one of the NPP's election promises, required plugging the major drain on the government's resources that the operation of this facility extracted.

The 60 percent increase in fuel prices early in 2001 had been an attempt to deal with this problem. Ghanaians were paying far less for fuel than its actual cost, and even with this increase there still remained a considerable subsidy. To make matters worse, in 2002 the price of petroleum began to increase. Inevitably the value of the cedi began to decline, so that by the end of the year it had gone from a 3 percent to a 13 percent depreciation rate. In 2000 the NDC had been faced with the same problem, but since it was an election year they had done nothing, and the economy had come near to collapsing. The NPP did not want to find itself in a similar dilemma, which had played an important role in the NDC losing in 2000.

Instead, in January 2003, well before the election, the government took the highly unpopular step of raising fuel prices by almost 100 percent.

The increase itself was not unexpected, but its size came as a shock. In one fell swoop the government sought to obtain full price recovery for the petroleum that Ghana was importing. The opposition maintained that this had been dictated by the IMF, which was unhappy with the government's economic performance and also wanted an increase in VAT.[35] The large increase in fuel prices was an attempt to make the latter unnecessary. The NPP remembered all too well how bitterly it had assailed this taxation when the NDC had first introduced it in 1995 and the riots that had followed in Accra. The government made a major effort to publicize the reasons behind the fuel increases. The gamble paid off, and even though there was considerable discontent with the new fuel prices, there were no riots. To ease the burden on the traveling poor, the government began importing double-decker buses from Europe. They were larger than the typical privately owned minibuses (*tro-tros*) that provide most public transport in the country, and consequently cheaper, but even more packed and uncomfortable to use. However, inevitably the dramatic increase in the price of fuel had a ripple effect all across the economy, and many business were left wondering how they would be able to stay in business with these new costs.[36]

In many ways an even more contentious issue involving cost recovery was the government's decision to invite private investors to participate in supplying water to the country's urban populations.[37] Opponents immediately attacked this "public-private partnership" (PPP) as a euphemism for privatization of the country's water-supply system.[38] Once again opponents of this plan saw the IMF and the World Bank as the masterminds behind what was seen as an attempt to commodify something so basic to life as water. Indeed, they maintained that water privatization was one of the conditions that the IMF and the World Bank had included if Ghana was to qualify for HIPC debt relief.[39] Beginning in the 1990s, these institutions had indeed been promoting this approach to dealing with the increasing challenge of providing enough water for rapidly expanding urban populations in the third world. The Second World Water Forum, held in The Hague in 2000 and attended by many of the multinational corporations that were engaged in providing these services, had echoed this "vision." The conference had called for "access to water at an affordable cost."[40]

However, by this time considerable opposition to this market-driven approach to the delivery of water had developed. A number of NGOs had come together to oppose privatization. In Ghana opposition came from a coalition of NGOs and civil society organizations, like churches and trade unions, that came together as the National Coalition Against the Privatization of Water (National CAP of Water). The most vocal of these NGOs was the Integrated Social Development Centre (ISODEC), a local NGO supported by Dutch funding and the publisher of the weekly *Public Agenda*. Initially ISODEC had been involved in assessing ways of improving water delivery in Ghana, but by 2001 they were locked in a heated "battle of nerves in the media" with the Water Sector Restructuring Secretariat, a newly formed bureaucracy to oversee private participation in the water sector.[41] ISODEC's fear was "that even the government [would] be incapable of controlling the monster monopoly it [was] in the process of creating."[42] They did not feel that the Public Utilities Regulatory Commission (PURC) would be up to this task.

There had also been considerable shift in the government's attitude. During the 2000 election campaign the NPP had opposed water privatization, but after assuming power it had quickly come to realize that it could not rely on the Ghana Water Company Limited (GWCL) to improve water delivery for Ghana's sprawling urban areas. Indeed, over the years there had been a number of attempts to address this situation. The Ghana Water and Sewage Corporation had been incorporated to form the GWCL. There had been a number of attempts to train and retrain personnel, and foreign consultants had been hired "to help with capacity building."[43] But it had all been to little avail. According to the GWCL's own estimates, about half of the urban water supply is lost to leakage and the illegal tapping of water mains.[44] The loss by leakage is hardly surprising, since many of these water mains are over 30 years old. There has been very little investment in the country's water system during this time. Only 60 percent of the nation's capital is served by pipe-borne water. Almost half the population relies on water tankers and pays as much as 10 times what the GWCL charges its commercial users.

Schemes to resolve this situation by inviting private capital to participate in the country's water sector have been in discussion since 1994, during the NDC era, and not surprisingly their opposition to privatization has been somewhat ambiguous. However, making participation in the water sector attractive to private companies presented a considerable challenge. Undoubtedly a great deal of expenditure will be necessary to modernize water-delivery systems in Ghana, and current water rates are far too low to ensure some profit on this investment. In 2001 the government tried to respond to this dilemma by increasing water tariffs in urban areas by 95 percent, trying to make that part of the water sector that could afford to pay market rates more attractive to private capital. This followed the World Bank strategy of "unbundling," where rural water supply, where cost recovery is much more difficult, would remain the responsibility of the government. There were also experiments in areas of Accra with pre-paid water meters installed by private companies that have been able to deliver water at cheaper rates than previously. However, the system has been subject to frequent breakdowns, and during the first three years of the project the cost of water has more than doubled.[45] According to CAP's campaign coordinator, Rudolf Amenga-Etego, water-privatization schemes have given rise to an increase in guinea worm, a parasitic infestation transmitted by contaminated water sources.[46]

Not surprisingly, unlike the opposition to the colonial government's Waterworks Bill of 1934, which was also aimed at cost recovery, the current protest against privatization cannot be dismissed as "loose thinking" on the part of Africans. This was how the secretary of state for the colonies, Sir Philip Cunliffe-Lister, had reacted to the 1934 delegation from the Gold Coast that had come to protest this legislation.[47] Instead, the NPP government has been forced to scale back its plans and embark on a public-relations program to win support for PPP. Beginning in April 2004, there have been a number of stakeholders' forums all over Ghana to draft a water policy for the country. With elections coming up in December, it is unlikely that any radical decisions will be made in the near future. Like the introduction of VAT, which required a new government before it was introduced, the same will no doubt be necessary before PPP can go forward.

The issue of private-sector participation (PSP) has also been controversial in other aspects of Ghanaian society that in the past have been dominated by the state. In 1997 the Post and Telegraph corporation, which had enjoyed a monopoly over telecommunications in the country, was officially privatized, with Telekom Malaysia acquiring 30 percent of the new company's stock. The Ghana government retained a 70 percent controlling interest in this new company, Ghana Telecom, but the hope was that the new partners would invest substantially in the operation. This did not happen, and Telekom Malaysia became little more than a management agency. The deal had been bitterly criticized by the NPP when it was in opposition for its lack of transparency, but in 2003 the NPP government entered into a similar arrangement with Telenor, a Norwegian telecommunications company, to replace what was seen as the failure of the Telekom Malaysia arrangement.[48] Once again the deal has been criticized for a lack of transparency. The suspicion is that promises have been made to Telenor that, if made public, would raise a storm of protest in a society that is already highly suspicious of multinational corporations.

Equally controversial have been attempts to seek cost recovery in the operation of the state's institutions of higher learning. There were a number of important reforms in the 1990s that began to reduce what had previously been the state's sole responsibility for financing the operation of the country's universities. Among the most important were the introduction of loan schemes and user fees, so that by 1998 the government was paying less than 40 percent of what it had been paying to support students in 1992.[49] At the same time, there was a considerable expansion in the number of institutions of higher learning and a quadrupling of the student population, with the result that the state's overall expenditure on higher education increased. The loan scheme was funded by the SSNIT, which in reality was highly subsidized by the state. High rates of loan defaulting, as many graduates have not been able to find employment upon graduating, have also compounded the state's financial burden.

In general, tertiary institutions are woefully underfunded, and many of their graduates, particularly in medicine and the sciences, the most expensive fields to fund, leave Ghana for greener pastures. In 2001 Professor Ivan Addae-Mensah, the vice-chancellor of the University of Ghana, indicated that the university intended to recover the full cost of training each student by introducing tuition fees.[50] So far this has not been implemented, but the plan has the support of the government, which recently has been reducing substantially the per-student subsidy it has contributed to the state universities.[51] Implementing changes within the Ghanaian university system has always been controversial and contested. Immediately after the vice-chancellor's announcement, the Students Representative Council (SRC) of the University of Ghana at Legon rejected outright the two-tiered tuition system he proposed.[52] Undoubtedly this change will continue to be controversial and contested. Ghana's university students, with the assistance of their union, NUGS, have a long history of opposing government reforms for higher education, but so far during the NPP administration there have not been any attempts to shut down the universities.

After considerable opposition, privatization of tertiary education has also began to transform higher education in the country. In the late 1990s the NDC government invited PSP in higher education. Many of the main religious organizations in the country have taken up this challenge, and a number of such institutions have come into existence. Apart from providing religious training, they invariably offer courses in career-oriented studies like business, accounting, and information technology. Their tuition fees are substantially higher than the user fees currently being charged by the University of Ghana. However, they come much closer to full cost recovery, which is significantly lower than for the state institutions, which have a history of being both overstaffed and underpaid. Not surprisingly, these private institutions have been able to lure away faculty from the state institutions with better salaries. Only about half of the students who seek admission to the state universities can be accepted, so the private universities, in spite of their much higher cost, have had little difficulty in meeting their enrollment goals.

From very hesitant beginnings in the PNDC era, when the issue of privatization of state-owned concerns became a major issue, it is not surprising that the pace of this process has picked up considerably in the NPP's Golden Age of Business. Recently there has also been talk of privatizing Ghana Airways, Ghana Railways, and even Ghana Commercial Bank. In the case of Ghana Airways their aircraft are old and uneconomical to operate. The airline has massive debts and a bloated workforce. It is hard to imagine any private investor offering more than a pittance for its assets, but with the country's tourist industry taking off, it might be "offering a potential gold mine on a sliver platter to the lucky investor(s)."[53] Selling the country's "patrimony and . . . heritage to outsiders" has always been politically sensitive in Ghana.[54] In the case of Ghana Airways, there are particularly sensitive memories, since the airline is still very much associated with the early days of independence, when it symbolized the country's coming of age. Privatizing the rail system might be less politically sensitive, but it is also badly run-down. It has never achieved cost recovery, even in colonial days, and it is hard to imagine it being attractive to any private investor. In general the country's banking industry also needs a major infusion of capital to modernize, but attempts at privatization would raise a storm of controversy.

Apart from facing considerable challenge over the question of privatization, like the NDC government, the NPP has also had to deal with serious ethnic unrest in the north. In March 2002 the *yaa-naa* of the Dagon Traditional Area, Yakubu Andani, was brutally murdered, along with 28 members of his palace administration, in his capital of Yendi in the Northern Region. The perpetrators were members of a rival "gate" (clan) who have been locked in a chieftaincy dispute that has been going on for more than a generation. The brutal nature of the murder and the importance of the *yaa-naa* in Ghana's chiefly hierarchy (he is the leading traditional authority in the north, and probably the second-most-important in the country after the *asantehene*) immediately made this an issue of national security. So sensitive was the issue that the government imposed official censorship on the Ghanaian media, which inevitably gave rise to "raging fires of conspiracy-making."[55]

The NPP responded with the well-established tradition of holding a commission of inquiry as well as appointing a mediation committee that included the new *asantehene*, Otumfuo Opoku Ware II, and a number of major chiefs from the north. More immediately, the government had to dispatch a military and police force to the area that a year later had cost the government 7 billion cedis (over $800,000) to maintain. Unrest in the Yendi area sparked unrest in other areas of the north, which has inevitably become linked to the country's main political parties. For two and a half years there was a state of emergency in all districts of the Yendi Traditional Area as well as in the Northern Region's capital, Tamale, which has only recently been lifted.[56] Ghanaians are well aware that what is happening in the north offers a frightening parallel to what happened in Sierra Leone and Liberia in the 1990s, where ethnic fighting began in similarly outlying areas and eventually came to engulf the entire country.[57] The large number of fragmented ethnic groups in the north, and their customs that seem outmoded to many other Ghanaians and spawn conflicts, make this area of Ghana particularly susceptible to unrest, which politicians of the major parties have found hard to resist exploiting. Just as the NDC was challenged to remain impartial after the conflict of 1994, the NPP has experienced similar difficulty in remaining neutral.

RUN-UP TO THE 2004 ELECTION

In December 2004 Ghanaians will once again go to the polls to select a new government. Six months before the election there are five parties officially registered with the EC, but as in previous elections of the Fourth Republic, it will undoubtedly come down to a race between the NPP and the NDC. Currently indications seem to favor an NPP victory. In the past, incumbency has been a potent advantage. Significantly, the NPP has won all of the seven by-elections in the last three and a half years, and its flag-bearer, President Kufuor, has acquired unrivaled stature in his party, similar to what Jerry Rawlings enjoyed when he was the flag-bearer for the NDC. Indicative of his regional status, he is now serving his second term as president of ECOWAS. He has played a pivotal role in the negotiations between the warring parties in neighboring Ivory Coast, and Ghana, along with Nigeria, has become the most important country in working for peace in the West African region.

President Kufuor has also been able to establish an international reputation for himself, as evidenced through the successful visits of British prime minister Tony Blair and German chancellor Gerhard Schroeder.[58] Blair's visit was the first by a British prime minister since Harold Macmillan's in 1960. Schroeder's was the first by a German leader since independence. Kufuor himself has worked hard to establish an international presence by doing his fair share of globetrotting and meeting many of the world's important leaders. He has enthusiastically embraced the program of the New Economic Partnership for Africa's Development (NEPAD), which was set up by the main industrialized nations (the G8) in 2002.[59] This initiative's call for trade and investment rather than loans and grants to spur development in Africa fits in well with his own ideas about the role of private capital. Similarly, he has been pan-Africanist by playing an important role in the formation of the African Union, which in 2002 replaced the OAU with an organization modeled after the European Union.

On the economic front, his government has been able to avoid many of the pitfalls that undermined the NDC's in 2000. It has done far better in reducing the rate at which the cedi has devalued. During 2003 it devalued at 4.7 percent and is currently devaluing at a slightly slower rate. This has been a significant achievement, since the world price of petroleum has risen far beyond what the government anticipated, and in spite of the massive increase in fuel prices in 2003 the government continues to provide a considerable subsidy to Ghanaian consumers. Not surprisingly, inflation has been harder to control. It peaked at 30 percent in April 2003 and then declined to a little under 24 percent by the end of the year, and in spite of crude-oil prices reaching even higher levels, by the end of the year inflation has continued to decline, so that in May 2004 it was only 11 percent, the lowest it has been in recent time.[60] Not surprisingly, in his address to Parliament on the 2004 budget, the finance minister, Yaw Osafo-Maafo, was upbeat on the overall state of the country's economy. He pointed out that the real-growth domestic product (GDP) had grown by 5.2 percent, which was better than the 4.7 percent that had been projected for 2003. The government had also come very close to meeting its target for an anticipated budget deficit, and consequently "domestic borrowing represented the best performance since 1995."[61]

High prices for Ghana's two most important exports, gold and cocoa, played an important role in enabling the economy to offset the shocks caused by the high cost of crude oil. Ironically, instability in the Middle East, which affected the price of crude oil, at the same time had weakened the U.S. dollar, and gold inevitably benefits from this development. Similarly, instability in the neighboring Ivory Coast, the world's largest producer of cocoa, has driven up the price of the commodity. In 2002 cocoa reached $2,000 per ton, which was a 15-year high.[62] This meant that the Ghana government has been able to raise the price paid to cocoa producers in the country to the point where they are currently getting almost 70 percent of the world-market price for their crop. Apart from cutting down on smuggling across the border to the Ivory Coast and Togo, where it is estimated 40,000 tons of Ghana's cocoa goes, an increased price for cocoa is calculated to help the NPP in the major cocoa-growing areas of the country.[63]

The NPP government has also been able to reach what the World Bank and the IMF describe as the "HIPC completion point." This means that the country has been able to bring its economic performance into line with standards established by these agencies, and it is now entitled to a maximum cancellation of debt owed to the World Bank and the IMF. In reality what this means is that funds that would have been spent servicing these debts can now be used to fund development projects in Ghana. Already this scaling back of debt repayment to these agencies has been happening. The NPP government has been deriving as much support as possible for its decision to join HIPC by indicating what recent projects have been funded through this initiative, even to the point of claiming some that political opponents claim were not.

Nevertheless, in spite of the economic achievements there still remains considerable opposition to how HIPC has enabled the IMF "to strengthen and entrench its control over economic policy management" in Ghana.[64] How long Ghana will remain "stuck in the HIPC fraternity" is a highly politically sensitive issue.[65] In general, though the World Bank and the IMF may be relatively satisfied with the country's economic progress, the increase in fuel costs, hikes in utility bills, stubbornly high unemployment rates, and a recent tax on earnings to fund a national health scheme have all added to a sense of disillusionment on the part of many ordinary Ghanaians that things are getting worse rather than better. The macroeconomic successes that donor agencies applaud seldom trickle down to the masses in ways that are easily recognized. Even infrastructure improvements, like road and sewage construction, have increased the already high level of congestion in many of the country's main urban areas and have added to this dissatisfaction. A wide array of newspapers and talk-radio shows have made it much easier than at any time in the past to express all kinds of discontent, and there are those, particularly in the urban areas, who see "no point spending hours in a queue to vote for a party where your reward will be no improvement in your living standard."[66]

However, it is debatable how much this potential voter apathy, or even outright criticism of "Kufuornomics," will help the opposition parties and the NDC in particular, since many of the current unpopular economic policies trace their roots back to the PNDC/NDC period. Not surprisingly, the NDC minority cooperates 90 percent of the time with the majority in Parliament.[67] Also, the NDC struggles with a reputation, stemming from its PNDC days, for authoritarianism and an arbitrary use of power. The recently completed NRC has if anything confirmed this opinion. Predictably, the highly emotional issue of the murder of the three high-court judges and the retired army officer came up during its hearings. Inevitably there were many attempts to link directly ex-President Rawlings and Kojo Tsikata, the former head of state security, with this atrocity. Not surprisingly, there were no startlingly new developments, since this horrific crime has been the object of intense scrutiny ever since it happened in 1982. Many of the witnesses who tried to implicate Rawlings and Tsikata had, even before the hearings, already undermined their own credibility. Nevertheless, there were more than enough sordid details about other atrocities to rake up unpleasant memories from this past. In contrast, the NPP administration has been constitutional and open to debate, and undoubtedly gains by comparison.

Instead, the NDC opposition has tried to make the issue of corruption in government a major element in its campaign. Ex-President Rawlings has been promising that if the NDC was successful in December it would begin trying the corrupt officials in the NPP administration.[68] Undoubtedly there have been scandals. Recently, the deputy minister for presidential affairs, Alhaji Bamba, was forced to resign for "indiscretion in his business dealings."[69] Other ministers have been involved in similarly shady operations, and a number were charged with crimes by the Serious Fraud Office. However, to NPP opponents it has seemed as if "zero tolerance for corruption" has been applied far more stringently to northerners than to Akans, and they have tried to use this to undermine support for the NPP in non-Akan areas.[70] The use of ethnicity in Ghanaian politics has tended to wax and wane in importance.[71] However, how successful it will be in this context is questionable, for the NDC's record is also not without blemish. More importantly, and once again like the NDC, the NPP government has been careful to spread development projects around the country. They have even used this record to challenge the Volta Region to give up its reputation as the "World Bank" of the NDC and join with the rest of the country.[72]

NOTES

1. This is how President Kufuor (former chief executive of Asante Kotoko soccer club) described Ghanaians at his recent presentation to the

CFA (Confédération Africain du Football) in support of Ghana's bid (successful) to stage the 2008 African Cup of Nations.

2. "Launching a 'Golden Age'," *West Africa,* January 15–21, 2001.

3. "Arguments over Kufuor Visit," *West Africa,* February 12–18, 2001.

4. Ibid.

5. "Kufuor Promises National Reconciliation," *West Africa,* February 26–March 4, 2001.

6. "Reopening Wounds or Reconciliation?," *West Africa,* June 25–July 1, 2001.

7. "Reburial for Executed Generals," *West Africa,* May 14–20, 2001.

8. "Ghana Buries (some of) its Past," *West Africa,* January 14–20, 2002.

9. "The 75-day Inquiry into the Missing $46,000 Ends Mallam Issa Jailed 4 yrs—Lawyer to Appeal," *Daily Graphic,* July 21, 2001. He was also fined and ordered to repay the money or face additional periods of imprisonment.

10. "Corruption, Justice and Party Politics," *West Africa,* December 17–23, 2001.

11. "Quality Grain Scandal can't be Justified," *Daily Graphic,* May 1, 2001.

12. One of the most important differences between them and the ordinary courts was that they had been computerized, in contrast to the latter, where judges laboriously transcribe the court's record in longhand.

13. "Ghana's Rice Scheme Trial: Judgment and Controversy," *West Africa,* May 5–11, 2003.

14. Ibid.

15. "The Question of Integrity," *West Africa,* May 5–11, 2003.

16. "Minimum Wage Now ¢5,500," *Daily Graphic,* May 1, 2001.

17. "What to do About Ghana's Debt?" *West Africa,* March 12–18, 2001.

18. Ibid.

19. Ibid.

20. "Kufuor Confident," *West Africa,* July 9–15, 2001.

21. "Writs Have Started Flying," *West Africa,* February 5–11, 2001.

22. "Ghana: Thousands Attend Soccer Disaster Memorial," *African Sun Times,* May 17–23, 2001.

23. "Reviving a Dead Debate," *West Africa,* October 15–21, 2001.

24. "We Can Live with each other in Peace," *West Africa,* September 9–15, 2002.

25. "Judges Back Move," *Daily Graphic,* October 5, 2001.

26. "Intelligence Service Under Fire," *West Africa,* June 18–24, 2001.

27. "Erasing 'Rawlings Day'," *West Africa,* June 11–17, 2001.

28. "Tough Political Battle Ahead," *West Africa,* July 1–7, 2002.

29. "Mode of Retirement from GAF Dangerous—Rawlings," *Daily Graphic,* June 6, 2002.

30. "Rawlings Becomes a Hot Issue," *West Africa,* August 26–September 1, 2002.

31. Ibid.

32. Ibid.

33. "NDC Chooses Mills Again," *West Africa*, January 13–19, 2003.

34. "Two Johns to Contest Again," *West Africa*, January 13–19, 2003.

35. "New Fuel Prices are Outrageous—NDC," *Daily Graphic*, January 20, 2003.

36. "Oil: Cost Recovery and the Suffering Public," *West Africa*, January 27–February 2, 2003.

37. "Ghana Water Privatization Controversy," *West Africa*, October 15–21, 2001.

38. It was also described as "private-sector participation" (PSP).

39. "Water Privatization is HIPC Condition," *Public Agenda*, September 27, 2001.

40. "Ministerial Declaration of The Hague on Water Security in the 21st Century," March 22, 2000. http://www.waternunc.com/gb/secwwf12.htm

41. "Ghana Water Privatization Controversy," *West Africa*, October 15–21, 2001.

42. Ibid.

43. "Water: Minister Defends Policy," *West Africa*, October 21–27, 2002.

44. "We are Committed to Making Water Safe," *West Africa*, April 7–13, 2003.

45. "Tema Residents Cry Foul Over Pre-Paid Meters," *CAP Water News*, July 16, 2004.

46. "Paying the Price for Clean Water," *West Africa*, April 7–13, 2003. In 2004 he received a Goldman Environmental Prize from this California-based environmental foundation.

47. "Are We Loose Thinkers?" *Daily Graphic*, July 12, 2004.

48. "Unease over Ghana Telecom Deal," *West Africa*, February 17–23, 2003.

49. Eboe Hutchful, *Ghana's Adjustment Experience: The Paradox of Reform* (Oxford: James Currey, 2002), 137.

50. "Call for Tuition Fees at Legon," *Daily Graphic*, October 22, 2001.

51. "Ghana's Universities Consider Full Cost Recovery," *West Africa*, March 31–April 6, 2003.

52. "Controversy Over Tuition Fees," *Daily Graphic*, October 23, 2001.

53. "Ghana Airways Will not Die," *Daily Graphic*, July 22, 2004.

54. Roger Tangri, "The Politics of State Divestiture in Ghana," *African Affairs* 90 (1991): 529.

55. "A Long-standing Conflict," *West Africa*, April 8–14, 2002.

56. "State of Emergency Lifted," *Daily Graphic*, August 17, 2004.

57. "NDC, NPP Tension in Tamale: Save Ghana from a Liberia Situation—Security Agencies Told," *Ghanaian Chronicle*, July 16, 2004.

58. Blair visited in February 2002, Schroeder in January 2004.

59. "Implementing NEPAD in Ghana," *West Africa*, May 5–11, 2003.

60. "Effect of Declining Inflation Rate on Economy," *Daily Graphic,* May 5, 2004.

61. "Budget 2004," *Daily Graphic,* February 7, 2004.

62. "Cocoa market Still Unpredictable," *West Africa,* September 23–29, 2002.

63. Ibid. This is equivalent to between 12 and 13 percent of the annual cocoa crop.

64. Charles Abugre (executive director of ISODEC), "Three Years into HIPC: What for Ghana?," (paper presented to the Legon Economic Students Society, Legon, Ghana, March 17, 2004), 4.

65. "NDC Disputes Minister's Claim Over HIPC," *Daily Graphic,* July 20, 2004.

66. "2004 General Election in Ghana," *Daily Graphic,* February 10, 2004.

67. "Minority, Majority in Parliament, so far so good, says Bagbin . . . As Minority Cooperates 90% with Majority Gov't," *Ghanaian Chronicle,* June 17, 2004.

68. "Jerry in His Element . . . Attacks NPP Gov't again . . . Says NDC Gov't will Imprison Corrupt NPP Officials," *Ghanaian Chronicle,* July 22, 2004.

69. "Alhaji Bamba Resigns," *Daily Graphic,* February 7, 2004.

70. "Kufuor is Pursuing Injustice and Nepotism, says Alhaji Dauda," *Ghanaian Chronicle,* July 19, 2004.

71. Carola Lentz and Paul Nugent, "Ethnicity in Ghana: A Comparative Perspective," in *Ethnicity in Ghana: The Limits of Invention,* ed. Carola Lentz and Paul Nugent (London: Macmillian Press, 2000), 22.

72. "NPP Enjoys Goodwill in the Volta Region," *Daily Graphic,* June 15, 2004.

Epilogue: Moving Forward, Looking Backward

In 1957, when Ghana became independent, in many ways it was at the same state of economic development as South Korea. Both countries were predominantly agricultural, they exported primary products including some mineral resources, they had experienced various forms of colonial rule, and they had per-capita incomes that were very similar. Today, South Korea is a newly industrialized nation with a per-capita income that is more than eight times that of Ghana's and ranks second in Asia after Japan. This startling difference in economic performance has long been a source of fascination to Ghanaian intellectuals, who have not failed to notice that in many respects Ghana in 1957 seemed a better candidate for development: it was significantly larger in size, not nearly as mountainous, possessed more mineral wealth, and, in contrast to the devastated state of the Korean peninsula after the recently concluded Korean War, enjoyed almost half a billion dollars in reserves.

In the 1960s and 1970s marxist explanations based on dependency theory were much in vogue to explain the failure of Third World countries like Ghana to develop. Underdevelopment in countries like Ghana, many of which had recently experienced European colonial rule, was the result of the capitalist nations of the world continuing to exploit the resources of the Third World to benefit their own economies, and preventing the development of integrated and competing economies overseas. By being restricted in the capitalist system to exporting primary products, Third World counties were doomed, in the words of one leading spokesman for this school of thought, to the "development of underdevelopment."[1] In the Ghanaian context this interpretation was best exemplified in Kwame Nkrumah's *Neo-colonialism: The Last Stage of Imperialism*, which argued that in this new stage of "neo-colonialism," states that enjoyed "all the outward trappings of international sovereignty" did "in reality [have their] economic systems and thus their political policy directed from outside."[2]

More recently, with the collapse of the socialist bloc, which seemed to offer an important alternative to capitalist development, and the rise of other "Asian Tigers," like Malaysia, Singapore, and Thailand, dependency theory has had to compete with other explanations. Instead, a new generation of critics now also point to far more internal explanations for the failure to develop, like "failed leadership," the "inability to mobilize human and financial resources," and "political instability."[3] Malaysia, particularly, offers striking parallels to Ghana but with a very different outcome. They are both tropical countries of similar population size with long histories of exporting primary products: tin and rubber for one, gold and cocoa for the other. Both were model British colonies with economies controlled by metropolitan conglomerates. Unlike South Korea, with a basically homogeneous population, Malaysia also possess considerable ethnic diversity, with the potential for serious conflicts, which in the late 1960s exploded with a ferocity not yet seen in Ghana. Nevertheless, by the late 1980s Malaysia was well on its way to becoming a major manufacturing exporter, with a per-capita income that was "approximately four times that of Ghana."[4] Today Malaysia is a middle-income country with a per-capita income that remains four times that of Ghana's.

Since its independence in 1957 Malaysia also followed a bewildering series of development strategies. Like Ghana, it began with private-sector development right after independence, then made an about-face to a state-dominated economy, and finally, like Ghana in the 1980s, reverted once again to privatization. Inconsistency of this nature has undoubtedly been a major obstacle in the path to development for Ghana. Along with the destabilizing influence of the coups and counter-coups that were an integral part of this experience, these economic changes contributed to making Ghanaians poorer in 1970 than they had been at the time of independence. Establishing a predictable order in this history of chaos may well be the PNDC/NDC's most important legacy. However, it was obviously not able to do so as effectively as was the case in Malaysia. There has undoubtedly been modest economic growth since the 1980s. For anyone familiar with Ghana over this period the changes have indeed been striking, but undoubtedly Ghana still remains very much a poor Third World country, and this situation has ensured that the debate over what direction Ghana's economic policies should take continues.

In his inauguration address in 2000 President Kufuor promised to transform the lives of Ghanaians within a decade and to make the country a middle-income nation. The example of the Asian Tigers looms large in this vision, but it offers no obvious and easy blueprint. Aspects of these Asian strategies have at times been at variance with those advocated by the World Bank and the IMF, which have become important players in shaping Ghana's future. Undoubtedly there have been mistakes, or at least false assumptions about what was possible, and all of this uncertainty has contributed to the lively debate that continues in Ghana today between those who are highly suspicious of what today is described as globalization, and those who, like President Kufuor, believe that "empowering the private sector is the only sustainable method to create wealth in a nation."[5] Once again the roots of this open-ended debate can be traced back to the PNDC/NDC era, but in the Kufuor administration it has become significantly more vigorous. The culture of silence has been replaced much more by a culture of lively debate and vocal dissent.

The pendulum has clearly swung in the direction of less state control of the economy, which characterized the colonial period. However, divestiture and privatization, which also began in the PNDC era, have not been easy. Even in what President Kufuor hopes will be a golden age of business, there still remains considerable suspicion of the entrepreneur in Ghana. Particularly is this so for foreigners, who all too often seem to outperform their Ghanaian counterparts. Unquestionably the latter have faced enormous odds. In the colonial era, the commanding heights of the economy were preserved for metropolitan conglomerates. Outsiders, like the Lebanese, Indians, and to a lesser extent Nigerians were able to establish a foothold in retail trading. Perhaps, like the Chinese in Malaysia, they might have later on been able to move into manufacturing, but like their Ghanaian counterparts they were victims of the very hostile climate to private enterprise that characterized the early years of independence.

Not surprisingly, attracting private foreign investment to a country where the issue of cost recovery, not to mention profit, is bitterly contested has been difficult. Most of the infrastructure development that has taken place in Ghana since the 1980s has been financed through donor agencies like the IMF/World Bank and government-to-government loans that are a burden on the country's general revenue. Only very recently have there been tentative attempts to impose user fees that will at least recover costs. As one observer has recently pointed out, the capital that has flowed into Ghana has functioned more like "welfare" than as investment to promote economic growth.[6] There has been some economic diversification, with the economy no longer as dependent on cocoa as was the case before, with tourism offering the brightest promise. But even this represents a mixed success. As cocoa production in Ghana stagnated during the 1970s and 1980s, the neighboring Ivory Coast expanded its production and now is responsible for 40 percent of the world's production, as once was the case for Ghana.

Instead, the most important source of foreign exchange in Ghana today comes from remittances from Ghanaians who have migrated to Europe, North America, Asia, and other African countries. In 2003, according to government figures, this amounted to $1.9 billion, which was equivalent to more than 80 percent of Ghana's total exports.[7] There is constant lamenting in Ghana today about the loss of skilled personnel to greener pastures overseas, but the money that they send back amounts to the most important source of "welfare" for the country. In a belated recognition of the importance of these Ghanaians in the diaspora, in 2002 the NPP government finally granted them the option of dual citizenship.[8] Apart from paying for basic necessities, a significant portion of money that comes back is invested in the acquisition of property, primarily as retirement family homes, which indicate how close the ties still remain with Ghana.

Undoubtedly over time this investment will diversify into more business-oriented ventures, but before this can happen some resolution of the highly contested issue of property ownership will be necessary. One of the many legacies bequeathed from the colonial past has been the confusion over property ownership stemming from competing systems of inheritance. Conflict between indigenous systems of inheritance based on matrilineal and patrilineal conceptions of the family have vied with one another as well as with Western concepts of the nuclear family and individual property. The colonial judiciary was never really able to resolve these conflicts and went back and forth from either favoring English common law or traditional law, which itself was highly varied. The result was that disputes over property could drag on for years before the colony's courts with judgments even being appealed all the way to the Privy Council in Great Britain. Today "land guards" function like a private police force to defend possession of disputed lands while these disputes still languish for years before the country's courts. Recently there has been talk of creating "fast-track land courts" to deal with what has become a state of paralysis in the regular courts.

The colonial past has also left unresolved the position of the chief in modern Ghanaian society. At the time of independence there were many observers who felt that this traditional institution would be swept away by the advancing waves of modernization.[9] This has not been the case, and today chieftaincy in Ghana is if anything more vibrant than it was in the heyday of indirect rule. Rather than conforming to the colonial stereotype of the illiterate chief as the norm, today "higher education has invariably become one of the qualifications for ascending to any stool in Ghana."[10] Nevertheless, disputes over chieftaincy issues have been at the heart of some of the potentially most destabilizing issues in Ghana today. Not only is this so for the north, which today is something of a flashpoint. Currently in the Central Region there are over 200 chieftaincy disputes before the country's various courts.[11] Periodically they can also become so inflamed that they explode, with resulting loss of life and property.

This is not unlike the situation that existed in the colonial period. Once again colonial policy oscillated from one extreme to another. Initially it was hostile to chiefs, particularly in the "civilized" areas of the coast, and favored direct rule. Then it changed to one of indirect rule through the chiefs, but at the end of the colonial period turned away from the chiefs in favor of locally elected officials. Neither has the independence period been any more consistent in its attitude toward traditional office holders. The Nkrumah government was extremely hostile to the chiefs, who it saw as having been "pro-British stooges."[12] In the Busia era they came back into favor and obtained their own deliberative body, the National House of Chiefs, and the government agreed to stop meddling in chieftaincy affairs. However, there was a reversal in the PNDC era when there was an attempt, once again, "to tame the chief."[13] PNDC Law 107 made the chiefs dependent on government recognition. Finally, in 1992, with the passage of the Fourth Republic's constitution, the chiefs once again were guaranteed an independent status not dependent on recognition from anyone, but barred from participating in party politics. With this checkered career it is hardly surprising that the institution has failed to crystallize into a stable form.

Creating macroeconomic stability in Ghana will continue to be of paramount importance to whatever party wins the election in 2004, but so too will resolving more individual and parochial issues, like property ownership and bringing stability to the institution of the chieftaincy. The two are closely linked, since a great deal of land in Ghana today is "stool land," or land under the control of the nation's chiefs, and most of the chieftaincy disputes inevitably revolve around disputes over the use of this land. At the onset of the independence struggle, Nkrumah enjoined his fellow Ghanaians to "seek ye first the political kingdom."[14] It obviously was not been that simple, and the vast projects of the early years of independence served to distract Ghana from its own domestic challenges. Now the pendulum seems to have swung back to the more modest expectations of the colonial past. Change will obviously be a much slower and more difficult than anticipated. It will also require flexibility rather than adherence to rigid plans that characterized the thinking of the early years of independence.

"Every wise man knows where he is going, but only the fool does not know where he is coming from" is the exhortation and admonition of the Sankofa bird. With its head turned backward and its body facing forward, this legendary creature from Akan mythology symbolizes the need to both learn from one's past experiences and to avoid its mistakes. Ghana stands in this position today.

NOTES

1. Gunder Frank, "Development of Underdevelopment," in *Latin America: Underdevelopment or Revolution: Essays on the Development of Underdevelopment* (New York: Monthly Review Press, 1969), 3–17.

2. K. Nkrumah, *Neo-colonialism: The Last Stage of Imperialism* (London: Nelson, 1965), ix.

3. H.E.A. Kyerematen (Ghana's ambassador to the United States), speech given at the Forty-fifth Annual Meeting of the African Studies Association, Washington, D.C., December 6, 2002. Similar criticisms were made by Dr. Paa Kwesi Nduom (minister for economic planning and regional integration), paper delivered at the Workshop on National Development Policy Framework, Washington, D.C., August 10, 2004.

4. Eboe Hutchful, *Ghana's Adjustment Experience: The Paradox of Reform* (Oxford: James Currey, 2002), 238.

5. "Interview with the President," *West Africa*, March 4–10, 2002.

6. D. Rimmer, "Learning about Economic Development from Africa," *African Affairs* 102 (2003): 477.

7. "Budget Speech," *Daily Graphic*, February 7, 2004.

8. As an indication of how substantial this migration has been, it has been estimated that by the middle of the 1990s the Ghanaian population in the United States was between 200,000 and 400,000. E. Akyeampong, "Africans in the Diaspora: The Diaspora in Africa," *African Affairs* 99 (2000): 211.

9. One of the best examples of this thinking is to be found in David Apter, *Ghana in Transition* (New York: Atheneum Press, 1963), 161.

10. Kwame Boafo-Arthur, "Chieftaincy in Ghana: Challenges and Prospects in the 21st Century," *African and Asian Studies* 2, no. 2 (2003): 132.

11. Ibid., 147.

12. George Padmore, *The Gold Coast Revolution: The Struggle of an African People from Slavery to Freedom* (London: D. Robson, 1953), 105.

13. Boafo-Arthur, "Chieftaincy in Ghana," 142.

14. This injunction was on the masthead of the CPP's newspapers in Accra, Cape Coast and Sekondi/Takoradi.

Notable People in the History of Ghana

Acheampong, Ignatius Kutu (1931–79), was born in Kumasi and educated at Catholic schools in Kumasi and Ejura and at the Central College of Commerce in Agona-Swedru. He was commissioned in the army in 1959 and attended military-training programs in the United Kingdom and Kansas. As a colonel he was the leader of the military coup in 1972, and became the head of state of the National Redemption Council from 1972 to 1978. In 1978 he was removed by his military colleagues, held in custody for a while, disqualified from holding public office again, and dismissed from the army without benefits. In 1979, at the time of the Armed Forces Revolutionary Council's coup, he was arrested, convicted of treason, and executed by firing squad.

Afrifa, Akwasi Amankwaa (1936–79), was born in Mampong and attended the Presbyterian Boys School in Mampong as well as Adisadel High School in Cape Coast. In 1956 he joined the army and trained in the United Kingdom. He was sent to the Congo in 1961 and became convinced that Nkrumah's polices were a threat to Ghana. Along with other officers he directed the coup that overthrew Nkrumah in 1966. At first he served as member of the Executive Council of the National Liberation Council, and then in 1969 he became head of state. He opposed the coup of 1972 against the Busia government and was arrested by the National Redemption Council. He opposed UNIGOV. In 1979 he helped to organize the United National Convention Party and was elected to Parliament. One week after his election he was executed by the Armed Forces Revolutionary Council.

Aidoo, Christina Ama Ata (1930–), was born near Saltpond in the Central Region and was educated at Methodist schools and at the University of Ghana at Legon. She also studied in the United Kingdom and the United States. In 1982 she became secretary of education in the PNDC government, and lasted for only a year in this position. She subsequently taught English literature in Zimbabwe and recently returned to Ghana. Her best-known work is *No Sweetness Here,* a collection of short stories published in 1970. Her many plays and novels focus on the roles assigned to women in Africa.

Akuffo, Frederick W. K. (1937–79), was born in Akuropon, Akuapem. He joined the army in 1957 and trained in the United Kingdom. He served in the Congo in 1961. By the time of the coup against Busia he was a colonel, and by 1976 he was a member of the Supreme Military Council and chief of the defense staff. In 1978 he seized power from Acheampong and became chairman of the Supreme Military Council. When Rawlings seized power in 1979 he was arrested and eventually executed.

Armah, Ayi Kwei (1939–), was born in Takoradi. He was educated at Achimota and then attended Groton School in Massachusetts and then Harvard University, where he received a degree in sociology. He then moved to Algeria and worked as a translator for the weekly *Revolution Africaine.* He then returned to Ghana and taught and worked for Ghana Television. In 1967 he enrolled in the writing program at Columbia University. He then worked for *Jeune Afrique* for one year and then accepted professorships in the United States and Tanzania. He has spent much of his later life in Senegal. He is best known for his earlier novels, which deal with Ghana right after independence. His later novels are more allegorical and less dependent on socially realistic detail.

Awooner, Kofi (1935–), was born in Wheta, in the Volta Region. He was educated at Achimota and got his B.A. in English from the University of Ghana. He subsequently received a Ph.D. in comparative literature from the State University of New York at Stony Brook in 1972. He taught there and at the University of Texas at Austin for a short while, and then returned to Ghana to teach at the University of Cape Coast. In 1975 he was arrested by the Supreme Military Council for being involved in a plot to overthrow the government. Eventually he was pardoned and released. He was appointed by the Provisional National Defense Council to be Ghana's ambassador to Brazil, and later in the 1990s he was the ambassador to the United Nations. He is one of Ghana's most prolific writers. His best known work is entitled *This Earth, My Brother* (1971).

Boahen, Adu A. (1932–), was born in Osiem in Akyem Abuakwa. He was educated at the Presbyterian School in Osiem, the Methodist School at Asokore in the Ashanti Region, and at Mfantsipim School, Cape Coast. In 1956 he received a B.A. Honors from the University College of the Gold Coast in history. He then obtained a doctorate in history from the School of Oriental and African Studies, University of London, in 1959. He returned to teach at what was then the University of Ghana, and eventually in 1971 he was promoted to the position of full professor. In 1983 he was elected president of the International Scientific Committee of the United Nations Educational, Scientific, and Cultural Organization (UNESCO) for publishing the eight-volume series *Africa under Colonial Domination, 1888– 1935*. In 1985 he retired from the University of Ghana and entered politics. His 1988 J. B. Danquah Memorial Lectures, which criticized the Rawlings government, are credited with playing a watershed role in the restoration of party politics in Ghana. He was a founding member of the New Patriotic Party and its presidential candidate in the 1992 election. After his defeat the party criticized the fairness of the election, and it seemed as though Boahen would challenge Rawlings again in 1996. However, he lost his party's nomination to be its flag-bearer. During his long academic career, Professor Boahen wrote six books, the most recent of which, *Mfantsipim and the Making of Ghana, 1876–1976*, won the prestigious Noma Award for Publishing in Africa (1997).

Botchwey, Dr. Kwesi (1943–), was born in Tamale, but his parents were originally from Agona in the Central Region. He attended Presbyterian Secondary School in Odumase-Krobo and also St. Augustine's College in Cape Coast. He obtained an L.L.B. from the University of Ghana Law School in 1967, an L.L.M. from Yale Law School in 1968, and a S.J.D. from the University of Michigan Law School in 1970. He taught at the University of Zambia, the University of Dar es Salaam, and the University of Ghana. In 1982 he became the secretary of finance and economic planning for the Provisional National Defense Council. In 1993, when the National Democratic Congress government took power, he was the minister of finance and economic planning. In 1995 he resigned from this position and went to work for the African Development Bank. He subsequently became the director of Africa research at Harvard University. For a short while he was with the Earth Institute of Columbia University. In 2003 he contested with Professor John Atta Mills for the position of presidential candidate for the NDC in the 2004 election. He was unsuccessful.

Botsio, Kojo (1916–2001), was born in Winneba and educated at Adisadel College, Cape Coast; Fourah Bay College in Sierra Leone; and Oxford University. On his return to the Gold Coast he taught at Akyem Abuakwa State College. He had met and become one of Nkrumah's close confidants while he was in England. He was one of the founders of the Convention People's Party and its first general secretary. He was arrested by the colonial authorities in 1950 as a result of the CPP's campaign of Positive Action. He was elected to Parliament in 1951 and became the first minister of education and social welfare in the new cabinet. He was to serve in a number of other ministerial positions in the CPP government. He spent some time in custody after the 1966 coup, and then he joined Nkrumah in his Guinean exile. He accompanied Nkrumah's body back to Ghana in 1972. The following year he was sentenced to death by the Acheampong government for plotting its overthrow, but this was commuted to life imprisonment. In 1977 he was released, and soon after he was director of operations and chairman of the Campaign Committee of the PNP for the 1979 election.

Brew, James Hutton (1844–1915), was born in Anomabu. His father was a successful merchant who sent his son, at the age of eight, to England for a liberal education. He returned to the Gold Coast in 1861 and practiced as a solicitor. In 1871 he was active in the Fanti Confederation Movement. In 1874 he founded the *Gold Coast Times* and became one of the leaders in seeking to raise national consciousness among Africans in the Gold Coast. In 1885 he organized another newspaper, the *Western Echo,* and used this paper to exhort his countrymen to get elected representation for Africans on the Legislative Council. He was one of the pioneers of early African nationalism in the Gold Coast.

Burns, Sir Alan Cuthbert Maxwell (1887–1980), was born in St. Kitts, West Indies, into a family of colonial civil servants who served in the West Indies and Africa. He began his career in the West Indies, but subsequently served on several occasions in Nigeria. Eventually, in 1941, he was appointed governor of the Gold Coast. Apart from dealing with war effort, he also was confronted with the crisis stemming from what in the colony was known as the "Kibi Murder," a ritual murder that took place after the death in 1943 of Nana Sir Ofori Atta. In 1946 Governor Burns introduced a new constitution for the colony that gave Africans a majority in the Legislative Council. Shortly after he retired from the governorship of the Gold Coast, he wrote his autobiography, *Colonial Civil Servant* (1949).

Busia, Dr. Kofi Abrefa (1913–78), was born in Wenchi in the Brong-Ahafo Region and was educated at the Methodist School in Kumasi, Mfantsipim, and Wesley College, Kumasi. In 1936 he taught at Achimota. He then went to the United Kingdom and eventually obtained a doctorate in social anthropology from Oxford University. On his return to the Gold Coast he was appointed an assistant district commissioner. In 1949 he joined the faculty of the new University College at Legon. While in this position he published a study of Ghanaian chieftaincy and a social survey of Sekondi-Takoradi. In 1951 he was elected to the legislative assembly, and by 1957 he was the leader of the United Party, which opposed the Convention People's Party. In 1959 he went into exile and was a professor at Oxford University. He returned to Ghana after the 1966 coup and eventually created the Progress Party, which won the elections of 1969. He became the president of Ghana's Second Republic, but in 1972 his government was overthrown by the military. He returned to his position at Oxford University.

Casely Hayford, Joseph Ephriam (1866–1930), was born in Cape Coast and received his secondary education at Fourah Bay College in Sierra Leone. After a brief spell of newspaper work in the Gold Coast he went to England to study law and was called to the Bar in 1896. On his return he joined the Gold Coast Aborigines Rights Protection Society, and from then onward combined a legal career with political and journalistic activities. In 1902 he established his own newspaper, the *Gold Coast Leader,* which was to remain one of the most important newspapers in the colony. In 1911 he published a quasi-intellectual autobiography entitled *Ethiopia Unbound* in which he advanced the ideas of the West Indian Wilmot Edward Blyden. In the same year he also published *The Truth about the West African Question,* in which he attacked colonial land policies. He was one of the first West Africans to realize the need for a pan–West African political agitation on the part of Africans, and after the First World War he was instrumental in the establishment of the National Congress of British West Africa. Its first meeting was held in Accra in 1920, and Casely Hayford was elected vice president. In 1916 he became an unofficial member of the Legislative Council, and he played a major role in its deliberations. However as a result of his leading role in the NCBWA and his opposition to the new constitution that Governor Guggisberg introduced for the colony in 1925, he had a major political falling out with the colony's leading chief, Nana Ofori Atta. In the period after the First World War, up until this falling out with Nana Ofori Atta, he was the most important African voice in the Gold Coast and British West Africa.

Danquah, Dr. Joseph Boakye (1895–1965), was born in Bepong, Kwahu, and was the half brother of Ofori Atta. He also studied in Basel mission schools and at the University of London, from which he obtained a doctorate in ethics in 1927. He also qualified as a barrister. While in London he published *The Akim Abuakwa Handbook, Akan Laws and Customs,* and the *Akim Abuakwa Constitution.* When he returned to the Gold Coast he founded the *West African Times,* later known as the *Times of West Africa,* which were daily newspapers. In 1937 he founded the Gold Coast Youth Congress, and in 1947 he was one of the founders of the United Gold Coast Convention. In 1948 he was arrested with Nkrumah and others as a result of the riots in the colony, but in 1949 the colonial government appointed him a member of the Coussey Committee. By this time he had parted ways with Nkrumah and he became one of his main opponents. He ran for election in 1954 and 1956, first for the National Liberation Movement and then for the United Party. In 1960 he was the candidate for the UP, but lost badly against Nkrumah. He was imprisoned in 1961, released in 1962, and imprisoned again in 1964. One year later he died while still in prison.

Freeman, Thomas Birch (1809–90), was born in Great Britain of an African father and an English mother. In 1838 he came to Cape Coast as a Methodist missionary. He was to play a major role in the spread of Methodism in the Gold Coast and Nigeria. He made three trips to the Asante capital of Kumasi and kept an extensive diary. He also kept accounts of his trips to Dahomey and Nigeria between 1839 and 1843, and they are important historical sources. During the 1840s and 1850s he served as the superintendent of the Methodist Mission on the Gold Coast. After he resigned as general superintendent he was for a while the civil commandant of the Accra District. The last 20 years of his life were spent primarily in Accra and Mankesim.

Gbedemah, Komla Agbelli (1912–), was born in Warri, Nigeria, of Ghanaian parents from the Volta Region. He attended secondary school in Cape Coast and completed his secondary education at Achimota. He then taught for a few years and then went into business. In 1948 he became the chairman of the Committee on Youth Organizations. He joined the United Gold Coast Convention and was to be a founding member of the Convention People's Party. While Nkrumah was in prison he ran the CPP and edited the party's newspaper, the *Evening News*. He won a seat in the 1951 election. From 1951 to 1952 he was the minister of health and labor, from 1952 to 1954 he headed the ministry of commerce and industry, and from 1954 to 1961 he was finance minister. When Nkrumah moved to the left the two became estranged, and eventually Gbedemah resigned. For a brief while he returned to his earlier position as minister of health, but in 1961 Nkrumah fired him, and he went into exile for five years. After 1966 he returned to Ghana, and after a short time as a businessman he once again returned to politics and organized the National Alliance of Liberals in the 1969 elections. He won a seat in the new National Assembly but was barred from taking it. After the coup of 1972 he was appointed a roving ambassador by the National Redemption Council, but eventually fell out over the issue of UNIGOV. He was briefly arrested and then barred from participating in the 1979 elections.

Griffith, Sir William Brandford (1824–97), was born in Barbados, West Indies, where he served as a member of that colony's legislature from 1861 to 1874. In 1880 he became the lieutenant governor of the Gold Coast. In 1885, when the Gold Coast was separated from Lagos, he became the governor of the colony, a position he was to hold until 1895. He was to be the longest serving of British governors. During his long governorship he did much to extend British authority on the Gold Coast, establishing boundaries with the Germans and the French and expanding British administration in general.

Guggisberg, Sir Frederick Gordon (1869–1930), was born in Canada and served in the British army. He did survey work in the Gold Coast from 1902 to 1908 and then became surveyor-general for Nigeria. After fighting in the First World War, he became governor of the Gold Coast in 1919. He believed that major infrastructure were necessary for the colony and offered a very ambitious 10-year development plan. During his 10 years as governor the Gold Coast acquired a deepwater harbor, new railroads, hospitals, a leading secondary school, water-supply systems, and many other such projects. He believed that Africans should be trained to fill positions in the civil service and that the colony's constitution should be changed to give Africans experience in responsible government. After his service in the Gold Coast he was posted to British Guiana, where poor health cut short his period of service.

Kotoka, Emmanuel Kwasi (1926–67), was born in Alakple in the Volta Region. He was educated in Catholic schools. In 1947 he enlisted in the Gold Coast Regiment. He was commissioned in 1954 and served for a time in England and Germany. He went to the Congo as a member of the UN Emergency Force. In 1965 he was the commander of the First Infantry Brigade in Kumasi and helped plan the coup that overthrew Nkrumah. After the coup he became a member of the National Liberation Council, commander of the Ghana armed forces, and minister of defense, health, labor, and social welfare. He was killed in the unsuccessful coup of 1969 in front of Accra Airport. A statue was erected on the spot where he died and the airport was named after him.

Kufuor, John Agyekum (1938–), was born in Kumasi. He received his secondary education at Prempeh College. He then enrolled in Lincoln's Inn, London, and was called to the Bar in 1961. He then entered Oxford University and obtained an Honors B.A. in 1964 in politics, philosophy, and economics. In 1967 he was appointed town clerk of Kumasi. He was a member of the 1968–69 and 1979 assemblies that drafted the constitutions of the Second and Third Republics. He was a founding member of the Progress Party in 1969, the Popular Front Party in 1979, and the New Patriotic Party. He was elected an MP in the Second and Third Republics, and served brief periods of detention after these governments were overthrown. He served for a short while as secretary of local government during the Provisional National Defense Council administration. In 1992 he contested unsuccessfully the leadership of the NPP, and did so again in 1996, when he was successful. However, he was defeated in the general election. In 1998 he was renominated as leader of the NPP, and in the election of 2000 he was elected Ghana's president. In 2004 he was again elected president of Ghana.

Limann, Dr. Hilla (1934–98), was born in Gwolu, Upper West Region. He received his early education at the Lawra Confederacy Native Authority School. For a while he taught in Tamale and also was a district councillor. In 1954 he ran as an independent for Parliament but lost. He then went to the UK and obtained a degree in political science from the London School of Economics; he then received a diploma in French from the Sorbonne, a B.A. in history from London University, and a doctorate from the University of Paris in political science and constitutional law. He taught for a short while after he returned, but then he joined the diplomatic service for the CPP. He was a member of the commission that wrote the Second Republic's constitution. In 1979 he was nominated by the People's National Party, a grouping of the Nkrumahists, to contend the election for the presidency of the Third Republic. In 1981 his government was overthrown by Jerry Rawlings and his fellow soldiers. Limann was arrested and held in protective custody until 1983. His last effort in politics was to try to bring the fractured Nkrumahists together, and he was chairman of their Unity Talks.

Mensah, Emmanuel Tettey (E. T.) (1919–96), was born in Accra. His talent for music was discovered while he was in school. After leaving school he teamed up with his brother and others in the Accra Rhythmic Orchestra. At that time, in the 1930s, musical tastes were highly European, but during the Second World War Ghanaian musicians came under the influence of African Americans and West Indians. There were also ex-professional European musicians and for a while he played with them. After the war he joined the Tempos Band, one of whose members had traveled to Europe and America. The band came under the influence of Afro-Cuban music. Out of these many inspirations, and the need to develop something that was based on African rhythms, emerged West African Highlife. In 1948 he formed his own band, and in 1950 they visited Nigeria. He also began recording and did so in many Ghanaian languages. In the 1950s and 1960s he was at the peak of his popularity, and was known as the "King of Highlife." In 1969 he traveled to London for a very successful tour. By the 1970s new forms of popular music began to challenge and replace Highlife.

Mills, Professor John Evans Atta (1944–), was born in Cape Coast and attended Achimota School. He then attended the University of Ghana, Legon, where he received a B.A. and a professional certificate in law in 1967. While he was earning the Ph.D. from the School of Oriental and African Studies at London University, he was selected as a Fulbright scholar at Stanford Law School. His first formal teaching assignment was as a lecturer on the faculty of law at the University of Ghana, Legon, where he spent more than twenty years. During this time he sat on numerous university boards and committees. He has also been a visiting professor at Temple University and Leiden University. He has published extensively in the field of taxation and investment. In 1988 he became the acting commissioner of the Internal Revenue Service of Ghana and was named commissioner in 1996. In 1997 he was named the vice president of the Republic of Ghana.

Nelson, Azumah (1958–), was born in Accra, and like many of the young boys who grew up in the Bokum section of Accra, he began to box at an early age. Also, his father had been a boxer. His first major crown was the featherweight title at the Commonwealth Games in 1978. After this success he turned professional, and after 10 victories he was the holder of the Ghanaian, African, and Commonwealth belts. In 1984 he won the World Boxing Commission featherweight title, which he held for three years. In 1988 he won the WBC super-featherweight title. He attempted to move up to the lightweight division but was defeated. He concluded his boxing career by losing and then reclaiming his super-featherweight belt. Eventually, in 1997, he lost his world title, and in 1998 he retired from the ring. Azumah Nelson was the greatest boxer to come out of Ghana. He was known in boxing circles as "the Professor" on account of his ability to teach his opponents a boxing lesson. In 2004 he was inducted into the International Boxing Hall of Fame.

Nkrumah, Kwame (1909–72), was born at Nkroful, a small village in the Western Region, and educated in the Roman Catholic schools in Half-Assini and Sekondi. He attended Achimota College and for a short while taught at this institution. He went to the United States in 1935 and attended Lincoln University in Pennsylvania, where he graduated with a degree in economics and sociology. He then received a M.A. from the University of Pennsylvania. In 1945 he went to the United Kingdom to study for a law degree and to complete a doctorate in philosophy. Instead, he soon became caught up in the anticolonial movement, and eventually he became the vice president of the West African Student's Union. In 1945 he was the joint secretary with George Padmore for the committee that organized the Fifth Pan-African Congress, held in Manchester, England. In 1947 he returned to the Gold Coast as the general secretary of the United Gold Coast Convention. After the riots of 1948 he was arrested along with the other five leaders of the UGCC. By this time he had fallen out with the UGCC, and in 1949 he formed the Convention People's Party, which demanded "Self-Government Now." As a result of the Positive Action the party called for in 1950, Nkrumah and other CPP leaders were arrested. While he was in prison he was elected to the legislative assembly. He was released from prison and in 1951 became the leader of government business. In 1952 he became prime minister. In 1953 he introduced his "Motion of Destiny" for Ghana's independence, but three years of bitter wrangling followed over what form of government should obtain, and two elections were necessary before Ghana became independent in 1957. Quickly his rule became more authoritarian. In 1958 his government passed the Preventive Detention Act. In 1959 the opposition was expelled from Parliament, and in 1960 Ghana became a republic. There were a number of attempts on his life. In 1962 Nkrumah became president for life, and in 1964 Ghana became a one-party state. In 1966, while he was away on a trip to China, there was a successful military coup. His main supporter, Sékou Touré of Guinea, proclaimed him copresident, and Nkrumah spent the rest of his life in Guinea. Nkrumah wrote many books, including his autobiography and an apologia while he was in exile in Guinea.

Ofori Atta I, Sir Nana (1881–1943), *okyenhene* of Akyem Abuakwa, 1912–43. He was educated in Basel Mission schools and at its seminary in Akuropon. He worked for several years as a clerk, and served in the West African Frontier Force, where he saw service during the Yaa Asantewaa War. In 1912 he was enstooled as the *okyenhene* of Akyem Abuakwa. In 1916 Governor Clifford appointed him to the Legislative Council. In 1920 he came into conflict with Casely Hayford over whether the intelligentsia or the traditional rulers, like himself, were the true leaders of the African people. He was the most influential traditional ruler in the Gold Coast and played a leading role in the passing of the Native Administration Bill of 1927. In the same year he was knighted. In 1943, just before he died, he was one of two Africans appointed to the Executive Council.

Owusu, Victor (1923–2000), was born in Agona-Asante and received his higher education at the University of Nottingham, the University of London, and at Lincoln's Inn. He was called to the Bar in 1952. During the Nkrumah years he developed a reputation as an outstanding lawyer. He was elected president of the Ghana Bar Association from 1964 to 1967. After the 1966 coup the National Liberation Council made him the attorney general and the commissioner of justice. He helped organize the Progress Party and won election to Parliament. First he was minister of external affairs, and then minister of justice and attorney general. After the coup of 1972 he was detained, but in 1978 he helped to organize opposition to UNIGOV. He was detained for a short time, but after Acheampong was forced out in 1978 he was released, but disqualified from standing for office. Nevertheless, he joined former PP members to form the Popular Front Party and was the unsuccessful presidential candidate for the party. During the Third Republic he continued as the leader of the PFP and tried to combine all the opposition parties. The Rawlings coup of 1981 put an end to these efforts.

Pele, Abedi (1964–), was born in Dome in the Volta Region. He began his career with Real Tamale United (RTU), and in 1982 he helped Ghana to win the African Nations Cup. He then left Ghana to play in Qatar, moved to F. C. Zurich, then returned to Ghana and played both for his old club, RTU, and Dragons of Benin. He moved to France to play in the French Second Division League. Eventually he joined Olympique Marsielle in the First Division and helped them to win the European Club Championship in 1993. He then played for AC Turin in the Italian League and finished his European playing career with TSV Munich. He was voted African player of the year in 1991, 1992, and 1993. In appreciation of his services to his country, the Ghanaian government awarded him the country's highest honor, the Order of the Volta (civil division), and he was the first Ghanaian sportsman to be so honored.

Prempeh I (Kwaku Dua III, Agyeman Prempeh (ca. 1873–1931), ascended to the Golden Stool of Asante in 1888 as Kwaku Dua III, but there was civil war in the kingdom and not until 1894 was he finally recognized. The British used the discontent in Asante as reason for their invasion of the kingdom in 1896. The state was declared dissolved, Prempeh was arrested, and he and his family were taken to Elmina and then to Sierra Leone. After the final revolt in Asante, the Yaa Asantewaa War of 1900, Prempeh and his entourage was sent to the Seychelles. He was only allowed to return in 1924, but as a private citizen. In 1926 the British did recognize him as *kumasihene*.

Quaque (Quacoe), Reverend Philip (1741–1816), was born in Cape Coast, son of a wealthy African slave trader. Along with three other young boys, he was sent to England to be trained as future clergymen in the Church of England and to serve the Christian community on the Gold Coast. He returned to the Gold Coast and established a school in Cape Coast and later in some of the other coastal towns. At this time the transatlantic slave trade was at its height, and it was a particularly difficult time to be a missionary. During Quaque's career he succeeded in converting only five people, but he played an important role in sowing the seeds of future Christian proselytizing success.

Rattray, Robert Sutherland (1881–1938), was born in India of Scottish parents. In 1906 he joined the Gold Coast Customs Service. In 1911 he became assistant district commissioner in Ashanti. He learned a number of native languages, and in 1921 he was appointed the head of the Anthropological Department. He held this position for nine years, and during this time did extensive field work studying the customs of the Asante and many of the ethnic groups in northern Ghana. His books on these subjects have become classics of Ghanaian anthropology.

Rawlings, Jerry John (1947–), was born in Accra. His father was Scottish and his mother was Ewe. He attended Achimota School. He then enrolled at the Military Academy at Teshi in 1968. He was commissioned a lieutenant in 1969, took flight training, and became a flight lieutenant in 1978. He took part in an attempted coup against the Supreme Military Council in 1978 and was arrested, went to prison but was released as a result of another coup in 1979, and became chairman of this new government, the Armed Forces Revolutionary Council. During its four months in power three former heads of state and five high-ranking military officers were executed. The AFRC relinquished power to an elected government, but in 1981 Rawlings led another coup, and once again became head of state of the Provisional National Defense Council. In 1992 Ghana acquired a new constitution, and the PNDC became the National Democratic Congress, with Rawlings this new political party's presidential candidate. He won the election that was held at the end of the year and became Ghana's fourth president. In 1996 his party won once again, and Rawlings remained the president of Ghana. The 1992 constitution permitted only two four-year terms for the president, and in 2000 Rawlings had to step down. Since this point he has remained the head of the NDC and a major force in Ghana's political life.

Sarbah, John Mensah (1864–1910), was born in Cape Coast, the son of the Honorable John Sarbah, prosperous merchant of Cape Coast and Anomabu. He received his early education in Cape Coast and in England. He studied law at Lincoln's Inn in London and was called to the Bar in 1887, the first African from the Gold Coast to achieve this distinction. He was one of the founders of the Gold Coast Aborigines Rights Protection Society, in 1897. He published *Fanti Customary Law* in 1897, *Fanti Law Reports* in 1904, and *Fanti National Constitution* in 1906. He helped in the creation of Mfantsipim School in 1904, which today is one of the premier secondary schools in Ghana. In 1901 he followed in his father's footsteps and was appointed a member of the Legislative Council, a position he held until his death. In his day he was the most important spokesman for African interests in the Gold Coast Colony.

Sekyi, William Esuman-Gwira, better known as Kobina Sekyi (1892–1956), was born in Cape Coast, where he attended Mfantsipim High School. He continued his education in London and by 1918 had obtained an M.A. in philosophy from London University and a B.L. in law. On his return to the Gold Coast he became involved with Casely Hayford and the National Council of British West Africa. Eventually the two men had a falling out over the question of the 1925 constitution. Sekyi became the most important critic of British policies of indirect rule and the most important "noncooperator" in the colony. He used the Gold Coast Aborigines Rights Protection Society as his main vehicle for opposing colonial indirect-rule policies, and after Casely Hayford died in 1930 his main African opponent became Nana Sir Ofori Atta. Sekyi represented a conservative nationalism, and as the nationalist movement gathered steam after the Second World War, he was overtaken by a new generation of radicals.

Sutherland, Efua Theodora, née Morgue (1924–98), was born in Cape Coast. After completing her teacher training in Ghana she attended Cambridge University, one of the first African women to do so. She founded the Drama Studio in Accra, which is now the Writers' Workshop in the Institute of African Studies at the University of Ghana at Legon. In 1992 she was the driving force behind the organization of the First Pan-African Historical and Theater Festival, which was held in Cape Coast. It is now held every two years. She was the author of several plays. Some of the best known are *Edufa, Foriwa,* and *The Marriage of Anansewa.*

Wallace-Johnson, Isaac Theophilus Akunna (1895–1965), was born in Freetown, Sierra Leone. In 1915 he joined the British Army, serving as a clerk in the Carrier Corps. In 1926 he joined the merchant marine and became involved in the United Kingdom National Seamen's Union. He eventually came to the attention of the Comintern and was invited to attend the People's University of the East in Moscow in 1931. Eventually, after a brief stay in England, he returned to Sierra Leone, but soon left for Lagos and eventually Accra, where he began to write for the *African Morning Post,* under the editorship of his Nigerian friend Nnamdi Azikiwe, and also to organize workers. In 1934 he was instrumental in the formation of the West African Youth League. He was convicted in 1936 of publishing seditious material but appealed to the Privy Council, which brought him to the attention of the British left wing. In 1938 he returned to Sierra Leone and continued his radical political activities. During the Second World War the colonial authorities considered him such a threat to security that they imprisoned him. After the war he continued to be a radical voice in Sierra Leonean politics.

Yaa Asantewaa (1863?–1921) was the queen mother of Ejisu, a town 10 miles east of Kumasi. She rallied the Asante against the British in 1900 when Governor Frederic Hodgson came to Kumasi to demand the Golden Stool. She was sent into exile in the Seychelles Islands with Prempeh I and his entourage in 1901 and died there in 1921.

Selected Bibliography

There is a long tradition of historical writing for Ghana that extends back to the nineteenth century. The earliest of the general histories was A. B. Ellis's *History of the Gold Coast of West Africa,* published in 1893. The Reverend Carl Christian Reindorf's *History of the Gold Coast and Asante,* which was published by the Basel Mission in 1895, also has an Akan/coastal focus. W. W. Claridge's *A History of the Gold Coast and Ashanti from Ancient Times to the Commencement of the Twentieth Century* (2 vols.), published in 1915, is the first really detailed history of the entire colony, but the emphasis is still very much on the coast and Asante. W. T. Balmer's *A History of the Akan Peoples,* published in 1925, has a coastal and Asante focus. In 1935 W.E.F. Ward published *A Short History of the Gold Coast,* which was to go through many editions as it became the standard history for Gold Coast schools. In 1948 he published *A History of the Gold Coast,* and in 1958 it was revised and published as *A History of Ghana.*

With the coming of independence there was a significant increase in general histories that focused on the development of the nationalist struggle. David Kimble's *A Political History of Ghana: 1850–1928* (1963), was the most magisterial of these works. There were others that were more general in focus, like Freda Wolfson's *Pageant of Ghana* (1958); J. D. Fage's *Ghana: A Historical Interpretation* (1959); J. E. Flint's *Nigeria and Ghana* (1966); Francis Agbodeka's *Ghana in the Twentieth Century* (1972); A. A. Boahen's *Ghana: Evolution and Change in the Nineteenth and Twentieth Centuries* (1975); Basil Davidson's *Ghana: An African Portrait* (1976); and K. F. Buah's *A History of Ghana* (1980). More recently there has been Kofi Awoonor's *Ghana: A Political History from Pre-European to Modern Times* (1990) and David Owusu-Ansah and Daniel McFarland's *Historical Dictionary of Ghana* (2nd edition, 1995).

One of the most important sources of historical information about Ghana, and indeed West Africa, has been the periodical publication *West Africa*. It was first published in 1917 and appeared basically every week until 1999, when it went bankrupt. The Daily Graphic Corporation of Ghana took it over in 1999, but it still continued to be published in London. The Graphic Corporation was not able to sustain the publication, and in the middle of 2003 it was discontinued. Ghana also has a long history of newspaper publication that dates back to the nineteenth century. This tradition includes newspapers like the *Gold Coast Times* and the *Western Echo* for the nineteenth century. In the twentieth century these publications, mostly weeklies, became more regular and long-lasting. The most important were the *Gold Coast Leader*, the *Gold Coast Independent*, the *Times of West Africa*, and the *African Morning Post*.

In the 1950s a number of dailies emerged, the most important of which were the *Daily Graphic*, which was owned by the London-based Mirror Group; the *Ghanaian Times*, which was established by the Convention People's Party government; and the *Evening News*, which was started in 1948 as a mouthpiece for the CPP. The *Daily Graphic* and *Ghanaian Times* have continued to this day; both of them are now government-owned newspapers, but in today's Ghana they exhibit considerable editorial independence. The *Daily Graphic* has a regular Web site (http://www.graphicghana.com/). In the 1990s, when the "culture of silence" ended, a number of independent newspapers emerged, and the most important among them continue to circulate in Ghana today, like the *Ghanaian Chronicle*, the *Free Press*, *Public Agenda*, the *Independent*, and *Ghana Palaver*. Some have an Internet presence, like the *Ghanaian Chronicle* (http://db.ghanianchronicle.com/) and *Ghana Palaver* (http://www.ghana-palaver.com/).

There are also a number of scholarly journals that publish articles on Ghana. Among the most important for contemporary studies are *African Affairs*, *African and Asian Studies*, the *Journal of Democracy*, and the *Journal of Modern African Studies*. Other journals, like *Africa*, *African Studies Review*, the *Canadian Journal of African Studies*, and *Comparative Studies in Society and History* publish both contemporary and sometimes more historical studies. The *Journal of African History* and the *International Journal of African Historical Studies* publish only historical studies.

What follows is a list of books, some of the more classic and others more recent, that deal with specific issues and periods in Ghanaian history.

Chapter 1: Introduction: Ghana in Perspective

Atta-Quayson, J., ed. *Macmillan Atlas for Ghana.* London and Basingstoke: Unimax Publishers and Macmillan Educational, 1995.

Birmingham, W., I. Neustadt, and E. N. Omaboe, eds. *A Study of Contemporary Ghana* 2 vols. London Allen and Unwin, 1966.

Dickson, Kwamina B., and G. A. Benneh. *New Geography of Ghana.* 2nd ed. London: Longmans, 1973.

Gould, Peter R. *The Development of the Transportation Pattern in Ghana.* Evanston, Ill.: Northwestern University Press, 1960.

Institute of Statistical, Social, and Economic Research. *The State of the Ghanaian Economy in 2002.* Legon, The Institute of Statistical, Social and Economic Research, University of Ghana, 2003.

Lentz, Carla, and Paul Nugent, eds. *Ethnicity in Ghana: The Limits of Invention.* New York: St. Martin's Press, 2000.

Chapter 2: Precolonial States and Societies

Adjaye, Joseph K. *Diplomacy and Diplomats in Nineteenth Century Asante.* Lanham, Md.: University Press of America, 1984.

Anquandah, James. *Rediscovering Ghana's Past.* Harlow, England: Longman Group, 1982.

Blake, John W. *West Africa: Quest for God and Gold, 1454–1578.* Totowa, N.J.: Rowman and Littlefield, 1977.

Bosman, William. *A New and Accurate Description of the Coast of Guinea.* 1704. Reprint, London: Frank Cass, 1967.

Braimah, J. A., H. H. Tomlinson, and O. Amankwatia. *History and Traditions of Gonja.* Calgary, Canada: University of Calgary Press, 1997.

Cardinall, A. W. *The Natives of the Northern Territories of the Gold Coast: Their Customs, Religion, and Folklore.* 1920. Reprint, New York: Negro Universities Press, 1969.

Crooks, J. J. *Records Relating to the Gold Coast Settlements from 1750–1874.* 1923. Reprint, London: Frank Cass, 1973.

Daaku, Kwame. *Trade and Politics on the Gold Coast, 1600–1720: A Study of the African Reaction to European Trade.* London: Clarendon Press, 1970.

Davis, K. G. *The Royal African Company.* London: Longmans, 1956.

DeCorse, C. R. *An Archaeology of Elmina: Africans and Europeans on the Gold Coast, 1400–1900.* Washington, D.C.: Smithsonian Institution Press, 2001.

Edgerton, Robert B. *The Fall of the Asante Empire: The Hundred-Year War for Africa's Gold Coast.* New York: Free Press, 1995.

Feinberg, Harvey. *Africans and Europeans in West Africa: Elminans and Dutchmen on the Gold Coast During the Eighteenth Century.* Philadelphia: American Philosophical Society, 1989.

Fyfe, Christopher. *Africanus Horton: West African Scientist and Patriot, 1835–1883.* New York: Oxford University Press.

Fynn, John K. *Asante and Its Neighbors, 1700–1807.* London: Longman, 1971.

Greene, Sandra E. *Gender, Ethnicity, and Social Change on the Upper Slave Coast: A History of the Anlo-Ewe.* Portsmouth, N.H.: Heinemann, 1996.

Hansen, Thorkild. *Coast of Slaves.* Trans. Kari Dako. Accra, Ghana: Sub-Saharan Publishers, 2002.

Horton, James A. *Letters on the Political Condition of the Gold Coast since the Exchange of Territory between the English and Dutch Governments on January 1, 1868.* 1870. Reprint, London: Frank Cass, 1970.

Kea, Ray A. *Settlements, Trade, and Politics in the Seventeenth Century Gold Coast.* Baltimore: Johns Hopkins University Press, 1982.

Kwamena-Poh, M. A. *Government and Politics in the Akuapem State, 1730–1850.* Evanston, Ill.: Northwestern University Press, 1973.

Lawrence, A. W. *Trade Castles and Forts of West Africa.* Stanford, Calif.: Stanford University Press, 1963.

Levtzion, Nehemia. *Muslims and Chiefs in West Africa: A Study of Islam in the Middle Volta Basin in the Pre-Colonial Period.* Oxford: Clarendon Press, 1968.

McCaskie, T. M. *State and Society in Pre-Colonial Asante.* Cambridge: Cambridge University Press, 1995.

Meyerowitz, Eva L. R. *The Early History of the Akan States of Ghana.* London: Red Candle Press, 1974.

Priestley, Margaret. *West African Trade and Coast Society: A Family Study.* London: Oxford University Press, 1969.

Rattray, Robert S. *Ashanti Law and Constitution.* London: Clarendon Press, 1929.

Reynolds, Edward. *Trade and Economic Change on the Gold Coast, 1807–1874.* London: Longman, 1974.

Savalesen, Leif. *The Slave Ship Fredensborg.* Trans. Pat Shaw and Selena Winsnes. Accra, Ghana: Sub-Saharan Publishers, 2000.

Vogt, John L. *Portuguese Rule on the Gold Coast 1469–1682.* Athens: University of Georgia Press, 1979.

Wilks, Ivor. *Asante in the Nineteenth Century: The Structure and Evolution of a Political Order.* London: Cambridge University Press, 1975.

———. *Forests of Gold: Essays on the Akan and the Kingdom of Asante.* Athens: Ohio University Press, 1993.

Wilson, Louis E. *The Krobo People to 1892: A Political and Social History.* Athens: Ohio University Press, 1991.

Wiltgen, Ralph M. *Gold Coast Mission History, 1471–1880.* Techny, Ill.: Divine World, 1956.

Chapter 3: Colonial Rule

Agbodeka, Francis. *African Politics and British Policy in the Gold Coast, 1868–1900: A Study in the Forms and Force of Protest.* Evanston, Ill.: Northwestern University Press, 1971.

Arhin, Kwame. *West African Traders in Ghana in the Nineteenth and Twentieth Centuries.* London: Longman, 1979.

Bartels, F. L. *The Roots of Ghana Methodism.* Cambridge: Cambridge University Press, 1965.

Berry, Sarah S. *Chiefs Know Their Boundaries: Essays on Property, Power, and the Past in Asante, 1896–1996.* Portsmouth, N.H.: Heinemann, 2001.

Casely Hayford, J. E. *Gold Coast Native Institutions: With Thoughts upon a Healthy Imperial Policy for the Gold Coast and Ashanti.* 1903. Reprint, London: Frank Cass, 1970.

Danquah, J. B. *Gold Coast: Akan Laws and Customs and the Akim Abuakwa Constitution.* London: G. Routledge, 1928.

Davies, P. N. *The Trade-Makers: Elder Dempster in West Africa, 1852–1972.* London: Allen and Unwin, 1973.

Debrunner, Hans W. *A History of Christianity in Ghana.* Accra, Ghana: Waterville Publishing House, 1967.

Dumett, Raymond. *El Dorado in West Africa: The Gold-Mining Frontier, African Labor, and Colonial Capitalism in the Gold Coast, 1875–1900.* Athens: Ohio University Press, 1998.

Ephson, I. S. *Gallery of Gold Coast Celebrities.* Accra, Ghana: Ilen Publications, 1969.

Field, Margaret J. *Social Organization of the Ga People.* London: Crown Agents for the Colonies, 1940.

Howard, Rhoda. *Colonialism and Underdevelopment in Ghana.* New York: Holmes and Meier, 1978.

Kay, Geoffrey B., ed. *The Political Economy of Colonialism in Ghana: A Collection of Documents and Statistics, 1900–1960.* Cambridge: Cambridge University Press, 1972.

Kimble, David. *A Political History of Ghana, 1850–1928.* London: Oxford University Press, 1963.

Kirk-Greene, Anthony, ed. *Gold Coast Diaries: Chronicles of Political Officers in West Africa, 1900–1919: Thora Williamson.* London and New York: Radcliffe Press, 2000.

Kuklick, Henrika. *The Imperial Bureaucrat: The Colonial Administrative Service in the Gold Coast, 1920–1939.* Stanford, Calif.: Hoover Institution Press, 1978.

McCarthy, Mary. *Social Change and the Growth of British Power in the Gold*

Coast: The Fante States 1807–1874. Lanham, Md.: University Press of America, 1983.

Metcalfe, George E. *Great Britain and Ghana: Documents of Ghana History, 1807–1957*. London: Thomas Nelson and Sons, 1964.

Parker, John. *Making the Town: Ga State and Society in Early Colonial Accra*. Portsmouth, N.H.: Heinemann, 2000.

Patterson, K. David. *Health in Colonial Ghana: Disease Medicine and Socio-Economic Change, 1900–1955*. Waltham, Mass.: Crossroads Press, 1981.

Pedler, Frederick J. *The Lion and the Unicorn in Africa: A History of the Origins of the United Africa Company, 1787–1931*. London: Heinemann, 1974.

Pfann, Helene. *A Short History of the Catholic Church in Ghana*. Cape Coast, Ghana: Catholic Mission Press, 1965.

Sarbah, John Mensah. *Fanti Customary Laws*. 1897. Reprint, London: Frank Cass, 1968.

———. *Fanti National Constitution and Fanti Law Report*. 1906. Reprint, London: Frank Cass, 1968.

Chapter 4: Politics and Protest in the Model Colony

Akyeampong, Emmanuel. *Drink, Power, and Cultural Change: A Social History of Alcohol in Ghana, c. 1800 to Recent Times*. Portsmouth, N.H.: Heinemann, 1996.

Allman, Jean, and Victoria Tashjian. *"I Will Not Eat Stone": A Women's History of Colonial Asante*. Portsmouth, N.H.: Heinemann, 2000.

Asante, S.K.B. *Pan-African Protest: West Africa and the Italo-Ethiopian Crisis 1934–1941*. London: Longman Group, 1977.

Bening, Raymond. *Ghana Regional Boundaries and National Integration*. Accra: Ghana Universities Press, 1999.

Crisp, Jeff. *The Story of an African Working Class: Ghanaian Miners Struggles 1870–1980*. London: Zed Press, 1984.

Edsman, Bjorn M. *Lawyers in Gold Coast Politics, c. 1900–1940: From Mensah Sarbah to J. B. Danquah*. Uppsala, Sweden: University of Uppsala, 1979.

Gocking, Roger S. *Facing Two Ways: Ghana's Coastal Communities under Colonial Rule*. Lanham, Md.: University Press of America, 1999.

Henige, David. *The Chronology of Oral Tradition: The Quest for a Chimera*. Oxford: Oxford University Press, 1974.

Hill, Polly. *The Migrant Cocoa Farmers of Southern Ghana*. Cambridge: Cambridge University Press, 1963.

Jeffries, Richard. *Class, Power, and Ideology in Ghana: The Railwaymen of Sekondi*. London: Cambridge University Press, 1978.

Philips, Anne. *The Enigma of Colonialism: British Policy in West Africa*. London: James Curry, 1989.

Rathbone, Richard. *Murder and Politics in Colonial Ghana.* New Haven, Conn.: Yale University Press, 1993.

Wraith, R. E. *Guggisberg.* London: Oxford University Press, 1967.

Wright, Martin. *The Gold Coast Legislative Council.* London: Faber and Faber, 1947.

Chapter 5: The Model Colony at War and the Aftermath

Acquah, Ione. *Accra Survey: A Social Survey of the Capital of Ghana, Formerly Called the Gold Coast, 1953–1956.* London: University of London, 1958.

Apter, David. *Ghana in Transition.* Rev. ed. Princeton, N.J.: Princeton University Press, 1972.

Austin, David. *Politics in Ghana: 1946–1960.* London: Oxford University Press, 1964.

Bonne, Nii K. *Milestones in the History of the Gold Coast: An Autobiography of Nii Kwabena Bonne II.* London: Diplomatist Publications, 1953.

Bourret, F. M. *Ghana: The Road to Independence 1919–1957.* Stanford, Calif.: Hoover Institution Press, 1960.

Busia, Kofi A. *The Position of the Chief in the Modern Political System of Ashanti: A Study of the Influences of Contemporary Social Changes on Ashanti Political Institutions.* London: Oxford University Press, 1951.

————. *Report on the Social Survey of Sekondi-Takoradi.* London: Crown Agents, 1950.

Collins, John. *Highlife Time.* Accra, Ghana: Anansesem Publications, 1996.

Danquah, Francis. *Cocoa Diseases and Politics in Ghana, 1909–1966.* New York: Peter Lang, 1995.

Mikell, Gwendolyn. *Cocoa and Chaos in Ghana.* New York: Pargon House, 1989.

Rathbone, Richard. *Ghana: Part One, 1941–1952; Part Two, 1952–1957.* British Documents on the End of Empire. London: University of London, 1992.

Chapter 6: The Convention People's Party and the Road to Independence

Allman, Jean. *The Quills of the Porcupine: Asante Nationalism in an Emergent Ghana.* Madison: University of Wisconsin Press, 1993.

Bankhole, Timothy. *Kwame Nkrumah: His Rise to Power.* London: Allen and Unwin, 1955.

Nkrumah, Kwame. *Ghana: The Autobiography of Kwame Nkrumah.* New York: International Publishers, 1957.

Owusu, Maxwell. *Uses and Abuses of Political Power: A Case Study of Continuity and Change in Politics of Ghana.* Chicago: University of Chicago Press, 1970.

Padmore, George. *The Gold Coast Revolution: The Struggle of an African People from Slavery to Freedom.* London: D. Robson, 1953.

Sherwood, Marika. *Kwame Nkrumah: The Years Abroad 1935–1947.* Legon, Ghana: Freedom Publications, 1996.

Tait, David. *The Konkomba of Northern Ghana.* London: Oxford University Press, 1961.

Wallerstein, Immanuel. *The Road to Independence: Ghana and the Ivory Coast.* Paris: Mouton and Co., 1964.

Chapter 7: Independence: The Nkrumah Years

Adamafio, Tawia. *By Nkrumah's Side: The Labour and the Wounds.* London: Rex Collings, 1982.

Alexander, Henry T. *African Tightrope: My Two Years as Nkrumah's Chief of Staff.* London: Pall Mall Press, 1965.

Appiah, Joe. *The Man, J. B. Danquah.* Accra, Ghana: Academy of Arts and Sciences, 1974.

Armah, Kwesi. *Africa's Golden Road.* London: Heinemann, 1965.

Bankole, Timothy. *Kwame Nkrumah from Cradle to Grave.* Evershot, England: Gavin Press, 1981.

Bing, Geoffrey. *Reap the Whirlwind: An Account of Kwame Nkrumah's Ghana from 1950–1966.* London: MacGibbon and Kee, 1968.

Birmingham, David. *Kwame Nkrumah: The Father of African Nationalism.* Rev. ed. Athens: Ohio University Press, 1998.

Bretton, H. *The Rise and Fall of Kwame Nkrumah: A Study of Personal Rule in Africa.* New York: Frederick Praeger, 1966.

Davidson, Basil. *Black Star: A View of the Life and Times of Kwame Nkrumah.* London: Allen Lane, 1973.

Dunn, John, and A. F. Robertson. *Dependence and Opportunity: Political Change in Ahafo.* London: Cambridge University Press, 1973.

Fitch, B., and M. Oppenheimer. *Ghana: End of an Illusion.* New York: Monthly Review Press, 1966.

Garlick, Peter C. *African Traders and Economic Development in Ghana.* London: Oxford University Press, 1971.

Hadjor, Kofi B. *Nkrumah and Ghana: The Dilemma of Post-Colonial Power.* London: Kegan Paul International, 1988.

James, C.L.R. *Nkrumah and the Ghana Revolution.* Westport, Conn.: Lawrence Hill, 1977.

Jones, Trevor. *Ghana's First Republic 1960–1966: The Pursuit of the Political Kingdom.* London: Methuen, 1976.

Nkrumah, Kwame. *Africa Must Unite.* London: Heinemann, 1965.

———. *Challenge of the Congo.* London: Nelson, 1967.

———. *I Speak of Freedom: A Statement of African Ideology.* London: Heinemann, 1961.

———. *Neo-colonialism: The Last Stage of Imperialism.* London: Nelson, 1965.

Omari, Peter T. *Kwame Nkrumah: The Anatomy of an African Dictatorship.* New York: Africana Publishing, 1970.

Peil, Margaret. *The Ghanaian Factory Worker: Industrial Man in Africa.* Cambridge: Cambridge University Press, 1972.

Phobee, John S. *Kwame Nkrumah and the Church in Ghana, 1949–1966.* Accra, Ghana: Asempa Publishers, 1988.

Powell, Erica. *Private Secretary, Gold Coast.* London: C. Hurst, 1984.

Rathbone, Richard. *Nkrumah and the Chiefs: The Politics of Chieftaincy in Ghana 1951–1960.* Athens: Ohio University Press, 2000.

Rimmer, Douglas. *Staying Poor: Ghana's Political Economy 1950–1990.* Oxford: Pergamon Press, 1992.

Rooney, David. *Kwame Nkrumah: The Political Kingdom in the Third World.* New York: St. Martin's Press, 1989.

Thompson, W. Scott. *Ghana's Foreign Policy 1957–1966.* Princeton, N.J.: Princeton University Press, 1969.

Chapter 8: From Military Coup to Second Republic

Afrifa, Akwasi A. *The Ghana Coup, 24th February 1966.* London: Frank Cass, 1966.

Asante, Clement E. *The Press in Ghana: Problems and Prospects.* Lanham, Md.: University Press of America, 1996.

Austin, Dennis, and Robin Luckham. *Politicians and Soldiers in Ghana. 1966–72.* London and Totowa, N.J.: Frank Cass, 1975.

Chazan, Naomi. *An Anatomy of Ghanaian Politics: Managing Political Recession, 1969–1982.* Boulder, Colo.: Westview Press, 1983.

Donkoh, C. E. *Nkrumah and Busia of Ghana.* Accra, Ghana: New Times, 1972.

Killick, Tony. *Development Economics in Action: A Study of Economic Policies in Ghana.* London: Heinemann, 1978.

Kilson, Marion. *African Urban Kinsmen: The Ga of Central Accra.* London: C. Hurst, 1975.

Le Vine, Victor T. *Political Corruption: The Ghana Case.* Stanford, Calif.: Hoover Institution, 1975.

Nkrumah, Kwame. *Dark Days in Ghana.* London: Lawrence and Wishart, 1968.

Pinkney, Robert. *Ghana under Military Rule, 1966–1969.* London: Methuen, 1972.

Schildkrout, Enid. *People of the Zongo: The Transformation of Ethnic Identities in Ghana.* Cambridge and New York: Cambridge University Press, 1978.

Staniland, Martin. *The Lions of Dagbon: Political Change in Northern Ghana.* New York and London: Cambridge University Press, 1975.

Chapter 9: Return of the Soldiers

Agbodeka, Francis. *A History of the University of Ghana: Half a Century of Higher Education, 1948–1998.* Accra, Ghana: Woeli Publishing Services, 1998.

Boahen, Adu A. *The Ghanaian Sphinx: Reflections on the Contemporary History of Ghana, 1972–1987.* Westport, Conn.: Greenwood Press, 1989.

———. *Mfantsipim and the Making of Ghana: A Centenary History, 1876–1976.* Accra, Ghana: Sankofa Educational Publishers, 1996.

Pellow, Deborah, and Naomi Chazan. *Ghana: Coping with Uncertainty.* Boulder, Colo.: Westview Press, 1986.

Petchenkine, Youry. *Ghana in Search of Stability, 1972–1992.* New York: Praeger Publishers, 1993.

Oquaye, Mike. *Politics in Ghana: 1972–1979.* Accra, Ghana: Tornado Publications, 1980.

Ray, Donald. *Ghana: Politics, Economics and Society.* Boulder, Colo.: Lynne Rienner, 1986.

Chapter 10: The Third Republic and the PNDC

Adjei, Mike. *Death and Pain Rawlings' Ghana: The Inside Story.* London: Black Line Publishing, 1994.

Gyimah-Boadi, E., ed. *Ghana under PNDC Rule.* Dakar, Senegal: Codesria, 1993.

Hansen, Emmanuel. *Ghana under Rawlings.* Oxford: Malthouse, 1991.

Herbst, Jeffrey. *The Politics of Reform in Ghana, 1982–1991.* Berkeley: University of California Press, 1993.

Huq, M. M. *The Economy of Ghana: The First 25 Years since Independence.* New York: St. Martin's Press, 1989.

Ninsin, Kwame A., and F. K. Drah. *Political Parties and Democracy in Ghana's Fourth Republic.* Accra, Ghana: Woeli Publishing Services, 1993.

Nugent, Paul. *Big Men, Small Boys, and Politics in Ghana: Power, Ideology, and the Burden of History, 1982–1994.* London: Printer Publishing, 1995.

Quantson, Kofi. *Ghana: National Security . . . The Dilemma.* Accra, Ghana: Napasvil Ventures, 2003.

Rothchild, D., ed. *Ghana: The Political Economy of Recovery.* Boulder, Colo.: Lynne Rienner Publishers, 1991.

Shillington, Kevin. *Ghana and the Rawlings Factor.* London and Basingstoke: Macmillan Press, 1992.

Stryker, J. D. *Trade, Exchange Rate, and Agricultural Pricing Policies in Ghana.* Washington, D.C.: World Bank, 1990.

Chapter 11: The First NDC Administration: 1993–97

Hutchful, Eboe. *Ghana's Adjustment Experience: The Paradox of Reform.* Oxford: James Currey, 2002.

Chapter 12: The Second NDC Administration: 1997–2001

Agyeman-Duah, Ivor. *Between Faith and History: A Biography of J. A. Kufuor.* Trenton, N.J.: Africa World Press, 2003.

Chapter 13: The NPP in Power: 2001–4

Asante, K. B. *Voice from Afar: A Ghanaian Experience.* Accra, Ghana: Graphic Packaging, 2003.

Index

About the Author

ROGER S. GOCKING is a Professor in the Civic and Cultural Studies Department at Mercy College. His main area of specialization is African colonial history with a focus on Ghana, West Africa. He has authored *Facing Two Ways: Ghana's Coastal Communities Under Colonial Rule*.

Other Titles in the Greenwood Histories of the Modern Nations

Frank W. Thackeray and John E. Findling, Series Editors